REGULATION THAT WORKS

This book explains what regulation is – and is not.

It clarifies how regulation actually works, and how it can be made better. It also sets out how regulation should be done given fundamental challenges and changes to how we have done it. What is regulation trying to achieve? Is there too much red tape? Does regulation impede growth and innovation? Does regulation provide protection, and stability, and fair behaviours? Is it effective? How do we know if it succeeds?

The book illustrates competing regulatory models, and how multiple tools work – but also how things need to work differently in the future.

Given the pace of change in new technologies, creating unknown and uncontrollable risks, and the global nature of these technologies, we can only keep ourselves safe if we modernise how we 'do' regulation and work in collaborative ecosystems in which everyone works together to identify and control new harms. We should be aiming to achieve multiple outcomes, including protection as well as fair markets, facilitating innovation, and economic growth and social cohesion.

The book elucidates how this is all possible – if we organise ourselves and behave in new ways. Examples show sectors where all of this is already being applied – in Australia, Canada, New Zealand, and the UK.

This is a revolutionary book, and a must-read for anyone who wants to effect change in their regulatory spaces.

Regulation That Works

*Transforming the Future of
Regulatory Spaces*

Christopher Hodges

·HART·
OXFORD · LONDON · NEW YORK · NEW DELHI · SYDNEY

HART PUBLISHING

Bloomsbury Publishing Plc

Kemp House, Chawley Park, Cumnor Hill, Oxford, OX2 9PH, UK

1385 Broadway, New York, NY 10018, USA

Bloomsbury Publishing Ireland Limited, 29 Earlsfort Terrace, Dublin 2, D02 AY28, Ireland

HART PUBLISHING, the Hart/Stag logo, BLOOMSBURY and the Diana logo are trademarks of Bloomsbury Publishing Plc

First published in Great Britain 2026

1

Copyright © Christopher Hodges, 2026

Christopher Hodges has asserted his right under the Copyright, Designs and Patents Act 1988 to be identified as Author of this work.

All rights reserved. No part of this publication may be: i) reproduced or transmitted in any form, electronic or mechanical, including photocopying, recording or by means of any information storage or retrieval system without prior permission in writing from the publishers; or ii) used or reproduced in any way for the training, development or operation of artificial intelligence (AI) technologies, including generative AI technologies. The rights holders expressly reserve this publication from the text and data mining exception as per Article 4(3) of the Digital Single Market Directive (EU) 2019/790.

While every care has been taken to ensure the accuracy of this work, no responsibility for loss or damage occasioned to any person acting or refraining from action as a result of any statement in it can be accepted by the authors, editors or publishers.

All UK Government legislation and other public sector information used in the work is Crown Copyright ©. All House of Lords and House of Commons information used in the work is Parliamentary Copyright ©. This information is reused under the terms of the Open Government Licence v3.0 (http://www.nationalarchives.gov.uk/doc/open-government-licence/version/3) except where otherwise stated.

All Eur-lex material used in the work is © European Union, http://eur-lex.europa.eu/, 1998–2026.

A catalogue record for this book is available from the British Library.

A catalogue record for this book is available from the Library of Congress.

ISBN:	PB:	978-1-50998-915-7
	ePDF:	978-1-50998-918-8
	ePub:	978-1-50998-917-1

Typeset by Compuscript Ltd, Shannon
Printed and bound in Great Britain by TJ Clays Ltd.

For product safety related questions contact productsafety@bloomsbury.com

To find out more about our authors and books visit www.hartpublishing.co.uk. Here you will find extracts, author information, details of forthcoming events and the option to sign up for our newsletters.

FOREWORD

As Chair of the Regulatory Horizons Council (RHC) as well as Emeritus Professor of Justice Systems at the University of Oxford, Chris Hodges plays an important role in the development of regulatory policy in the UK. All of us involved in regulatory reform are fortunate to be able to draw on his deep understanding of the underlying issues.

This book is a valuable account of his thinking. He envisages a regulatory system developing with more co-operative exchange between the different participants. As well as setting out this high-minded optimistic vision he has good practical advice en route such as do not regulate too soon when standards often come first. He argues we need to focus on outcomes not process.

Hodges reminds us of the need to think of regulation as an overall system in which we need to understand the behaviour and incentives of all the participants. It is refreshing for such a distinguished jurisprudentialist to embrace insights from economics and the science of human behaviour. These perspectives enrich the account in this latest addition to his series of books on the intellectual framework under-pinning regulation.

David Willetts
Rt Hon Lord Willetts FRS

PREFACE

What sort of person are you?

Have you ever felt that the rules you are supposed to follow are a real pain and they stop you doing what you want or need to do? There is too much red tape. It's not only too costly, but the rules are also stupid and prevent sensible activities, business and innovation.

Or ...

Have you ever felt that an awful catastrophe, in which many people died or got hurt, was totally preventable – and should have been prevented? The Grenfell fire, the Post Office disaster, global warming, the Global Financial Crisis, sewage polluting rivers and beaches, blood infected with HIV and other viruses, buildings with asbestos, rogue landlords, a nurse killing babies, unaffordable energy prices, train cancellations, online scams, children being abused online, PPI being mis-sold ... there's no need to go on.

Both these views are valid. But what do we do about it?

This book tries to explain *why* both views are valid: that 'regulation' can help, but also that 'how we do regulation' has to change radically if we are to succeed in achieving better outcomes.

We frequently take regulation for granted. It works unseen to deliver protection all the time – safe drinking water (no cholera or other diseases), safe food, effective vaccines, good education and training, professional medical and trade staff, fair behaviour by traders, traffic management, the extraordinary safety of flying ... The list is long. This is not to say that some difficult challenges remain.

The problem is that there is overwhelming evidence that the traditional authoritarian way of managing employees and of regulating are both obsolete. Systems and organisations need to be approached holistically. There are significant implications for spreading good practice not only across market sectors but also down supply chains. This points to the need for development of meta governance models. The vision involves the integration of public and private tools in both personal and organisational behaviour and culture.

The situation is serious since many things are changing. The pace of change brought about by science and technology is now so fast that traditional regulatory regimes and practices will fail to deliver adequate levels of protection. We cannot regulate AI or quantum technologies by the equivalent of requiring a person to walk in front carrying a red flag, or requiring operators to pass a test. How can children be kept safe online and information and political debates be accurate and fair? It's easy to deliver absolute safety – close things down, ban them! But don't we need the internet? Should children be banned from all online activity? Is that effective or reasonable? How will we identify harms so as to be fast enough in responding to them to prevent widespread damage? Does imposing fines on multinationals actually get them to introduce changes or prevent people being harmed?

In recent years, the policies of many governments have seesawed between the opposing goals of increasing protection after a scandal and of deregulating in order to support business and economic growth. Attempts to create a 'third way' by adopting Better Regulation have run out of steam. The trouble is that if one reduces controls, one can increase risk (and that means causing harm) and litigation (which is rising in the USA and various other countries). Is there a better way?

This book argues that there is.

It's not matter of 'either/or': it's a matter of doing things differently! The book aims to be both an objective overview of the current state of 'regulation' and also a summary of the new approaches and future development of effective regulation. The premise is that we can achieve both protection and prevention if we change the way we do things. Regulators and regulatees need to evolve beyond traditional models. Some sectors have evolved very successfully to a new approach that establishes the achievement of common outcomes through a cooperative approach. This can seem counter-intuitive the first time one hears it, but the ideas are underpinned by extensive scientific evidence that changes policies, practices, behaviours, techniques and cultures.

When I started writing this book, regulation was being criticised by politicians who thought that it was impeding the economic growth of their nation. Regulation had become a dirty word. Regulation and regulators were the problem and needed to be 'fixed'. Red tape needed to be removed (again).

'Let's pull a lever and fix the regulators' was a common cry. 'Let's regulate the regulators.' That was somewhat ironic, given that the supposed idea was to *remove* 'red tape' rather than increase it. But these calls were all failing to understand what regulation is, how it works, why it doesn't work, and how it can be done better. They had missed the trick.

A lot of the problems were consequences of regulatory systems that had been created by politicians through legislation that constrained regulators and regulatees – and no one could see that the root causes of many problems lay with the *system* rather than what regulators were doing (which was actually what we required them to do). However, if we look to change the system, to a better one, we can avoid so many problems.

However, the apple cart was well and truly upset by President Trump in early 2025 when he removed whole regulatory regimes in the USA and introduced tariffs that profoundly destabilised markets. People started to value certainty, stability and predictability in commercial markets – because they were no longer there. Maybe, after all, we do need protection from arbitrary actions if we want daily life and activities of many kinds to continue? The wrecking ball has demolished previous certainties, and we need to build a new system.

This is an opportunity to base a new approach on sound scientific foundations. It will need some rethinking of how things should be done. But we can build an effective and resilient new system. The key ideas are: outcomes, data, collaboration, trust, values, a systemic approach. This book sets out the problems and the evidence on what we should do. The prescription, if we are bold enough to do it, is summarised in the last chapter.

OVERVIEW OF THE BOOK

This book aims to set out a concise statement of what regulation is and how it is done. The aim is to inform about a subject that often appears complex. The information here is also intended to form the basis of a syllabus for teaching those involved in regulation. but since so many fundamental aspects of regulation are currently subject to change, the book also aims to set out a blueprint for how regulation should be done in future, if it is to be based on all the currently available knowledge and evidence.

This book is written as a concise overview of, and introduction to, regulation. It does not aim to be comprehensive. There are various issues raised here that bear much deeper analysis, or are hardly touched on. For those who are interested, there are more extensive books written by me and others!

Part A starts by establishing the purpose(s) of regulation, namely delivering protection of various types, and the basic public and private structures that exist for doing this (chapter 1). It summarises the Legal and Economic Models that have been used as structures for regulation, and notes their inadequacies. Chapter 2 summarises the scientific evidence on human behaviour that has transformed approaches to regulation, especially away from just focusing on enforcement and deterrence. Chapter 3 then focuses on the importance of viewing regulation as a system, and sets out the Regulatory Functions Model that such a regulatory system should comprise. Chapter 4 identifies new models for regulation: the Regulatory Delivery Model (RDM, especially focusing on achieving desired outcomes) and the Outcome-Based Collaboration (OBC) Model. Chapter 5 looks in greater detail at the OBC Model and the elements necessary for its achievement.

Part B sets out more detail on how to operate an evidence-based regulatory system approach. Chapter 6 first explains the transformation of the practice of enforcement and interventions. Chapter 7 then analyses the regulatory tools that are used in three phases of regulatory controls, which can be summarised as 'before, during and after' marketing or problems arise. An evidence-based approach to regulatory delivery policy is set out.

Part C examines the criticisms, problems, challenges and future solutions of regulation. A range of common criticisms and challenges, plus attempts to control regulation itself, are summarised in chapter 8. The specific challenge of how to regulate innovation is discussed in chapter 9. Finally, chapter 10 summarises the transformations that are needed in regulation, in order to operate an effective system. Amongst future challenges that remain is the need to address global coordination.

Regulation is a global phenomenon. It exists in many countries and also, to some extent, globally or across groups of countries. This book aims to give an overview of the regulatory phenomenon and how it works everywhere. However, although some examples are quoted from different countries, the basic model used is the one that exists in the United Kingdom. The aim has been to provide readers with a general introduction, and to try to cover many variables and examples would have turned it into an encyclopaedia.

THANKS

The ideas and evidence set out here are a summary of much more extensive material published elsewhere. So many friends have contributed information and knowledge, and deserve warm thanks. Particular thanks in relation to this book are due to Graham Russell (the originator of the RDM), and to Srikanth Mangalam, who has moderated a succession of OBC projects. Both have kindly contributed thoughts and some text to this project. Thanks also to Ruth Steinholtz for her pertinent comments and for updating her Ethical Frameworks and to Joyce Tait for her PAGIT expertise. Of course, I should stress that the contents of this work are my sole responsibility.

As always, I owe deep thanks to Fiona for her unstinting support while this book and associated work have been undertaken. I am also delighted to thank Roberta Bassi and Tom Adams once again for their kind support and encouragement on yet another book and David Stott for eagle-eyed copy editing.

I hope that you, reader, will find this illuminating and useful. It's time to do things differently.

CONTENTS

Foreword v
Preface vii
Overview of the Book xi
Abbreviations xxi
List of Figures xxiii
List of Tables xxv

PART A
THEORIES, MODELS, REGULATION AS A SYSTEM

1. What is Regulation? 3
   What is the Purpose of (and Justification for) Regulation? 4
   Predictability, Stability, Social and Economic Goals 5
   Areas Subject to Regulation 8
   Safety Regulation – And Risk 11
   Markets, Competition and Economic Regulation 13
   Some Definitions of Regulation 16
   Structure and Hierarchy of Regulations 17
   The Landscape of Regulatory Authorities 18
   The Legal Model: Rules and Enforcement 19
   The Economic Model: Rational Profit Maximisation and
       Deterrence 21
   Rules, Procedures and Systems 22
   Problems with the Legal and Economic Models 23
   Public and Private Modes of Regulation 26
   Standards, Conformity Assessment, Certification and
       Accreditation 27
   Advantages and Drawbacks of Private Regulation 31
   Achieving Both Protection and Freedom 32
   Precautionary or Proportionate Risk? 33
   What is a Regulatory System for? 35

2. Scientific Evidence on How Humans Behave 39
   Factors Affecting Human Actions 40
      The Power of Internal Motivation 41
      Morality, Ethics and Values 41
      The Power of Social Influence, Culture and Ethics 43
   The Causes of Disasters 45
      Inquiries into Disasters 45
      Systemic and Behavioural Risk Factors 46
      Scientific Research into Accidents 48
   The Psychological Basis of Actions: Self-Determination
      Theory 50
   Business Research into Good Management Practice 52
      Psychological Safety 53
   Cooperation and Trust 53
   Why and How do We Comply with Rules? 55
   Make Rules Simple to Assist Compliance 57
   Social Punishment and Maintaining Group Cohesion 57
      Authoritarian Punishment and Maintaining the
         Commons 58
   What do People Want When Things Go Wrong? 59
   Conclusions: Differentiating a Supportive Fair Cooperative
      Culture from Enforcement 60

3. A Regulatory System and its Functions 74
   Regulation as a Coordinated Means of Delivering Protections 74
   Regulation as a System 76
   The Concept of a 'Regulatory Space' 78
   The Core Functions of the Regulatory Space: The Regulatory
      Functions Model 79
      Achieving Outcomes 81
      Delivering the Functions 82
   Key Elements of the Regulatory Functions Model 86
      A Collaborative System 86
      Actors 86
      Scope of the Ecosystem 89
      Accountability 89
      Trustworthiness 89
      Data 90
      Risk and Responding 91
   The Basic Operational Challenges Around Risk and Harms 91

    Bespoke Regulatory Spaces 93
    Governance of a Regulatory System 94
    Coordinating Multiple Systems 96

4. New Models 98
    From Theories to Science, and Rules to Outcomes 99
    A Modern Regulatory Authority: The Regulatory Delivery
       Model 100
       RDM Prerequisites 101
       RDM Practices 103
    The Significance of Transformation under the RDM 106
       Outcomes 106
       Intervention Choices 108
    A Systemic Behavioural Approach: Open and Just Culture 111
    The Outcome-Based Collaborative Regulation (OBCR) Model 112
       Trust and Ethics 113
    The Potential for Consistency between the Goals of Regulatees
       and Regulation 114
    Combining Two Different Universes 115
    Conclusion: A Time for Reform 117

5. How to do Outcome-Based Collaborative Regulation 121
    The Value of Collaborating 121
    How People Collaborate 123
       The Mechanism of Trust 123
       Values 124
       Trust Structures 125
       Evidence of Trustworthiness 125
       Evidence List for Trust in Organisations 127
       Evidence of Ethical Organisational Culture 129
    Creating an OBC System 131
       The Stakeholders: Who has to be Involved? 131
       Identifying the Outcomes 131
       Achieving the Outcomes 131
       Monitoring 131
       System Architecture 132
       Building Collaboration Through Trust 132
       Comments on the Creation Process 132
       Data 134

Aspects of the OBC Approach 134
   Motivation 134
   Commitment 135
   Responsibility and Accountability 135
Examples of Outcome-Based Cooperative Systems 137
   Open and Just Culture in Aviation Safety 137
   OBCR Case Studies 139

PART B
OPERATING A REGULATORY SYSTEM APPROACH

6. Transformation of Practice on Interventions and Enforcement 149
   The Traditional Legal Enforcement Architecture 150
      Categorisations and Differences between Criminal/
         Administrative/Civil/Private Law 150
      Sanctions 153
   Purposes and Justifications of Enforcement of Rules 156
   Traditional Principles Justifying Regulatory Action 156
   Principles of Fair Enforcement 157
      Proportionality: Mitigating and Aggravating Factors in
         Calibrating Sanctions 158
      The Relevance of Harm 160
      Competence 161
      Compliance Programmes 161
      Regulating Discretion and Flexibility 163
      OECD's Best Practice Principles for Enforcement and
         Inspections 164
   An Example of an Enforcement Policy 166
   Applying the Science 169
      The Sociological Function of Enforcement 169
      Philosophy of Punishment and Democracy 170
      Evolution in Understanding of Enforcement and
         Intervention 171
      Moves Towards Classification of Behavioural Motivations 173
      Better Regulation and Regulatory Delivery 174
      Adding Behavioural Science: Evolution from Enforcement
         to Supportive Interventions 174
   Restatement of Policy on Regulatory Intervention 177

7. Tools for a Regulatory System 184
   The Purpose of Tools in a Regulatory System: From Compliance
     to Outcomes 185
   A. Before: Pre-Marketing..186
   Objectives of Regulation before Marketing or Undertaking
     Activities 186
   Licensing, Approval, Permits, Registration, Notification 187
   Private Assurance Schemes...188
   Professional Competence..189
   Authorised Competent Persons 190
   Economic Regulation 191
   Safety Regulation in General 191
   Products 192
   Testing 193
   Sandboxes 194
   Information and Disclosure 194
   Financial Products and Services 195
      Principles for Businesses..195
      Senior Managers and Certification Regime (SM&CR) 197
      Culture 199
      Limitations in Harnessing Culture as a Regulatory Tool 203
   Open and Just Culture in Aviation Safety..204
   Regulatory Culture..204
   Using Trust as a Regulatory Tool 205
   B. During: Monitoring and Surveillance 207
   The Objectives of Monitoring and Surveillance...................................207
   Data Collection 209
   Some Examples of New Approaches 210
      Ombuds 210
      Safe Food Production Queensland..211
      UK Food Standards Authority...212
      Future Opportunities 213
   Markets and Economic Regulation 213
   C. After: Responding to Problems...215
   The Objectives of Regulatory Interventions..215
      Comments on the Objectives..216
      Markets and Economic Regulation 217
   Distinguishing between Actors: Two Modes...217
      Supportive Intervention Mode 217
      Protection Mode 218

Private Regulatory Schemes 219
Ensuring that Change Occurs 219
   An Inadequate Feedback System 221
Redress 222

PART C
PROBLEMS, CRITICISMS, CHALLENGES AND FUTURE SOLUTIONS

8. Problems and Criticisms of Regulation 231
   Too Much Regulation? 231
      Too Many Rules and Procedures 232
      Cumulative Effects 233
      Resource Problems for Regulators 234
      Regulatory Creep 234
      Gaps and Silos – Inconsistency between Regulators 235
      Specific Issues Arising with Economic Regulation 236
      Impeding Growth and Investment 238
   The Underlying Issues 239
      Proportionality 239
      Risk Perception 240
      Risk: Attitudes and Appetite 241
      Many Decisions are Political 243
   Attempts to Control Regulation 245
      Reduction Techniques 246
   Better Regulation Techniques 252
      Make Better Regulations 252
      Regulatory Reform Principles 252
   Regulation of Regulators 253
      Codes, Duties and Steers 254
      'Performance' of Regulators 255
      Regulatory Relationships: Enforcement or Support? 256
      Consistency, Networking 256
      Regulatory Delivery: Do it Better 257
   How Much does Regulation Cost? 258
   Challenges of Globalism 259

How to do Regulation Better 261
    Remember Why 261
    How to Address the Real Problems 262

9. New Regulatory Systems to Support Innovation 269
    Challenges in Regulating Innovation 269
    Principles 271
        Precautionary and Other Principles 271
        Principles and Responses in Regulating Innovation 272
    Stages of Maturity 274
    Tools 276
        Building Pathways: Standards and Private Accreditation
           Mechanisms 276
        The PAGIT Framework 277
        Responsible Innovation 280
        Risk Appetites and Competing Values 281
        An Ecosystem for Identifying and Responding to Harm ... 282
        Agility 283
        New Tools for Examining Risks 284
        Opportunities from Collaboration 285

10. The Future of Regulation (and What We Need to do) 290
    A Time of Transformations 290
    Background: Failures in the Traditional Models 290
        A More Sophisticated Model: Adding Behavioural Science
           to Legal and Economic Assumptions 290
        Duties or Outcomes? 292
    Solutions and the Way Forward 293
        Solutions from Human Science 293
        The Power of Outcomes 294
        The Power of a Regulatory *System* 295
        A Quick Checklist 297
        Refreshment 298
        A Systemic Solution to Risk 298
        The Power of Collaboration 298

Index *301*

ABBREVIATIONS

AI	Artificial Intelligence
BCPs	Basel Core Principles
BCBS	Basel Committee on Banking Supervision
BSI	British Standards Institution
CAB	conformity assessment body
CEN	European Committee for Standardisation
CENELEC	European Committee for Electrotechnical Standardisation
CFTC	US Commodity Futures Trading Commission
CPD	Continuous Professional Development
ETSI	European Telecommunications Standards Institute
EU	European Union
FENSA	Fenestration Self-Assessment Scheme
GATT	Global Agreement on Tariffs and Trade
GDPR	General Data Protection Regulation(s)
HP	Human Performance
IAEA	International Atomic Energy Agency
IASC	International Accounting Standards Committee
ICAO	International Civil Aviation Organisation
ICH	International Conference on Harmonisation of Pharmaceuticals for Human Use
IEC	International Electrotechnical Commission

IMDRF	International Medical Device Regulators Forum
IMO	International Maritime Organisation
IOSCO	International Organisation of Securities Commissions
ISO	International Organization for Standardization
ITU	International Telecommunication Union
NAO	The National Audit Office
NGO	Non-governmental Organisation
NQI	National Quality Infrastructure
OBC	Outcome-Based Collaboration
OBCR	Outcome-Based Collaborative Regulation
OECD	Organisation for Economic Cooperation and Development
OPSS	Office for Product Safety and Standards
PBR	Performance-Based Regulation
RDM	Regulatory Delivery Model
RHC	Regulatory Horizons Council
RFM	Regulatory Functions Model
SMS	safety management system
UK	United Kingdom
UKAS	United Kingdom Accreditation Service
UNCITRAL	United Nations Commission on International Trade Law
UNCTAD	United Nations Commission on Trade and Development
USA	United States of America
VUCA	volatile, uncertain, complex and ambiguous
WEF	World Economic Forum
WHO	World Health Organization
WIPO	World Intellectual Property Organization

LIST OF FIGURES

Figure 3.1 Vertical and Horizontal Modes of Authority 76
Figure 3.2 The Regulatory Functions Model 81
Figure 3.3 Public Risk Management – Multi Stakeholder Context 88
Figure 4.1 Combining the Legal and Behavioural Models 117
Figure 6.1 Enforcement Pyramid of the Civil Aviation Authority 2012 155
Figure 6.2 Segmentation of Offenders: Spectrum of Compliance (Scottish Environmental Protection Agency) 173

LIST OF TABLES

Table 5.1	Characteristics of Trust Evidence	127
Table 5.2	The Ethical Practice Frameworks	130
Table 6.1	Intervention Tools for Specific Objectives	154
Table 7.1	Powers Needed to Deliver Specific Objectives	209
Table 9.1	Technology Readiness Levels (TRLs)	274
Table 9.2	Routine, Company-specific RI Elements related to Standard Business Practice	278
Table 9.3	Project-specific Elements of RI Requiring Active Consideration and Monitoring as a Project Evolves	279
Table 9.4	Consolidated RI Framework	280

PART A

Theories, Models, Regulation as a System

1

What is Regulation?

What is the purpose of regulation, and the justification for it? Basically, it is to deliver protection of various kinds – not just protection from physical, environmental or economic harm, but also to provide predictability and stability in human activities, and thereby provide the conditions for effective human social and economic activity.

Regulation covers a huge range of activities. It comes in various broad families – especially safety, environment, competition, economic regulation of markets. This gives rise to many definitions of regulation.

Regulation is typically made and imposed by a state (public regulation) through laws and legal requirements and sanctions, usually administered by a specific regulatory authority. But private actors (such as professions or trades) can have their own 'self-regulatory' requirements, especially around technical competence. Some hybrid arrangements exist.

There are two traditional models of regulation:

(1) The Legal Model: rules/requirements, duties, compliance, identification of non-compliance, enforcement/imposition of sanctions.

(2) The Economic Model: theories of rules/compliance and deterrence.

Standards and private certification and accreditation schemes (sometimes run by state entities) are widely used.

What is the Purpose of (and Justificiation for) Regulation?

Most discussions of regulation start with definitions of what it is, and we can then get lost in technical detail. It is more important to ask first: 'Why regulation?' – What's it for?

The principal purpose of regulation is *protection*. This means protection from the occurrence of unacceptable harm. Harm can arise from carrying out many human activities, and the goal is to try to carry out regulated activities in such a way that avoidable, unacceptable harm is prevented or minimised. Risk cannot be avoided in life, and there is no such thing as absolute safety. The avoidance or reduction of *unacceptable* risk of harm, and of unacceptable harm itself, not only makes people and things safer, avoiding damage, but also reduces the cost of remedying harm suffered, through rectification and compensation, and the cost of insurance.

There are various aspects of harm that regulation aims at. Broadly, the objectives are to avoid harm by achieving the following goals:

(a) *Safety*: avoidance of injury and harm, notably physical, mental, economic or reputational, usually as caused by products or services that are of acceptable quality.

(b) *Fair markets* (fair trading, eg fair prices, fair treatment of consumers and small businesses), *stable markets* (capital adequacy) and *fair competitive markets* (no abuse of market position, or collusion, especially on concentrations and prices; ability for new entrants to join).

(c) *Quality and competence* in responsible activities, such as research, education, professions, and also proper operation of companies and charities.

(d) *Public goals* (eg education, equality and human rights, charities) and *social goals* (fair, principles-based government and treatment of citizens by the state).

(e) *Sustainability of the natural environment*, and of the planet.

All of these goals are in fact about achieving the same thing: protection. Underlying all aspects is the need for trust between different actors in society and its relationships and markets. If people do not trust the safety, competence, fairness or sustainability of others and institutions, the resultant lack of faith will undermine productive activities, markets and societies. Hence, effective regulation is essential to healthy human societies and states.

Since human activity encompasses so many manifestations, multiple sources of harm might arise and could be prevented – if we want to. Regulation is therefore aiming to protect the safety, fairness and sustainability of almost all of the different forms of human activity, whether commercial, professional, economic, markets, and the natural environment – and regard to others as well as ourselves. We can see this from looking at the number of areas that are subject to regulation.

Predictability, Stability, Social and Economic Goals

Why do we need to deliver protection? Without effective regulation, there would be more harm – to people, society, markets, the environment, and so on. Some of the harm might be caused deliberately, and some because people didn't think enough about what they were doing, or had inadequate competence or resource. If we fail to invest some effort into protection and controlling risk in advance, we would have to pay large liability bills to compensate for the harm after it has been caused. We might risk a collapse in trust between people who would otherwise collaborate. Hence social and economic structures would be undermined or even unable to operate. Regulation is not, therefore, about imposing costs; it is about allocating costs wisely.

Although protection is the primary goal of regulation, and its primary justification, there are numerous other benefits that can be obtained through regulation (if it is done appropriately), including: economic and market benefits, such as predictability, stability, growth, innovation, and wider social benefits, such as consumer and citizen empowerment, support for vulnerable or disadvantaged groups, and achievement of the Sustainable Development Goals (SDGs). Let's look at some of these benefits and consequences more closely.

Stability over time. Both those subject to regulation and those who use or may be affected by products, services, markets and the environment should ideally have confidence that the same values, rules, behaviours and outcomes are shared to a significant extent by everyone. This is the basis of trust in a stable society. It is supported where there is confidence that those who intentionally break the rules or are incompetent in observing them will not be allowed to rock the boat and cause harm to others. Psychological research shows that the stability of social groups rests on this sense of security, and confidence that everyone else in the group(s) to which we belong is playing to the same rules, or shares the same basic values. The same is true in relation to markets, or other areas of behaviour. If we have confidence that the same rules apply to our fellow citizens, professionals, companies, competitors or sports colleagues then we should have sufficient confidence that the endeavours of each of us will take place on a fair and level playing field. A sense of fairness, justice and consistency is a core human need. These perceptions build senses of security, cohesion and confidence in action.

Economic prosperity, growth and innovation. Stability and predictability promote not only engagement but also investment, growth and innovation. Stability in many markets, especially financial markets, is frequently said to be essential. Companies and their investors need stability and confidence in order to plan and invest over an adequate time period. Consumers need confidence in the people they are buying things from. Traders also want to have confidence that their competitors are playing by the same rules as they are, in other words that markets are fair.

Regulation may also support the delivery of *public goods*. This is the rationale for regulation of water, energy, railways and so on when they are privatised (see below).

Confidence is also necessary for people to buy ('Is this what I need? Is it of the right quality/price/safety etc? Will the seller provide ongoing support if anything goes wrong?'). Empowerment of consumers, tenants and citizens (whether vulnerable or not) in exercising informed choice and obtaining value and redress when faced with powerful traders and government are all important goals and outcomes. These benefits are encapsulated in 'Consumer Principles' of Access, Information, Choice, Safety and Quality, Fairness and Equity, Value for Money, Redress and Representation.[1]

All these aspects of healthy, fair transactions support confidence, trust, predictability and stability in commercial and social relationships, markets and societies. Those elements therefore underpin economic prosperity by producing *social capital* and *economic capital*, through growth and innovation. It can also support the wider and swifter adoption of new things (innovation), through providing a relevant degree of standardisation and predictability.

All of this means that regulation itself should be predictable. Although we often think of regulation as being about commercial activities, it is equally important to deliver the benefits of information, choice, safety, fairness, redress and so on in relation to the activities of governments or publicly-owned services. This would cover social security, healthcare, social housing, police, fire and rescue, water, energy, waste and recycling, postal services, prisons and so on. Public services raise additional regulatory challenges over and above commercial situations, given that consumers theoretically have a choice whether to buy a good, whilst the provision of most public services fulfils basic human needs and can be essential. Hence, issues arise of unfairness in provision (generally and to individuals), such as inequitable distribution and availability, and balancing the cost to public funds, as well as efficiency and respectful, fair behaviour. We will touch on these issues further in chapter 8.

Outcomes. We will emphasise throughout this book that having principles and goals is essential but only a starting point. We need to be clear that the principles and goals are being delivered in practice. This needs a focus (which is only just appearing as a relevant issue in regulation) on whether the right outcomes are being achieved through regulation. Are the good outcomes of the activities that are being regulated delivered or impeded? Are we empowering or impeding? Also, if people are being exposed to significant risk, or widely hurt, what is the point? Focusing on outcomes inevitably raises questions about how we can tell if they are being achieved by the system, and if things are getting better or worse. This needs data, and the need for reliable and comprehensive data raises the issue of who holds it, and how it is shared.

Government policy. Given the positive and negative effects that regulation can have on socio-economic goals, governments can try to use regulation primarily as a tool to deliver governmental policy. This idea can become an obsession and sometimes distort the regulatory environment. It is true that regulation can be a barrier to innovation and economic growth. It can also be a means of supporting those and many other goals. But the idea that regulation is essentially a tool by which governments can achieve their political goals is fundamentally to misunderstand that regulation is primarily about protection rather than anything else, and it inevitably involves constraints. It is possible in certain circumstances that multiple outcomes can be achieved through using regulation in the right way. But the trick here is in how regulation is delivered, which is not widely understood. The achievement of the multiple outcomes of different actors – each with their own focus, goals, activities, cultures and so on – requires an approach based in coordination, rather than in top-down authoritative control.

What is Regulation?

Areas Subject to Regulation

We rely on regulation extensively, and often take it for granted. Many areas of life are underpinned by regulation in keeping us safe.

The following is a list of major areas that are subject to formal state regulation in advanced states (a regulator exists for each of them in the UK). It is not a complete list, but it illustrates the breadth of everyday activities where regulation applies to provide protection. The areas are listed under a few brief headings (safety, markets, professions and so on) so as to make the list more readable. The categories used here are not exclusive (some areas could be listed under several headings or different descriptions, and could be subdivided further).

Safety

AI
Animal and Plant Health
Biometric Material
Building Safety
Civil Aviation
Drinking Water Quality
Driver and Vehicle Licensing, Standards and Certification
Education, Children's Services and Skills
Food Standards
Gambling
Health and Safety in Workplaces
Health and Social Care Services and Improvement
Health Research
Human Fertilisation and Embryology
Human Tissue
Information and Data Privacy
Oil and Gas
Medicines and Healthcare Products
Nuclear Safety
Product Safety
Security Industry
Social Housing
Sports Grounds
Traffic

Economic and Markets

Anti-Money Laundering
Consumer Protection
Communications
Competition and Fair Markets
Education Funding
Employment Agencies Standards
Energy
Equality and Human Rights
Fair Access to Benefits (products, services, markets, public goods)
Financial Reporting
Financial Services (Conduct and Prudential)
Gas and Electricity Markets
Higher Education Funding
Immigration Services and Visas
Labour: Gangmasters (non-permanent and part-time workers)
Organised Sports: Football, Rugby, Cricket, various others
Pensions
Payment Systems
Politicians' Expenses
Public Houses
Qualifications and Examinations
Rail and Road
Revenue and Customs
Rural Payments
Small Businesses
Students
Supermarket Sales
Water Services

Professional Services

Accountants
Architects
Constabulary and Fire & Rescue Services
Farriers
Forensic Science
Goldsmiths and precious metals, Hallmarking
Lawyers (Bar, Solicitors, Legal Executives, Will Writers, Licensed Conveyancers, etc)

Insolvency
Medical (Chiropractic, Dental, Medical, Midwifery, Nursing,
Opticians, Osteopathic, Pharmacy, Surgical, Social Work etc)
Police Conduct
Security Industry
Statistics
Teachers

Corporate and Civil Society Organisations

Charities
Community Interest Companies
Companies Registration
Media, including social media
Digital and Cryptocurrency Assets
Cultural Heritage

Natural and other Assets

Coal
Forestry
Land Registration and Property Rights
Environment
Historic Buildings and Monuments
Homes and Communities
Intellectual Property: Patents, Designs and Trademarks
Lighthouses
Marine Management
Maritime and Coastguard
Natural Environment and Assets
Planning
Religious Buildings (Faculties)

Public

Electoral System
Public Benefits

There are so many situations subject to regulation that to use the single word 'regulation' to encompass them all is pretty misleading. As we shall see later, the mechanisms by which we are kept safe, or which try to keep us safe, differ depending on the context. One consequence of this is that criticisms of 'regulation' are meaningless if they are not precise about the context that is being criticised.

Let us now look at some of the main types of regulation (safety, economic and so on) in greater detail.

Safety Regulation – And Risk

Safety regulation is typically about prevention of *physical harm* (economic harm has its own category, discussed below) to people or things. A major element of what we are trying to do here is to rectify a power imbalance. We intervene to protect the vulnerable who are unable to protect themselves from many sources of harm that are caused, or can be controlled, by more powerful actors. The latter are more able to affect things like the number and complexity of the causes of risk, the availability of information about the risk and how to avoid harm, or the ability to exercise informed choice in avoiding the risk.

As an example, a long list of potential 'digital harms' has been produced – and note here reliance on the concept of *outcomes*. Within each category, the taxonomy describes the digital harms in one of two ways:[2]

- As a harmful outcome for consumers, ie, the direct harm experienced by consumers.
- As a practice that can lead to harmful outcomes for consumers, ie, actions by firms/individuals that can result in direct harm to consumers.

However, *safety is never absolute*. There is always the potential for something to go wrong and cause harm. So, another way of looking at safety regulation is that it is about *risk*. We are trying to control and reduce risk. It is inherent that some harm may occur in human life, since no one can control all the multiple sources of actions in nature and human activity. This means that we have to come to terms with the concept of relative risks, and engage with which risks, and what levels of risk, are *acceptable*. This raises the *risk appetite* of society. How much do we value achieving the benefits and avoiding the risks?

So, the objective of regulation is to reduce unacceptable risk to a level that is acceptable. Of course, numerous difficulties arise. First, your willingness to accept particular risks, or levels of risk, may differ from anyone else's. If a regulator is to take this decision on behalf of us all, who is to say that the decisions taken are right? What level of risk is acceptable to different people, or to a particular society, and who decides?

Second, the sources of harm and of risk can be many and complex. It is not always possible to 'control' every aspect of a system that might make a key contribution to causing some harm, and the possibility and incidence of harm might not be predictable. Third, can a single regulated institution, or a single regulator, adequately identify or control multiple risk factors? Do we not need to be able to control a system that comprises many actors?

Fourth, if we suffer harm that is deemed to arise from an unacceptable risk, or level of risk (or activity, or breach of the rules), will someone compensate us (and who and how?), and who is going to be accountable, and perhaps punished, for having caused the harm (or breach)?

An example of these points is medicines. By definition, medicinal substances can be powerful, and might produce unintended as well as intended effects, especially in different individuals. At the heart of regulation of medicines is the idea that since safety is a relative concept, the regulatory decision has to *balance the risks and benefits* of a product, based on the known data about risks and benefits from experiments on toxicology in animals, then clinical trials involving healthy volunteers and then patients, supplemented after marketing by continuous data from clinical use. We continue to discover new effects and interactions between human systems, disease states, and the range of food and drugs that circulate in individuals. The reality is that evaluation of safety has to be continuous and based on the collection and evaluation of ever-growing sets of data, drawn from multiple sources.

In an ideal world, a settled regulatory regime should be based on a 'steady-state' that delivers predictable and consistent control of risk and prevention of harm. For example, the major risks would be known, even if they may be unpredictable in particular situations, and the means of controlling them are known. Thus, it ought to be the case that complying with a specific set of rules and/or procedures will result in an adequately low level of harm arising from use of the regulated products, services, activities and markets. But unfortunately, life is not that simple. The whole point about risk is that it is uncertain. This is even more true these days, where many aspects of life are being transformed by new science and technologies. As we discuss in chapters 4 and 9, new and unknown risks (and harms) arise all the time. Existing approaches to regulation might not (will not) adequately control them. And the pace of change is so fast that we need to find new ways of doing things pretty quickly.

Markets, Competition and Economic Regulation

If the central concept of safety regulation is safety, that of markets is fairness. The objectives are to see *fair competition* – especially avoidance of monopolies, which tend to distort markets, innovation and prices – and *fair behaviour*. Despite the 'principles of individual freedom' and 'freedom of contract', governments have increasingly intervened to protect those who may be harmed where there is an *imbalance of power*. The anti-monopoly objective is about avoiding concentrations of economic power, thereby maintaining a 'level playing field'. The traditional justification for regulatory intervention is said to be market failure,[3] ie a failure of private mechanisms to deliver adequate protection, manifested by unfairness, abuse of power by stronger players over those more vulnerable. This produces an absence of fairness and trust. The assumption is that the incentives and competitive forces on private actors who operate in markets are inadequate to control some harms.

The underlying issue is one of power. Unduly powerful companies, or groupings of traders, acting monopolistically, can lead to inefficiencies and waste in delivery, exploitative behaviour, excessive prices, unresponsiveness to market forces that would otherwise reduce inefficiencies, providing inadequate information to customers and users, oppressive behaviour, poor service, squashing of competition, lack of innovation, and harm to third parties (externalities) that can be hard to repair. Hence, ensuring that traders behave fairly in markets and to customers and others is self-explanatory. A major focus is on consumer protection, especially in relation to ensuring fairness in pricing or other behaviour towards customers. Where the market consists of a small number of traders, the competitive forces can lead to inadequate observance of safety, quality or behaviour, and an absence of effective means of ensuring that rules are observed by all. This may result not only in failure by some actors to behave well and take appropriate steps to control the risks that they generate, but also a 'race to the bottom' in terms of behaviour and controls, thereby increasing risks. So, it is argued, one needs mandatory rules that apply to all, plus enforcement mechanisms.

As a matter of policy, governments are traditionally reluctant to step in to control market behaviour; actors are free to make their own decisions and make their own bargains and mistakes. Thus civil law has a general principle of *caveat emptor* and is based on parties having the freedom to agree whatever contract terms they wish. However, requirements for fair and honest trading, or at least control of dishonest or fraudulent trading, go back many centuries, especially with the increase in open markets and trade from the Middle Ages. But such controls have typically been introduced primarily by professional associations, rather than by government.

Three broad legal domains can be distinguished: competition law, economic regulation, and consumer protection.

Competition law can apply to any actors, in relation to any anti-competitive practices, such as secretly sharing information on pricing, or illicitly agreeing not to compete openly (a cartel). Mergers between large companies are subject to reporting, review and approval (perhaps subject to conditions) if the resulting concentration of market power is considered to be unacceptably large. Hence, the principal objectives of competition law are to address:

- abuse of a dominant position, for example where companies try to restrict supply, or segment a market, or to control prices;
- cartels – unfair sharing of information that partitions markets and keeps prices artificially high;
- mergers that concentrate a market to an unacceptable degree, which is addressed by either banning or imposing conditions on a merger, or requiring the break-up of a concentration.

Economic regulation[4] applies specific techniques of control in relation to a specific sector in which there is, or may be a tendency towards, a natural monopoly in a public good that may lead to undesirable practices. This is important in relation to provision of public *utilities* like water, energy, rail and communications. There are two main types of interventions. First, interventions can focus on the *structure* of an industry, limiting the number of firms that can trade (even to one firm), or separating particular activities in a supply chain, or requiring that access to infrastructure (an energy grid or rail or communications network) be given to other traders. Where the benefits to one user of a network (such as in payments systems, transport, energy and communications networks, and digital platforms) are dependent on others, or the behaviour of groups, then the system may need to be policed so as to avoid unacceptable 'network effects' that would also harm ultimate users of the network (such as consumers). These ideas lead to using regulation as a means of administration of the long-term contracts that are needed to deliver effective utilities.[5] Second, interventions are aimed at affecting the *behaviour* of firms, in order to protect consumers and order a market, such as decisions on prices, investment, coverage of service, quality and behaviour of service, and the terms on which access is provided to others.

Consumer protection has expanded since the 1960s to protect consumers as a class (occurring in parallel with an increased emphasis on human rights). This is a further example of trying to control unacceptable imbalances of power between powerful traders and individual consumers (who may have limited information, or ability to exercise choice, and may be exploitable through their biases or be vulnerable in various ways). Consumer protection legislation was extensive in the West by the 1990s, including laws against unfair contract terms, misleading and unfair advertising, unfair business practices generally, and improved means of obtaining redress. Similarly, legal protection of tenants has also increased, but has developed slowly. Principles of fair trading have also spread more recently beyond consumers to some *vulnerable business groups*, such as small businesses. Examples are farmers and small food suppliers (the Groceries Code Adjudicator), tied pub tenants (the Pubs Code Adjudicator), and late payment to small businesses (the Small Business Commissioner).

This trend towards ethical behaviour in business and society generally has slowly gathered momentum, such as through the extensive adoption of Codes of Business Conduct, evolving into Codes of Ethical Behaviour and Practice, which have been adopted by trade associations and increasingly as a result of the desire to maintain the good reputation of traders, spreading as legal requirements in sectoral regulatory regimes. The same trend has produced in financial services the introduction in 2022 of a legal 'duty of care' by banks towards customers.

In all these three domains – competition, economic regulation and consumer protection – it follows from adequate regulation of safety, fair behaviour, fair markets and other aspects of protection, that regulation can assist business and innovation by providing *clarity* and *certainty* over the requirements that society and a given nation expects for actors. This supports predictability and stability in markets.

Some Definitions of Regulation

Against this background, it's interesting to reflect that there are many definitions of regulation. Some definitions focus just on its mechanics, rather than on its fundamental purpose. Thus, some may think of regulation as 'a system of rules and enforcement'. Philip Selznick's definition is the 'sustained and focused control exercised by a public agency over activities that are valued by the community'.[6] This is a restricted concept since it focuses just on the activities of the state, although it is illuminating in referring to 'activities that are valued by the community'. That would distinguish a valued activity, which we try to regulate, from a criminal or undesirable activity, which we ban.

Roger Brownsword says that regulation is about the public channelling of conduct, designed to advance some valued purpose, and involving standard-setting, monitoring for compliance, and responding to deviance (directing, detecting, and correcting).[7] His approach builds on a baseline of law and legality, involving a set of procedural requirements. He notes that this accords with Lon Fuller's view that 'the rules and standards set should be general, promulgated, prospective, clear, non-contradictory, (reasonably) constant, and not impossible to comply with'.[8] Brownsword also suggests that 'it [is] of the essence of the rule of law that enforcement should be congruent with the rules and standards so promulgated.'[9] However, Brownsword notes that law may actually not be required as the foundation, since regulation can be considered to arise from social values, norms and practice, illustrated by studies of societies in Bukowina (part of the Austro-Hungarian empire)[10] and ranchers and farmers in Shasta County, California.[11]

A widely quoted definition is that of Julia Black: regulation is 'the sustained and focused attempt to alter the behaviour of others according to standards or goals with the intention of producing a broadly identified outcome or outcomes, which may involve mechanisms of standard-setting, information-gathering and behaviour-modification'.[12] This definition is notable in focusing on *behaviour* and *outcomes*, themes that we will pick up later.

One point is worth remembering above all: regulation should be about achieving *the public good*.

Structure and Hierarchy of Regulations

Regulation typically exists in a hierarchy of controls. Structurally, there are government/Ministers, regulatory authorities, those subject to regulation (regulatees), and the beneficiaries of regulation (consumers, other traders) – which we can view as a hierarchy of power.

Politically (ie in terms of power), at the top of the structure are Parliament and government, with executive authority exercised by Ministers and assisted and implemented by civil servants in their Departments. They make policy on regulation, setting the rules and procedures through legislation. Ministers 'sponsor' a regulatory authority, which in practice usually means they exercise the right to appoint and sack the Chairs of the Board and the CEO of an authority. Ministers also make and approve secondary legislation, and impose 'policy steers' in instruction letters to authorities. Ministers control the funding of regulators. General requirements on regulators may also be imposed by government through mechanisms like a Civil Service Code and a Regulators' Code, which apply horizontally to multiple regulatory authorities.[13]

Regulatory authorities are created by legislation, which gives them powers (to issue licences, make conditions, or to enforce breaches of rules through public enforcement mechanisms, such as fines) and duties (such as to protect people from harm, hold businesses to their responsibilities, support responsible businesses and fair markets).[14] Being public bodies, they are subject to private actions for judicial review of their use of powers and performance of duties.

Authorities are typically viewed as operationally independent of government. But this can be something of a mirage, given the extent of ultimate power that can be exerted by government over their senior officers.

Public accountability of authorities is exercised in theory by Parliamentary Select Committees and requirements to publish policies and reports. We will return to whether these mechanisms are effective in chapter 6.

Regulations themselves are issued in either primary or secondary legislation (by Parliament or Ministers respectively) or in documents issued by regulatory authorities themselves, such as by policies (priorities, enforcement policies, annual reports etc) or guidance documents. Codes of practice or behaviour can (confusingly) be issued either by government, or by authorities, or sometimes by professional or trade bodies (and may be approved by an authority or by government, or made mandatory for a particular group of traders).

The Landscape of Regulatory Authorities

The traditional method of imposing regulation on a sector is to create a regulatory authority with duties and powers, including powers of imposing (or initiating) enforcement sanctions on those subject to regulation. In many states, a single regulatory authority exists for each area that is subject to regulation – and this can create inconsistencies and gaps.

At the national level, most regulatory authorities are public bodies, created by statute as individual entities that are separate from government. However, some regulatory authorities can exist within a Government Department and therefore be formally part of government. An example in the UK is the Office for Product Standards and Safety (OPSS). Further, some regulatory authorities can be private sector bodies, created as private corporations, often as not-for-profit entities or owned by a trade association. An example in the UK is the Advertising Standards Authority, the independent regulator of advertising across all media, applying codes that are written by the Committees of Advertising Practice.[15]

Each public regulatory authority comes under the oversight and sponsorship of a particular Government Department, and of its associated Parliamentary Committee. This has positive and negative aspects. The logic of oversight in a democratic state on behalf of the populace has obvious logic. However, in practice, the landscape of control over the many regulatory authorities leads to a complex matrix in which consistency of policy, approach, culture, practice and behaviour, especially over time, can give rise to significant inconsistencies. The diffusion can lead to confusion on the part of regulated actors, who may be subject to markedly different approaches by different regulators.

A further issue is that local authorities also play a role in aspects of regulation, especially in local authorisations, inspections and enforcement activities. The principal actors here are the Trading Standards and Environmental Health Departments of local authorities. Once again, the potential for inconsistencies arises, whether between national and local level approaches, or between different local authorities, or even different departments in a single local authority. Conflicts here can give rise to inconsistency and confusion for businesses that operate nationally or span several local areas.

A major problem with the traditional approach is that the technique of having a single authority that is subject to duties and powers omits the ability to adopt a more systemic approach that involves all relevant actors more productively, and also omits using a focus on achieving *outcomes*.

The Legal Model: Rules and Enforcement

State regulation is based firmly on a legal model. The legislative power of the state creates the following key elements of a regulatory system by legislation:

(1) A regulatory authority, which has duties to oversee the regulatory system and powers to act, including to take enforcement action if the rules are broken.
(2) Rules and requirements with which regulatees must comply.
(3) Where non-compliance with particular rules is identified, action instituted by the regulator to enforce compliance with the rules, usually through imposition of sanctions.

These elements form a simple linear, reactive sequence: rules, identification of non-compliance, enforcement. Thus, the basic functions of a traditional regulatory system are:

- to set the rules,
- to ensure that the rules are followed, and to identify non-compliance, and
- to enforce compliance with the rules.

The system is mechanistic: it focuses on compliance with rules. It assumes that adequate protection will arise if people comply with general and specific rules; that compliance delivers protection. The theoretical mechanistic assumption is that enforcement will *deter* future non-compliance with the rules, and that deterrence will be the basic (even, the only) tool that will deliver maximised compliance by all. But, as we will see below, there are serious problems with deterrence as a (and especially, the only) theory of controlling behaviour.

This is an authoritarian model. What we see in the Legal Model is a relic of an authoritarian state that contains echoes from many centuries ago, where power is centralised in a monarch who is all-powerful and feared. That authoritarian model is now applied in the context of the more recent idea of an all-powerful 'Westphalian' nation state, adopting an authoritarian 'command and control' mode.[16] The basic tools are power and coercion, exercised by a state, inducing fear in citizens to incentivise compliance with the state's rules, in the context of 'the rule of law', based on the assumption that compliance with a set of rules is all that is required. As summarised by legal anthropologist Professor Fernanda Pirie, 'Laws provide tools with which rulers can order and control their societies.'[17] The authoritarian mode aligned with Western philosophy of individual responsibility, with its focus on individuals obeying commandments, attaching blame to an individual who could be held responsible for adverse events.

There are big problems with the assumptions here. If one starts with the idea that we are dealing with people rather than theories, and we ask how and why people behave in particular ways, we should start with *the science of people*, ie psychology and sociology, instead of assumptions based on people theorising philosophically in the absence of empirical and scientific evidence. We should insist on scientifically verifiable answers to why people and institutions do or do not do things, especially things that cause harm. Further, the starting point for this scientific inquiry does not revolve around why people obey or break legal rules, since law is a human-made artifact. It starts with how and why people behave in particular ways. We should also ask, if we are thinking about regulation, what the purpose of a regulatory regime is (protection), and how and why it is able to deliver the required *outcomes*.

The legal system focuses on responding to breach of a *single* rule (a 'tick box' approach). This fails to give an overview of the risk of an activity or enterprise. Shifting to focus on the holistic competence of actors and a system – and especially on whether desired outcomes are being achieved – gives a better framework. The strength of the systemic cultural approach in aviation safety is that it shifted from a compliance-based approach to a performance-based approach, focused on achieving the outcomes that planes stay in the sky and people perceive that flying is safe.

The rule of law has been a fundamental constitutional principle in modern states. It has achieved much good. It supports democratic societies, challenges dictatorship and arbitrary or unfair action, and supports the rights of everyone. But it has not always existed – and, if that is so, is it immune to evolution? The construct of 'the rule of law' assumes that a rule, in the form of a law, is the only relevant criterion for judging action. But law is not the only tool that is capable of motivating or regulating society, behaviours and markets. It inherently also leads to concepts of enforcement and punishment, equated with the idea of the moral responsibility of an individual, but also requiring the exercise of power. What about norms, especially ethical norms? Are they not more fundamental than rules? What about means of organisation that are less authoritarian and more collaborative, where power is genuinely shared between multiple actors? How do we control things in those contexts?

The Economic Model: Rational Profit Maximisation and Deterrence

The primacy of deterrence as the theoretical mechanism that controls behaviour is fundamental in economic theory. The classic economic theory has been that individuals and commercial organisations are rational selfish economic actors, driven by maximising personal wealth and avoiding losses. They can, therefore, be controlled through economic incentives, so as to maximise their personal economic advantage. The principal lever here is simply (and only) money. If people break laws or cause harm, the imposition by the state of fines or damages would remove the economic advantage gained by law-breaking, re-incentivise profit maximisation, and hence deter future non-compliance. Thus, deterrence was quoted almost exclusively as the objective and justification for criminal, regulatory and civil enforcement.

The theory has obvious attractions in the context of profit-seeking companies. But it has quite a few flaws. Firstly, decisions by humans and even by companies are not taken solely on the basis of automaton-like profit maximisation. Many human factors and influences are often involved. Even if these are realised, an analytical approach of 'behavioural economics' in which the core framework is cost incentives rather than behavioural drivers and motivations is inadequate.

Secondly, the focus on enforcement and deterrence is wholly misleading. It is assumed that rational actors would avoid the loss caused by enforcement and hence be motivated to maximise their assets by complying in the first place. There are so many flaws in that assumption; we do not need to repeat what has been said elsewhere.[18]

Thirdly, there is a time-delay problem. The assumption is that imposing a financial penalty *after* an event will affect actors' rational calculations *before* they act, as they will know that certain actions will cost them money. But there are various problems with that thinking, starting with the point that people need to perceive that there is a high likelihood that their illicit gain will be totally and irrevocably removed from them, so that the wrongful activity is not worth it. As we shall refer to below, a major problem is that people (and organisations) do not act solely on the basis of rational calculation (emotions, values and culture are highly relevant) or in fact of profit maximisation, important as that is to businesses. This wider realisation – especially the relevance of psychology, sociology and ethics – is a major factor in the evolution of regulation and enforcement in recent decades.

In recent years, there has been a realisation that the basis of action by humans and organisations is far more complex than simple theories might suggest, and hence that the approaches and tools that are effective in achieving both this widening of relevant ideas and their substance raise real challenges for delivering good outcomes through external means (regulation and enforcement), as well as internal means (organisational management and culture). This realisation calls for a rethink about both the purposes and methods of what we mean by enforcement, and how we do it.

Fourthly, since the currency of enforcement is money, it is assumed that private enforcement and public enforcement achieve the same goals and can be interchanged: fines and damages are equivalent as levers in producing deterrence. This is also untrue in real life. A consequence of deregulation of public controls, notable especially in the US legal system, is that private enforcement rises, so there is more litigation.

Rules, Procedures and Systems

Individual systems may impose a large number of *rules*:

(a) *general rules*; rules on what actions or activities may or may not be done;

(b) standards; where agreed or formal standards and conditions are to apply (or able to be applied) to certain goods, services, traders, distributors, other actors or markets; or that certain legal requirements will be deemed satisfied if certain standards are applied.

Rules come in many shapes and sizes. They can be:

- private or public; formal (law) or informal (guidance) or hybrid (standards, codes); general rules or principles and specific detailed rules, which may be contained in legislation or as licence conditions;
- standards (and guidance) – private rules, agreed practice developed by consensus amongst technical experts;
- codes of practice and behaviour, typically based on (ethical) norms.

Both standards and codes are typically private but can be assimilated into public legal requirements. Rules need to be simple if they are going to be understood, not confused, be remembered, and applied.[19]

At a higher level than rules, there is often a focus on *procedures and processes* (such as design, manufacture, distribution, advertising, monitoring, surveillance and complaints). Indeed, the OECD has set out various principles for the governance of regulators themselves, which are: clarity of roles, preventing undue influence, sound decision-making and governing body structure, accountability and transparency, engagement, appropriate funding, and performance evaluation.[20]

There is a focus not just on the safety of individual products and services but also on the *systems* that contribute to safety, such as a quality management system, testing system, post-marketing surveillance system. The importance of looking at regulation as a *system* is a central focus on this book.

Problems with the Legal and Economic Models

The theory behind enforcement action in both traditional legal theory and classical economic theory is that enforcement will produce deterrence, and it is (solely) deterrence (generated by enforcement action) that will achieve compliance with the rules. The idea of deterrence is so widespread that until recently it has been heretical to challenge it. But the facts are, first, that people observe or break rules for many reasons, and the threat of enforcement and sanctions is not a major factor in inducing compliance with rules and, second, that humans may be entirely irrational or unconscious, and act in accordance with complex motivations, where they break rules. There is extensive empirical and scientific evidence on these points, which we summarise in chapter 2. Yet legal and regulatory systems and theories have not yet been updated to reflect the clear scientific evidence.

Two serious problems with traditional theories of enforcement are that they assume that everyone (including organisations) behaves the same way and does so all the time, for example is motivated by 'rational profit maximisation' (ie selfishness, calculation and greed), and that imposing punishment will prevent that behaviour. In reality, people behave differently, with different motivations and at different times. Yuval Feldman's extensive review of the evidence on 'behavioural ethics' and law[21] led him to differentiate between the motivations of 'good' and 'bad' people and to call for a clear differentiation in the mechanisms used to regulate and 'enforce' against each.[22]

Empirical research on enforcing rules in a regulatory context supports findings of psychology in relation to the consequences of people focusing on certain goals or rules, the phenomenon of crowding out, resentment of overload and feelings of diminished autonomy and trust, and so on.

In any case, a fundamental objection to the traditional Legal and Economic Models is that citizens should not nowadays be ruled by fear. We do not live in the Middle Ages or in dictatorships. Inducing fear is the essence of the theory of generating compliance through deterrence. Compliance with the rules is supposed to be produced through fear of being punished for not following them. It is inherently authoritarian – a top-down exercise of power. That is political theory and practice that does not stand up in 21st century democracies.

The traditional models are in real trouble – but this is not widely recognised. The World Economic Forum (WEF) recognised in 2021 the 'inability of conventional governance [by law] to achieve desired outcomes after the Fourth Industrial Revolution':[23]

> Rule-based legal governance models such as existing governmental institutions have traditionally held primary responsibility for defining rules and achieving trust in society. These traditional systems, however, tend to be rigid and slow to react to change. For example, legislative amendments may take years to pass, during which the external environment, expectations and

requirements may have evolved. This causes friction that inhibits innovation or fails to fully respond to societal challenges.

Traditional methods of periodic monitoring, ascribing liability and enforcement are also poorly suited to systems involving multiple actors that are engaged in complex and fluid interactions, especially where decision-making and actions are made autonomously by AI with little or no immediate human oversight. For instance, the information in company annual reports or monthly status reports lags behind the actual situation, and may not be suitable for use in autonomous systems that need to function in real time. Enforcement by on-site inspections may not be practicable where infrastructure is located in different geographies, such as when physical servers are located in various jurisdictions ...

As a way forward, the WEF recognised the influence on behaviour of social norms, markets and a goal-based approach, and suggested a system of governance involving 'consensus-building, monitoring, transparency and verifiability assurance functions', in which a Trust Governance Framework would be 'formed by accumulated evidence under trusted governance'.

A number of implications arise from the limitations of law as the basic tool, and certainly as the only tool. Is it right that compliance with legal rules is all that is required for delivering adequate protection from harm, achieved through controlling the behaviours of many actors and systems? The counter proposition is that rules are not the only mechanism, and have their limitations. Values, ethics, and principles have profound relevance. The need for *both* legal rules and codes of ethical behaviour is increasingly being recognised in many regulatory and commercial contexts. The findings of anthropologists are illuminating on the evolution of concepts and institutions involving law and values, such as the reliance by rulers on legal rules and courts, and the deeper reliance by societies on ethical values embodied in religions. They also note that as religions have waned in some Western nations, there is a need to reinvent ethical values, codes, and institutions such as Ombuds, if social cohesion is to be reinforced.

The distinguished anthropologist Joseph Henrich has strongly criticised civil law's basis on 'rights':

> the particular idea of endowing individuals with 'rights' and then designing laws based on those rights only makes sense in a world of analytical thinkers who conceive of people as primarily independent agents and look to solve

problems by assigning properties, dispositions and essences to objects and persons.[24]

In contrast, where we conceive of people as cooperative and interdependent, working together in coordinated relationships, concepts of legal rights may be seen as less important tools than fundamental ethical values and principles. Also, formal institutions need to fit the cultural psychology of the population in question.[25]

The same myopia exists about public regulatory law and its assumption that a basis on rules-sanctions-compliance is all that is necessary. This is not to say that law is irrelevant or useless. We can view the use of law anthropologically as a necessary stage in the evolution of humanity. People find legal rules, legal institutions and enforcement by their state to be useful. In providing protection from those with criminal intent or from those who incompetently cause risk and harm, a formal, trusted process based on legal principles of justice is essential. But it should be instructive to reflect that as forms of human societies evolve, different tools may be relevant. A simple example is that the Ten Commandments were a set of rules, whereas the later approach of Christianity is based on ethical values.

Public and Private Modes of Regulation

Regulation is usually thought of as an activity carried out by the state. A state is able to use its power to take enforcement action against non-compliance with its rules. However, regulation is also extensively carried out by private actors – without the backing of state enforcement mechanisms, but sometimes with other sanctions. The various modes of 'regulation' are largely classifiable into public, private, or social mechanisms. The typology includes the following range of options:[26]

(1) *Formal state regulation*, involving laws made by the state (by Parliament or under delegated powers), typically authorising an authority with defined remit, duties and powers, such as to undertake investigations, and to enforce non-compliance with the rules by imposing sanctions or institute prosecutions in the courts, and specifying legal rules to which those subject to the rules must observe (eg requirements, duties, prohibitions).
(2) *Self-regulation*, where a group of private sector actors (eg sectoral trade or professional associations, or civil society bodies such as

Fairtrade, WWF) voluntarily observe obligations arising under a code of practice of their association. The arrangement might sometimes involve complaint mechanisms, and perhaps some form of sanctions, such as a reprimand or ultimately (but rarely) exclusion from the association.

(3) *Co-regulation*, involving some combination of state regulation and self-regulation. There are various possible modes. One mode might make observance of a private code mandatory for all defined types of traders. Another mode is *mandated self-regulation*, in which traders are required by law to join an association and/or be subject to its code or rules. Another element might involve reliance on one or more private accreditation and assurance or certification schemes.

(4) *Information, guidance and education*, whether for traders or consumers/customers, and whether provided or mandated by public or private actors and mechanisms. The purpose is usually to try to rectify an imbalance of power between purchasers and one or more traders, so that the former can exercise informed and free choice in purchasing, or be properly informed about how to use a product safely or perform an activity safety.

(5) *Economic instruments*, such as exclusion from a professional body, or requirements to pay fees for membership of a professional body or dispute resolution scheme, training requirements (initial and/ or continuing), financial penalties for breaching rules, civil law requirements to make good damage caused.

(6) *Informal, social and reputational levers* that influence traders' behaviour by providing consumers with better information on what they should ask or choose, and nudging them towards traders with greater reliability.

(7) *Inspection and grading* where the technique of inspection typically does not lead to enforcement, intervention or support but to public grading. This model has given rise to significant problems but can also deliver results.

Standards, Conformity Assessment, Certification and Accreditation

Private forms of 'regulation' have developed independently from state regulation. The principal mechanisms are standards, conformity assessment, certification and accreditation. These mechanisms have evolved in most states into being created and administered by formalised bodies, such as national standards and certification authorities, but the private and public streams remain separate and distinct. (The USA does not have a national system: anyone can write a standard in a non-collaborative way.) However, they both share the ultimate need to support trust in activities.

In order to increase efficiency in how different people do the same things, to help them converge on the best way of doing something, and to enable efficient and accurate checking (for commercial and regulatory purposes) of what has been done, recognised *standards* are widely used.[27] A standard is a document, established through a collaborative process and approved by a recognised body. It provides rules, guidelines or characteristics for activities or their results so that they can be repeated.

A related mechanism is a professional or trade association's *code of behaviour*, which specifies the behaviours that are expected of a group of professionals or companies, typically based on a set of agreed fundamental ethical norms and principles. Some codes have been created by trade bodies, or are approved[28] or imposed by governments. However, the more independent and democratically collective they are, in relation to both co-creation and operation, the more they will be trusted.

National standards bodies assist in the discussions on drafting standards across an extremely wide range of subject matter. They operate on the basis of facilitating expert discussion and consensus. Standards can be adopted voluntarily, and formally at national, supra-national (eg EU) or international levels. Examples of international standards adopted by the International Standards Organisation (ISO) are:

- Quality management standards to help people work more efficiently and reduce product failures, eg ISO 9001:2015 *Quality management systems – Requirements*.
- Environmental management standards to help reduce environmental impacts, reduce waste and be more sustainable, eg ISO 14001:2015 *Environmental management systems – Requirements with guidance for use*.
- Health and safety standards to help reduce accidents in the workplace, eg ISO 45001:2018 *Occupational health and safety management systems – Requirements with guidance for use*.

Standards, Conformity Assessment, Certification and Accreditation 29

- Energy management standards to help cut energy consumption, eg ISO 50001 *Energy management*.
- Food safety standards to help prevent food from being contaminated, eg ISO 22000 *Food safety management*.
- IT security standards to help keep sensitive information secure, eg ISO/IEC 27001:2022 *Information security, cybersecurity and privacy protection – Information security management systems – Requirements*.
- ISO 37001:2025 *Anti-bribery management systems – Requirements with guidance for use*
- ISO/IEC 42001:2023 *Information technology – Artificial intelligence – Management system*

Major standardisation bodies include: the British Standards Institution (BSI), European Committee for Standardisation (CEN), European Committee for Electrotechnical Standardisation (CENELEC) and European Telecommunications Standards Institute (ETSI), and at international level, the International Organization for Standardization (ISO), International Electrotechnical Commission (IEC) and International Telecommunication Union (ITU).

A standard is not 'regulatory' as such, but it may be *designated* by a government, with the consequence that a manufacturer who claims compliance with the standard can claim compliance with the 'essential requirements' of the relevant law. Compliance gives a 'presumption of conformity' (which can be countered by evidence) with the corresponding essential legal requirements. Designated standards do not replace the essential requirements, and manufacturers retain full responsibility for ensuring the applicable law is met. But this alternative means of demonstrating compliance is widely used, and can be efficient in combining commercial and regulatory objectives.

A body may claim that its products, services or activities conform to a specific standard (subject to complying with legal prohibitions on making false marketing statements). But it is common to demonstrate compliance by having one's conformity with a standard assessed and confirmed by an independent third party. Thus, *conformity assessment* and *certification* of compliance provide assurance that what is being supplied meets the expectations specified or claimed. These activities are carried out by specialist *conformity assessment bodies*. Conformity assessment can be applied to a product (which, for these purposes, includes a service), a process, a management system, a body or persons and includes activities such as testing and inspection before issuing certification. Accreditation is specific to the requirements or activities covered under the relevant standard.

The conformity assessment body should, of course, be independent of the body whose claimed conformity is being assessed and certified. In various fields, the potential for conflicts of interest can remain a concern. A conformity assessment body may itself demonstrate its competence and compliance with international conformity assessment standards by being formally recognised as *accredited* under a distinct approval process. Such approval is granted by an independent *accreditation body*, which may be independent or a sole governmental body (as in the UK, where the national body is the United Kingdom Accreditation Service (UKAS), which operates under a Memorandum of Understanding with the UK Government). Thus, the accreditation process determines, in the public interest, the technical competence and integrity of organisations such as those offering testing, calibration and certification services.

The International and European standards bodies have facilitated the use of conformity assessment by the development of standards for the operation of various types of conformity assessment bodies (CABs) and for accreditation bodies. Agreements within the regional and international accreditation fora (eg European cooperation for Accreditation, International Accreditation Forum, and International Laboratory Accreditation Cooperation) have also facilitated the international acceptance of accredited conformity assessment. These 'multilateral arrangements' are based on the peer assessment of national accreditation bodies and help to establish the equivalence of accredited conformity assessment. In some sectors, mutual acceptance schemes have been developed, based on the peer assessment of individual CABs, negating the need for duplicate testing. Mutual recognition agreements between regulators can also facilitate trade by enabling business to source its conformity assessment in the exporting market.

The UK refers to its National Quality Infrastructure (NQI) as comprising standardisation, measurement, conformity assessment, accreditation and market surveillance.

In some states, public regulatory systems and requirements have adopted private mechanisms into their architectures, which supports increased efficiency and avoids some duplication. An example is the option of manufacturers applying harmonised standards in many EU laws on regulation of product types. Another example is use of 'regulated self-assurance':[29]

> 6.5. Regulated self-assurance can work through a variety of mechanisms:
> - assurance schemes (eg Red Tractor);
> - industry-run registers (eg the Gas Safe scheme of registered gas engineers or the Fenestration Self-Assessment Scheme (FENSA), the register of window installers);
> - regulator supervision of industry/professions' self-regulation (eg Financial Reporting Council supervision of accountancy bodies);
> - accredited voluntary registration (eg the Professional Standards Authority accreditation of bodies like the British Acupuncture Council or the Association of Child Psychotherapists); and
> - company self-regulation (eg water companies are responsible for monitoring water quality and reporting adverse incidents, with every stage of the process being accredited, likewise medicines approval and testing).

Advantages and Drawbacks of Private Regulation

A private regulatory system is usually much quicker to create than one involving legislation, and quicker to amend and update. It can leverage practical expertise and knowledge that focuses on delivery.[30]

But a private regime might not include everyone, so may have limited force, and might potentially be anti-competitive, excluding some or new actors. Hence, there is a need for a level playing field, consistency for all, and for independent and transparent governance. A 2019 study undertaken for the Government of a number of UK self-regulatory and co-regulatory initiatives concluded that 'those initiatives considered to be the most successful have leveraged a range of tools and incentives to encourage both participation and compliance among members.'[31]

The major difference between public and private regulation is in relation to the consequences where non-compliance with the rules is identified, and the requirements are enforced. Different tools are used. Public enforcement may involve a range of sanctions based on the state's criminal law, from imprisonment, fines, disqualification as a director or professional, and various other consequences. Private sanctions are typically more restricted, such as reprimand or censure, disqualification from certain activities, and ultimately expulsion from membership of the professional or trade body. Criticisms are heard that private bodies can be reluctant to impose sanctions on their own members (a form of 'capture'), whereas public regulators should enforce the rules without fear or favour.

There has been a significant cross-fertilisation of sanctions between the public and private worlds in recent decades, and some attempts are now being made to review the entire landscape and produce an effective matrix of sanctions. Some private sanctions, such as withholding certification, can bring highly significant consequences, which can produce swift focus on taking actions to remedy problems so as to regain the ability to trade or practice.

In deciding which modes of regulation to employ, it is logical to start by compiling all relevant evidence of the various potential risks and harms that may be caused by the activity, and the incidence and severity of each risk. From that evidence base, the objective is to analyse and compare the relevant regulatory options, and conclude what level of regulatory intervention seems appropriate to respond to each risk, so that it is likely to be at an acceptable level. It will be necessary to evaluate the effectiveness of the relevant optional interventions in adequately identifying, preventing, responding to, and controlling the relevant risks(s) and harm(s). As we discuss further in chapter 4, it is also logical to carry out an analysis of how the various functions in the relevant regulatory space can be fulfilled most efficiently and effectively.

Recent UK Government policy on regulation is not only to carry out full consideration of all options (public, private, do nothing),[32] and their advantages and disadvantages, using an impact assessment based on available evidence, but also to seek to avoid unnecessary formal regulation if acceptable alternatives exist.[33]

Achieving Both Protection and Freedom

Regulation is inherently about constraining some activities or things, or the way that things are done, so as to prevent harm and reduce risk. But constraints unavoidably interfere with personal freedoms. So, regulation does present a barrier to activities, especially for any person who wants to undertake commercial activity. In simple terms, the situation here is that the activity is inherently legal (it is not inherently classed as criminal) but how it is done, and the outcomes that it produces, are required to be controlled. Hence, regulation may involve some costs and delay in undertaking activities.

Given the inherent conflict between, on the one hand, the principle of freedom of individual action and commerce, and, on the other hand, the principle of delivering adequate protection from harm and risk, control systems need to achieve a *balance* that adequately delivers positive outcomes. The 'right' balance needs to be set between benefits and risks, between freedom and constraint, between prosperity and protection. How should that balance be set and achieved, and who sets this?

The balance is ultimately a matter for each society, based on its common values. In relation to what is the 'right' balance, views can, of course, differ and can change over time. We must expect debate and evolutions in consensus on what is appropriate. We should design fora and institutions to accommodate such debate and evolution. These factors can make the life of regulators (and regulatees, beneficiaries and the public) particularly challenging. They often get blamed, when they are just trying to do what society has asked them to do (deliver protection) by acting within the constraints that Parliament has given them.

But it is also true that people and organisations have their own reasons for controlling what they do and how they do it. Rational businesses and investors would not want to waste time or money on activities that fail to produce good outcomes because they involve unacceptable risk. Hence, commercial organisations operate internal mechanisms such as management systems, private accreditation systems, audits, and controls on research and development, manufacturing, marketing, and post-marketing surveillance and customer care. The ideal is for the requirements of internal and public controls to be aligned, so as to optimise outcomes and efficiency. A good business or regulated activity should itself spontaneously be controlling risk, harms and outcomes in order to operate in a self-sustainable way as if external regulatory requirements were inherently part of good internal practice.

Precautionary or Proportionate Risk?

We have said that regulation of safety unavoidably involves engaging with the concept of risk. How much risk is a society prepared to accept? Do people expect that everything will be completely safe, and that a regulator will achieve complete safety, without any harm occurring? Many people do think that. But in what circumstances is it realistic?

Societies have different risk appetites. Some states can decide not to allow some activities unless and until all risks are known and quantified. Other states may prefer to accept some risks in order to gain advantages from innovation. These different viewpoints are illustrated by political statements about precautionary or proportionate approaches. A leading example of the former is the EU's 'precautionary principle'. The approach is that where there is significant scientific uncertainty about the potential risks and their level of significance, a precautionary approach should be adopted.[34] But governments can call for greater acceptance of risk in order to achieve improved growth and innovation. These points are examined further in chapter 8.

It follows that a society or group should ideally know what its appetite is for risk – including for different types of risk and uncertainty. Psychology research shows that most people are influenced by particular aspects of perceived risk, that can strongly affect their emotional responses to risk. Factors that will affect humans' perception of risk and its probability include: how the risk or harm is framed or presented; its proximity in space and time, likelihood, severity, type; personal exposure.[35] Risk can be undervalued when focusing on some other task. A logical approach is to construct a consensus on a framework of different risks, based on both data on incidence and severity.

Since one cannot avoid all risk in this world, it is axiomatic that the degree of constraint imposed by regulation needs to be proportionate, so as to balance the benefits and the potential risks. Regulators (both in companies and state authorities) have the challenging task of striking the right *balance* on a daily basis. This needs a mechanism for decision, and may give rise to controversy over both the mechanisms (who decides, and on what basis) and individual decisions. The traditional constitutional mechanism has been that Parliament is the institution that should reach such political or controversial decisions. But in reality, decisions are now largely delegated to regulatory authorities or committees, but remain subject to criticism by the media and commentators of many kinds. These considerations highlight the advisability of encouraging widespread and transparent debate in many regulatory situations, certainly those which involve high controversy.[36] An example is the need for widespread trust in new technologies, and in the systems and institutions that govern them, if they are to be taken up effectively.

What is a Regulatory System for?

If regulation is about protection, a regulatory *system* is aimed at ensuring that regulated activities achieve the desired *outcomes* that ensure that the desired levels of protection are achieved. In other words, undesired harms are prevented (in both incidence and severity) and risks are controlled. So, *outcomes are the point*. Are prices and markets fair? Are people kept safe? Are people harmed? Are regulated people and entities delivering useful productive products, services innovation and growth? Are risks identified, avoided, mitigated, and people warned?

Too many traditional regulatory regimes and systems totally fail to focus on whether they are achieving the desired outcomes at all, let alone whether things are improving or getting worse. In the popular consciousness, regulation is largely about blaming people and imposing sanctions. The scientific evidence in chapter 2 shows why that approach is bound to fail. Instead, we should be measuring the outcomes that we produce. Do planes stay in the sky? Is AI safe? Are new medical techniques and treatments safe and effective? Are professionals competent and behaving well? Are we achieving net zero? We can only start to know the answers to so many questions like these if we establish what the desired outcomes are and then collect and examine the data that proves if they are being achieved, or if our efforts are being effective or not. So, *outcomes need data*.

Where do we get the data from? We need a system that collects all the relevant data. Often regulatory regimes are far from comprehensive in collecting data. Digital technology has opened huge opportunities to collect relevant data, and AI has the ability to scrutinise it highly effectively to identify what we want to know. So, we need to modernise our regulatory systems. This almost certainly means that more people and places that have data need to be involved as data sources. So, we need a wider and more collaborative system. The following chapters will explain how we should design and operate an effective regulatory system on these lines.

Key Points

- Regulation is about protection.
- It is also about predictability and stability, supporting fair markets and social relationships necessary for fair, stable and vibrant societies and growing economies.

- Regulation is everywhere, and essential for ensuring that many human activities are safe and fair.
- Regulation inevitably restricts freedom. But you can achieve both if you do things well.
- Many organisations and activities share the desire for protection so regulatory requirements should be akin to a checklist of good practice.
- Doing this well should allocate costs efficiently, and avoid both causing unnecessary harm and incurring the costs of putting things right (redress and compensation).
- It's tempting – but wrong – to criticise 'regulation'. Given the variety of contexts, tools and behaviours that are used across many different regulatory regimes, we need to be far more specific when seeking to identify problems and solutions.
- Two traditional models of regulation – the Legal Model and the Economic Model – have serious limitations.
- New technologies pose significant risks, and traditional regulatory regimes will not deliver adequate protection from new harms.
- We need to revise how we do regulation. Please read on …

---

[1] See *United Nations Guidelines for Consumer Protection*, http://unctad.org/system/files/official-document/ditccplpmisc2016d1_en.pdf.

[2] *Digital consumer harms – A taxonomy, root cause analysis and methodologies for measurement*. Prepared for DCMS by LSE & Plum Consulting, January 2023, www.gov.uk/government/publications/digital-consumer-issues-research.

[3] AI Ogus, *Regulation: Legal Form and Economic Theory* (Clarendon Press, 1994); R Brownsword, *Rethinking Law, Regulation, and Technology* (Edward Elgar, 2022).

[4] C Decker, *Modern Economic Regulation. An Introduction to Theory and Practice*, 2nd edn (Cambridge University Press, 2023).

[5] ibid.

[6] P Selznick, 'Focusing Organizational Research on Regulation' in Roger Noll (ed), *Regulatory Policy and the Social Sciences* (Berkeley: University of California Press, 1985) 363 at 383.

[7] R Brownsword, *Rethinking Law, Regulation, and Technology* (Edward Elgar, 2022).

[8] LL Fuller, *The Morality of Law* (New Haven: Yale University Press, 1969). For an application of the Fullerian principles to particular instances of cyberlaw, see C Reed, 'How to Make Bad Law: Lessons from Cyberspace' (2010) 73 *MLR* 903, esp at 914–16. As Reed summarises it (at 927): 'Complexity makes laws hard to understand, contradictory rules make compliance impossible and frequent change compounds these difficulties.'

[9] R Brownsword, *Rethinking Law, Regulation, and Technology* (Edward Elgar, 2022).
[10] E Ehrlich, *Fundamental Principles of the Sociology of Law* (New Brunswick: Transaction Publishers, 2001 [1913]).
[11] RC Ellickson, *Order Without Law* (Cambridge, Mass: Harvard University Press, 1991).
[12] J Black, 'What is Regulatory Innovation?' in J Black, M Lodge, and M Thatcher (eds), *Regulatory Innovation* (Cheltenham: Edward Elgar, 2005) 1 at 11.
[13] In the UK, the Regulators' Code (www.gov.uk/government/publications/regulators-code) was made under the Legislative and Regulatory Reform Act 2006.
[14] See *Delivering protection and confidence in a strong, green economy. OPSS Product Regulation Strategy 2022 to 2025* (Office for Product Safety & Standards, 2022).
[15] Other UK private sector 'regulators' include:

Association of Chartered Certified Accountants (ACCA)
British Board of Film Classification
Chartered Institute of Public Finance and Accountancy
Chartered Institute for the Management of Sport and Physical Activity
College of Policing
The Complementary and Natural Healthcare Council (CNHC)
Engineering Council
The Faculty Office of the Archbishop of Canterbury
Fundraising Regulator
Independent Press Standards Organisation (IPSO)
Institute of Chartered Accountants in England & Wales
The Institute and Faculty of Actuaries
The Association of Professional Pension Trustees (APPT)
Prescription Medicines Code of Practice Authority (PMCPA)
Royal Institution of Chartered Surveyors
Many other sectoral professional associations, such as in law and healthcare.

[16] TC Daintith 'The techniques of government' in J Jowell and D Oliver (eds), *The Changing Constitution*, 3rd edn (Oxford University Press, 1994); TR Tyler, 'The psychology of self-regulation: normative motivations for compliance' in C Parker and VL Nielsen (eds), *Explaining Compliance. Business Responses to Regulation* (Edward Elgar, 2012).
[17] F Pirie, *The Rule of Laws. A 4,000-Year Quest to Order the World* (Profile Books, 2021).
[18] See C Hodges, *Law and Corporate Behaviour* (Hart, 2015); Y Feldman, *The Law of Good People* (Cambridge, 2018); B van Rooij and A Fine, *The Behavioral Code* (Beacon Press, 2021); TR Tyler, *Advanced Introduction to Law and Psychology* (Edward Elgar, 2022).
[19] See ch 2 below.
[20] *OECD Best Practice Principles for Regulatory Policy. The Governance of Regulators* (OECD, 2014).
[21] See also MH Bazerman and AE Tenbrunsel, *Blind Spots: Why We Fail to Do What's Right and What to Do about It* (Princeton University Press, 2011); AE Tenbrunsel and D Chugh, 'Behavioral Ethics: A Story of Increased Breadth and Depth' (2015), 6 *Current Opinion in Psychology* 205; B van Rooij and DD Sokol (eds), *The Cambridge Handbook of Compliance* (Cambridge University Press, 2020).
[22] Y Feldman, *The Law of Good People. Challenging States' Ability to Regulate Human Behavior* (Cambridge University Press, 2018).
[23] *Rebuilding Trust and Governance: Towards Data Free Flow with Trust (DFFT)* (World Economic Forum, 2021), para 2.2.
[24] J Henrich, *The Weirdest People in the World. How the West Became Psychologically Peculiar and Particularly Prosperous* (Allen Lane, 2020) 84–85.
[25] ibid 219.

[26] See *Reducing Regulation Made Simple: Less regulation, better regulation and regulation as a last resort* (HM Government, 2010). *Recommendation of the Council on Regulatory and Policy Governance* (OECD, 2012), Recommendation 4. The descriptions attached to each type above are those of Professor Christopher Hodges.

[27] This section is based on website statements by the UK Government and the International Standards Organization on standards, conformity assessment, certification and accreditation. See www.gov.uk/guidance and www.iso.org/home.html.

[28] *Consumer Codes Approval Scheme. Core Criteria and Guidance* (Office of Fair Trading, 2008), OFT 390.

[29] *Regulatory Futures Review* (Cabinet Office, 2017).

[30] J Rowan-Robinson, P Wachtman and C Barker, *Crime and Regulation. A Study of the Enforcement of Regulatory Codes* (Edinburgh, T & T Clark, 1990).

[31] K McEntaggart, J Etienne and J Uddin, *Designing Self-and Co-Regulation Initiatives: Evidence on Best Practices: A literature review*, BEIS Research Paper Number 2019/025.

[32] *Guidance: The Green Book (2022)* (Government Finance Function and HM Treasury, 2022).

[33] ibid para 7.9.

[34] Treaty on the Functioning of the European Union (TFEU), Art 191. *Understanding and Applying the Precautionary Principle in the Energy Transition* (OECD, 2023).

[35] D Kahneman, *Thinking Fast and Slow* (Allen Lane, 2011); C Hodges, *Law and Corporate Behaviour* (Hart, 2015) 18–25.

[36] A recent idea is that Boards of regulators would have a different attitude to risk (and commercial benefits) if there were more business experience around the table (to counteract the default of focusing solely on risk and harm). Equally, the voice of those who are concerned about safety issues and unknowns is relevant.

2

Scientific Evidence on How Humans Behave

> This chapter summarises several streams of research on the psychology and sociology of human motivation and behaviour, and socio-legal studies into why and how people obey or break laws. It summarises a vast quantity of scientific and empirical research relevant to what makes people observe social and legal rules, what makes people break such rules, how the risk that people and organisations may break rules can be reduced, and hence how internal and external regulatory systems, and enforcement regimes, should best be designed and operated. The evidence now comprises several different streams, which together form a coherent and convincing corpus. A number of books contain summaries of much of this material.[1]
>
> We achieve more if our intrinsic motivation is engaged, rather than if external incentives or forces try to influence us. Self-Determination Theory is a key unifying theme: the objective of supporting (not undermining) autonomy, competence and relatedness. Powerful forces are the ethics of ourselves and our groups, and the social norms of our groups. Trust and trustworthiness are powerful, based on an internal ethical compass that is inherent in (almost) all of us.
>
> These findings have been applied in business practice to drive successful companies, and with astounding success across multiple organisations in aviation safety (Open & Just Culture). Key elements are motivation, support, encouragement, psychological safety, and the size of groups. The findings here inform good practice in leadership of organisations, in interventions and enforcement of rules, and form the basis of the OBC (Outcome-Based Collaboration) model.
>
> If the point is to affect human behaviour, should we not start with human science rather than legal/economic theories?

Factors Affecting Human Actions

Human behaviour is not in fact rational but (predictably) *irrational*.[2] We are each affected by our individual heuristics and biases.[3] We can react quickly and automatically in situations that are perceived to be familiar (System I thinking) without thinking objectively (System II). If given time to think or to react to challenge, we tend to act more carefully.

Our thought and actions are influenced by the effects of different personalities,[4] mental abilities and injuries, exposure to experiences, depth of knowledge,[5] and conditions (such as emotional states[6] and tiredness). Feldman refers to differences in personalities affecting behaviour, relating to moral identity,[7] level of moral disengagement,[8] and moral firmness,[9] and context-specific measures.

Good people can make mistakes, break rules and can act badly, quite frequently. Yuval Feldman concludes that legal systems have wrongly focused on assuming that people break the law because they are bad people, whereas he lists extensive evidence that many (good) people make mistakes.[10] This can be for many reasons, including not realising that what we are doing is unethical,[11] or where actions are driven by emotion,[12] or acting in circumstances where the focus on achieving certain goals, or the lack of focus on risks and adverse consequences, causes temporary ethical blindness.[13]

Humans are able to persuade themselves that breaking a rule is consistent with their ethical values and sense of self-worth (*cognitive dissonance*, which is the discomfort that we feel in the face of conflict between different values and hence actions).[14] When we are confronted with evidence that challenges our deeply held beliefs, which therefore threatens our self-worth, we are more likely to *reframe* the evidence,[15] and deny that we have acted unethically, than we are to accept self-censure. For a behaviour to lead to a cognitive or attitude change, we must first experience taking responsibility for bringing about an adverse event (dissonance arousal) and then accept personal responsibility for the consequences of the behaviour (dissonance motivation).[16] Thus, many good people often cheat – but only to a limited extent.[17] Studies found that the level of dishonesty dropped when people paid more attention to honesty standards, and climbed with increased categorisation malleability.[18]

We can focus on particular goals (eg sales or performance targets, or bureaucratic processes) and forget to apply ethical principles or other goals (crowding out).

The Power of Internal Motivation

Numerous researchers have identified that internal motivation is more powerful than external motivation. Experiments by Dan Ariely and colleagues found that introducing or raising incentives does not necessarily improve performance – it can even make it worse.[19] They and Teresa Amabile concluded that tasks that involve algorithmic effort (production of similar items on a production line, as long as the operator does not get tired) *can* be motivated by external incentives like contingent rewards and punishments, but they can cause 'devastating' impairment of performance for heuristic *cognitive* (right brain, judgmental) tasks (such as adding numbers or problem solving).[20] Amabile summarised the conclusion: 'Intrinsic motivation is conducive to creativity; controlling extrinsic motivation is detrimental to creativity.'[21] Ernst Fehr predicts that external incentives that use monetary rewards or punishments may undermine internal motivation to comply.[22] The theory that specific (ethical) values and intentions can be 'crowded out' by other incentives or distractions has been widely supported.[23]

Feldman suggests that an incentive-based approach fails to engage with many behaviours, and that the whole focus of the criminal and regulatory enforcement systems is incorrect and ineffective, because it uses the wrong tools on the wrong people.[24] He suggests that too little attention has been paid to the role of internal motivation.

Morality, Ethics and Values

Our sense of morality strongly affects actions. Psychologist Jonathan Haidt describes morality as 'the extraordinary human capacity that made civilization possible'.[25] Nicholas Christakis cites studies showing humans' inherent moral sense, even from birth.[26] The effect is both innate (the product of automatic intuitions, that vary between individuals depending upon our brains) and learned (influenced by our application of those intuitions in a particular social culture).[27] Ethics and morality are based on our values, personally and those of our group.

Solomon identified the three most basic business virtues as honesty, fairness and trustworthiness.[28] Since the 1990s at least, statements have been made about virtue-based personal and organisational business ethics.[29] Many corporations have issued mission and values statements.

But it has been found that official statements are of little value in affecting the behaviour of staff unless the values are demonstrated and supported throughout an organisation.[30] You have to 'live the values'.

Values are highly stable in individuals[31] but can evolve.[32] However, our *application* of our values is not as immutable as we may think. Shalom Schwartz identified 10 clusters of basic personal values that are recognised across cultures in 44 countries: self-direction, stimulation, hedonism, achievement, power, security, conformity, tradition, benevolence and universalism.[33] He mapped these in a circle of opposing values that are present in all humans, but are enhanced depending on our emotional response to different situations. An example might be feeling altruistic when content but feeling aggressive when threatened. The most recent survey of moral attitudes was published in 2019 by Curry, Mullins and Whitehouse, who analysed records of cooperative behaviours from anthropological data from 60 societies across the world and coded them into seven types.[34] The seven basic moral rules were all held almost universally in common: help your family, help your group, return favours, be brave, defer to superiors, divide resources fairly, and respect other people's property.

Values have the sociological function of supporting individuals interacting in groups by providing a prescription for what to do.[35,36,37,38] Values can constrain the self-interests of an actor, by having to take the legitimate interests of others into account.[39] There is mounting evidence of the effect of values on controlling human activity in groups, and on the origins and need for this mechanism. Many recent sociologists have asserted that values are defined by the community or group as immutable ideas (principles) to govern the behaviour of the individuals of that group.[40] Without this accepted but inherent mental discipline, it is argued that individuals could not cooperate in cohesive groups.

Value commitments are part of a society's culture, which is 'an ever-shifting pattern of values, beliefs, traditions, projects and allegiances holding ... communal networks together'.[41] 'Values-related issues are often magnified when coupled with group identities, where winning or the domination of a group can be more important than living up to one's own values.'[42] Organisational values can be embedded within organisations through diffusion by different stakeholders at multiple hierarchical levels with whom they are internalised.[43]

Jonathan Haidt asserts that moral reasoning is a synthesis based on three mechanisms: how groups create social solidarity, the existence of affective behaviour, and social persuasion.[44] The first element rests on extensive evidence of in-group activity, which binds people into groups, builds the group, and also blinds the members to other influences. The second element is based on the alleged primacy of affective intuitions in humans, and the argument that concerns of justice, care, loyalty, authority and purity are all best characterised as moral intuitions or emotions. Haidt argues that these affects, or emotions, are more powerful than moral reasoning as they are triggered more quickly (pre-rational) and are hence primary. The third element posits that the object and hence rationale of moral thinking is to persuade others in a social context and enable the individual to succeed in the social order.

Christakis considers that the development of human evolution is based on the *need* to cooperate, and that the inter-relationship of genes and cooperative culture has produced, and is continuing to produce, a movement towards humans inherently becoming more ethical.[45] He concludes that the arc of our evolutionary history 'bends towards goodness', ie that humans tend overall to behave more ethically, because we learn (and accordingly our genes adapt) that moral behaviour is better for cooperation.[46] Frans de Waal's insight is that 'When we became cooperative animals, we abandoned the right-of-the-strongest principle and moved on to a right-of-the-contributor principle.'[47]

The Power of Social Influence, Culture and Ethics

We are significantly affected by social influences, ie by the actions and perceptions of others. This is based on an inherent need to conform to the culture of a group. Roy Baumeister identified our powerful motivation to form and sustain at least a minimum number of social connections ('Need-to-Belong Theory'). He explains self-esteem as an internal measure of a person's chances of having good relationships.[48] Baumeister noted women's emphasis on close, intimate relationships and men's orientation towards larger networks of shallower relationships. He also noted research that showed that rejection, thwarting the need to belong, could produce emotional numbness and even aggression. He concluded that culture depends on belongingness.

Self-esteem is thought by Mark Leary to be a psychological gauge of the degree to which people perceive that they are relationally valued and socially accepted by others.[49] He found that actions appearing to protect or increase a person's self-esteem are usually motivated by protecting or enhancing their relational value to others, and thus increasing the likelihood of interpersonal acceptance. Feldman's overview concluded that the importance of group identity and the individual's need to belong is beyond debate.[50] The motivation to fit into a group is a powerful motivator that can counteract an individual's self-interest and intrinsic values.[51] Kahan said that we may need to believe that other members of society share the same commitment to the law, so as to maintain our own commitment to society and its rules.[52]

Social cooperation and the success of groups is strongly associated with shared values and ethical culture. The culture of an organisation, or a sub-group, is a powerful influence on how people typically behave, since it influences processes, instinctive reactions, and which ethical values are applied. Joseph Henrich, Professor of Human Evolutionary Biology at Harvard, considers that 'Psychological changes induced by culture can shape all manner of subsequent events by influencing what people pay attention to, how they make decisions, which institutions they prefer, and how much they innovate.'[53]

Surveying extensive literature on how institutions influence and shape behaviour, Christoph Engel and Elke Weber[54] note that institutions typically resort to routines, procedures and problem-solving cycles,[55] as well as skill sets and professionalism,[56] to assist rational decision-making (Kahneman's Type II reasoning rather than the Type I intuitive heuristic). Introducing a need to justify actions tends to make an individual aware of complexities of a task,[57] makes accountability salient,[58] and typically also raises the stakes. Higher stakes and risk tend to induce greater preparation,[59] to be more open to facts,[60] to take more of the available information into account,[61] to show greater internal consistency,[62] and to become more risk averse.[63]

Yuval Feldman suggests that the situational factor is much more influential than the personal factor in causing wrongdoing.[64]

In summary, social norms can override ethical norms, as occurs in criminal gangs and the Mafia (social network theory).[65] The mechanism here is that we have an inherent need to protect the social groups to which we belong. Historically, we have used punishment, ostracism and expulsion for those who threaten the cohesion of our group by flouting its values, identified as breaking its rules. Law and a legal system have played a helpful role, but at the expense of de-emphasising ethical values and genuine inclusivity.

The Causes of Disasters

Inquiries into Disasters

The list of major disasters is long and constantly growing. It also provides a wide range of contexts for examining human behaviour and why harm occurs. Some well-known examples are:

- transport: Challenger space shuttle; Herald of Free Enterprise ferry capsize;
- energy and nuclear plants disasters: Three Mile Island;[66] Chernobyl;
- financial: collapse of significant institutions, such as the secondary banking crisis in the 1970s; BCCI in 1991;[67] Barings in 1995;[68] Equitable Life;[69] Payment Protection Insurance; selling sub-prime mortgages, and derivatives; hence the Global Financial Crash;[70] fixing LIBOR;[71] 1DB; Wirecard 2020; Australian examples;[72] unauthorised accounts created in Wells Fargo;[73] people *around* a Ponzi scheme, eg around Madoff;
- corporate: ENRON and World Com;[74] Austrian wine contamination; melamine infant formula contamination in China; Volkswagen diesel emissions fraud; Boeing 737 MAX;[75]
- healthcare: a succession of failures in care, especially in maternity care, elderly care homes, and child safeguarding; failures of care, of oversight, and of responses;[76]
- public organisations: Post Office: multiple prosecutions for fraud against innocent sub-post office workers, based on reliance on a faulty computer system whose unreliability was known early on, plus corporate behaviour on investigations and oversight that treated victims as guilty throughout and failed to respond to warning signs or evidence plus cover-ups;[77] provision of infected blood to patients; failures of care, information, oversight, covering up;[78]
- fire: the Grenfell Tower fire and inability to act on unsafe cladding that was known to be a fire risk; issue of fraudulent certificates of compliance; failure of public oversight mechanisms.[79]

So much of the classical analysis of disasters and the allocation of blame is focused on *individuals*. This overlooks the profound effects of behavioural, group and systemic factors on causing harm (and non-compliance with rules). Behavioural analysis found that individuals behaved in ways that were entirely *predictable*, given their context – too little time, too tired, too much focus on particular targets and issues rather than the ability to stand back and take a common-sense holistic view of risk and what they were doing. *Any* human would probably have acted in the same way. So, what does that say about individual responsibility, wrongdoing, or 'bad apples'? It could have been any of us. A frequent observation is that the *culture* of the organisation is critical in affecting the behaviour of individuals in and around it. Further, analysis into the root causes of these disasters identifies problems with *systems* rather than with individuals.

There are few indications that the constant reoccurrence of problems has been stemmed – especially by punishment and deterrence. Research into criminology does not support the effectiveness of punishment in deterring crime – the impact of harsh regimes involving blame and fines may be intuitive for political and media commentators, but science shows that it is a myth. The longer people cling to the myth, the more the 'hamster wheel' effect of constantly repeating disasters without learning and improvement will recur.

Systemic and Behavioural Risk Factors

Studies of the causes of numerous major disasters and of breaking rules indicate that the following are major risk factors:

(a) Lack of competence and capability.
(b) Lack of resource and capacity.
(c) System design and operation:
  – complexity of multiple parts or people, or
  – siloism and inadequate interaction,
  – hence, failure to trigger a warning of impending risk.
(d) Psychological factors, leading to lack of focus, fear or blindness, eg:
  – distraction, focus on specific targets, groupthink, and crowding out (focus or emphasis on particular goals at the expense of a wider balanced perspective; incentivisation to meet specific targets especially if income, status or job is conditional on these),
  – focusing staff attention significantly on financial targets for themselves and their remuneration,

- not allowing enough time for reflection and co-creative consideration before acting,
- arbitrary termination of employment for those who fail to reach financial targets,
- under-estimation of risk, recklessness, over-confidence,
- lack of objectivity; blindly following a system without standing back and considering objectively and critically a system's effectiveness, or information about a potential risk or about harm that is occurring.

(e) Organisational culture(s) and entrenched behaviours that:
- fail to support adequate or critical thinking about risks, harm or the system,
- are authoritarian, unfair or abusive.

(f) Motivation: criminal selfish intention based on deliberately or recklessly maximising personal gains or causing harm to others.

Thus, these are the sorts of behavioural, cultural and systemic factors that individuals, organisations and regulatory systems should be aiming to eradicate. It is also relevant to try to identify particular risks and behaviours in the context of different sectors. A study of misconduct in global financial markets covering 14 jurisdictions from 1814 to 2022 identified a relatively consistent pattern of six core behaviours that occur most frequently:[80]

(1) Price manipulation
(2) Circular trading
(3) Misuse of inside information
(4) Reference price influence
(5) Improper order handling
(6) Misleading customers and/or markets.

An effective response to this information would be to design the system and its data flows and behavioural cultures to deliver effective prevention and identification of each issue. Where has this been done? Most regulatory regimes plod onward by continuing to apply traditional sanctions. But so much evidence shows that that mode of 'enforcement' just does not work.

Given that these causes of failures are well-known, and can give rise to major systemic disasters, and should therefore be identified and avoided,

48 Scientific Evidence on How Humans Behave

the question arises *how* current rules, procedures, cultures and enforcement practices identify and prevent these dangers? Does current practice even scratch the surface of the problems? To start to answer those questions, we need to look at the sciences of human behaviour (rather than theoretical legal or economic models).

Scientific Research into Accidents

Professor James Reason's extensive work on analysis of the causes of errors identifies major categories as absent-minded slips and lapses,[81] failures in planning, and (deliberate) violations.[82] He categorises violations into types: corner-cutting or routine violations; thrill-seeking or optimising violations; necessary violations (such as over-specification); and exceptional violations. He identifies the coexistence of three levels of performance: skill based, rule based (where one has to think and apply a pre-packaged solution) and knowledge based (where one has no pre-packaged solution).[83] Organisational accidents, Reason notes, share the following characteristics:

- Many of the contributing factors were present within the system before the actual catastrophe occurred, sometimes for many years.
- All of the systems had multiple defences, barriers and safeguards designed to prevent known hazards from coming into damaging contact with people or assets.
- The disasters occurred because an unforeseen concatenation of latent conditions – human unsafe acts and local triggers – defeated the many defences, creating a trajectory of accident opportunity, causing damage and loss.

Proactive safety management involves regular monitoring of the system's 'vital signs'. Reason says that one of the key features shaping a system's robustness is its culture.[84] He agrees with Weick and colleagues that the power of a safe culture lies in instilling a 'collective mindfulness' of the many entities that can penetrate, disable or bypass a system's safeguards.[85]

Common themes in multiple reports from contrasting situations (space, nuclear, mining, transport, NHS, financial, frauds, GFC, etc), are poor organisational culture, focus on imposed targets, poor management, and cultures of blame and hence lack of focus on teamwork, objectivity, and suspension of ethical behaviour. Reason identified various ways in which an inadequate safety culture can adversely undermine a complex system's protective layers.[86]

Reports into the causes of disaster after disaster showed that they were often predictable in hindsight, which raised the issue of why they could not be prevented in advance. A frequent finding highlights causes related to 'systems and thinking' that are too rigid: tick box or compliance culture.

It is important to carry out root cause analysis on the systemic causes of a problem, rather than to blame a proximate hapless individual. Systems are more relevant than individuals. The issue is rarely 'Is this person to blame?' but 'Why would any human in these circumstances behave (predictably) like this?'

Professors Benjamin van Rooij and Adam Fine analysed why the corporate cultures at BP, Volkswagen and Wells Fargo had become 'toxic', and concluded that the causes were less to do with deliberate law-breaking but lay in the fact that the accumulated strength of the social norms and culture overpowered the external legal rules.[87] In all three companies studied, the causative combination of factors was described as leading to cultures (a) that condoned, neutralised, or enabled rule breaking; (b) that disabled and obstructed compliance systems; and (c) where actual practices contrasted with expressed compliant values. They noted literature on unethical climates that highlighted (a) the way organisations deal with errors and their type of management culture; (b) how differentiation between employees can be perceived as unfair and give rise to envy and disengagement; and (c) dysfunctional ethical climates.[88] They concluded that organisations should address the *structures, values, and practices* that enable violations and obstruct compliance within an organisation, as well as move away from a singular focus on liability management (ie, assigning blame and punishment) to an approach that prioritises promoting transparency, honesty, and a responsibility to initiate and sustain actual cultural change.

A 2012 meta-review of the evidence suggested that higher levels of *integrity* are correlated with commercial success in many contexts.[89] Corruption can become normalised in groups.[90] Companies with anti-corruption programmes and strong *ethical* guidelines were found to suffer up to 50% fewer incidents of corruption than those without such programmes.[91]

The Psychological Basis of Actions: Self-Determination Theory

There are numerous theories of human behaviour, although many have similar principles.

Ryan and Deci's Self-Determination Theory (SDT) emphasises the need for humans to feel competent, autonomous, and related to others.[92] They define their three basic concepts like this.

> *Competence* is the feeling of satisfaction that accompanies the achievement of effects on one's environment.[93] This encompasses ownership of causational efficacy and the acquisition and application of skills.
>
> *Autonomy* means behaving freely in accordance with the self's own overarching values, needs, and interests.[94] This does not mean individualism as complete freedom, nor being free from external influences, or proximal stimuli. It means that actions are accepted, valued and endorsed by the self as a matter of self-determination and 'self-compatibility'.[95] Since experience is always *of* something other than the self, the self is conceived to be '*self-as-process*', a set of spontaneous, integrative processes that are fluid and emergent, 'aids in regulating action and adapting to circumstances'.[96]
>
> *Relatedness* is 'the feeling of belonging, a basic need to feel responded to, respected, and important to others, and conversely, to avoid rejection, insignificance, and disconnectedness'.[97] The most powerful forces derive from the quality of experiences of partners within close relationships.

Ryan and Deci assert that humans need to satisfy the three psychological needs as a *functional* requirement, so its satisfaction or frustration will affect functioning and wellness respectively for better or worse. Positive or negative outcomes are, therefore, produced spontaneously by effects on autonomy, competence or relatedness,.[98] The *balance* of the three elements is important to wellness and adjustment. Other needs can also be relevant in some circumstances, such as deficit needs (for security and self-esteem) or thwarting of growth needs, which emerge as most salient under adverse conditions.[99] Ryan and Deci suggest that an individual 'has multiple identities, all being managed by values and regulations that have been more or less fully integrated into a single, coherent self'.[100] 'The more integrated an identity is, the greater its benefit is for individual flourishing.'[101]

There are many studies into situations where the three needs are affected. The results are strikingly consistent across how managers, public authorities, friends, teachers and so on behave towards others. The clear conclusion is that supporting subjects' intrinsic motivation (through supporting feelings of competence, autonomy, and relatedness) is far more effective than attempting to exert control through external motivation or authoritarian intervention, since the former tends to support the essential needs, whereas the latter tends to diminish them.

In constant interacting with others in a social world, individuals constantly process external influences, internalising values, beliefs, practices or behavioural regulations from external sources and transforming them into their own.[102] The extent to which this *internalisation* process occurs determines the extent to which individuals are able to carry out behaviours *on their own*, in the absence of immediate contingencies or surveillance. The outputs fall along a spectrum of autonomous or controlled behaviour. 'The more fully integrated a value or goal is, the more the person is effective in self-regulation.'[103] A person can also not be motivated to behave, or behave in a way that is not mediated by intentionality (amotivation).[104]

Ryan and Deci hold that behaviour that is regulated through more autonomous or integrated forms of internalisation will tend to display higher performance, persistence and quality. The social situation should support a person's need for relatedness, competence and autonomy. The opposite will apply to the extent that the context is more controlling, and that needs are thwarted.[105] More integrated functioning (mindfulness) is promoted by greater focus on intrinsic goals relative to extrinsic goals.[106] Thus, workers should be empowered, not overpowered.[107] The SDT framework explains why some incentives, rewards, evaluations, directives and feedback systems work and others backfire.[108] Culture is 'perhaps the most pervasive influence on human behaviour, as well as the most complex to conceptualize and measure'.[109] This means respecting the perspectives, values, and concerns of all participants,[110] and avoiding authoritarian and controlling behaviours and culture.[111]

The analysis illustrates the difference between a totalitarian or fascist regime and a democratic society.[112] Legitimacy is increased by fairness in the *process* of enacting and applying laws, and the *content* of the laws and policies.[113] Inequality and income distribution in a society has a negative effect on cohesion and autonomy. Wilkinson and Picket conclude: 'We have seen how inequality affects trust, community life, and violence, and how – through the quality of life – it predisposes people to be more or less affiliative, empathic or aggressive'.[114]

'Considerable research has shown that when people are more focused on competition and attaining money, they are likely to be less autonomously motivated[115] and more likely to display a variety of negative social behaviors and a lower relatedness to their community.'[116] The more hierarchical the power structure of a group is, the *less* prone are lower ranked members to cooperate.[117]

Self-Determination Theory is consistent with other strands of research. Tom Tyler, the leading expert in psychology and law, puts forward this conclusion: 'Disrespect and humiliation have a real cost, and affirmation and respect from others are valued gains.'[118] He also says: 'People need to have feelings of self-confidence and competence to motivate them to make decisions; without such feelings they would be less willing to take risks and less likely to obtain rewards.'[119]

Business Research into Good Management Practice

There are extensive studies by business schools on corporations, and how to get the best out of employees in commercial or private organisations. The conclusions have evolved over several decades, passing through ideas on the importance of a unifying goal through to the effectiveness of an ethical, cooperative culture,[120,121,122] with motivating organisational purposes and satisfaction of personal needs.[123]

An extensive line of research by Lee Treviño, Jennifer Chatman, Charles O'Reilly and colleagues has analysed the cultures of business organisations, especially highlighting the importance of cultures based on ethical values.[124] Studies by Ann Tenbrunsel and colleagues conclude that an organisation's ethical infrastructure, culture and climate are far more important than individual factors in supporting the moral awareness of staff[125] and conversely can generate significant unethical behaviour if they are inadequate in this respect.[126] Lee Treviño and colleagues have highlighted the influence of messages received by employees through formal and informal systems, and identified the following five aspects of ethical culture that had a profound effect on employee behaviour:[127] orientation of ethics and compliance programmes,[128] ethical leadership,[129] ethical climate,[130] fairness,[131] and trust.[132]

Psychological Safety

Individuals need to feel psychological safety[133] if they are to share essential information and cooperate well in a team. A 2017 meta-analysis of 117 studies suggested that psychological safety is a facilitator of employee performance in general, including being positively related to positive leader relations, work engagement, task performance (especially when the outcome measure was subjective rather than objective), a supportive work context, commitment, satisfaction, information sharing, citizenship behaviours, creativity, and learning behaviour.[134]

Organisations and nations that rule by fear will generate lack of support and social cohesion, and will ultimately collapse. Contrary to the assumption that organisational compliance systems will be adequate to deliver the outcome of compliance, this primarily manifests a controlling, distrusting approach[135] that conflicts with supporting operators' senses of competence, autonomy and relatedness (Self-Determination Theory), especially in complex management and organisational contexts,[136,137,138] and empirical studies show limited effectiveness of compliance programmes in improving levels of compliance.[139,140] Adding more rules complicates processes and may constrict mental focus,[141] can induce resistance,[142] and organisations can construct for themselves an internal meaning of both compliance and law.[143] The inescapable context of authoritarianism and punishment that hangs over a compliance regime has been said to lead to 'mindless compliance rather than quality behaviour'.[144]

Cooperation and Trust

Human beings achieve more when they cooperate. David Johnson's research indicates that the mode of interdependence between human beings determines outcomes.[145] His three modes are:

(i) Individualism – (*no interdependence*): a situation in which individuals perceive that they can reach their goal regardless of whether other individuals in the situation attain or do not attain their goals.
(ii) Competition – (*negative interdependence*) exists when individuals perceive that they can reach their goals if and only if the other individuals with whom they are competitively linked fail to reach

their goals. Participants, therefore, obstruct each other's efforts to achieve their goals.

(iii) Cooperation – (*positive interdependence*) exists when individuals perceive that they can reach their goals if and only if the other individuals with whom they are cooperatively linked also reach their goals. Participants, therefore, promote each other's efforts to achieve the goals.

Johnson said that conflict arises in both competitive and cooperative modes – possibly even more in the cooperative mode, since differences of perspectives, goals and means should arise more freely. 'The issue, therefore, is not how to eliminate or prevent conflict, but rather how to make it productive or, at the very least, how to prevent it from being destructive.'[146]

David and Roger Johnson's study of cooperation and conflict led them to identify the following characteristics of effective cooperative situations:[147]

1. Individuals focus on mutual goals and shared interests.
2. Individuals are concerned with both self and others' well-being.
3. Individuals adopt a long-term time orientation where energies are focused on both achieving goals and building good working relationships with others.
4. Effective and continued communication is of vital importance in resolving a conflict. Within a cooperative situation, the communication of relevant information tends to be open and honest, with each person interested in informing the other as well as being informed. Communication tends to be more frequent, complete, and accurate.
5. Perceptions of the other person and the other person's actions are far more accurate and constructive. Misperceptions and distortions such as self-fulfilling prophecies and double standards occur less frequently and are far easier to correct and clarify.
6. Individuals trust and like each other and, therefore, are willing to respond helpfully to each other's wants, needs, and requests.
7. Individuals recognize the legitimacy of each other's interests and search for a solution that accommodates the needs of both sides. Conflicts tend to be defined as mutual problems to be solved in ways that benefit everyone involved.

Trust in other individuals, organisations and institutions is a critical driver of behaviour and cooperation. Trust is essential if cooperation and outcomes are to be maximised. Trust is a state of mind, in which we place (levels of) trust in the future actions of others where complete information is unavailable. Our decision to trust another is based on the evaluation of the complete body of evidence available to us. The anthropologist Edward Wilson concluded that we constantly evaluate evidence against our internal value systems, which are based on our inherent ability to distinguish between right and wrong (unless psychopathic or sociopathic). He said that this automatic mechanism arose from a critical genetic mutation that gave the species *homo sapiens* this unique powerful advantage over other species.[148]

A successful relationship built on justified trust requires *both* trust and trustworthiness. This is because if we place trust in someone or something that is without trustworthiness, we misplace trust, and, conversely, if the object is trustworthy but not trusted, that is unjustified mistrust.[149]

Why and How do We Comply with Rules?

Tom Tyler, Professor of Law and Psychology at Yale, has undertaken a lifetime's work on why and how we comply with social or legal rules, or break them.[150] He summarises the principal factors for observing rules as follows:

(a) The rules are made through a fair *process*; where people feel that they have had involvement, or a possibility for voice and input.
(b) The *substance* of the rule is perceived to be fair by the individual and most of the community, even if individuals do not agree with it.
(c) The rule accords with their sense of *values*; namely the values of the individual, the particular community or social group or organisation.
(d) The rule is *applied* fairly by/to all.
(e) Most people are *observing* the rule.

The concept and value of *fairness* applies to all elements. Those subject to the regime and its rules need to hold perceptions of fair process,[151] fair substance and fair application if they are to want to observe one or more rules and regard the regime as legitimate. For example, enforcement has to be perceived to be done fairly if it is to promote respect and observance. This has been demonstrated in relation to public law[152] and in private organisations.[153] Indeed, many scholars regard the set of elements as adding up to the extent to which a regime and its rules are perceived as legitimate.[154] Similarly, in the workplace, evaluations of the procedural justice of performance appraisals were found to influence judgments of overall workplace fairness, perceptions of management legitimacy, and employee rule-adherence behaviour more strongly when employees believed fairer workplace procedures were required by law.[155] Fairness can clearly dominate the motivation of self-interest.[156] Authorities in the USA have been described as having tried to widen the base of their perceived legitimacy in the past two decades.[157]

If the quality of *legitimacy* exists, people will be motivated voluntarily to observe the rules, even if they think that some aspects are unfair or they otherwise disagree with them.[158] The psychological basis for evaluating process, substance and application as fair and legitimate is based on individuals' ethical values and moral principles,[159] as discussed further in chapter 5.[160] Indeed, it is well established that people do not need to know the wording of a rule in order to observe a general ethical principle or a specific behaviour or action in a concrete situation.[161] People make guesses about specific content, based on their values and experience.[162] The relevance of moral and emotional drivers on making decisions that can be against a person's self-interest has long been recognised.[163]

People may, of course, hold differentiated and varying views on the extent to which process, substance and application of both individual rules and the system are fair and legitimate. It is possible for individuals to believe that some aspects are far from ideal, but nevertheless to regard a regime and individual rules as fair, legitimate and hence for them to be subject to an internal obligation to observe them. However, factors such as corruption, bias, inequality, and failure by an authority to follow the rules or to behave fairly, reduce compliance. On the other hand, perceptions that tax authorities are part of the same community as taxpayers, and perform a polite (and not antagonistic) service to the community, influence the level of tax compliance[164] and provide a foundation based on trust.[165]

The last factor – *observance* – is the critical point in the context of 'enforcement'. The point is not that people perceive that a rule is enforced – there may be many reasons why constant and complete enforcement does not occur – but that most people *are observing* it and think that it is *fair and legitimate* to observe it. If people think that others are not observing a rule, it can lead to questioning why one should oneself, because the legitimacy and fairness of the regime or rule, or one's sense of moral obligation, is called into question. It is clear that seeing others not observing a rule will undermine intrinsic motivation voluntarily to observe a rule: there are many examples of this, from Covid examples of wearing masks, social distancing and getting vaccinated, to popular protests and revolutions against states which are perceived to have lost their legitimacy. Fair *outcomes* can override people's views on an unfair process and vice versa (interactional justice).[166]

Despite the focus above on observance of others' and one's own observation of *rules*, the strength of intrinsic motivation, senses of fairness and legitimacy of rules and regimes do clearly motivate observance even when no-one is watching.[167] In other words, intrinsic motivation can play a major role, for many people and possibly for much of the time.

Make Rules Simple to Assist Compliance

If you want to make someone do something, then make it easy for them. Cognitive overload and conflicting values and priorities make life more difficult, leading to crowding out, lack of focus and confusion. Recent research on regulatory rules found that the more components (what is in the rule) or connections (how the rule inter-relates to other rules) a rule had, the greater the likelihood of non-compliance.[168]

A focus on 'compliance' might not direct attention to achieving general improvements in performance, behaviour or culture, or new ways of doing things. Individuals tend to simplify information that can distort its meaning and implications.

Social Punishment and Maintaining Group Cohesion

Research into the phenomenon of 'peer punishment' suggests that the motivation of 'harming or hurting others marks an escalation of conflicts, this punishment is motivated by anger, greed, and aggression. It is primarily used to hold others down, to exploit them, to weaken them, to get rid of them.'[169] Further research found that the best performing people do not use punishment, unlike the worst-performing: 'winners do not punish, losers do'.[170] It was also found that although both punishment and reward responses led to cooperation, cooperation and rewards led to much higher payoffs.[171] If both reward and punishment were on offer, then the winning groups did not use punishment, which was both costly and ineffective. Rewards went further than punishment in both benefitting the public good and in building cooperation, despite the efforts of free riders. Nowak concluded that the ability of people to gain a reputation was powerful: 'Cooperators in the public goods game gain a reputation, which makes them more attractive partners for other cooperators in private – one to one – dealings.'[172] Interestingly, repeating these experiments with students in different countries produced striking national differences, with freeloaders responding to loss of tokens becoming more cooperative in the UK, Switzerland and the USA, but seeking retribution or becoming generally uncooperative in Greece and Russia.[173]

The language has changed here as well as the concepts. Game theory research uses concepts of defectors and free riders. Social research talks instead of non-cooperators, selfishness or altruism. The law is typically concerned with assumed states of mind of an individual – intentional, reckless, negligent, without care – in categorising behaviour that triggers criminal or civil sanctions. But the root causes of harm and infringement of rules occurs for many reasons.

Authoritarian Punishment and Maintaining the Commons

Garrett Hardin showed that where multiple individuals all act so as to preserve their own interests, common goods are inadvertently destroyed in a 'Tragedy of the Commons'.[174] The original examples were forests and other natural habitats and species, but the point is universal – and clearly illustrated by climate change. Elinor Ostrom showed that positive steps need to be taken to preserve the common good, especially though redesign of actions and incentives,[175] recognising that this can be challenging to achieve.[176]

Publicly-organised enforcement is widely used by states as a tool to prevent anti-social behaviour, based on breach of legal rules. As Tom Tyler concluded:[177]

> One of the main functions of the law is to regulate the behaviour of the citizenry by maximizing the likelihood that people will comply with

normative standards of conduct, i.e. with socially shared definitions of acceptable conduct as they are enshrined in rules, norms, and laws. If the law is to be effective in fulfilling its regulatory role, most citizens must obey most laws most of the time.

Nowak accepts that there have been few game theory studies to illuminate what is going on in hierarchical 'institutional punishment'.[178] He summarised the evidence from the well-known Prisoner's Dilemma experiments as finding that although punishment is one mechanism that can counter the selfishness of natural selection that leads to a 'Tragedy of the Commons' destruction of common public goods, it is very inefficient and does not help people cooperate much. A much better mechanism for achieving the maintenance of public goods is to 'reward fellow cooperators by establishing mutually beneficial private interactions with them' such that 'the public cooperators gain a reputation that makes them more attractive prospects to fellow cooperators', and private cooperation can support public cooperation.[179] Hence, transparency and ability to advertise good private cooperation is essential.

Imposing severe penalties, for example on an exemplary basis, turns out to have less effect than may commonly be thought. It is important to distinguish severity from likelihood, and to consider the effect from the perception of an individual offender.[180] A consistent finding from behavioural research is that it is an individual's *perception of the risk of being identified* in doing something wrong, and hence subject to shame, reputational damage, harm or punitive sanction, that affects the action, rather than the *perception of the severity* of a sanction.[181]

What do People Want When Things Go Wrong?

A well-recognised response to the occurrence of harm is to say: 'Who is to blame? They should be punished.' As discussed below, such a response is a protective reaction to the maintenance of both personal safety and group cohesion. But we now know that such a response prevents us sharing information, learning and taking steps to improve. Such a response in fact impedes reducing future risk.

There is considerable evidence on what people really want when they suffer personal injury or major loss, such as following consumer or natural disasters.[182] The basic desire is for the same thing not to happen to others, in other words for there to be learning, change, improvement and future prevention. There is extensive research on what people want when healthcare causes harm. Sonia Macleod and I summarised the evidence like this:[183]

> The findings are consistent and clear. People expect healthcare systems to demonstrate qualities of openness, caring and improvement. They expect individual apologies and care. They show remarkable stoicism in relation to personal adversity, which they are prepared to cope with provided that lessons are learned and performance improves, so that the same thing does not happen to others. Hence, they expect that the individual professionals and the system within which they operate will demonstrate improvement in performance.

Conclusions: Differentiating a Supportive Fair Cooperative Culture from Enforcement

The major conclusions from the scientific evidence summarised above are:

(1) Managers and regulators 'enforcing' rules should clearly *differentiate* between those who are well-intentioned and those who are not. These two groups must be managed and responded to differently.

(2) For those who are not well-intentioned, the need to ensure protection from their doing harm to others may call for firm enforcement measures. Groups and societies need to take effective steps to protect themselves and their members from harm caused by those who are not ethically self-motivated cooperators. Here, the concept of enforcement using 'hard' tools remains fully valid. For example, civil aviation authorities can resort to removal or limitation of licences to operate. Criminal courts can remove people's liberty. These measures demonstrate to others that the law is being upheld, and that the same rules apply equally to all, thereby supporting feelings of self-motivation in other group members to follow the rules. But this is positive reinforcement, rather than fear-induced deterrence. Empirical findings indicate that deterrence is often ineffective in affecting future behaviour. Procedures should be perceived to be fair. Sanctions or processes that are perceived (by victims or society

members) as unfair will tend to induce resentment and less willingness to comply in future.

(3) However, use of hard 'enforcement' tools on those who believe they are well-intentioned is likely to reduce desire to comply and reduce actual compliance. The focus solely on 'enforcement', including on those who think of themselves as being good citizens, also turns out to be not only ineffective but to tend to undermine adherence to the norms and rules.

(4) For the well-intentioned group, usually comprising the majority of people, the basis of the approach rests on Self-Determination Theory (SDT), taking steps to address issues of improvements in competence, focus, motivation, behaviour, culture and systems by supporting feelings of competence, autonomy and relatedness, and not undermining those feelings. Strong cohesion around achieving shared goals can be created. But they will not share information unless they feel psychological safety. Thus, processes of learning, improvement and achieving outcomes will be prevented by threatening, authoritarian cultures. The concepts and language of punishment, enforcement, sanctions, accountability, which may remain valid where protection from criminals and the incompetent is required, need to be evolved for others.

(5) Powerful self-motivation forces operate automatically in most humans to maintain their senses of behaving ethically and of self-worth and reputation, satisfying their need to belong to a social or work group, including an organisation of nation. If such people feel that they are (all) treated fairly, and subject to fair and fairly made and applied norms and rules, in a culture of psychological safety and cooperation, they will be strongly motivated to share information on where things have gone wrong and contribute to making changes so as to improve things. It follows that a regime that is perceived as punishing or controlling through fear will not be constructive for most people. It will undermine and ultimately destroy senses of competence, autonomy, relatedness, fairness and cooperation. Hence, concepts such as support and intervention to increase competence, autonomy and increased performance are required. Concepts such as punishment, deterrence and enforcement will not be helpful.

(6) Based on the evidence that humans achieve more when they cooperate, and that approaches that build trust and involve behaviour

based on SDT principles support cooperation, the ideal is to build relationships, behaviour and cultures in which those who demonstrate that they are trustworthy are involved as equal stakeholders in achieving agreed common purposes, objectives and outcomes. My recent conclusions were that the science supported the development of a society and systems on the basis of the Outcome-Based Cooperation model.

Regulation, therefore, has two distinct components. First, it is essentially about affecting behaviour, so as to reduce risk. This can be done by building on a coalition of motivated actors to jointly achieve common goals. Reliance on ethics and hence codes of behaviour will be important tools. Secondly, it is about ensuring protection from criminals and the incompetent. Different, more forceful responses may be required to deliver protection, based on legal tools. A successful regulatory system will need to encompass both these two elements.

---

[1] Overview books are: C Hodges, *Law and Corporate Behaviour* (Hart, 2015); F Blanc, *From Chasing Violations to Managing Risks* (Edward Elgar, 2018); Y Feldman, *The Law of Good People* (Cambridge, 2018); B van Rooij and A Fine, *The Behavioral Code* (Beacon Press, 2021); TR Tyler, *Advanced Introduction to Law and Psychology* (Edward Elgar, 2022).

[2] N Mazar, O Amir and D Ariely, 'The Dishonesty of Honest People: A Theory of Self-Concept Maintenance' (2008) 45(6) *Journal of Marketing Research* 633–44; D Ariely, *The (Honest) Truth about Dishonesty. How We Lie to Everyone—Especially Ourselves* (HarperCollins, 2012).

[3] T Gilovich, D Griffin and D Kahneman (eds), *Heuristics and Biases: The Psychology of Intuitive Judgment* (Cambridge University Press, 2002); D Kahneman and A Tversky (eds), *Choices, Values, and Frames* (Cambridge University Press, 2000); D Kahneman, *Thinking, Fast and Slow* (Allen Lane, 2011).

[4] PT Costa and RR McCrae, 'The five-factor model of personality and its relevance to personality disorders' (1992) 6(4) *Journal of Personality Disorders* 343–59. See also D Nettle, *Personality: What makes you the way you are* (Oxford University Press, 2007), noting RR McCrae and PT Costa Jr, 'A Five-Factor Theory of Personality' in LA Pervin and OP John (eds), *Handbook of Personality: Theory and Research* (Guilford Press, 1999): Neuroticism, Extraversion, Openness to experience, Agreeableness, and Conscientiousness. See also EO Wilson, *The Social Conquest of Earth* (Liveright Publishing, 2012) categorised the very large array of personality traits into five broad domains: extroversion versus introversion, antagonism versus agreeableness, conscientiousness, neuroticism, and openness to experience. But see A Bandura, 'A social cognitive theory of personality' in L Pervin and O John (eds), *Handbook of Personality*, 2nd ed (Guilford Publications, 1999).

[5] MFH Schmidt, H Rakoczy and M Tomasello, 'Young children enforce social norms selectively depending on the violator's group affiliation' (2012) 124(3) *Cognition* 325; MFH Schmidt and M Tomasello, 'Young children enforce social norms' (2012) 21(4) *Current Directions in Psychological Science* 232–36.

[6] KJ Eskine, NA Kacinik and J Prinz, 'A Bad Taste in the Mouth: Gustatory Disgust Influences Moral Judgment' (2011) 22(3) *Psychological Science* 295–99; E Ghelfi at al, 'Reexamining the Effect of Gustatory Disgust on Moral Judgment: A Multilab Direct

Conclusions 63

Replication of Eskine, Kacinik, and Prinz' (2020) 3(1) *Advances in Methods and Practices in Psychological Science* 3.

[7] A Reed II and KF Aquino, 'Moral identity and the expanding circle of moral regard toward out-groups' (2003) 84(6) *J of Personality and Social Psychology* 1270.

[8] A Bandura, 'Moral disengagement in the perpetration of inhumanities' (1999) 3(3) *Personality and Social Psychology Review* 193–209.

[9] S Shalvi and D Leiser, 'Moral firmness' (2013) 93 *J of Economic behaviour* 400–07.

[10] Y Feldman, *The Law of Good People. Challenging States' Ability to Regulate Human Behavior* (Cambridge University Press, 2018).

[11] MH Bazerman and AE Tenbrunsel, *Blind spots: Why we fail to do what's right and what to do about it* (Princeton University Press, 2011).

[12] J Haidt, 'The emotional dog and its rational tail: A social intuitionist approach to moral judgement' (2001) 108(4) *Psychological Review* 814.

[13] N Mazar, O Amir and D Ariely, 'The dishonesty of honest people: A theory of self-concept maintenance' (2008) 45(6) *Journal of Marketing Research* 633–44; DM Bersoff, 'Why good people sometimes do bad things: Motivated reasoning and unethical behaviour' (1999) 25(1) *Personality and Social Psychology Bulletin* 28–39; RM Kidder, *How good people make tough choices: resolving the dilemmas of ethical living* (Harper, 2009); DD Cremer, RV Dick and J Murnighan, 'When good people do wrong: Morality, social identity, and ethical behavior' in *Social psychology and organizations* (Routledge, 2012); J Hollis, *Why good people do bad things: Understanding our darker selves* (Gotham Books, 2008); MR Banaji and AG Greenwald, *Blindspot: Hidden biases of good people* (Penguin, 2008).

[14] L Festinger, *A Theory of Cognitive Dissonance* (Row, Peterson, 1957).

[15] M Syed, *Black Box Thinking. Marginal Gains and the Secrets of High Performance* (John Murray, 2015) 80.

[16] J Cooper, 'Cognitive Dissonance Theory' in PAM Van Lange, AW Kruglanski and ET Higgins, *Handbook of Theories of Social Psychology* (SAGE, 2012) ch 18.

[17] N Mazar, O Amir and D Ariely, 'The Dishonesty of Honest People: A Theory of Self-Concept Maintenance' (2008) 45(6) *Journal of Marketing Research* 633–44.

[18] J Dana, RA Weber and JX Kuang, 'Exploiting Moral Wiggle Room: Experiments Demonstrating an Illusory Preference for Fairness' (2007) 33 *Economic Theory* 67–80.

[19] D Ariely, U Gneezy, G Loewenstein and N Mazar, 'Large Stakes and Big Mistakes' (2009) 76 *Review of Economic Studies* 451.

[20] TM Amabile, *Creativity in Context* (Westview Press, 1996) 119; JC Kaufman and RJ Sternberg (eds), *The International Handbook of Creativity* (Cambridge University Press, 2006) 18; DH Pink, *Drive. The surprising truth about what motivates us* (Riverhead Books, 2009); E Deci, R Ryan and R Koestner, 'A Meta-Analytic Review of Experiments Examining the Effects of Extrinsic Rewards on Intrinsic Motivation' (1999) 125(6) *Psychological Bulletin* 659; A Kohn, *Punished by Rewards. The Trouble with Gold Stars, Incentive Plans, A's, Praise, and Other Bribes* (Houghton Mifflin, 1993 and 2018).

[21] TM Amabile, *Creativity in Context* (Westview Press, 1996) 119.

[22] E Fehr and S Gächter, *Do incentive contracts undermine voluntary cooperation?* (2002) University of Zurich Working Paper No 34; E Fehr and B Rockenbach, 'Detrimental effects of sanctions on human altruism' (2003) 422(6928) *Nature* 137. General review: BS Frey, *Not just for the money: An economic theory of personal motivation* (Edward Elgar, 2007).

[23] S Bowles, 'Policies designed for self-interested citizens may undermine the "moral sentiments": Evidence from economic experiments' (2008) 320(5883) *Science* 1605–09.

[24] U Gneezy, S Meier and P Rey-Biel, 'When and why incentives (don't) work to modify behavior' (2011) 25(4) *The Journal of Economic Perspectives* 191–209.

[25] J Haidt, *The Righteous Mind. Why Good People are Divided by Politics and Religion* (Penguin Books, 2012). See previously J Haidt and J Graham, 'When morality opposes

justice: Conservatives have moral intuitions that liberals may not recognise' (2007) 20(1) *Social Justice Research* 98–116.

[26] NA Christakis, *Blueprint. The Evolutionary Origins of A Good Society* (Little, Brown Spark, 2019).

[27] J Haidt, *The Righteous Mind. Why Good People are Divided by Politics and Religion* (Penguin Books, 2012). See previously J Haidt and J Graham, 'When morality opposes justice: Conservatives have moral intuitions that liberals may not recognise' (2007) 20(1) *Social Justice Research* 98–116.

[28] R Solomon, *The Joy of Philosophy* (Oxford University Press, 1999).

[29] RC Solomon, *Ethics and Excellence* (Oxford University Press, 1992); RC Solomon, *A Better Way to Think About Business: How Personal Integrity Leads to Corporate Success* (Oxford University Press, 1999); RC Solomon, 'Business with Virtue: Maybe Next Year' (2000) 10 *Business Ethics Quarterly* 319–31; RC Solomon, 'Aristotle, Ethics and Business Organizations' (2004) 25 *Organization Studies* 1021–43; RC Solomon, *It's Good Business: Ethics and Free Enterprise for the New Millenium* (Rowman & Littlefield, 1997).

[30] LS Paine, *Value Shift. Why Companies Must Merge Social and Financial Imperatives to Achieve Superior Performance* (New York, McGraw-Hill, 2003); S Killingsworth, 'Modeling the Message: Communicating Compliance through Organizational Values and Culture' (2012) 25 *Georgetown Journal of Legal Ethics* 961.

[31] *Values and Identities. A Policymaker's Guide* (European Commission Joint Research Centre, 2021) 12.

[32] OR Goodenough, 'Values, Mechanism, Design, and Fairness' in PJ Zack, *Moral Markets. The Critical Role of Values in the Economy* (Princeton University Press, 2008).

[33] SH Schwartz, 'Universals in the content and structure of values: Theory and empirical tests in 20 countries' (1992) 25 *Advances in Experimental Social Psychology* 1; S Schwartz, 'Are there universal aspects in the structure and content of human values?' (1994) 50(4) *Journal of Social Issues* 19–45.

[34] OS Curry, DA Mullins and H Whitehouse, 'Is it good to cooperate? Testing the theory of morality-as-cooperation in 60 societies' (2019) 60(1) *Current Anthropology* 47.

[35] M Rokeach, *The nature of human values* (Free Press, 1973).

[36] R Cotterrell, 'Theory and Values in Socio-Legal Studies' (2017) 44 *Journal of Socio-Legal Studies* S19. He quotes Weber that values are held for their 'own sake': M Weber, *Economy and Society: An Outline of Interpretive Sociology*, transl E Fischoff et al (1968) 25–26.

[37] R Barrett, *The Values Driven Organization*, 2nd ed (Routledge, 2017) 3.

[38] R Reber, *Critical Feeling. How to Use Feelings Strategically* (Cambridge University Press, 2016) 83.

[39] LT Hosmer, 'Trust: the connecting link between organizational theory and philosophical ethics' (1995) 20(2) *Academy of Management Review* 379.

[40] Yuval Noah Harari asserts that in the millennia following the Agricultural revolution, humans organised themselves in mass-cooperation networks by creating imagined orders and devising scripts, which together filled the gap left by our biological inheritance. Yuval Noah Harari, *Sapiens. A Brief History of Humankind* (Vintage, 2015) 149.

[41] R Cotterrell, 'Theory and Values in Socio-Legal Studies' (2017) 44 *Journal of Socio-Legal Studies* S19.

[42] *Values and Identities. A Policymaker's Guide* (European Commission Joint Research Centre, 2021) 11.

[43] WS Harvey, S Osman and M Tourky, 'Building Internal Reputation from Organisational Values' (2022) 25 *Corporate Reputation Review* 78.

[44] J Haidt, *The Righteous Mind: Why good people are divided by politics and religion* (Knopf Doubleday, 2012).

⁴⁵ NA Christakis, *Blueprint. The Evolutionary Origins of a Good Society* (Little, Brown, Spark, 2019).
⁴⁶ See also R Bregman, *Humankind, A Hopeful History* (Bloomsbury, 2020).
⁴⁷ FBM de Waal, 'How Selfish an Animal?' in PJ Zack, *Moral Markets. The Critical Role of Values in the Economy* (Princeton University Press, 2008) 66.
⁴⁸ RF Baumeister and MR Leary, 'The need to belong: Desire for interpersonal attachments as a fundamental human motivation' (1995) 117(3) *Psychological Bulletin* 497; RF Baumeister, 'Need-to-Belong Theory' in PAM Van Lange, AW Kruglanski and ET Higgins, *Handbook of Theories of Social Psychology* (SAGE, 2012) ch 32.
⁴⁹ MR Leary, 'Sociometer Theory' in PAM Van Lange, AW Kruglanski and ET Higgins, *Handbook of Theories of Social Psychology* (SAGE, 2012), ch 33.
⁵⁰ Y Feldman, *The Law of Good People. Challenging States' Ability to Regulate Human Behavior* (Cambridge University Press, 2018), 108.
⁵¹ MB Brewer and RM Kramer, 'Choice behaviour in social dilemmas: Effects of social identity, group size, and decision framing' (1986) 50(3) *Journal of Personality and Social Psychology* 543.
⁵² DM Kahan, 'Trust, collective action, and law' (2001) 81 *Boston University Law Review* 333.
⁵³ J Henrich, *The Secret of Our Success: How culture is driving human evolution, domesticating our species, and making us smarter* (Princeton University Press, 2016); see also J Henrich, *The Weirdest People in the World. How the West Became Psychologically Peculiar and Particularly Prosperous* (Allen Lane, 2020).
⁵⁴ C Engel and EU Weber, 'The impact of institutions on the decision how to decide' (2007) 3(3) *Journal of Institutional Economics* 323-349.
⁵⁵ eg JV May and AB Wildavsky, *The Policy Cycle* (Sage, 1978).
⁵⁶ A Gehlen, 'Mensch und Institutionen' in A Gehlen (ed), *Anthropologische Forschung: Zur Selbstbegegnung und Selbstentdeckung des Menschen* (Rowohlt, 1960) 69-77, 71; WM Goldstein and RM Hogarth, 'Judgment and Decision Research. Some Historical Context' in WM Goldstein and RM Hogarth (eds), *Research on Judgement and Decision Making* (Cambridge University Press, 1997) 3-65, 29.
⁵⁷ G Cvetkovich, 'Cognitive Accommodation, Language, and Social Responsibility' (1978) 41 *Social Psychology* 149-55; R Hagafors and B Brehmer, 'Does Having to Justify one's Judgments Change the Nature of the Judgment Process?' (1983) 31 *Organizational Behavior and Human Decision Processes* 223-32; E Weldon and GM Gargano,'Cognitive Loafing: The Effects of Accountability and Shared Responsibility on Cognitive Effort' (1988) 14 *Personality and Social Psychology Bulletin* 159-71.
⁵⁸ R Hagafors and B Brehmer, 'Does Having to Justify one's Judgments Change the Nature of the Judgment Process?' (1983) 31 *Organizational Behavior and Human Decision Processes* 223-32.
⁵⁹ PE Tetlock, 'Accountability and Complexity of Thought' (1983) 45 *Journal of Personality and Social Psychology* 74-83.
⁶⁰ JS Lerner, JH Goldberg and PE Tetlock, 'Sober Second Thought: The Effects of Accountability, Anger, and Authoritarianism on Attributions of Responsibility' (1998) 24 *Personality and Social Psychology Bulletin* 563-574.
⁶¹ PE Tetlock, 'Accountability and the Perseverance of First Impressions' (1983) 46 *Social Psychology Quarterly* 285-92; PE Tetlock and R Boettger, 'Accountability: A Social Magnifier of the Dilution Effect' (1989) 57 *Journal of Personality and Social Psychology* 388-98.
⁶² R Hagafors and B Brehmer, 'Does Having to Justify one's Judgments Change the Nature of the Judgment Process?' (1983) 31 *Organizational Behavior and Human Decision Processes* 223-32; RH Ashton, 'Effects of Justification and a Mechanical Aid on Judgment Performance' (1992) 52 *Organizational Behavior and Human Decision Processes* 292-306.

[63] JM Blatt, 'The Utility of Being Hanged on the Gallows' (1979) 2 *Journal of Post Keynesian Economics* 231–39.
[64] Y Feldman, *The Law of Good People. Challenging States' Ability to Regulate Human Behavior* (Cambridge University Press, 2018) 127.
[65] D Palmer and C Moore, 'Social networks and organizational wrongdoing in context' in D Palmer, K Smith-Crowe and R Greenwood (eds), *Organizational Wrongdoing: Key Perspectives and New Directions* (Cambridge University Press, 2016); SE Asch, 'Effects of Group Pressure Upon the Modification and Distortion of Judgments' in H Guetzkow (ed), *Groups, Leadership and Men* (Carnegie Press, 1951); DJ Brass, KD Butterfield and BC Skaggs, 'Relationships and unethical behaviour: A social network perspective' (1998) 23 *Academy of Management Review* 14.
[66] JV Rees, *Hostages of Each Other: The Transformation of Nuclear Safety since Three Mile Island* (1994); JV Rees, 'Development of Communitarian Regulation in the Chemical Industry' (1997) 19 *Law & Policy* 477.
[67] *Report of the Inquiry into the Supervision of the Bank of Credit and Commerce International* (2991) HC 192.
[68] Strong criticism of the Bank of England was made in *A New Approach to Regulating and Developing Singapore's Financial Sector* (Singapore, Monetary Authority of Singapore, 1997); Board of Banking Supervision, *Report of the Board of Banking Supervision Inquiry into the Circumstances of the Collapse of Barings* (London, Bank of England, 1995).
[69] The Equitable Life Payments Scheme, and various progress reports, information at www.gov.uk/government/collections/equitable-life-payment-scheme-documents; *Administering the Equitable Life Payment Scheme* (NAO, April 2013).
[70] M Carney, 'Turning Back the Tide', speech given to FICC Markets Standards Board Conference, 29 November 2017; *Banking Conduct and Culture. A Permanent Mindset Change* (Group of Thirty, 2019); A Nesvetailova and R Palan, *Sabotage. The Business of Finance* (Allen Lane, 2020).
[71] S Miller, 'The Libor Scandal: Culture, Corruption and Collective Action Problems in the Global Banking Sector' in J O'Brien and G Gilligan (eds), *Integrity, Risk and Accountability in Capital Markets. Regulating Culture* (Hart Publishing, 2013) (referring to institutional corruption). See *LIBOR, Public Inquiries and FSA Disciplinary Powers* (House of Commons Library, SN/BT/6376, July 2012); *The Wheatley Review of LIBOR: initial discussion paper* (HM Treasury, August 2012); *Fixing LIBOR: some preliminary findings* (House of Commons Treasury Select Committee, HC 481–I, August 2012), Volume I: Report, together with formal minutes and Volume II: Oral evidence; *The Wheatley Review of LIBOR: final report* (Martin Wheatley, September 2012); *Wheatley Review of LIBOR – Written Ministerial Statement* (HM Treasury, October 2012); *LIBOR, Public Inquiries and FSA Disciplinary Powers – Commons Library Note* (SN/BT/6376: House of Commons Library, November 2012); *Internal Audit report: A review of the extent of awareness within the FSA of inappropriate LIBOR submissions* (FSA, March 2013); Press release, *LIBOR Becomes a Regulated Activity* (BBA, 02/04/2013).
[72] D Gentilin, *The Origins of Ethical Failures. Lessons for Leaders* (Abingdon and New York, Routledge, 2016).
[73] *Banking Conduct and Culture. A Permanent Mindset Change* (Group of Thirty, 2019); Press release, 'Wells Fargo Agrees to Pay $3 Billion to Resolve Criminal and Civil Investigations into Sales Practices Involving the Opening of Millions of Accounts without Customer Authorization', Department of Justice, February 21, 2020, www.justice.gov/opa/pr/wells-fargo-agrees-pay-3-billion-resolve-criminal-and-civil-investigations-sales-practices.
[74] JC Coffee Jr, 'Understanding Enron: It's the Gatekeepers, Stupid' (2002) 57 *The Business Lawyer* 1403–20; JC Coffee, Jr, *Gatekeepers. The Professions and Corporate Governance* (Oxford University Press, 2004); B Soltani, 'The anatomy of corporate fraud: a comparative

analysis of high profile American and European corporate scandals' (2014) 120(2) *Journal of Business Ethics* 251–74.

[75] P Robison, *Flying Blind: The 737 MAX Tragedy and the Fall of Boeing* (Penguin Business, 2021).

[76] See J Cumberlege, *First Do No Harm: The report of the Independent Medicines and Medical Devices Safety Review* (2020), available at www.immdsreview.org.uk/Report.html.

[77] See *Post Office Horizon IT Inquiry. Report Volume 1*, HC 11119 (2025), available at www.postofficehorizoninquiry.org.uk/volume-1-post-office-horizon-it-inquirys-final-report. N Wallis, *The Great Post Office Scandal* (Bath Publishing, 2021).

[78] *Infected Blood Inquiry. The Report*, HC 569-1 (2024), available at www.infectedbloodinquiry.org.uk/reports/inquiry-report.

[79] *Grenfell Tower Inquiry: Phase 2 Report: Report of the Public Inquiry into the Fire at Grenfell Tower on 14 June 2017* (2024), HC 19-1, available at https://assets.publishing.service.gov.uk/media/66d817aa701781e1b341dbd3/CCS0923434692-004_GTI_Phase_2_Volume_1_BOOKMARKED.pdf.

[80] *Behaviour-pattern Condict Analysis: Market misconduct through the ages* (Financial Markets Standards Board, 2022).

[81] J Reason, *Human Error* (Cambridge University Press, 1990); J Reason, 'Stress and cognitive failure' in S Fisher and J Reason (eds), *Handbook of Life Stress, Cognition and Health* (Wiley, 1989) 405–21.

[82] J Reason, *A Life in Error. From Little Slips to Big Disasters* (Ashgate Publishing, 2013).

[83] ibid.

[84] J Reason, *A Life in Error. From Little Slips to Big Disasters* (Ashgate Publishing, 2013) 76; J Reason, 'Achieving a safe culture: Theory and practice' (1998) 12 *Work & Stress* 293.

[85] KE Weick, KM Sutcliffe and D Obstfeld, 'Organising for high reliability processes of collective mindfulness' (1999) 21 *Research into Organizational Behavior* 23–81.

[86] J Reason, *A Life in Error. From Little Slips to Big Disasters* (Ashgate Publishing, 2013), 83.

[87] B van Rooij and A Fine, 'Toxic Corporate Culture: Assessing Organizational Processes of Deviancy' (2019) 8(3) *Administrative Sciences* 23.

[88] See summary at W Scholten and N Ellemers. 'Bad apples or corrupting barrels? Preventing traders' misconduct' (2016) 24 *Journal of Financial Regulation and Compliance* 366–82.

[89] PM Nichols, 'The Business Case for Complying with Bribery Laws' (2012) 49(2) *American Business Law Journal* 325.

[90] BE Ashforth and V Anand, 'The Normalisation of Corruption in Organizations' (2003) 25 *Research in Organisational Behaviour* 1.

[91] PricewaterhouseCoopers, *Economic Crime: People, Culture and Controls: The Fourth Biennial Global Economic Crime Survey* (2007) 33, www.whistleblowers.org/storage/documents/pwc_survey.pdf.

[92] RM Ryan and EL Deci, *Self-Determination Theory. Basic Psychological Needs in Motivation, Development, and Wellness* (Guilford Press, 2017).

[93] This draws on RW White, *Ego and reality in psychoanalytic theory: A proposal regarding independent energies* (International Universities Press, 1963) 185.

[94] RM Ryan and EL Deci, *Self-Determination Theory. Basic Psychological Needs in Motivation, Development, and Wellness* (Guilford Press, 2017) 55–75.

[95] ibid 56. RM Ryan and EL Deci, 'Autonomy is no illusion: Self-determination theory and the empirical study of authenticity, awareness, and will' in J Greenberg, SL Koole and T Pyszczynski (eds), *Handbook of experimental existential psychology* (Guilford Press, 2004).

[96] RM Ryan and EL Deci, *Self-Determination Theory. Basic Psychological Needs in Motivation, Development, and Wellness* (Guilford Press, 2017) 79.
[97] ibid 96.
[98] ibid 248.
[99] ibid 255.
[100] ibid 400.
[101] ibid 392.
[102] RM Ryan, JP Connell and EL Deci, 'A motivational analysis of self-determination and self-regulation in education' in C Ames and RE Ames (eds), *Research on motivation in education: The classroom milieu* (Academic Press, 1985).
[103] ibid 189.
[104] ibid 190.
[105] ibid 202–08.
[106] RM Ryan and EL Deci, *Self-Determination Theory. Basic Psychological Needs in Motivation, Development, and Wellness* (Guilford Press, 2017) 289.
[107] ibid 534, citing N Doshi and L McGregor, *Primed to perform: How to build the highest performing cultures through the science of total motivation* (HarperCollins, 2015).
[108] M Gagné, EL Deci and RM Ryan, 'Self-determination theory applied to work motivation and organizational behavior' in DS Ones, N Anderson, HK Sinangil and C Viswesvaran (eds), *The SAGE Handbook of Industrial, Work, and Organizational Psychology*, 2nd ed (Sage, 2017).
[109] RM Ryan and EL Deci, *Self-Determination Theory. Basic Psychological Needs in Motivation, Development, and Wellness* (Guilford Press, 2017) 565.
[110] RG Craven, RM Ryan, J Mooney, RJ Vallerand, A Dillon and F Blacklock, 'Toward a positive psychology of indigenous thriving and reciprocal research partnership model' (2016) 47 *Contemporary Educational Psychology* 32–43; RJ Wlodkowski and MB Ginsberg, *Diversity and motivation: Culturally responsive teaching* (Jossey-Bass, 1995).
[111] RM Ryan and EL Deci, *Self-Determination Theory. Basic Psychological Needs in Motivation, Development, and Wellness* (Guilford Press, 2017) 589.
[112] CM Gonzalez and TR Tyler, 'The psychology of enfranchisement: Engaging and fostering inclusion of members through voting and decision-making procedures' (2008) 64(3) *Journal of Social Issues* 447–66.
[113] See eg A Mankad and M Greenhill, 'Motivational indicators predicting the engagement, frequency and adequacy of rainwater tank maintenance' (2014) 50 *Water Resources Research* 29–38.
[114] RG Wilkinson and KE Pickett, *The spirit level: Why equality is better for everyone* (Penguin, 2010) 236.
[115] eg EL Deci, R Koestner and RM Ryan, 'A meta-analytic review of experiments examining the effects of extrinsic rewards on intrinsic motivation' (1999) 71(1) *Review of Educational Research* 1–27; J Reeve and EL Deci, 'Elements of the competitive situation that affect intrinsic motivation' (1996) 22(1) *Personality and Social Psychology Bulletin* 24–33.
[116] RM Ryan and EL Deci, *Self-Determination Theory. Basic Psychological Needs in Motivation, Development, and Wellness* (Guilford Press, 2017) 610.
[117] KA Cronin, DJ Acheson, P Hernández and A Sánchez, 'Hierarchy is detrimental for human cooperation' (2015) *Scientific Reports* 5, available at www.nature.com/articles/srep18634.
[118] TR Tyler, *Advanced Introduction to Law and Psychology* (Edward Elgar, 2022) 14.
[119] ibid 19.
[120] EH Schein, *Organisational Culture and Leadership*, 5th edn (John Wiley & Sons, 2017). See earlier EH Schein, 'Coming to a New Awareness of Organizational Culture' (1984) 25(2) *Sloan Management Review* 3.

[121] G Hofstede, *Culture's Consequences*, 2nd edn (McGraw-Hill, 2001); G Hofstede, GJ Hofstede and M Minkow, *Cultures and Organizations: Software of the Mind* (McGraw-Hill, 2010).

[122] RJ House, PJ Hanges, M Javidan, PW Dorfman and V Gupta, *Culture, leadership, and organizations: The GLOBE study of 62 societies* (Sage, 2004).

[123] LK Treviño, J Haidt and AE Filabi, 'Regulating for ethical culture' (2017) 3(2) *Behavioural Science and Policy* 57–70.

[124] See especially C O'Reilly, 'Corporations, Culture, and Commitment: Motivation and social control in organizations' (1989) 31(4) *California Management Review* 9; C O'Reilly III, J Chatman and DF Caldwell, 'People and Organizational Culture: A profile comparison approach to assessing person-organization fit' (1991) 34 *Academy of Management Journal* 487–516; LK Treviño et al, 'Managing Ethics and Legal Compliance: What Works and What Hurts' (1999) 41 *California Management Review* 131; C O'Reilly, 'Corporations, Culture, and Commitment: Motivation and Social Control in Organizations' (2008) 50(2) *California Management Review* 85–101; LK Treviño, NA den Nieuwenboer and JJ Kish-Gephart, '(Un)ethical Behavior in Organizations' (2014) 65 *Annual Review of Psychology* 635.

[125] A Tenbrunsel and K Smith-Crowe, 'Ethical decision making: Where we've been and where we're going' (2008) 2(1) *Academy of Management Annals* 545–607.

[126] A Tenbrunsel and D Messick, 'Ethical fading: The role of self-deception in unethical behavior' (2004) 17 *Social Justice Research* 223–36.

[127] LK Treviño, J Haidt and AE Filabi, 'Regulating for ethical culture' (2017) 3(2) *Behavioural Science and Policy* 57–70.

[128] See LK Treviño, GR Weaver, DG Gibson and BL Toffler, 'Managing ethics and legal compliance: What works and what hurts' (1999) 41(2) *California Management Review* 131–51.

[129] ME Brown, LK Treviño and DA Harrison, 'Ethical leadership: A social learning perspective for construct development and testing' (2005) 97 *Organizational Behavior and Human Decision Processes* 117–34.

[130] Drawing on B Victor and JB Cullen, 'The organizational bases of ethical work climates' (1988) 33 *Administrative Science Quarterly* 101–25; and KD Martin and J Cullen, 'Continuities and extensions of ethical climate theory: A meta-analytic review' (2006) 69 *Journal of Business Ethics* 175–94. However, ethical climate alone was found in a later study to be insufficient to lead to ethical behaviour: A Arnaud and M Schminke, 'The ethical climate and context of organizations: A comprehensive model' (2012) 23 *Organizational Science* 1767–80.

[131] See also M Ambrose and M Schminke, 'The role of overall justice judgments in organizational justice research: A test of mediation' (2012) 94 *Journal of Applied Psychology* 491–500.

[132] Treviño et al referred to the seven item scale developed in FD Schoorman and GA Ballinger, 'Leadership, trust and client service in veterinary hospitals' (2006) Working paper, Purdue University, West Lafayette, IN; FD Schoorman, RC Mayer and JH Davis, 'An integrative model of organizational trust: Past, present, and future' (2007) 32 *Academy of Management Review* 344–54.

[133] A Edmondson, 'Psychological safety and learning behavior in work teams' (1999) 44 *Administrative Science Quarterly* 350–83 and a number of subsequent studies. See recently AC Edmondson, *The Fearless Organization* (John Wiley & Sons, Inc, 2019).

[134] M Lance Frazier, S Fainshmidt, RL Klinger, A Pezeshkan and V Vracheva, 'Psychological Safety: A Meta-Analytic Review and Extension' (2017) 70(1) *Personnel Psychology* 113–65.

[135] GP Miller, 'The compliance function: an overview', NYU Law and Economics Research Paper No 14-36 (November 18, 2014), at: www.law.nyu.edu/sites/default/files/upload_documents/The%20Compliance%20Functiion%20an%20Overview.Miller.pdf.

[136] With multiple functions such as performance management, product planning, and financial controls: JA Chatman and CA O'Reilly, 'Paradigm lost: Reinvigorating the study of organizational culture' (2016) 36 *Research in Organizational Behavior* 199–224; CA O'Reilly and JA Chatman, 'Culture as social control: Corporations, cults, and commitment' (1996) 18 *Research in Organizational Behavior* 157; CA O'Reilly and JA Chatman, 'Culture as social control: Corporations, cults, and commitment' in BM Staw and LL Cummings (eds), *Research in organizational behavior: An annual series of analytical essays and critical reviews, Vol 18* (Elsevier Science/JAI Press, 1996) 157–200.

[137] C Parker and S Gilad, 'Internal corporate compliance management systems: structure, culture and agency' in C Parker and V Lehmann Nielsen (eds), *Explaining Compliance. Business Responses to Regulation* (Edward Elgar, 2012).

[138] GC Gray and SS Silbey, 'Governing inside the organization: interpreting regulation and compliance' (2014) 120(1) *American Journal of. Sociology* 96–114.

[139] A Prakash and M Potoski, *The Voluntary Environmentalists: Green Clubs, ISO 14001, and Voluntary Environmental Regulations* (Cambridge University Press, 2006); W Ge, A Koester and S McVay, 'Benefits and Costs of Sarbanes-Oxley Section 404 (b) Exemption: Evidence from Small Firms' Internal Control Disclosures' (2017) 63(2-3) *Journal of Accounting and Economics* 358; JJ Kish-Gephart, DA Harrison and LK Trevino, 'Bad Apples, Bad Cases, and Bad Barrels: Meta-Analytic Evidence About Sources of Unethical Decisions at Work' (2010) 95(1) *Journal of Applied Psychology* 1; NM Schell-Busey, 'The Deterrent Effects of Ethics Codes for Corporate Crime: A Meta-Analysis', unpublished PhD dissertation (University of Maryland, 2009), http://drum.lib.umd.edu/bitstream/handle/1903/9289/SchellBusey_umd_0117E_10313.pdf?sequence=1.

[140] M Jenkins, *The relationship between business integrity and commercial success* (Chr Michelsen Institute, 2017), available at www.u4.no/publications/the-relationship-between-business-integrity-and-commercial-success.pdf.

[141] DW Lehman, B Cooil and R Ramanujam, 'The Effects of Rule Complexity on Organizational Noncompliance and Remediation: Evidence From Restaurant Health Inspections' (2020) 46(8) *Journal of Management* 1439–68.

[142] R Huising and SS Silbey, 'From Nudge to Culture and Back Again: Coalface Governance in the Regulated Organization' (2018) 14 *Annual Review of Law and Social Science* 91–114, citing KW Sandholtz, *When legitimacy becomes a constraint: lessons from an ethnographic study of human resources work*, PhD dissertation, (Stanford University, 2013); N Gunningham and D Sinclair, 'Integrative regulation: a principle-based approach to environmental policy' (1999) 24(4) *Law and Society Inquiries* 853.

[143] LB Edelman and SA Talesh, 'To comply or not to comply – that isn't the question: how organizations construct the meaning of compliance' in C Parker and V Lehmann Nielsen (eds), *Explaining Compliance. Business Responses to Regulation* (Edward Elgar, 2012) 103.

[144] *IBE Response to Corporate Governance Consultation* (Institute of Business Ethics, 2017).

[145] DW Johnson, *Constructive Controversy. Theory, Research, Practice* (Cambridge University Press, 2015).

[146] ibid 13.

[147] DW Johnson, *Constructive Controversy. Theory, Research, Practice* (Cambridge University Press, 2015) 11–12. Citing M Deutsch, *The Resolution of Conflict, Constructive and Destructive Processes* (Yale University Press, 1973); DW Johnson and RT Johnson, *Cooperation and competition: Theory and research* (Interaction Book Company, 1989); DW Johnson and RT Johnson, 'New developments in social interdependence theory' (2005) 131(4) *Genetic, Social, and General Psychology Monographs* 285; G Watson and DW Johnson, *Social psychology: Issues and insights*, 2nd edn (Lippincott, 1972).

[148] EO Wilson, *The Social Conquest of Earth* (Liveright Publishing, 2012); J Haidt, *The Righteous Mind. Why Good People are Divided by Politics and Religion* (Penguin Books, 2012).

[149] *The roadmap to an effective AI assurance ecosystem – extended version* (HMG, December 2021).

[150] An excellent summary is: TR Tyler, *Advanced Introduction to Law and Psychology* (Edward Elgar, 2022).

[151] R Paternoster, R Brame, R Bachman and W Sherman, 'Do fair procedures matter? The effect of procedural justice on spouse assault' (1997) 31 *Law and Society Review* 163; DG Pruitt, RS Peirce, NB McGillicuddy, GL Welton and LM Castriano, 'Long-term success in mediation' (1993) 17 *Law and Human Behavior* 313; EA Lind and TR Tyler, *The social psychology of procedural justice* (Springer Science & Business Media, 1988); JW Thibaut and L Walker, *Procedural justice: A psychological analysis* (Erlbaum Associates, 1975).

[152] TR Tyler, JD Casper and B Fisher, 'Maintaining Allegiance towards Political Authorities: The Role of Prior Attitudes and the Use of Fair Procedures' (1989) 33(3) *American Journal of Political Science* 629; TR Tyler, 'Citizen Discontent with Legal Procedures: A Social Science Perspective on Civil Procedure Reform' (1997) 45(4) *The American Journal of Comparative Law* 871; TR Tyler, 'Social Justice: Outcome and Procedure' (2000) 35(2) *International Journal of Psychology* 117–25.

[153] R Cropanzano, DE Rupp, CJ Mohler and M Schminke, 'Three roads to organizational justice' (2001) 20 *Research in Personnel and Human Resources Management* 1–113; R Cropanzano, B Goldman and R Folger, 'Deontic justice: the role of moral principles in workplace fairness' (2003) 24 *Journal of Organizational Behaviour* 1019–24; CT Kulik and Y Li, 'The Fork in the Road: Diversity Management and Organizational Justice' in RS Cropanzano and ML Ambrose (eds), *The Oxford Handbook of Justice in the Workplace* (Oxford University Press, 2015); R Miles, *Culture Audit in Financial Services* (KoganPage, 2121).

[154] TR Tyler, *Why People Obey the Law* (Yale University Press, 2006); TR Tyler, 'Psychological perspectives on legitimacy and legitimation' (2006) 57 *Annual Review of Psychology* 375–400; J Sunshine and TR Tyler, 'The role of procedural justice and legitimacy in shaping public support for policing' (2003) 37 *Law and Society Review* 513; TR Tyler and YJ Huo, *Trust in the Law* (Russell Sage Foundation, 2002); JM Darley, TR Tyler and K Bilz, 'Enacting justice: The interplay of individual and institutional perspectives' in MA Hogg and J Cooper (eds), *The Sage Handbook of Social Psychology* (Sage, 2003); JT Jost and B Major, 'Emerging perspectives on the psychology of legitimacy' in JT Jost and B Major (eds), *The Psychology of Legitimacy* (Cambridge University Press, 2001); TR Tyler and SL Blader, 'Can businesses effectively regulate employee conduct? The antecedents of rule following in work settings' (2005) 48 *Academy of Management Journal* 1143; TR Tyler and SL Blader, *Cooperation in Groups: Procedural Justice, Social Identity, and Behavioral Engagement* (Psychology Press, 2000).

[155] Y Feldman and TR Tyler, 'Mandated Justice: The potential promise and possible pitfalls of mandating procedural justice in the workplace' (2012) 6(1) *Regulation & Governance* 46.

[156] D Kahneman, JL Knetsch and RH Thaler, 'Fairness and the assumptions of economics' (1986) 59(4) *Journal of Business* S285–S300; E Fehr and KM Schmidt, 'A theory of fairness, competition, and cooperation' (1999) 114(3) *Quarterly Journal of Economics* 817–68; Y Feldman and TR Tyler, 'Mandated justice: The potential promise and possible pitfalls of mandating procedural justice in the workplace' (2012) 6(1) *Regulation & Governance* 46–65.

[157] T Tyler and J Jackson, 'Popular Legitimacy and the Exercise of Legal Authority: Motivating Compliance, Cooperation and Engagement' (2014) 20(1) *Psychology, Public Policy and Law* 78.

[158] HC Kelman, 'Patterns of personal involvement in the national system: A social-psychological analysis of political legitimacy' in J Rosenau (ed), *International Politics and Foreign Policy* (Free Press, 1969); JT Scholz and N Pinney, 'Duty, fear, and tax compliance: The heuristic basis of citizenship behavior' (1995) *American Journal of Political Science* 490–512; HC Kelman, 'The role of national identity in conflict resolution' (2001) 3 *Intergroup Conflict, and Conflict Reduction* 187; DA Strauss, Reply: Legitimacy and obedience' (2005) 118(6) *Harvard Law Review* 1854; TR Tyler, *Why People Obey the Law* (Yale University Press, 2006).

[159] See PH Robinson and J Darley, *Justice, Liability, and Blame* (Westview, 1995); TR Tyler and JM Darley, 'Building a law-abiding society: Taking public views about morality and the legitimacy of public authorities into account when formulating substantive law' (2000) 28 *Hofstra Law Review* 707.

[160] See also TR Tyler, 'Psychology and the Law' in *The Oxford Handbook of Law & Politics* (Oxford, 2008).

[161] C Engel, 'Learning the Law' (2008) 4(3) *Journal of Institutional Economics* 275–97.

[162] JM Darley, KM Carlsmith and PH Robinson, 'The ex ante function of the criminal law' (2001) 35(1) *Law and Society Review* 165.

[163] RH Frank, *Passions with reason: The strategic role of the emotions* (WW Norton, 1988).

[164] E Kirchler, *The economic psychology of tax behavior* (Cambridge University Press, 2007).

[165] E Kirchler, E Hoelzl and I Wahl, 'Enforced versus voluntary compliance: The "slippery slope" framework' (2008) 29 *Journal of Economic Psychology* 210–25.

[166] RW Hamilton, 'When the means justify the ends: Effects of observability on the procedural fairness and distributive fairness of resource allocations' (2006) 19(4) *Journal of Behavioral Decision Making* 303–20.

[167] S Lindenberg, 'Are there sanctions that work even when nobody is watching? Value protecting versus egoistic sanctions', unpublished Working Paper (University of Groningen, 2018), quoted in E Fehr, *Behavioral Foundations of Corporate Culture*, UBS International Center of Economics and Justice, University of Zurich, Paper 7 (2018).

[168] E Fehr, *Behavioral Foundations of Corporate Culture* (UBS International Center of Economics in Society, November 2018), UNS Center Public Paper 7.

[169] M Nowak with R Highfield, *SuperCooperators. Beyond the Survival of the Fittest. Why Cooperation, not Competition, is the Key to Life* (Canongate Books, 2011) 225.

[170] A Dreber, DG Rand, D Fudenberg and MA Nowak, 'Winners don't punish' (2008) 452 *Nature* 348.

[171] DG Rand, A Dreber, T Ellingsen, D Fudenberg and MA Nowak, 'Positive Interactions Promote Public Cooperation' (2009) 325 *Science* 1272.

[172] M Nowak with R Highfield, *SuperCooperators. Beyond the Survival of the Fittest. Why Cooperation, not Competition, is the Key to Life* (Canongate Books, 2011) 231.

[173] S Gächter, B Herrmann and C Thöni, 'Antisocial punishment across societies' (2008) 319 *Science* 1362.

[174] G Hardin, 'The tragedy of the commons' (1968) 162 *Science* 1243.

[175] E Ostrom, *Governing the Commons: Evolution of Institutions for Collective Action* (Cambridge University Press, 1990).

[176] E Ostrom, 'A diagnostic approach for going beyond panaceas' (2007) 104(39) *Proceedings of the National Academies of Science USA* 15181–87; E Ostrom, 'Beyond markets and states: polycentric governance of complex economic systems' (2010) 100 *American Economic Review* 1–33.

[177] TR Tyler, 'Psychology and the Law' in *The Oxford Handbook of Law & Politics* (Oxford, 2008). See TR Tyler, *Why People Obey the Law* (Yale University Press, 2006).

Conclusions 73

[178] M Nowak with R Highfield, *SuperCooperators. Beyond the Survival of the Fittest. Why Cooperation, not Competition, is the Key to Life* (Canongate Books, 2011) 234.

[179] M Nowak with R Highfield, *SuperCooperators. Beyond the Survival of the Fittest. Why Cooperation, not Competition, is the Key to Life* (Canongate Books, 2011) 233–35, 218.

[180] RJ MacCoun, 'Drugs and the law: a psychological analysis of drug prohibition' (1993) 113 *Psychological Bulletin* 497; PH Robinson and J Darley, *Justice, Liability, and Blame* (Westview, 1995); PH Robinson and J Darley, 'The utility of desert' (1997) 91 *Northwestern University Law Review* 452; HL Ross, *Deterring the Drinking Driver* (Lexington Books, 1982).

[181] DS Nagin and R Paternoster, 'The preventive effects of the perceived risk of arrest' (1991) 29 *Criminology* 561; R Paternoster, 'The deterrent effect of the perceived certainty and severity of punishment' (1987) 4 *Justice Quarterly* 173; R Paternoster and L Iovanni, 'The deterrent effect of perceived severity' (1986) 64 *Social Forces* 751; R Paternoster, LE Saltzman, GP Waldo and TG Chiricos, 'Perceived risk and social control: Do sanctions really deter?' (1983) 17 *Law and Society Review* 457.

[182] See summaries in C Hodges, *Delivering Dispute Resolution* (Hart, 2019) ch 3.

[183] S Macleod and C Hodges, *No-Fault Approaches in the NHS* (Hart, 2023) 266.

3
A Regulatory System and its Functions

> Regulation should be thought of – and designed and operated – as a *system* – a coordinated means of delivering protections.
>
> A regulatory system should contain certain essential functions, as specified in the Regulatory Functions Model (RFM).
>
> The precise arrangements (of public and private techniques) will differ between different regulatory spaces and systems. This requires and empowers bespoke design choices. But having all the relevant data will be essential.
>
> The system, and public and private elements, need appropriate governance arrangements.
>
> In practice, multiple regulatory systems need effective coordination.

Regulation as a Coordinated Means of Delivering Protections

As we saw in chapter 1, the traditional model of regulation envisages regulation as a hierarchical exercise of power aimed at controlling the behaviour of entities to comply with hierarchies of rules. Thus, government aims to control regulators, and regulators aim to control regulatees. But if we change the vision of what is happening, we can achieve a far more powerful and effective model, that delivers better outcomes. The trick is to look at *regulation as a system*. The system necessarily involves all relevant actors – governments, regulators, regulatees, bystanders, and citizens. Each need to play their role if the system is to work.

This chapter looks at how regulation works *as a system*. We have said in chapter 1 that the *purpose* and *function* of regulation is to provide *protection* from unacceptable risks and harms (including unfairness) produced by activities that are otherwise not illegal. We tend to talk about a number of distinct regulatory *systems*, such as those for particular professions or types of product or services, or for markets or activities such as financial services, energy, water and so on. Each system is individual and distinct, and has particular features, even though the architecture and details of what might be called families are similar. But each exists as a distinct system (and we will need to look at the problems that this gives rise to in chapter 4).

How does a regulatory system operate? How does it deliver the desired level of protection from harm and risk? We start by identifying the core *functions* that every regulatory system should deliver – but many fail to. The essence of delivering protection is that adequate arrangements need to be in place from (in fact, before) the start, and usually to operate throughout an activity, so that risk is identified and controlled, and any harms that arise are either prevented (or controlled to an acceptable level) or identified quickly and then stopped and controlled, and that damage is repaired.

This vision of the functions of a regulatory system is wider than some traditional models of regulation. It is holistic and comprehensive about controlling activities and risks. It ought to be what every responsible company or trader or professional does anyway – the overlay of a more comprehensive regulatory system is ultimately aimed at doing things better by using the combined knowledge and resource of all actors who are carrying out similar activities, so as to share data and good practice and provide consistent and effective responses to risk and protection. This approach accepts that some risks will occur – especially unknown risks. So it aims to be *responsive* when they do occur, and to put things right. The aim is to be able to identify and respond to known and unknown risks swiftly and effectively, through acting together in a coordinated *system*.

This approach contrasts with the idea that a regulatory authority regulates individual actors by imposing sanctions if they break particular rules. That might have been what people thought some decades ago, but we now have a deeper understanding of what we are trying to do through using a regulatory system. We have moved from a legal model – a vertical, authoritarian model – to a more collaborative model – because the evidence is that the latter works far better than the former.

Regulation as a System

In popular imagination, regulation is about requiring, and sometimes forcing, people to comply with rules that are established by a dominant group, such as the state. It is inherently authoritarian, an exercise in power, operating on a top-down basis, involving identifying breaches of rules, imposing sanctions and withholding or removing licences.

But a better way to think of regulation is as a *system* that achieves desired protections, avoiding harm and achieving desired outcomes. Viewed as a system, a regulatory space inherently becomes *a collaborative enterprise* between the relevant actors. It is only possible to make a system work, and to achieve all the desired outcomes, if all of those who perform core functions within the system, however modest they may be, perform their roles adequately. Otherwise, the system will not work. Achieving effective collaboration means that we have to think of regulation as a horizontal exercise, in which different actors engage with each other, in order to achieve their shared goals and outcomes. Such collaboration requires mutual respect and trust between the actors if it going to achieve much.

Thus, if our conception of regulation is shifting from an authoritarian mode to a system mode, we need to shift the focus from the vertical to the horizontal. As illustrated in Figure 3.1, the power moves from an authoritarian source to being shared between all actors and stakeholders. It needs to apply learning about when people trust each other.

Figure 3.1 Vertical and Horizontal Modes of Authority

VERTICAL MODE	HORIZONTAL MODE
Government ↓ Authority ↓ Actor	Government – Authority – Actors – Users – Others

We can illustrate the significance of this shift in various simple ways. Let's say that a regulatory system needs to be able to identify incidents of major harm that occur, especially if they are unexpected. The traditional way of doing this is to impose a requirement on, say, a manufacturer or distributor to report to the regulatory authority incidents of particular severity. The authority will then decide whether it will enforce the law by imposing sanctions on those who are deemed to have caused harm, or not complied with rules whose breach led to the harm. But will everyone report the relevant information? Would you report something if you might be prosecuted or sued? Will the authority have a complete picture of risks and harms? What about issues that are not reported because they (could be argued to) fall outside the strict definition of what needs to be reported?

By contrast, if we want to operate a system that identifies what is actually happening, and what harms are occurring, we need something more effective. If we want a system that captures all data on the use, risks and harms of multiple products and services, and traders' behaviour towards consumers or users, as well as issues arising in a market, all those involved would voluntarily contribute information, as part of a collaborative effort, so that a complete picture can be revealed, and issues swiftly identified. They would be motivated to do this, and benefit from having a reputation for contributing to the combined enterprise, their trustworthiness being evidenced.

Dona Meadows, an expert in systems, gave this definition: 'A system is an interconnected set of elements that is coherently organised in a way that achieves something. ... [It needs] three kinds of things: *elements, interconnected,* and a *function* or *purpose.* ... Many of the interconnections in systems operate through the flow of information.'[1]

The New Zealand Government not only considers its regulatory regimes to be systems, but it has also introduced legislation requiring all chief executives of public service agencies to have 'stewardship responsibility' for their systems.[2] On the basis that the Government 'uses regulation to protect the community from harm and to improve the living standards of its people', regulatory stewardship 'aims to ensure that all the different parts of a regulatory system work well together to achieve its goals, and to keep the system fit for purpose over the long term'.[3] That Government's expectations for regulatory stewardship manifest as responsibilities in three areas:

- monitoring, reviewing and reporting on existing regulatory systems;

- robust analysis and implementation support for changes to regulatory systems;
- good regulatory practice.

The responsibilities begin with describing the system and stating the roles of responsibilities of all organisations that actively contribute to it – but these are only *public* organisations: the *private* regulatees or beneficiaries of the system are (I suggest wrongly) not in focus. Further, is a wider, independent review focus necessary? There is also a problem that regulators themselves usually do not have power to amend the system within which they work, and this needs legislation from government or changes by those who are regulated.

The Concept of a 'Regulatory Space'

The idea that provides the flexibility that is needed in designing a regulatory regime is that of a 'regulatory space'. This contrasts with a regulatory regime that consists solely of a public regulatory authority (that enforces compliance with the rules on all actors under its jurisdiction). A 'regulatory space' is more flexible because it can accommodate a particular configuration or number of actors or particular subject matter. It can also combine different tools depending on the nature and severity of the different types of risk that it is intended to control. This can especially combine elements of public and private tools.

Hence, different regulatory spaces may have particular mixtures of public and private actors (which may well be efficient and effective), but the combination of actors in any space should all, collectively, work together to deliver the required functions and outcomes. For example, in a system that regulates safe and healthy property, and fair rents and behaviours, the system can use the contributions of landlords, agents, tenants, mortgagors and local authorities. Each makes their own particular contribution, operating within an holistic system. A contemporary model might include these features:

(a) A public portal, providing a register of properties, each giving details of landlord, agent, uploaded certificates of insurance, fire safety and so on, which acts as an efficient and consistent register

of all regulatory requirements but also as a source of information for all actors and the basis of a level playing field.
(b) A set of legal requirements, which set the boundary between acceptable and unacceptable behaviour and competence, breach of which may trigger public sanctions.
(c) A set of Codes of Behaviour, which state expected norms of fair and respectful behaviour by landlords, agents and tenants, leaseholders, commonholders, and authorities. An example is a Decent Homes Standard.
(d) An independent Ombuds, who acts as both data controller and resolver of disputes (together with the Property Tribunal for aspects of law). As data controller, the Ombuds collects and aggregates all data on behaviours arising from complaints and from the questions and searches that people make on websites. This provides the core source of information on behaviours in the market and individual relations, and identifies types of problems as well as individuals who may cause them.
(e) A feedback system that gives support to landlords, tenants and agents who could benefit from benevolent third party assistance (intervention), whilst also activating traditional enforcement in providing protection from criminal or incompetent actors.

Thus, this system is a mixture of formal and self-regulatory requirements.

The central coordinating activity here is regulation of a *system*. thus, there is a need for a *system regulator*, rather than a traditional regulator of those who are regulated (and subjected to enforcement). the focus is not on sanctioning people for breaking rules, it is to identify problems and drive improvement in behaviours, outcomes and performance where that is possible, whilst reserving firm measures against those who do not or cannot contribute properly and fairly to the system.

The Core Functions of the Regulatory Space: The Regulatory Functions Model

What is needed is to regulate a *system* that comprises multiple elements and actors. If the idea is to regulate a system of multiple actors, a fundamentally different approach is required. One of the consequences is the need for a different type of regulator – a 'system regulator'.

The starting point of looking at a system is to identify all the *actors*, who will be involved in making it work. This involves not just a public regulatory authority and the individuals and/or organisations who are subject to regulation, but also the intermediaries who contribute to it (accreditation, auditing, data), the beneficiaries of the regulatory protection or of the activities of those who are subject to regulation (including users, citizens, consumers, competitors, bystanders, commentators).

The second objective is to identify all the *functions* that will be necessary so that the system will work. Then one identifies who is involved in delivering each function, and how. How do they contribute to operating the system?

The basic functions of a regulatory system, it is suggested, are:

(1) To agree the purposes, norms and outcomes of the system.
(2) To establish the system and its functions, including procedures and rules, and ensure that they are fit for purpose and that the culture shared by the actors is appropriate.
(3) To identify problems, such as by inspecting and verifying, and monitoring data (for example from customer feedback and complaints).
(4) To investigate and identify the root cause of every significant problem.
(5) To agree what action should be taken to rectify any problem, to stop it continuing, and to reduce future risk.
(6) To undertake repair and deliver redress for any damage caused.
(7) To monitor the situation to determine if the desired changes have been made, and are effective or need to be amended.
(8) To do this continuously.

An effective system should aim to operate so as constantly to perform the *functions* identified above (of risk identification, acceptability, action and restoration) on a constant basis of improving performance. The ideal is a constant system that can be illustrated as a continuous circular cycle: a Regulatory Functions Model, illustrated in Figure 3.2.

Figure 3.2 The Regulatory Functions Model

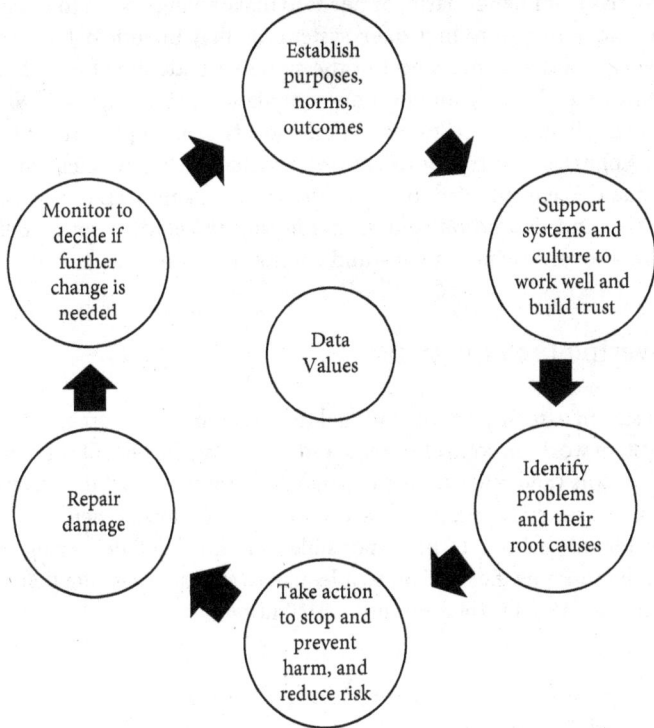

Achieving Outcomes

The basic objectives here are to operate a consistently effective system, which not only achieves the outcomes and constantly maintains and improves performance of the system and its actors, but also identifies problems and solves them. It is not (just) to identify non-compliance with rules (so that sanctions may be imposed). If we just focus on rules, we miss the goals of achieving improvements in performance, achieving outcomes, and addressing the root causes of problems. Non-compliance with one or more rules is relevant for the more fundamental purpose of identifying if there are more important problems that need addressing, such as that an actor does not have their system under control (so cannot control risk), or intends harm, or needs to make changes so as to improve performance in controlling their system, or that unanticipated harms or inadequacies in some aspect of the system are identified (so need to be addressed). Just identifying non-compliances with rules fails to get deep enough into more fundamental aspects. The approach outlined here recognises that trying to control a system through rules alone is inadequate. We need to adopt a holistic, systemic approach to achieving objectives and desired outcomes, monitoring risk and harm as well as performance and achievement – and continuously improving.

Delivering the Functions

Let us summarise the core operational functions at slightly greater depth. The system works in controlling risk and delivering the benefits of regulation if people (and relevant institutions) perform their part in delivering each of the *functions* properly. In each regulatory space, therefore, one has to identify who is to be responsible (and how) for delivering each function (and how they will do so adequately, and demonstrate that they are doing it). What is their unique contribution?

(1) Establishing the Purpose of the System and its Agreed Outcomes

The first step in identifying the features of a regulatory system is to agree what it is intended to do. What are the purposes of the various actors involved, are they all valid, and how are they to be translated into concrete outcomes that can be measured? Outcomes required by all the different actors are likely to include ones that need to be validated and aligned with others. For example, how are making profits and ensuring protection to be integrated and aligned? What levels of profits and protection are reasonable so that they do not conflict? What other outcomes are to be included, such as safety, fairness, risk, development, growth, sustainability, and so on? All agreed outcomes should be integrated into an agreed delivery plan, with appropriate measurable milestones. This step is the 'what?'; the next step is 'how?'.

(2) Establishing a System and Culture that will Deliver the Functions and the Outcomes

Who, and which institutions and arrangements, are needed to enable the various functions to operate effectively, so as to deliver the outcomes? The answer is likely to differ between regulatory regimes, but still be recognisably the same model. Delivery of each function could be by different public or private actors (or differing combinations of them). This affords a 'deregulatory' opportunity to shift from public bodies to trusted private bodies, or rules. An interesting example is the Delegated Administrative Authority model in Canada where private not-for-profit organisations are invested with regulatory functions and powers.[4]

System governance should be centred on an oversight body of all actors (Stakeholder Council), including state, regulatory, private and civil society actors, including consumer and citizen representation. Exact membership will vary depending on the context, but it should be inclusive. An interesting model in the Netherlands is that of periodic meetings between business and consumer representatives under the aegis of the Council of State, with detailed discussions sometimes being chaired by an independent expert or academic, thereby signifying the official collaborative nature of the discussions.

Operational management of the system is also necessary, and its complexity will vary depending on context. Much of this may be delivered by a traditional regulatory authority, although other models could be relevant.

Given that effective collaboration will be built on trust and respect, standards on the nature and extent of evidence of trustworthiness that different actors agree to produce about themselves will be needed. Again, variations and evolution will occur. Traditional sources of evidence will continue to be relevant (such as independent auditors, standard-setting bodies, accreditation and compliance bodies) but supplemented by other forms of evidence. Since trust is based on the human understanding of the difference between right and wrong, a society's ethical norms and values are fundamental here. Hence, Codes of Ethical Practice and Behaviour are likely to be helpful. Detailed technical rules can be made at subsidiary levels, such as by regulatory or standards bodies, involving suitable consultation with all stakeholders.

(3) Monitoring the Performance of the System, and Identifying Problems and their Root Causes

How do we know that the system is working well? How are different harms or problems in operation or performance of the system to be identified? What oversight, controls, audit, data, investigations and so on are necessary? Who produces the data and how is it shared?

The use of data from all relevant sources will be essential, and systems should be designed to produce relevant and coherent data.[5] Various means of identifying problems should be in place, from internal and external evidence, and a culture of psychological safety[6] that facilitates the raising of issues, monitoring activities, tests, inspections and audits. A key advance is to adopt frameworks and practices that support and maintain an ethical culture in organisations and hence trust between them and the people involved.

This 'root cause' approach is now widely adopted in technical contexts. It aims to identify the real – and often multiple and systemic – causes of a problem, rather than just the individual who was closest to 'causing' an incident or breaching a rule. The deeper question might be what circumstances surrounded certain behaviour: why would any human in that position have behaved in that way? The objective is to be as effective as possible in addressing the problem, rather than to sanction breach of a rule and hence fail to take more effective or widespread action.

(4) Responding: Taking Action to Improve, to Stop and Prevent Harm, and to Reduce Future Risk

What needs to change so as to make improvements, or adequately to control the occurrence of harm and ongoing risk? *What* changes are required and *how* will specific improvements be made so as to deliver improved *outcomes*? Many possible actions may be relevant. Action might be taken at 'ground level' by immediate actors, or more systemically at organisational level, or externally by a regulator. Whenever appropriate, relevant information and action should be notified to, and discussed and agreed between, responsible people at relevant levels, whether internal or external. As discussed in chapters 6 and 7, different approaches may be effective, ranging from spontaneous or agreed voluntary action to various interventions to traditional compulsive enforcement measures.

(5) Repairing Damage

The previous function is prospective, aimed at reducing future risk, whilst this function is retrospective, aimed at restoring things back into balance and repairing harm. It may involve making repairs, recalling dangerous products, restoring the environment, paying compensation for loss, or similar actions. Removing illicit gains as well as making good losses is required in markets so as to restore a balanced, level playing field.[7] Efficient systems should be in place to achieve these outcomes swiftly and economically.

The *restoration* objective is one that has traditionally been left to private action (usually through civil courts) rather than being seen as a responsibility of regulators. But it is critical in supporting confidence in the operation of the system. People will trust a system that involves major risk if they have confidence that harm will be identified quickly and solved, and that they will be cared for if they are hurt. It is also more effective and swifter if a regulator aims to ensure that redress is made as part of a complete resolution of the 'regulatory' risk issues. Since around 2000, a number of regulatory authorities in Europe, especially the UK, have used redress powers with great success, delivering redress or restitution swiftly, effectively and efficiently, resolving all issues at the same time as part of a holistic approach.

The holistic resolution of all issues of behaviour/culture and of redress simultaneously is highly efficient, delivers rectification of markets and redress to consumers speedily, and provides an incentive for businesses to behave ethically.[8] These techniques have been approved by UNCTAD.[9] An important objective is to *demonstrate* to the public and to market actors that fairness and effective outcomes are achieved in the system as a whole, so as to maintain confidence and legitimacy, and to support intrinsic motivation to behave in ways that support society's ethical values.

(6) Monitoring the Situation and Action Taken to See if Any Further or Corrective Action is Needed

Such corrective action might involve changes to the system, or its architecture or rules and approaches. It might involve cultural measurement over time to determine if cultural transformation efforts are succeeding. Thus, the model is circular, representing continuous activity (rather than activity just based on individual activities, such as inspections, identifying breaches and imposing sanctions).

Key Elements of the Regulatory Functions Model

Let us now highlight some of the essential – and non-traditional – aspects of the system, especially those that are unfamiliar from the classic Legal Regulatory Model. The critical focus is on achieving *outcomes*.

A Collaborative System

The analysis of defining the *functions*, then agreeing what institutions and systems are to fulfil them, and what each actor will contribute to the ecosystem within which they operate, necessarily involves two other aspects: a *collaborative* approach, within which an ecosystem works because everyone does their bit in delivering the sequence of functions, and a collective focus on *outcomes*, which show whether the agreed common desired protections and economic and social objectives are being achieved or not.

How do you ensure that the necessary stakeholders collaborate as required? Under a traditional system, the (vertically aligned) mechanism is that some traders report certain adverse events to a regulator. Is that going to work quickly enough in identifying the occurrence of serious harm? Increasingly, no. As we face fast-moving new technologies, situations and risks, we need a system that responds more quickly. The collaborative model emphasises that the approach actually involves everyone working together to deliver the core functions of 'identify, respond and restore'. This is why, in consumer markets, Ombuds act as data aggregators for all consumer feedback, and a comprehensive data system needs the input of *all* stakeholders – users, bystanders, traders, data controller, regulators – all acting together in an integrated, coherent way.

Actors

Involvement of all stakeholders in co-creation has the following advantages:

- It builds *ownership of the achievement of the purposes and outcomes* and accountability for observance of the principles and rules on the part of those who have to apply them. It maximises individuals'

internal motivation for achieving them. This powerfully supports compliance and with innovation in performance.
- It builds in the *support of citizens*, civil society and those who are the intended beneficiaries of the system. This facilitates both challenge and support for the outcomes and actions that follow.
- It draws together the *knowledge and expertise* of all relevant parties, especially government, regulators, academia, business, intermediaries, not just in agreeing the desired outcomes but also in ways of achieving them. It captures ideas and overcomes silos, enabling the development of joined-up thinking.
- It provides *challenge to established thinking*, which is necessary for testing and developing ideas. The tone of the discussion can be carefully moderated, within a culture of respect for the contributions of all stakeholders and mutual trust, so as to facilitate relevant debate but maintain joint cooperation and achievement of the core goals.
- It should enable the *identification of barriers and gaps* that impede achievement of the purposes and outcomes.
- It bases behaviours, rules and cultures on *principles that the society values* and encourages debate and balance between potential conflicts in values, purposes and outcomes at an early stage, so as to provide clarity in implementation.

If harm occurs, it is likely that users or bystanders are the ones who will suffer this or be aware of it. How is that information passed on, accurately and fully, to those who oversee the operation of the system? If this is not done, and information flows do not occur swiftly, or such that multiple small individual pieces of information are not aggregated, the system will not respond to the occurrence of harms, or be capable of learning. Easy routes for passing on, collecting and aggregating data, and using AI and other analyses, are nowadays required. Traditional mechanisms of requiring only, say, licensed manufacturers to report certain types of information to a regulator, perhaps annually, are now inadequate. We will look further at data below, but the point here is that *everyone* can be regarded as contributors to a regulatory system. This has implications not only for how the system is designed functionally, but also for involvement in its governance. Stakeholders need to be involved in governance. They may have valuable observations about how the functioning of a system may work, which challenges the views of regulatees and even regulators. Their involvement should be positive, and guard against capture.

Figure 3.3 illustrates that multiple actors are involved in risk issues. This mapping approach not only assists in identifying the stakeholders but also the relationships and interrelations that are necessary to enable the system to function effectively. Further, it helps in determining their level of influence in achieving the objectives. The intensity of the colour indicates differences in the level of influence over, and responsibility for, controlling risk. The roles, responsibilities and levels of accountability are generally directly proportional to the level of their influence on the system. From a systems perspective, it should be understood that not all of the system objectives are necessarily achieved through regulatory mandates. For example, education may be a better form of intervention to address unhealthy food practices.

Figure 3.3 Public Risk Management – Multi Stakeholder Context[10]

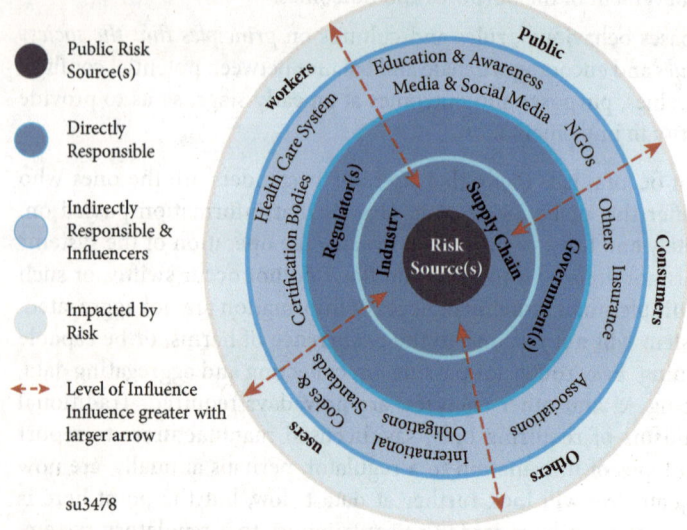

(NGOs = non-governmental organisations)

Key Elements of the Regulatory Functions Model

Scope of the Ecosystem

It follows that a regulatory ecosystem needs to involve relevant stakeholders so as to be able to capture all relevant data. Sometimes, regulatory regimes are too limited or siloed. For example, separate regulatory systems for manufacture of construction products, builders and construction (including use of construction products), use and operation of buildings, and governance of residency rights (owner/occupier issues), performance of managing agents, and so on, need to *function* in a unified fashion. Some of the individual regimes may differ in involving public or private 'regulatory' mechanisms or institutions, but much of the same data can be used in each element to identify issues around safety, quality, reliability, performance, competence, behaviour, culture, harms and problems.

Accountability

All of the activities involved (operating your system, identifying issues, feeding back data, instituting changes, continued monitoring) involve actors assuming *accountability* for their performance in contributing to make the system work. This concept is discussed further below.

The various actors also form *joint stakeholders* in the joint collaborative enterprise. This means that they inherently assume an element of power and responsibility for the enterprise; they play a role in its governance, and in its achieving its goals and outcomes.

Trustworthiness

Membership of this collaborative enterprise is predicated on actors being trustworthy. They can be trusted to perform their collaborative contributions. They can – and should – be questioning and critical about what is going on, but others will only collaborate with them and allow them to remain trusted actors in the group, if they produce evidence that demonstrates that they can be trusted. This includes evidence relating to motivation, capability, having appropriate resources and systems to perform their roles, and exhibiting appropriate behaviours. Since the basis of trust is the observance of a set of *values* by a group, and its constituent members, the values should be shared, agreed and (in a 21st century democracy) ethical.

Data

Data on outcomes, capacities, behaviours and performance are essential elements of a successful system. It tells us if we are capable of achieving outcomes and actually doing so, and identifies problems and risks in the operation of the system. Adequate and relevant data needs to be made available and collected in relation to the performance of each function and actor. In order to do this, the data system has to be essentially simple, holistic and unified. There needs to be a convincing answer to the question: Where do we get the data from? In many regulatory regimes, manufacturers, suppliers, retailers, professionals and so on have data on the safety, quality, performance, reliability etc of their products and services. This can be supplemented by data from quality systems, audits on compliance with standards, complaints, and so on.

Data could be derived from multiple sources, eg self-monitoring, remote monitoring (Internet of Things), inspections, conformity assessment bodies or complaints (platforms and Ombuds). In many consumer markets (in some countries), Ombuds have performed the function of data controller very effectively by aggregating the data on the nature and number of complaints. They have fused two or even three functions. In the dispute resolution context, they perform an efficient complaint management and resolution system, which is easily identified by consumers, and attractive to them, whilst remaining independent and hence trusted, and reducing cost to businesses who fund the service. In the regulatory context, Ombuds aggregate all micro data received from consumers and others.

Review of the data should be undertaken by relevant public and/or private groups, followed by implementation of relevant action to reduce risk, improve performance, or enforce law. In complex networks of organisations, such as supply chains, it may be appropriate that different data sets are collated and monitored by different entities – since it may be impossible for a single 'top down' authority, whether public or private, to control or have access to all data.

Risk and Responding

This approach accepts that risk is unavoidable, so it aims to achieve consistent, effective, acceptable and proportionate control over known risks, and to identify and quickly control unknown risks. Identification of unknown or unexpected risks is achieved through everyone working together, contributing their observations, data and control efforts, in an holistic collaborative system. The data is collated, aggregated and constantly reviewed. Appropriate interventions are agreed upon, undertaken, and evaluated to ensure that they provide adequate protection against harm. Learnings are fed back and applied, so that future risk is reduced. We discuss pre- and post-marketing and economic tools in chapters 6 and 7.

The Basic Operational Challenges Around Risk and Harms

The same questions lie at the heart of every regulatory system – as they do in managerial systems in private companies. Although the contexts in which different systems operate can differ considerably, and the solutions may differ, the core questions are the same. The essential questions that arise in operating the system in relation to its problem-identification function are:

(1) *Identification.* Can you identify all of the different risks that may arise from this activity, or use of these products, services, activities and markets? *How* will you identify the risks and potential harms? Further, how will you achieve the agreed outcomes? How will you know if you are making acceptable progress towards achieving your outcomes or not?

(2) *Acceptability.* How can you show what risks/harms will be viewed as *acceptable* and which as unacceptable? This has a technical aspect (how much risk) and an ethical aspect (what should we accept). One aspect of this is the extent to which damage is reversible. Another aspect is the risk culture of the community.

(3) *Action.* Can you demonstrate how unacceptable harms will be *stopped* from continuing? How can you provide confidence that all

relevant actors will take appropriate and swift *action* in response to evidence of unacceptable harm or risk? *What changes* should occur to reduce ongoing risk, and how will they occur? Exactly how will learning lead to changes in behaviour, and systems?

(4) *Restoration.* How will those who are harmed be *restored* to the position they would have been in before the harm occurred? How will those who need care or support be assisted? How will harm be repaired, rectified, redressed? How will markets be returned to fair, level playing fields?

These questions are fundamental in the case of all new technologies. In short, how do you control the risks and build trust in the technology and relevant actors, by showing that the risks are acceptable, and that serious risks will be either prevented or stopped early, and that people will be protected and looked after? What is your ecosystem for identifying harm when it occurs?

Take AI as an example. AI will be used in many ways and situations. Some applications will produce real and transformative benefits. Other applications will produce harm – possibly new types of harm that we cannot predict or guard against in advance. The key question is: How will we identify when harm occurs and what is going wrong? What is the ecosystem for doing this? Traditional regulatory systems (the rules-compliance-sanction model outlined in chapter 1) will not respond quickly or effectively enough. Do we just ban various activities, products, services and so on, or do we try to 'regulate' in new ways? Or are controls too costly, and we don't want to pay for them? Mark Zuckerberg accepted in January 2025 that the relaxation of content moderation and removal of in-house content assessors by Meta meant that 'we're going to catch less bad stuff'.[11] So more children, women and minorities would predictably suffer harm. Is this acceptable?

These questions need to be answered holistically, and with some imagination, since traditional answers (such as those that divide responses into discrete compartments like enforcement, civil liability, and courts) do not necessarily deliver convincing resolutions and complete outcomes. The answers to these questions ought to align business/investment risks and regulatory risks (ie everyone should be interested in the same issues, data and answers).

Bespoke Regulatory Spaces

Although the functions of every regulatory space should be the same, as summarised in Figure 3.2, the exact design of how each function is delivered may differ in practice between different systems, depending on their individual natures and architectures. In particular, the configuration of public and/or private actors who perform each function may differ. This model opens opportunities for a move away from the essential functions (identification of breaches and enforcement of rules) by a single public authority, and opens up considerable flexibilities for the involvement of private tools of standards, codes and assurance schemes, plus data control facilities – provided all actors satisfy the required levels of competence, governance and trustworthiness. Thus, a shift from a traditional regulatory model to a fresh regulatory space may well bring opportunities for greater efficiency (ie cutting costs).

There is also scope for fine-tuning a regulatory regime in order to match the nature and level of particular risks. A regime may provide adequate controls on behaviour and outcomes (the risk and occurrence of harm) through a 'light' mechanism, such as information and education, or self-regulation through a code of practice written by a trade association. But if the level of risk, in terms of the severity and likelihood of occurrence of harm, is high, then it is necessary to have a system of formal regulation, involving legal rules enforceable by state institutions and applicable to all who come within the stated ambit.

A regulatory system can also differentiate between different types of risk. Hence, some risks might only need 'light touch' controls, whereas other more serious risks may need formal regulation. A differentiated approach is, therefore, theoretically possible between different issues, for example, issues relating to capital adequacy, provision of information, achieving adequate understanding and control by parties, avoiding unacceptable levels of influence or decision-making by non-parties, and so on. Hence, modern practice is to design a 'regulatory space'[12] that might combine various techniques, whether they are public or private.

There are various examples of fused approaches. The global aviation safety framework integrates international standards (approved by ICAO), national oversight, and private safety audits. Financial supervision and regulation are subject to the global standards agreed in the Basel Core Principles (BCPs), which combine global standards with national adaptation and private risk models. The EU medical devices regime, created in the 1990s,[13] integrated the techniques that industry had previously widely adopted for private accreditation of quality management systems, and product standards (which had also been integrated into the UK's public regulatory requirements) were included in the EU legal system's architecture for many types of medical devices. Only high-risk devices (Class III) were required to be approved by a process involving a public authority. For all other Classes, manufacturers were empowered to self-certify (and apply CE marking) if they held the required set of approvals from private accreditation bodies (notified bodies). The EU data protection regime (the GDPR) blends mandatory public rules with private compliance certifications.

By contrast, in the food sector, businesses continue with private accreditation regimes, which they find useful commercially, in supply chains and as a means of obtaining information and support on improving their performance. These are separate from the public regulatory regimes established by governments, which differ across the globe in the extent to which they include elements of private conformity and accreditation. The continuation of both public and private regulatory systems appears unnecessary and costly. For operators such as food businesses and farmers, the need to obtain several sets of approvals is confusing, can involve inconsistencies between them, and is certainly time-consuming and costly.

In shifting every existing regulatory regime to a functions-based model, we should involve all stakeholders in answering the questions of whether and how each of the functions is adequately performed, and what more effective and efficient ways of performing them there might be. This should fill in existing gaps, nudge the adoption of new technologies that use more and better data, and probably replace some public law aspects with private mechanisms and actors.

Governance of a Regulatory System

In a traditional Legal Model, Ministers and Parliament create and oversee regulatory authorities. The latter are supposed to be independent authorities, and many have Boards that include independent non-executive directors, but authorities are accountable to their political masters. Political control is exercised, first, through powers of *appointment* of Chairs of Boards and Chief Executives, even where independent public appointment panels sieve candidates, and, second, through the imposition of *duties* on authorities (discussed in chapter 8).

In a Regulatory System Model based on OBC principles, the creation and oversight of the system is co-owned by all the stakeholders. They have joint responsibility for governance and effective operation of the *outcomes* that they agree. The primary governance mechanism is, therefore, a 'stakeholder council', comprising all of the stakeholders, or their representatives. The principles here are that those responsible for the design, operation and functioning of the system should be democratically involved in its governance and oversight. However, it is often useful to have an independent chair (and secretariat, if the system needs this), so as to provide independent and objective challenge.

At an operational level, the cohort of public and private actors who perform the various functions need to assume responsibility for performing their allotted tasks as contributors to the system as a whole, and hence need to adhere to relevant norms and rules of practice, performance and behaviour. There needs to be a mechanism for oversight of the performance of the system, and hence of all contributing actors. This may be a public or private authority, or council (perhaps the same as the governing stakeholder council), but arrangements can differ depending on the scale and nature of the system. The principles here are that the functional actors have to contribute appropriate expertise, knowledge and capacity so that all of the functions work together as a system.

Certain elements may still need to be created by the state, such as a public authority and legislation that makes rules mandatory for all those who are subject to regulation in the defined space, including being subject to codes, standards and the decisions of an Ombuds.

The risk of capture can arise in a traditional system as between a regulator and one or a group of regulatees. But this risk is mitigated through the involvement of *all* stakeholders in the System Model, coupled with transparency and an independent chair or further non-executives. The opposite phenomenon of relationships that are too close is resistance to involvement, especially to sharing information. Here Dona Meadows' experience was succinct: 'Bring in all the actors and use the energy formerly expended on resistance to seek out mutually satisfactory ways for all goals to be realized – or redefinitions of larger and more important goals that everyone can pull toward together.'[14] That releases the collective power of all the stakeholders and actors through working together systematically. Among Meadows' principles for 'Living in a World of Systems' are: 'Honour, respect and distribute information. Pay attention to what is important, not just what is quantifiable. Make feedback policies. Go for the good of the whole. Locate responsibility in the system. Stay humble – stay a learner. Celebrate complexity. Expand time horizons. Defy the disciplines. Expand the boundary of caring. Don't erode the goal of goodness.'[15]

Coordinating Multiple Systems

In reality, it is necessary to provide for the integration of multiple systems. The traditional approach of creating distinct regulatory systems tends to produce a world of separate regulatory silos. This makes interplay, let alone coordination, between the regulatory silos very challenging. What is needed is a mechanism of integrating, both within and across systems.

For example, food safety needs to be looked at in the overall context of food security; SDG Target 2.1 says, 'By 2030, end hunger and ensure access by all people, in particular the poor and people in vulnerable situations, including infants, to safe, nutritious and sufficient food all year round.' If one were to regulate some of those outcomes, one would need to be regulating across systems. We will return to this challenge in chapter 8.

Key Points

- Regulation is not 'a regulator and rules' but a system. The system perspective transforms the effectiveness of a regulatory regime.
- The Regulatory Functions Model specifies the elements that need to be present if a regulatory system is going to function well.
- In particular, functions of identification of harm, effective reaction to problems, and providing redress/repair are critical elements (and often given inadequate attention).
- A system that delivers all these functions well will be capable of coping with much unknown risk – it will be truly 'agile'.
- Delivering an effective system, and achieving its desired outcomes, as well as monitoring its performance and identifying problems, requires data. The sources of such data will be widely spread across different actors and stakeholders in a system. Designing

- for access to all relevant data requires fresh thinking. This is a huge opportunity of a digital age, and should be transformative.
- In designing a bespoke regulatory system, there can be a choice between whether some elements are delivered by public or private entities and arrangements.
- But either approach needs fully independent governance (and this is something that many private arrangements currently lack).
- A major challenge lies in how we coordinate multiple systems – domestically but certainly globally.
- So, a fundamental reconfiguration of how we do regulation is called for – but will be transformative.

---

[1] DH Meadows, *Thinking in Systems. A Primer* (Chelsea Green Publishing, 2008).

[2] State Sector Act 1988, introduced in 2013, amended by the Public Sector Act 2020.

[3] *Starting out with regulatory stewardship: A resource* (New Zealand Government, 2022).

[4] See S Mangalam, 'The Delegated Administrative Authority Model, a Radical Alternative Governance Framework from Ontario, Canada' in G Russell and C Hodges (eds), *Regulatory Delivery* (Hart, 2019).

[5] *Use of New Technologies in Regulatory Delivery – Summary Note and Case Studies Organization* (PRISM Institute, Deutsche Gesellschaft für Internationale Zusammenarbeit and World Bank Group, 2019); *Data-Driven, Information-Enabled Regulatory Delivery* (OECD, 2021).

[6] AC Edmondson, *The Fearless Organization* (John Wiley & Sons, Inc, 2019).

[7] C Hodges, 'Encouraging Enterprise and Rebalancing Risk: Implications of Economic Policy for Regulation, Enforcement and Compensation' (2007) 18 *European Business Law Review* 1231–66; C Hodges, 'A Market-Based Competition Enforcement Policy' (2011) 22(3) *European Business Law Review* 261.

[8] C Hodges and S Voet, *Delivering Collective Redress: New Technologies* (Hart, 2018); C Hodges, 'Collective Redress: The Need for New Technologies' (2019) 42 *Journal of Consumer Policy* 59–90.

[9] *Manual on Consumer Protection* (UNCTAD, 2018), chs 6 and 11.

[10] Underwriters Laboratories, UL 2984: Guideline for Managing Risks in the Public Interest.

[11] M Sellman, 'Zuckerberg warned over illegal content', *The Times* (13 January 2025), 8.

[12] A phrase coined by F Vibert, *The New Regulatory Space: Reframing Democratic Governance* (Edward Elgar, 2014).

[13] Originally Directives 90/385/EEC, 93/42/EEC, 98/79/EEC.

[14] DH Meadows, *Thinking in Systems. A Primer* (Chelsea Green Publishing, 2008) 116.

[15] ibid ch 7.

4
New Models

We are at a critical point of evolution in regulation and business from traditional to new models about 'how to do' regulation. There are currently huge opportunities to change how we do things and thereby generate *both* better protection from risk *and* increased prosperity.

The development of new models of regulation shows how to overcome drawbacks with the Legal and Economic Models:

(1) The Regulatory Delivery Model, especially focusing on outcomes, and on interventions rather than (just) enforcement.
(2) The Outcome-Based Collaborative Model.

Having established that regulation affects many aspects of daily life, and not just commercial activities, we turn to look at how it works. This chapter looks at the broad tools that are used in regulation. Every regulatory regime has its own tools and particular design, but there are many similarities and some broad families of approaches. But before we look at them, it is instructive to set the scene by identifying the broad theories that have led to the creation of the various toolboxes and influence how they are used.

We start with two theories that have dominated regulation and other disciplines until recently: legal theory and economic theory. We then focus on two recent models: the Regulatory Delivery Model (RDM) and the Outcome-Based Collaborative Model (OBC). In order to understand the evolution in thinking between these theories and models, we summarise some concerns and insights that arose from scientific research about behaviour and how to motivate and control it. This leads to noting important concepts like trust and trustworthiness. We then widen the gaze even further by looking at, namely, changes in political and social contexts that are relevant to the evolutions in thinking about behaviour and regulation.

> We are at a major turning point in regulation. The traditional model based on the *theories* of law and economics has proved to be inadequate, and behavioural *science* has provided the basis for a new model. But the implications for what needs to be changed, and how, have not yet been widely understood. The nature of the changes is significant. For some, the necessary changes to implement an evidence-based approach will be startling and even revolutionary. But the evidence and implications are clear.

From Theories to Science, and Rules to Outcomes

The objectives of both the Legal and Economic Models are to make people comply with rules. But the evidence is that those Models widely fail to achieve compliance, and are not focused on achieving protection from harm as such. Is compliance with rules all we want or need? Is compliance and sanctioning effective in underpinning modern behaviour, markets and states? If the fundamental purpose of regulation is about delivering desired levels of protection from harm, don't we need to focus explicitly on how we deliver objectives and outcomes such as adequate levels of safety and fairness? In addition, if we want to use regulation as a tool to assist in achieving other goals like innovation, a sustainable planet and vibrant economies, and not to impede those goals, do theories like pursuing compliance with rules, and by doing so through imposing sanctions on violations, actually work?

A 'compliance mindset' fails to respond to how people and systems improve their performance, especially *above and beyond* mere complance with particular standards, or to focus on responsiveness to actual risk and to changes in risk, or on innovative technologies that do not comply with existing rules (see chapter 9). Further, compliance focuses on breaches of a particular rule, rather than on whether the underling activity and behaviour tends to achieve the desired outcomes or to increase risk and cause harm. Imposition of a sanction is dependent on the wording of the rule, so that someone may do something awful but escape because the rule fails to prohibit it exactly.

As we have said above, the coherence of human beings in groups and societies is fundamentally based on mutual trust. Evidence of compliance with rules, or breach of a particular rule, usually provides some evidence of trustworthiness, but there is much more relevant evidence that could be used if it were available. Values are more important than rules. We need to know that members of the group to which we belong share and observe the same values, and are trustworthy, so that we can trust them and work together with them.

This all needs a wider focus. It needs a change in concepts and theories. Fortunately, useful developments have occurred, in at least part of the regulatory landscape, even if they are not yet embedded widely.

A Modern Regulatory Authority: The Regulatory Delivery Model

Dissatisfaction with a focus solely on regulatory *design* (and a rules-based Legal Model) led to a shift in thinking to regulatory *delivery*. The questions were: Is regulation delivered? Does the traditional system work as intended? Does it reduce harm, achieve its protection goals, disproportionately adversely affect freedom, prosperity, innovation and so on? In seeking to provide a framework for regulatory authorities to operate in a way that provided effective solutions to these questions, experienced officials led by Graham Russell and colleagues proposed a Regulatory Delivery Model (RDM) on how an effective authority should be constituted and operated.[1] The RDM was based on extensive engagement with regulatory regimes and practices in the UK and across the world.

The RDM has the following elements:

- Prerequisites:
  - Governance framework
  - Accountability
  - Culture
- Practices:
  - Outcome measurement
  - Risk-based prioritisation
  - Intervention choices

We summarise the significance of these six elements below.

RDM Prerequisites

Governance Framework

Governance is the manner in which control is exercised – the collective set of rules and relationships that define the regulatory agency, and which establish a framework within which the agency operates. The governance framework of a regulatory agency has multiple external constituents including the law that establishes it; its outward-facing role; and its defined relationship to others. These are part of establishing an effective authorising environment, which is further strengthened by aspects of accountability. These external constituents are internalised by regulatory agencies through their strategies, policies and procedures. The governance framework should comprise:

(1) the *purpose* of the agency, which should be clearly set out by government and legislation, and transparently and clearly communicated;
(2) the regulatory agency's *structures*, such as its decision-making capability and processes;
(3) the agency's *position within the wider regulatory landscape*, with clarity of responsibilities and appropriate arrangements for collaborating with other agencies;
(4) the agency's *powers and responsibilities*, which should be appropriate to its role and purpose, clearly communicated and effectively governed and monitored.

Accountability

Accountability, in the context of regulation, can be defined as 'the obligation to account for regulatory activities to another body or person'. It is understood within the RDM in terms of the empowerment of stakeholders to participate in the regulatory process and to challenge the regulatory agency. It is important as a constraint on the behaviour of the regulatory agency, but it is also an enabler, since the creation of confidence and the use of trust strengthens the authorising environment. The RDM encourages a wide consideration of accountability, with a focus on three parties in particular: the state; the 'beneficiaries' of regulation (those whom the law aims to protect and those who articulate concerns on their behalf); and businesses and others that are regulated.

102 New Models

Key aspects of accountability within the RDM are:

(1) the approach to transparency adopted by a regulatory agency, whether communications are effective and if the approach to transparency builds trust;
(2) whether mechanisms to hold the regulatory agency to account are effective, tailored appropriately to different audiences and accessible;
(3) the need for recognition by regulatory agencies that they have a responsibility for *building the capability* of those to whom they are accountable.

The fact that a regulator is accountable to multiple constituencies can be seen from the following summary by the UK National Audit Office:[2]

Accountability arrangements

Robust accountability arrangements help to ensure regulators are held to account for their efficiency and effectiveness. Key parts of the accountability system include the following.

- **Parliament**: Parliamentary accountability includes scrutiny by Select Committees, debates and oral and written questions. Most regulators are directly accountable to Parliament through their own accounting officer, who must personally 'be able to assure Parliament and the public of high standards of probity in the management of public funds'.
- **The National Audit Office (NAO)**: The NAO supports Parliament by auditing regulators' financial accounts and examining and reporting on the value for money of their activities.
- **Government departments**: Regulators are often sponsored by a government department and accountable to its secretary of state. The secretary of state may have a role in appointing the regulator's chair and non-executive board members, or providing a strategic direction to the regulator. The level of involvement will depend on the level of statutory independence the regulator has and the type of body it is.
- **Regulator boards**: Regulators are held to account internally by their boards, often including a publicly appointed chair and non-executive board members.
- **Citizens and consumers**: Citizens hold regulators to account by seeking redress for poor service, such as through ombudsman services or advocacy bodies.
- **Judicial review**: Companies and citizens may be able to hold the regulator to account through court action.

Culture

Culture in the RDM is a collective understanding and purpose that manifests itself in the visible behaviour of the regulatory agency: 'the way things are done around here'. It is the general style or description of how people tend to behave in an organisation or relationship. It is a generalised description of an environment, intended to summarise many behaviours. It is an outcome that is produced by the behaviours of the people within the organisation, and cannot be imposed on the organisation from outside. So, culture is very difficult to 'regulate'. But it has a profoundly powerful effect on how regulation is 'done' and whether its outcomes are good and as desired, or not. Culture determines how the regulatory agency will respond to the forces of governance and accountability and supports improvement. It demands particular attention by regulatory agencies because, as noted under governance, the absence of commercial influences and a regulatory agency's authorisation to exercise the coercive power of the state mean that culture plays a crucial role in determining how powers are exercised.

The aspects of culture explored within the RDM are:

(1) the nature of the *leadership* of the regulatory agency, including the leadership drive to build an outcome-focused culture;
(2) the *values* of the regulatory agency, including their appropriateness to the regulatory task of the agency and the extent to which these are shared values;
(3) the *competency* of staff to deliver the purpose of the regulatory agency, including whether knowledge, skills and behaviours are proportionate to the level of discretion.

RDM Practices

Outcome Measurement

It should be self-evident that any organisation needs to know what its intended outcomes are and to be able to understand whether it is making progress towards them. Well-communicated outcomes are equally important, internally, to give staff a clear sense of purpose, and, externally, to establish a foundation for trust and confidence in the agency. Where the regulatory agency understands and measures the impact of its activities, it is then able to make informed decisions, shifting resource allocation to those activities that are contributing effectively and efficiently. But the indirect nature of the regulatory agency's contribution, the multiplicity of contributors, the time lapse between activities and outcomes, together with the difficulties in establishing a counterfactual, make it challenging to identify the contribution to long-term outcomes. Measures such as the number of inspectors, inspection frequencies, or numbers of prosecutions, when taken as indicators of success, can have a perverse effect.

The aspects of outcome measurement explored within the RDM are:

(1) the *identification* of appropriate outcomes, from strategic to operational, including communication of these outcomes and the approach to managing conflicts;
(2) the regulatory agency's understanding of its *contribution* to outcomes resulting from its direct actions and the articulation of this contribution internally and externally;
(3) the approach to *measurement* of progress towards outcomes including appropriate indicators, adequate analysis capacity and continuous improvement in data access.

Risk-based Prioritisation

Risk-based prioritisation addresses the question of where the regulatory agency chooses to direct its resources. The role of a regulatory agency involves managing risks to regulatory outcomes by reducing their likelihood and/or their impact. The role of reducing risk requires the regulatory agency to ensure that its decision-making, at all levels, is based on an informed assessment of risk and that it prioritises on the basis of that assessment. It should be remembered that some risks are unknown.

Regulatory agencies exist because there is a risk of harm that would not be properly managed without their intervention. Over time, the purpose of the regulatory agency is to manage that risk by reducing the likelihood or impact of harm (or both). In making decisions about resource allocation, the regulatory agency faces the challenge of assessing and comparing different threats, and potential threats, to the regulatory outcomes that it is working towards. The concept of regulatory risk provides a means of assessing different challenges to desired regulatory outcomes. It provides a structured way of thinking about relative impacts, positive or negative, and comparing them so that the regulatory agency can direct its efforts in proportion to the risk. We could say that 'risk is the currency of regulation'.

The aspects of risk-based prioritisation explored within the RDM are:

(1) the importance of effective *identification and assessment* of risks to the regulatory agency's outcomes at all levels, from strategic to operational;
(2) the need to use all available *data, information and intelligence* to identify and assess risk, a proactive approach to closing data gaps and effective data sharing;
(3) the approach to *using risk*, including the risk frameworks used, the link between risk and prioritisation and the transparency of the risk-based prioritisation approach. This raises the issue of a society's *risk appetite*, which is discussed further below.

Intervention Choices

The question of how a regulatory agency, being clear on its outcomes and having decided where to direct its resources, should best use them is considered within the RDM in terms of its intervention choices. The task of regulatory agencies, while often expressed in terms of enforcement, controlling or mitigating risk or ensuring compliance with regulation, is fundamentally about changing the behaviour of regulated entities. The question for a regulatory agency is therefore what will be most effective in ensuring the desired behaviour amongst those it regulates.

A wide range of interventions are available to most regulatory agencies that can be used in conjunction with or as alternatives to traditional licence, inspection or investigation-based approaches. These might include, for example, initiatives to raise awareness and understanding of requirements amongst those they regulate; oversight of industry compliance initiatives; and initiatives to empower the beneficiaries of regulation, particularly those most at risk. Where a regulatory agency uses a narrow range of interventions, it is less likely to be effective. Comparisons and choices between interventions should be based on evidence of the effectiveness of different intervention strategies – whether these have been previously used by the regulatory agency itself or by other regulatory agencies.

New Models

The aspects of intervention choices explored within the RDM are:

(1) the *range and shape* of interventions available to a regulatory agency and its capability to choose interventions effectively;
(2) the need to focus on *building compliance* of regulated entities, including understanding motivations and capability and assessing the impact of interventions;
(3) the *use of sanctions* to drive appropriate outcomes, including monitoring to assess their impact.

The Significance of Transformation under the RDM

Both individually and collectively, adoption of the elements of the RDM open the door to profound transformation in regulatory practice. For example, the idea of the requirement of having the right *culture* in regulation (and a regulatory authority) is fundamentally new and challenging. There are in fact several cultures that are relevant, starting with the culture within a regulatory authority, the (probably different) cultures of each regulated entity, and the 'regulatory culture' as between regulator and regulatees. One should go on and add the cultures of users, and the media and politicians who comment on the system, and so on.

It is particularly significant to examine the impact of adopting an approach based on outcomes and interventions.

Outcomes

First, the importance of a focus on *outcomes* cannot be overstated. As we have noted above, the traditional legal model does not do this: it imagines a constricted world in which people look just at whether rules are complied with or broken. It might be that compliance with some rules might lead to the achievement of good outcomes – but it might not do so. Surely, the objective of a regulatory system is to achieve good outcomes, like safety and fair markets and protection of a sustainable environment. Are these goals and outcomes not the whole point? What are we trying to achieve – should we not be focusing on that? It is extraordinary that almost no statute establishing a regulatory system or authority mentions anything about outcomes or how they are to be set, achieved or measured. This is a pretty strong fault in the legal model. And it needs to be rectified. Valid, desired outcomes – and their achievement – need to be put at the centre of regulation.

Outcomes and impacts need to be distinguished from *outputs*, such as number of licences revoked, inspections undertaken, prosecutions instigated (or won), total monetary value of fines imposed, number of people sent to prison and total number of years. Those metrics do not clarify whether the fundamental goals are being achieved.

The Challenge of Competing Goals

In practice, different objectives and outcomes, which can conflict, have to be managed simultaneously. For example: do we want safe food, or healthy food, or sustainable food (and planet), and fair incomes for developing world farmers, or innovative foods? Emphasising one objective over others may adversely affect attainment of the others – and of levels of protection from risk. Do we want regulators to maintain protection, or to support economic growth? If we emphasise growth, does this not involve a reduction in protection, and increase in risk, and probably the occurrence of avoidable harm, leading to injury and lengthy litigation about compensation and (possibly unfair) prosecutions?

We might well want all of these goals and their associated outcomes. But a system of rules-plus-enforcement, which does not engage with the need to debate and prioritise particular goals and outcomes at particular times, will not succeed. What is needed is an approach that is realistic in recognising the potential for conflicts, and provides a mechanism for multi-stakeholder debate about how to balance and manage the competing goals and outcomes on an ongoing basis (and this is provided by an outcomes-based collaborative approach, discussed below).

Related challenges are risk-risk trade-offs and therefore jurisdictional issues as between different regulatory regimes. One example would be harm to building residents from construction versus harm from criminal activities such as fraudulent certification of construction materials. Another example may be whether food is safe when produced but unsafe when served, where each aspect may be regulated by different authorities; so is food safe or not? The key point

108 New Models

is that when we move into an outcomes space, the limitations and boundaries of individual regulatory systems become a risk in themselves. We need to evolve. Which approach would you prefer? Which approach is going to produce better outcomes?

Intervention Choices

The second major transformation here is the reference to *intervention choices* – rather than to enforcement. The logic is to *intervene* to achieve the desired outcomes. These may be to provide protection from criminal or dangerous activities (which is akin to tradition enforcement) or to support improvement and reduce risk by more engaged and effective means. We will develop these ideas in chapters 6 and 7.

Interventions in activities can occur at three different stages, which define a 'regulatory shape' for a specific regulatory regime.[3] The principal categorisation is:

(a) *before* regulated activity commences, for example, through business registration or licensing, or testing (pre-entry authorisation) – before a risk exists, or to reduce its likely incidence;
(b) *during* the undertaking of the regulated activity, for example through market surveillance or inspection (in-service supervision) – while the risk exists, to reduce it and to identify the occurrence of harm;
(c) *after* the regulated activity has resulted in an undesired incident, especially occurrence of unacceptable harm, for example through investigation and intervention or enforcement (post-event investigation and future-focused risk-reduction) – after a risk has materialised into harm.

Intervention at stages (a) and (b) is aimed at reducing risk by preventing harm occurring. Intervention at stage (c) cannot prevent the harm from occurring but can reduce future risk that it, or something similar, might occur in future, and can repair harm that has been caused. Stage (c) can have two components: backward-looking and forward-looking. The backward-looking focus might be to impose 'accountability' in the form of identifying what happened, but also to impose sanctions for wrongdoing (or causing harm), ultimately motivated by ideas of punishment or even revenge. The forward-looking focus would be to learn from identifying the root causes of what happened so as to learn how to reduce the future risk of the same sort of thing happening again in future (reducing future risk). We will look at these contrasting focuses in chapter 7 – they can be in conflict, and ideas about what is important and how to achieve the best outcomes are changing.

We will look at intervention and enforcement in chapter 6, but we can note here that the objectives of intervention are the following, covering the three dimensions of time (present, past and future):

(1) To cease ongoing harm to society (*cessation*).
(2) To prevent future similar harm (*prevention*).
(3) To repair harm caused (*restoration*).
(4) To signal that relevant consequences are occurring and that society is upholding its rules (*cohesion* and *just culture*).

Some other aspects deserve notice:

Independence

The whole idea of creating regulatory authorities that are separate from government is to allow independent operational decisions to be taken. Hence, the legislation creates a separate entity that is endowed with its own duties and powers. But as soon as anything goes wrong, goverments criticise regulators, thereby deflecting criticism from themselves to a convenient scapegoat. This is keenly resented by regulators, as a profession, as being unfair.

Expertise, Professionalism and Resource

Regulatory authorities often face challenges in attracting staff who are sufficiently trained and keeping them – the private sector usually offers far better salaries and benefits. This can often give rise to limitations on technical expertise, sufficient resource to address policy, undertake inspections, offer advice, process applications, and so on. In addition, there can be limitations on what an authority is allowed to do because of constraints on its scope and powers contained in legislation.

Corruption, Bias, Capture

These are issues for any public body that has to exercise power where decisions may differentiate between different constituents or beneficiaries. Any decision-maker whose decisions can affect the financial interests of others can be subject to lobbying, undue influence or even bribery and corruption. This is a potential risk for all politicians and all public officials. In the regulatory world, the major risk is that relationships between regulators and those subject to regulation can become too 'cosy' and lack objectivity and cause inertia. Proximity can affect the independence of thought and judgement of regulators.

Solutions include strong public ethics, with Codes of Standards in Public Life supported by strong ethical cultures and leadership, openness and transparency, plus the ability to provide an account of objectives, actions and outcomes to all constituents, from Parliamentary committees to the beneficiaries of regulation. Any collaborative work needs to include balancing stakeholders and transparency.

Evolution

The RDM is a revolutionary way of thinking. But it is not (yet) mandated for any regulator or by legislation. Instead of questioning the dominance of the legal rule-enforcement model head on, the RDM focused on *how* regulatory authorities could achieve better outcomes if they adopted different approaches and techniques – all of which could be done without the need to change any governing legislation. Some supportive changes were subsequently made in the UK through the liberalised environment of stating some broad principles in a Regulators' Code.[4] (To some extent, these changes mirrored evolutions in the Corporate Governance Code, although closer alignment there would be productive.)

Recently, as governments have been increasingly concerned with economic success and supporting innovative science and technology, Regulators' Codes and 'Ministerial steers' have been used as levers to require regulators to prioritise growth. Since 2014, most UK regulatory authorities have been tasked, under the Regulators' Code, to 'carry out their activities in a way that supports those they regulate to comply and grow'.[5] Growth was the Labour Government's 'number one priority' from 2024.

However, there is often no reason why regulators cannot shift to focusing on outcomes without legislative permission, although it would help. The RDM, therefore, was something of a 'work around' the traditional Legal and Economic Models. But before long, the need for more fundamental reform became clear. All six of the RDM's elements are important, and inter-connected, but the transformational power lies in three fundamentally important elements that mark a shift in thinking and practice from the

Legal Model to an Outcomes-Based System Model: outcomes, intervention and culture. The existence of a totally new (but largely unknown) system in aviation safety was a profoundly important innovation. In that sector, all the actors agreed on the need for them to collaborate in an 'open and just culture'. Research into the behavioural underpinning of that collaborative culture led to a model that provided a generalised methodology – the Outcome-Based Cooperative Regulation (OBCR) Model.

A Systemic Behavioural Approach: Open and Just Culture

High risk sectors have produced striking transformations in how firms operate, integrated with cooperative relations between private actors and with public regulators. A classic example is civil aviation, where there is an overriding need constantly to control very serious risk. Leaders in this sector adopted a fundamentally new approach, based on advice from psychologists,[6] which created an 'open and just culture' involving every person and organisation working together in a cooperative manner to share all relevant information relating to safety and risk, so as constantly to monitor and improve performance, and identify and reduce risk. The culture draws a line between acceptable and unacceptable behaviour. 'A wilful violation is not acceptable. An honest mistake is.'[7] Standards of behaviour require professional competence, openness, sharing, and taking responsibility for one's mistakes by correcting them and improving.[8] There is a long-stop legal protection, but one which rejects punishment:[9]

> a culture in which front line operators or others are not punished for actions, omissions or decisions taken by them that are commensurate with their experience and training, but where gross negligence, wilful violations and destructive acts are not tolerated.

Variations in culture across organisations or nations,[10] especially involving cultural,[11] authoritarian or punitive tendencies, will undermine the entire safety enterprise.[12] A Manual on Human Performance (HP) produced by the global aviation safety coordinating organisation ICAO in 2021[13] set out five HP principles:[14]

> Principle 1: People's performance is shaped by their capabilities and limitations;
> Principle 2: People interpret situations differently and perform in ways that make sense to them;

Principle 3: People adapt to meet the demands of a complex and dynamic work environment;

Principle 4: People assess risks and make trade-offs; and

Principle 5: People's performance is influenced by working with other people, technology, and the environment.

The 'open and just culture' approach does not focus on identifying an individual to blame for acting wrongly and causing harm, but, assuming that all actors in the industry are well-intentioned, focuses on what collection of factors were the root causes of the outcome, and why *any* humans in the same position would have behaved in particular ways, so that those root causes can be addressed and changes made to reduce future risk. These findings challenge legal systems that blame individuals for systemic harms, and that punish individuals who may not have been 'at fault', morally blameworthy, or causative of harm.

Further, the focus is always on identifying the root causes of problems, rather than assuming that an individual is the only factor. The question is never: 'Why did that individual do that?', but 'Why would any human in that situation behave like that? And how can that behaviour be prevented in future?' There is, of course, individual accountability for personal performance of tasks, subject to the relevant degree of training, competence, and resource.

The Outcome-Based Collaborative Regulation (OBCR) Model

The OBCR model focuses on what we are trying to do – objectives, goals, purposes – but also on whether we are succeeding, by achieving the right outcomes. How we perform in achieving the outcomes is scrutinised and demonstrated empirically, by setting metrics at the start and monitoring relevant data as we go along (rather than responding to some instances of non-compliance with particular rules).

The OBCR approach is to define the core regulatory functions as:

- to set the desired outcomes, such as safety or fairness;
- to ensure that the desired outcomes are being achieved; and
- to intervene to prevent harm, repair it, and to reduce risk.

The Outcome-Based Collaborative Regulation (OBCR) Model

The OBC model is based on extensive science on how humans actually behave, rather than inherited theories about this. The scientific evidence on how we can work together to achieve more is summarised in chapter 2. The model is also based on the evidence that humans achieve more when they cooperate. The model is a mechanism or technique for maximising collaboration and desirable outcomes. It has considerable flexibility in application to different circumstances. In order to maximise sensible values-based cooperation, building on the scientific evidence summarised in chapter 2, the key elements are as follows:

(1) To agree prioritisation of purposes, objectives and *outcomes*, involving everyone (all stakeholders) in a collaborative co-creative exercise.

(2) To *support* people to behave well and constantly improve performance, relying on stimulating *intrinsic motivation* with supportive interventions rather than externally imposed authoritarian control (which is reserved for those from whom society needs to be protected).

(3) To build *trust*, based on actors producing a convincing and adequate body of *evidence* that they have good intentions, competences, understanding, resources, and demonstrate *behaviours* that they do the right thing (based on ethical values), such as asking for help, reporting problems, cooperating to implement fixes. Hence, they are trustworthy and can be expected to do the right thing. This is achieved by:

   (a) actors producing evidence that they can be trusted to behave well (are trustworthy);
   (b) agreeing common codes of ethical values and principles to guide and evaluate behaviour, hence providing evidence that stakeholders are trustworthy and can be trusted.

Trust and Ethics

The collaborative model can only achieve legitimate, ethical outcomes as between actors who are trustworthy and trusted. The model therefore maintains an enforcement-based approach against those actors who are not trustworthy, and who cause harm. Others need to be protected from them. But the OBC model (which can be applied in regulatory contexts as OBCR) is open to those who demonstrate that they are ethically motivated and behave well, and hence acts as an inspiring incentive for them. OBCR may present considerable challenges in some situations, but where it can be done, it should achieve more desired outcomes.

Trust is so frequently invoked as being of fundamental importance in any human interactions. People constantly talk about trust, or the lack of it, by the public in regulators, by regulators in regulatees, and of everyone in politicians. Inspectors often approach an inspection with a formal checklist of points on which to check compliance, yet they are significantly influenced by their feeling of the level of trust they have in the people and institution being inspected. Extraordinarily, the concept of trust has almost no practical application or manifestation, for example as a practical criterion in any regulatory system. The question arises: if trust is so fundamental in regulation, and the decisions and relationships that arise in regulation, why do we not use the concept of trust more concretely and effectively?

Humans' decisions on the extent to which they can trust others is based on evidence of how others behave. We constantly assess the evidence we see of what others are doing against our inherent, automatic values compass of right and wrong. We could say that this 'ethical' mechanism occurred as a genetic mutation at the origin of the *homo sapiens* species, and is what enabled our ancestors to make reliable decisions on whom they could collaborate with or not. This mechanism led to the formation of tribes and larger groupings, distinguished from enemies. So, the trust mechanism is fundamental, operates cost-free and permanently in humans that have emotional intelligence, but is significantly under-used as a mechanism.

If you have data on, first, trustworthiness of actors and, second, actual outcomes and issues, you can redesign and streamline traditional regulatory systems, and make then react more quickly.

The Potential for Consistency between the Goals of Regulatees and Regulation

It is not only states that try to regulate risk. Any sensible business should also share that aim. Good businesses strive for success not just through selling goods and services of predictable and consistent quality, at fair prices, but also by recognising the reputational value in attracting a committed and supportive workforce, customers, investors, communities and states. They also need protection from criminal businesses if markets are to be fair.

Viewed from this insight, the goals and outcomes of good business and good regulation should be aligned – and hence the same checklists and procedures for achieving business success and regulatory success should be basically identical. This would enable efficiency as between regulation and business. But that simple view includes various assumptions that may distort what happens in reality. People can focus on other goals or matters that distract attention from safety or fairness. The histories of disasters, such as the Space Shuttle Challenger, the Global Financial Crisis, VW's Dieselgate, the Boeing 737 Max, the UK Grenfell fire and Post Office Horizon scandal, illustrate remarkably consistent root causes centred on closed minds, lack of curiosity, groupthink, achieving targets, corporate reputation, remuneration, personal or personnel issues – and sometimes conscious concealment or fraud.

Combining Two Different Universes

At the present time, we are in the confusing situation of having two universes of 'how to do regulation': the Legal Model and what might be called the Supportive Behavioural Model. We also have two further models: the RDM and the OBCR. Different regulators are at different stages in adopting some or all of the more modern approaches. So, we are in a state of flux, and no governments have yet grasped the transforming potential of the new approaches. Strong elements of traditional modes exist, whereas some sectors are shifting into a wholly different environment. Further confusion is caused by the fact that important elements of both approaches are needed but in different contexts.

The traditional regulatory universe rests on rules and enforcement in response to breaches of those rules. It assumes that compliance with the rules is all that is required to deliver effective regulation. It does not aim to achieve particular outcomes, but imposes duties on regulators – which are often conflicting duties and so difficult for regulators to manage. It is an inherently authoritarian system, using power in attempting to control behaviour. It has a strong undercurrent of allowing people freedom to do as they wish as long as they do not break rules. You are OK to do what you like, as long as you stay within the boundary of the circle. But it has a fatal disconnect between the idea of a system of complying with rules and the delivery of ongoing protection as things evolve. It cannot respond well to new ways of doing things, or disruptive technologies, until it has established all the relevant rules, so it will always be 'playing catch up'. (We have noted in chapter 1, and will return to in chapters 6 and 7, the problems that arise from a system based only on enforcement. An inability to identify and respond quickly enough to crises is inherent in the traditional model. We are subject to recurrent unexpected crises, to which we respond poorly and slowly.)

There are two keys to understanding the transition that is occurring:

(1) The shift from compliance to outcomes.
(2) The shift from law to behaviour.

The second point can be illustrated by reference to a new viewpoint on the Regulatory Functions Model (RFM) (Figure 3.2), and is illustrated in Figure 4.1. Outside the boundary, we need laws to protect ourselves from criminal or incompetent behaviour. Breach of (non-compliance with) a legal rule will trigger formal enforcement action by an authority, in accordance with legally fair and predictable procedures that apply formal valid rules. In contrast, inside the circle are people and organisations who are essentially well-intentioned but whose activities may sometimes cause harm. Here, the objective remains that of protection from harm, but also to support improvements in performance and control of risk. This area is about encouraging competence and good behaviour, especially through engagement in a collaborative (series of) ecosystem(s) that are aimed at achieving the society's desired outcomes. It is an area where the goals of profit, economic growth and protection from harm (and various other goals and outcomes) are all valid and shared. Achieving those goals and outcomes through a legalistic approach is simply to use the wrong tool. One needs to use more outcome-focused, motivational, collaborative approaches.

Thus, completely different tools are needed inside and outside the circle. Outside, we need law and enforcement. Inside, we need codes, ethics and culture aiming at achieving the agreed outcomes, based on ethical behaviour and a learning mindset, through an integrated system managed by stakeholders.

Figure 4.1 Combining the Legal and Behavioural Models

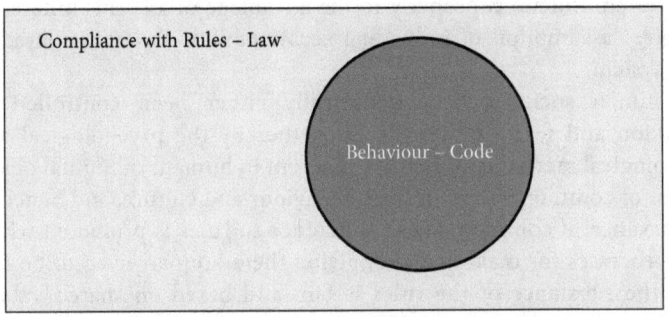

But this is usually not 'either/or'. In many sectors and situations, we need the two regimes: a legal/outside system of law, backed by legal enforcement powers; and a behavioural/performance/inside system, with mechanisms to monitor, capture and feedback learning and implement improvements. There is considerable scope for integrating the two universes of inside and outside the circle. The data collection system for both systems, and some of the mechanisms and institutions, could operate in two modes across both inside and outside modes. The critical point is to differentiate between the two *modes* (enforcement and support) and not confuse them. We then need to (re-)design out systems to ensure that we have the right institutions and arrangements to facilitate both modes, and to ensure that they operate both individually and collectively in an effective and efficient way. The mechanisms and institutions that are needed for both modes should be those that deliver the *functions* set out in the RFM (Figure 3.2).

Conclusion: A Time for Reform

A collaborative system aims to enlist all actors in jointly managing risk. By focusing on outcomes, it provides measurable evidence of whether goals are being achieved – or not. It challenges and motivates the various stakeholders to play their individual parts as essential components in a unified system. Their involvement is predicated on producing evidence that they can be trusted and will play their relevant roles, however modest they may be in the overall scheme of things, so that the system functions properly to the advantage of all. This inherently involves assumption of individual accountability. Power is shared in this system.

Human societies have historically either been controlled by coercion and fear, or been held together by the psychological and sociological mechanisms that are inherent in humans of mutual observance of common values in their behaviour and culture, and hence by observance of common rules. Adherence to rules is promoted where the processes for making and applying them are perceived to be fair, and the substance of the rules is fair, and based on shared values, ideally values that are considered to be ethical. The mechanisms that states have developed to deliver these functions are based on 'enforcement' of laws by imposing sanctions in response to breaches of rules.

However, we now know more about how to promote social and commercial cohesion and the observance of ethical behaviour that will support enhanced cooperation and achievement of desired outcomes. The scientific knowledge suggests that it is timely to reconsider the concepts, language and practices around how we 'enforce' laws, by drawing on other mechanisms that promote adherence to ethical social behaviour.

There are further reasons why a new approach is needed. First, it is assumed that adherence and compliance are produced by sanctions imposed by a state. As mentioned, this theory is now shown to be largely wrong. Secondly, activities are increasingly carried out on an international basis, across multiple states, and are no longer controllable by any individual state, or even by a number of states acting in similar or coordinated manners. Thirdly, levels of trust in important states are poor at best, so the mechanism is not trustworthy.

Fourthly, the pace of change of science and technology is now so fast that attempts at regulation by states, especially through legislation, are perpetually behind the curve and inadequate. The speed at which technologies develop and change things is now so fast that waiting for Parliaments to pass laws is pre-historically inadequate. We are going to need much faster systems, approaches and responses. The effect that AI will have on how we trust others is also going to need profound rethinking.

Key Points

- Regulation is traditionally operated through a Legal Model: rules, identification of breach of rules, imposition of sanctions (enforcement). The assumptions are, first, that compliance with rules is the only relevant requirement and, second, that enforcement will produce such compliance.
- Both those assumptions are incorrect and limiting in scope.
- We do need protection from deliberate and incompetent wrongdoing.
- But we also need to support the constant improvement of activities, performance and (multiple) outcomes.
- Models are now available that can achieve those goals, especially through focusing on outcomes and on achievement, performance and collaboration.
- The immediate task is to integrate the Legal and Outcomes models in every regulatory system.

---

[1] G Russell and C Hodges (eds), *Regulatory Delivery* (Hart, 2019).
[2] *An Overview of Regulation for the new Parliament 2023-24* (National Audit Office, November 2024).
[3] G Russell and H Kirkman, 'Intervention Choices' in G Russell and C Hodges (eds), *Regulatory Delivery* (Hart, 2019).
[4] *The Regulators' Code* (HM Government, 2014), first drafted c 2006.
[5] *Regulators' Code* (Department for Business Innovation & Skills, 2013).
[6] JT Reason, *Managing the Risks of Organizational Accidents* (Ashgate, 1997); S Dekker, *Just Culture. Balancing Safety and Accountability* (Ashgate Publishing, 2007); S Dekker, *Just Culture. Restoring Trust and Accountability in Your Organization*, 3rd edn (Ashgate Publishing, 2017).
[7] S Dekker, *Just Culture* (Ashgate Publishing, 2007) 15.
[8] D McCune, C Lewis and D Arendt, 'Safety Culture in Your Safety Management System' in AJ Stolzer, CD Halford and JJ Goglia (eds), *Implementing Safety Management Systems in Aviation* (Ashgate, 2011) 195.
[9] Commission Regulation (EU) No 691/2010 of 29 July 2010 laying down a performance scheme for air navigation services and network functions and amending Regulation (EC) No 2096/2005 laying down common requirements for the provision of air navigation services, Art 2(k).
[10] N McDonald, S Corrigan, C Daly and S Cromie, 'Safety management systems and safety culture in aircraft maintenance organisation' (2000) 34(1-3) *Safety Science* 151.
[11] P O'Connor, A O'Dea, Q Kennedy and SE Buttrey, 'Measuring safety climate in aviation: A review and recommendations for the future' (2011) 49 *Safety Science* 128-38;

M-Y Liao, 'Safety Culture in commercial aviation: Differences in perspective between Chinese and Western pilots' (2015) 79 *Safety Science* 193–205; H-B Lee and J-W Park, 'Comparative study on hazardous attitudes and safe operational behaviour in airline pilots' (2016) 54 *Journal of Air Transport Management* 70–79.

[12] AJ Lawrenson and GR Braithwaite, 'Regulation or criminalisation: What determines legal standards of safety culture in commercial aviation?' (2018) 102 *Safety Science* 251–62; J Woodlock and Håkan Hydén, 'Lex Avionica; How Soft Law Serves as an Instrumental Mediator Between Professional Norms and the Hard Law Regulation of European Civil Aviation Maintenance' (2020) 121 *Safety Science* 54.

[13] *Manual on Human Performance (HP) for Regulators* (International Civil Aviation Organization, 2021), Doc 10151.

[14] ibid para 1.4.

5

How to do Outcome-Based Collaborative Regulation

> Operating an effective regulatory system, and especially producing data from all relevant sources, requires people and organisations to *collaborate*. Humans achieve more when they collaborate.
>
> Humans collaborate best when they *trust* each other. Trust in another rests on an evaluation of the evidence you have about the future actions of that other. The evaluation is inherently framed in terms of whether behaviour is right or wrong (ie ethical).
>
> We can maximise collaboration by producing adequate evidence that we are trustworthy. This goes beyond evidence that we have good systems or compliance, and adds an unavoidable element of ethical behaviour and culture.
>
> This chapter outlines the Outcome-Based Collaborative (OBC) Model, and gives examples of its operation in OBC Regulation contexts.

The Value of Collaborating

The point of collaborating is to achieve desired outcomes where that achievement depends on input from different actors. You will not achieve your goals or outcomes without input from others. This is the essence of a system – cooperated inputs from multiple actors. How do you get others to work with you? Order them about? Or create a system of mutual collaboration in which you and the others all achieve a 'big vision', which realises the (different or shared) desired outcomes of everyone? In essence, it's a sophisticated form of 'I'll help you if you help me' but in which we're all motivated by achieving something big.

Groups that cannot cooperate are incapable of learning, evolving or innovating.[1] Competition *within* a group will ultimately be destructive, whereas moderate competition *between* groups can be inspiring. However, stimulating cooperation through intrinsic motivation of individuals and groups will be the most effective strategy in achieving performance and transformation. In simple terms, cooperation is ultimately vital for sustaining life and group activities, whereas competition can be destructive.

We do not learn unless we spontaneously share information, and we will not do that if we fear criticism or sanctioning (ie in a 'blame culture'[2]), so the best performing groups and organisations operate with cultures of psychological safety.

Some anthropologists and sociologists say that the history of our species has (slowly!) followed an historical trajectory away from defensive and aggressive competition towards increasing cooperation. Nicholas Christakis' research concludes that the cooperative mode of (social) interaction has developed integrally, linked with developments in our psychological reliance on ethical values, forms of engagement (institutions) and the evidence supporting levels of trust that others will act as expected. As we have evolved, so have our mechanisms. There is a trajectory towards our becoming less aggressive, more cooperative, and more ethical. The arc of our evolutionary history 'bends towards goodness', because we learn (and accordingly our genes adapt) that moral behaviour is better for cooperation.[3] Unmoderated competition is coming under attack for producing undesirable social and economic outcomes.[4] Humans have inherently competitive impulses, which can lead to great attainments, but the way that market and legal competition has been operated, linked with 'rugged individualism' per Martin Luther King, leaving the poor to struggle for themselves whilst permitting a 'bounty of gifts for the wealthy',[5] has led to toxic results and 'drained any ethical or moral content'.[6] Noble competition has been devalued. Garrett Hardin and Elinor Ostrom have identified that the destruction of essential common goods (the tragedy of the commons) arises inevitably from selfish behaviour, and coordinated control is required to prevent this, not least by creating the right institutions.[7]

The OECD's review of regulation in late 2021 identified an 'urgent need for a transformation of the way rules are made and implemented', and that 'results-oriented systematic performance assessment holds the key to improving regulatory oversight'.[8] The OECD called for lessons from behavioural insights to be applied, and emphasised that regulatory delivery is critical, ie how regulation is practised. It said that governments need to rebuild trust in regulation and regulatory services, and that improved oversight and coordination is required, noting that 'regulators with a stronger degree of independence use more good-practice accountability mechanisms, which enhances confidence'.

The power of a systematic approach to achieve intended outcomes and respond to harms and risks is intended to be far more effective, and far quicker, than a model that just focuses on identifying particular instances of non-compliance with rules. A system based on collaboration means that the various actors must trust each other, otherwise they will face real challenges in collaborating effectively. So, the ongoing involvement of actors in the system requires evidence that each actor is trustworthy. It may be challenging to switch from a system based (just) on identifying instances of non-compliance with rules to one based on trustworthiness. But is it not worth doing if it is much more effective, efficient and swift in achieving good outcomes and responding to risks?

How People Collaborate

The Mechanism of Trust

The mental mechanism that supports whether and how humans cooperate is our reliance on the mental bridge of *trust*. Trust enables us to plan and act where we have adequate belief that others will act in a particular way, so that we can make our own plans and actions.[9] The mental state of trust bridges the gap caused by *lack* of knowledge. A belief that we can trust someone else (in other words we can have confidence how they will behave in future) is based on our evaluation of *evidence* of how they have acted and are acting, and therefore how we expect them to act in the future. Humans constantly evaluate the evidence they see against an *internal moral compass*: the ability to distinguish between right and wrong based on an internal system of ethical/moral values of what is 'right and wrong'.[10]

Spontaneous altruistic actions build stronger trust and social capital than transactionally negotiated trust. 'When we became cooperative animals, we abandoned the right-of-the-strongest principle and moved on to a right-of-the-contributor principle.'[11] Linda Molm and colleagues found that reciprocal exchange (often spontaneous) produces stronger trust and affective commitment than negotiated exchange, and that behaviours signalling the partner's trustworthiness have greater impact on trust in reciprocal exchange.[12] This explains why a society in which individuals engage in spontaneous acts of giving will generate stronger trust and affective commitment[13] than markets that are based on contractual arrangements supported just by a legal system. Molm and colleagues concluded that, ironically, the very mechanisms that were created to reduce risk in *transactions* – the negotiation of terms and strictly binding agreements – have the unintended consequence of reducing trust in *relationships*. Thus, the forms of social and relational exchange affect the extent of trust and social cohesion. A generous warm society is preferable to an individualist contractual society.

It should simplify evaluation of whether we can trust others if people and organisations take clear steps to produce evidence of *their* competence, resources, motivations, achieved outcomes and general behaviour and cultures. This is what the OBCR model aims to deliver, whereby actors themselves produce evidence that they can be *trusted*. Such evidence should comprise all those elements, proportionate to size, resource, and state of development and sophistication.

Values

Trust is ethically neutral (it is the basis of cooperation in criminal gangs) and it has to be moderated by ethical criteria.[14] Values involve a 'co-primacy of right and good'.[15] In moral terms, there is a great deal of difference between those who intend to achieve their own goals by breaking the law (eg stealing, scamming, abusing, killing) and those who intend to do the right thing but make mistakes or act temporarily in a risky way.

Nicholas Christakis asserts that the evolutionary trajectory of transmitted genes and behaviour is towards increased cooperation, and towards increasing reliance on strong ethical values, since these elements are inextricably linked.[16] He argues that the trajectory of evolution of human social and mental dispositions is to reduce competition and favour cooperation, which necessarily involves increasing emphasis on ethical values 'bend[ing] towards goodness'.[17]

Higher levels of integrity are correlated with commercial success in many contexts.[18] This is recognised by major investors.[19] Countries that have high trust relationships have high social capital,[20] commercial cooperation and success (eg Germany[21] and Japan[22]).

Trust Structures

Edward Wilson and Jonathan Haidt believe that it was the genetic mutation in being able to distinguish right from wrong that occurred at the evolution of *homo sapiens* as a species that was the critical element in enabling our species to cooperate and hence to dominate all others.[23] The evidence of anthropology is that humans have evolved their modes of social organisation and institutions in order to cooperate in ever larger groups, whether in political organisations, such as nations, or in trade or other forms of cultural exchange. There is constant co-evolutionary interplay between the factors that support humans working socially in groups, such as psychology, institutions and culture.[24]

It is striking that ethical businesses find that internal organisational structures tend to be flat rather than hierarchical, and decisions are made by empowered staff, rather than by a limited number of managers.[25] They achieve more when operating in an open, trusting and ethical environment of psychological safety.[26]

The UK has introduced an accreditation system based on adherence to a trust framework for digital methods of proving personal identity. This was achieved through 'open and collaborative engagement with stakeholders across the public and private sectors, academia, and civil society'.[27]

Evidence of Trustworthiness

The idea in the OBC model is to operate a system that *encourages cooperation* based on ethical behaviour. This would differentiate between those who are cooperators and aim to do the right thing, and those who are not or are indifferent. In responding to evidence and signals of non-cooperation – such as the occurrence of harm, and lack of observance of ethical norms – we should differentiate between trusted cooperators and aim at protection and reduction of risk. However, this is not a binary categorisation, but one that contains multiple aspects observed over time and a sliding scale of trust. Nevertheless, there are two extremes – those who deserve trust and those who don't. This suggests a possible differentiation in those actors who are, or are not, treated as stakeholders who deserve to be involved in the governance of a regulatory space, or in its relevant marketplace:

(1) *Trust-based*. Pre-existing commitment to taking responsibility for achieving desired common outcomes through contributing relevant effort, accepting accountability – providing (in a context of open and just culture) an open account of what people did and what happened, and commitment to instituting appropriate retrospective restorative and prospective preventative actions.

(2) *Non-trusted*. A legal operation but without production of evidence of trustworthiness, of an ethical culture and commitment to achieving the agreed common outcomes and avoiding undesirable outcomes, or of evidence of outcomes. The traditional matrix of rules, breaches, investigation and sanctions aimed at providing protection should apply.

Thus, we can strengthen trust by producing more evidence that we can be trusted, based on our history of behaviour and our present competences and intentions. This is the unique tool that opens the opportunity of multiple stakeholders collaborating in the OBC model to achieve their multiple outcomes.

Various sets of criteria for characteristics of trust evidence can be built on,[28] such as competence, predictability, moral benevolence, ethical integrity, and concern for safety. These criteria have driven the type of evidence that people and organisations that wish to be trusted try to produce about themselves so as to build a convincing and consistent narrative. Thus, businesses rely on brand reputation and endorsements, regulatory systems include quality management and inspections mechanisms and consistent results over time, advisers rely on professional integrity mechanisms and rituals, and traders rely on contracts and legal systems.

We can strengthen trust by producing more evidence that we can be trusted, based on our history of behaviour and our present competences and intentions. Various sets of criteria for characteristics of trust evidence have been suggested, of which that by McKnight and Chervany is a leading example:[29]

Table 5.1 Characteristics of Trust Evidence

Trust-related characteristic	Second-order conceptual category
1. Competent 2. Expert 3. Dynamic	Competence
4. Predictable	Predictability
5. Good, moral 6. Good will 7. Benevolent, caring 8. Responsive	Benevolence
9. Honest 10. Credible 11. Reliable 12. Dependable	Integrity
13. Open 14. Careful, safe 15. Shared understanding 16. Personally attractive	Other

Evidence List for Trust in Organisations

Does the Organisation have a Purpose?

- What is its purpose?
- Does it state a clear purpose?
- Is it a purely selfish or does it also reflect a social purpose?
- What actions and behaviours demonstrate it acts in accordance with the purpose (or run counter to it)?

Does the Organisation Operate Ethically?

- Does it have a statement of organisational values?
- Were they identified and integrated by involving all the staff or just imposed from the Board/Executive?
- Does it have a Code of Ethics or similar document regularly referred to and communicated to all staff?
- Is there a means of asking questions or reporting concerns and a policy against retaliation?
- Do the Board and Senior Management regularly refer to the values and ethical policies in discussions with staff?
- Does the evidence demonstrate ethical behaviour or not?
- Are reasonable resources devoted to values, ethics and compliance, including Board-level sponsorship and adequate and proportionate personnel?
- Is there evidence of compliance (or non-compliance) with legal and ethical norms?
- What compliance and ethical frameworks does it have?
- What happens when things go wrong?
- Is there an established procedure for conducting root cause analysis of mistakes and failures, that is utilised at all levels?
- What level of transparency exists? Or does not exist? What is made public or hidden?
- What outcomes does the organisation deliver?

What Happens to the Money?

- Is the model profit or not-for-profit?
- Who gets what? How much do investors, directors, staff, suppliers, consumers, customers get?
- Are people incentivised or paid by output targets or behavioural results? How rather than what?
- What is the differential between top, bottom and median pay?
- Are staff happy and self-motivated? What is the evidence on this? Does the organisation do a Cultural Values Assessment?

- Are customers happy? What is the evidence? What is the level and type of complaints? How easy is it to complain or feed back?
- Are suppliers happy and not abused?
- Are investors supportive? Are they identifiable? Do they support ethical behaviour?

Evidence of Ethical Organisational Culture

The simple ideas of 'let's all do the right thing', plus 'if we're not sure, ask' and 'let's all prove that we are trying to do the right thing', have been shown to be an extraordinarily powerful strategy in achieving a group's objectives. A pithy description of culture is that it is 'an operating system' for organisations.[30]

How does an organisation strive to create, maintain, and demonstrate that it has, an ethical culture? In the Ethical Business Practice (EBP) model,[31] Ruth Steinholtz prescribes two organisational frameworks, or focus areas, in updated form:

(a) A *Cultural and Leadership Framework*, which covers the foundational principles underpinning an effective ethical culture, aspects relating to leadership and employee involvement and the importance of aligned systems and processes, in which 'ethics is everyone's responsibility' and managing the organisational culture is an essential task of management and a concern of all staff and investors.

(b) A *Values-based Ethics and Compliance (or Integrity) Framework*, which places greater emphasis on the shared ethical values of those working in the organisation, as well as outlining a different approach to the procedural aspects of compliance that encourage critical thinking and individual as well as collective responsibility based on the belief that this will produce compliance as an outcome rather than the sole approach. Historically, compliance focused on highly complicated and legalistic tick the box policies and procedures have often proved ineffective.

These two Frameworks, summarised in Table 5.2, mirror the two domains of law and behaviour described above in Figure 4.1. We need both: we need to move from having just the legal component to adding a strong behavioural component.

Table 5.2 The Ethical Practice Frameworks

Cultural and Leadership Framework: A holistic approach to organisational culture in all its aspects	Values-based Ethics and Compliance (or Integrity) Framework: The 'usual suspects done differently'

• Starting with a strong foundation:
  • Understanding that ethics/integrity is everyone's responsibility and that a healthy ethical culture is the basis for success.
  • Authentic core values identified through internal consultation, clearly defined and regularly used in decision making.
• People who commit to fostering a healthy ethical culture:
  • Leaders who embody the values and walk the talk.
  • Leadership development of relevant professional skills to improve relevant attitudes and competencies.
  • Psychological safety at all levels, fostered by focusing on learning not punishment.
  • A 'just culture' taking learnings from an enlightened approach to safety management (see below).
• Aligned systems and processes of all types, including performance management and incentives to ensure the culture is not undermined by unintended consequences.
	• Values-based Code and policies, developed through consultation, which are accessible to all staff (ie understandable as well as available).
	• Regular risk assessments, focused not only on systems but also on behaviour and cultural factors.
	• Engaging communication of values, behavioural norms and legal and regulatory requirements, wherever possible through face-to-face awareness and training opportunities; a network of ethics ambassadors/values champions or similar who help promote ethical decision making; instead of large central compliance departments.
	• Avoid 'compliance' and 'officer' titles and department names: language matters.
	• Ethical Decision-Making Models and scenario practice.
	• An emphasis on openness, and the ability to speak up in psychological safety rather than relying solely on whistleblowing.
	• Third party engagement, due diligence.
	• Sharing of stories of good practice, evidence for learning and trust building.
	• Use of innovative and creative methods that also involve obtaining feedback on effectiveness and incorporate improvements identified.

Creating an OBC System

How does one create a system that is based on OBC principles? The following outlines the experience that Srikanth Mangalam and I have had in nurturing a series of new or refreshed approaches in contrasting situations across the globe.

The Stakeholders: Who has to be Involved?

(1) Who occupies the current landscape?
(2) Which associations or groupings currently exist?
(3) Who has to be involved in delivering, or benefitting from, the ecosystem and its outcomes (good or bad)?
(4) Are the leaders of all the important stakeholders, or groups, supportive of adopting an OBC approach?

Identifying the Outcomes

(5) Get people together who need to cooperate to achieve the outcomes.
(6) They should define the outcomes they seek, for themselves and collectively.

Achieving the Outcomes

(7) How will each stakeholder achieve its outcomes?
(8) Who do you need to work with to achieve your outcomes?
(9) Does achieving the outcomes not necessarily involve everyone working together?
(10) Who needs to do what in order to achieve the outcomes?

Monitoring

(11) What metrics/data will tell you if you are achieving the outcomes and the system is performing well?

(12) Who has the data? Who needs to produce what? How will they do this?
(13) How will the system identify harms? What data and controls are needed to do this? Who needs to share what data with whom, and how?

System Architecture

(14) What functions are needed to make your ecosystem work?
(15) Do these equate to the circle of functions in the RFM?
(16) Are there any gaps in the functions?
(17) Who is best placed to perform the essential functions, either singly or in collaboration with others?
(18) Does it matter which institutions are public, private, or not-for-profit?
(19) Check that all the functions in the RFM are covered, so the system is going to work to deliver the outcomes, and identify harm/problems/performance.
(20) Drawing everything together, what is the agreed plan for the system, that all can commit to?

Building Collaboration Through Trust

(21) Everyone should ask themselves: Can I be trusted? What evidence do I need to show that I can be trusted? To whom? What do others say about whether I can be trusted?

Comments on the Creation Process

Initiation

Anyone can initiate the creation of an OBC or RFM approach. Our experience is that initiation can come from any stakeholder who wants to operate in a better system that the authoritarian and under-achieving traditional mode. Some regulators may feel inhibited in doing this absent governmental permission. But there is rarely any prohibition on different stakeholders talking to each other about creating such as system: it is not anti-competitive. It is often beneficial for independent experts to facilitate discussions about the creation of a new system.

Governance

Governance is shared amongst stakeholders. The form of power allocation is more horizontal than vertical. It aligns with Foucault's insight that power circulates amongst actors.[32] Governance of the ecosystem typically rests in a *Stakeholder Council*. A collaborative approach means that relevant people need to be *involved* in the systematic activities, hence involved in co-creation, co-operating, co-monitoring, and co-responding so that the system works.

The operational oversight of the system may be delegated to a different forum or body, such as a traditional regulatory authority. Where an OBC approach is constructed within the space of a pre-existing state-based regulatory system, various accommodations may occur, with an existing regulatory authority continuing to play a core and more traditional role (in any event, it needs to exercise enforcement authority based on its legal mandate and powers endowed by the state), although perhaps over time evolving towards a full stakeholder model. The transparent involvement of all stakeholders collaborating about operating a better system is not collusion or capture.

Agreeing Outcomes

Discussion of the desired outcomes acts as an opportunity for all stakeholders to test whether they can work together, and whether their outcomes are appropriate for the community at large. It is frequently transformatory to have to define what you actually want to achieve, and to define your outcomes, rather than to continue to operate on a 'business as usual' basis. Achieving inputs or outputs is irrelevant: it is outcomes and impacts that matter.

After the 'what' comes the 'how' question. How is each actor going to achieve its outcomes? The process of identifying mechanisms frequently leads to the realisation that almost every actor cannot achieve what they want effectively without the cooperation of others. Further, the achievement of various outcomes can be achieved more effectively if they form a combined package, in which everyone contributes.

The process of discussing and agreeing outcomes should also identify that not everything can be achieved at once. Hence, some prioritisation, and achievement in stages, will be relevant. What are the milestones?

Measuring Performance and Achievement of Outcomes

Then comes the 'how do we know?' question. It is salutary to ask how we are to know if we are achieving the desired outcomes, how we know if harm is occurring, how we know if the system is performing as it should, and if any function is underperforming or missing. What monitoring control, and what data, is needed to answer these points?

Data

Future systems can operate on the basis of instant availability of data on what occurs. This brings huge power to understand what is happening, if a system is performing, and what is unexpected. In essence, we are digitising a regulatory system, replacing previous methods of sampling incomplete data, reporting requirements, rare inspections, and slow responses. The reliability and completeness of the data will be important. What data is needed, who has it, and how is it shared? Is governance of the data adequately secure and independent? How will having this data affect risk appetite, and traditional mechanisms of trust? How are those aspects affected where data is generated by AI? Solutions to all these points are available, but satisfactory answers need to be implemented.

Aspects of the OBC Approach

Motivation

The objective of a Regulatory System approach is to enable people to focus on achieving high performance, acceptable risk, and desired outcomes. This is the psychological outcome of leveraging intrinsic motivation and enthusiasm to achieve positive good outcomes, rather than attempting to rely on external control of actions through mechanisms based on fear.

The former will always be more effective than the controlling, interventionist and punishing approach that typifies the latter. People should want to achieve the inspiring goals and outcomes. Actors should be accountable for how their contribution assists in achieving the outcomes. The coordinator's job is to maximise self-motivation, to encourage performance, and to intervene where there are problems, and deliver protection where it is needed, especially against those who fail to behave in an ethical manner.

Commitment

An OBC project will not succeed unless the leaders of all major stakeholders or groups are committed to the project. Time spent at the start on gaining and confirming commitment will always be well spent, if not essential. Leaders must understand, approve, support and advocate for an approach focused on achieving outcomes through investment of multiple stakeholders in a respectful, trust-based and hence collaborative environment. Hints of authoritarianism, control and enforcement mentalities amongst the cohort will defeat the enterprise.

It is a prerequisite that all relevant actors are committed to achieving the objectives and outcomes. Such commitment should be demonstrated. Signing up to an agreed plan can be powerful evidence. But if genuine collaboration is required on a daily operational level, this needs to be manifest in appropriate behaviours. It can be helpful for stakeholders to spontaneously produce evidence that they are trustworthy, and for there to be an agreed Code of Ethical Conduct. A Code, which is often found amongst professional and trade associations, typically sets out the common values, behaviours and expectations of members. It constitutes the overarching mode of consensual cooperative engagement in achieving the desired purposes and outcomes.

Responsibility and Accountability

Under the OBC and RFM approaches, individual stakeholders assume *responsibility* for performing their activities in order to ensure that the agreed outcomes are achieved, and that the agreed system operates well and effectively, on the basis that their contributions will be reliable and they are trustworthy. They assume *accountability* by accepting:

(a) *responsibility for performing* a function or role or activity that they undertake or is under their control, so that it is performed well and desired outcomes are achieved;
(b) that they will *give an account* of the performance and whether the outcomes have been achieved, of what they have done and not done, and the extent to which unintended, especially adverse, outcomes occurred;[33] and
(c) that they will *play a meaningful role* in assisting in the ongoing processes of learning and improvement in relation to their systems, functions, roles or activities, so as to constantly improve performance, reduce risk and achieve desired outcomes – and will share all relevant information.

Merely giving an account on its own is not enough as a regulatory or compliance technique. Giving an account of what has occurred is only an initial step in the circular problem-solving RFM. Equally, accountability in the sense of imposing retributive sanctions as the standard response where rules have been broken is now known to be ineffective and is an inaccurate use of the word 'accountability'. Responsible stakeholders will hold *themselves* to account.

The Financial Conduct Authority has described its Senior Managers and Certification Regime (SM&CR) (see chapter 7) as being based on accountability and responsibility, clearly distinguishing ethical from unethical conduct, and recognising that competent people make mistakes:[34]

> The basic principle of the SM&CR is about accountability and responsibility. A senior manager has to take responsibility for the activities under their control. Likewise, they should be accountable for that responsibility.
>
> ...
>
> *Lack of integrity*
>
> There is no universally agreed definition of integrity, but the courts have given useful guidance about what a lack of integrity might include. While it can involve deliberate or dishonest misconduct, it can also occur if someone acts recklessly or their 'ethical compass' points them in the wrong direction to a significant extent. If we find dishonesty or lack of integrity this is usually sufficient for us to prohibit an individual.

Lack of competence and capability
Here, the position is more nuanced; competent people make mistakes. In many situations, it would be disproportionate or inappropriate for us to prohibit an individual for a mistake, unless the mistake was particularly serious, or was made repeatedly and/or over a long period of time and never corrected. Where we find no evidence of lack of honesty or integrity, we generally focus on conduct that demonstrates sufficiently serious, repeated, prolonged and/or obvious failures, and measure that conduct against the standards expected of the person at the time and in the circumstances.

Examples of Outcome-Based Cooperative Systems

Open and Just Culture in Aviation Safety

The Performance-Based Regulation (PBR) model operated in aviation safety is mandated by the global coordinating authority, the International Civil Aviation Organisation (ICAO).[35] An essential element in maintaining aviation safety is the 'open and just culture' that exists across every organisation, encompassing regulators, engineers, airlines, airports and air traffic controllers. All information relevant to safety is shared freely (an 'open culture') supported by the knowledge that this occurs within a 'just culture'. A just culture means that everyone will have confidence that there are always *consequences* in response to new information, and these are aimed at everyone making a common contribution to improving performance and safety. Standards of behaviour require professional competence, openness, sharing, and taking responsibility for one's mistakes by correcting them and improving.[36]

In contrast to a quality system, which focuses on output and continuous improvement, a process-based aviation *safety management system* (SMS) approach focuses on monitoring performance (quality assurance activities) to ensure that the system is capable of reliably producing an acceptable level of output[37] and constantly of improving how people and the system are performing in a risk-based world. The SMS is operated constantly by organisations to identify hazards and take action to address them,[38] especially the constant checking of procedures and states, and sharing of information. It includes the documented, repeatable processes of a quality management system. It comprises four components: *safety policy, safety risk management, safety assurance* and *safety promotion*.

The typical consequences that arise in a traditional legal system are essentially irrelevant in the aviation system, on the basis that people demonstrate their commitment to the outcomes of increased safety, performance and learning. Indeed, adopting an authoritarian, legalistic and certainly punitive response after an accident, even just to how an investigation is conducted, will deter the free flow of vital information, in relation to finding out what happened, what the true contributory causes were, and how they can be avoided in future, both in relation to the particular incident and systemically in future.[39] However, the culture draws a line between acceptable and unacceptable behaviour. 'A wilful violation is not acceptable. An honest mistake is.'[40] There is a long-stop legal protection, but one which rejects punishment:[41]

> a culture in which front line operators or others are not punished for actions, omissions or decisions taken by them that are commensurate with their experience and training, but where gross negligence, wilful violations and destructive acts are not tolerated.

The culture is essentially blame-free and non-punitive[42] but does rest on individual responsibility and accountability.[43] Everyone takes responsibility for performing their tasks professionally and is accountable for their contributions, including contributing information on safety and performance. The regulatory system imposes personal responsibility for safety on the Chief Executive of an organisation, who is responsible for ensuring that their work cultures are based on socially supportive, open and just principles. The internal culture requires not just sharing of information but also training, listening, prompts, reminders, questioning and the constant mutual support of all staff and managers.[44]

All operators are constantly socially accountable to their peers to be open, to share information, to question and to check, all in a non-hierarchical way.[45] Sidney Dekker, an expert in 'just culture', identifies critically contrasting viewpoints:

> Backward-looking accountability tries to find a scapegoat, to blame and shame an individual for messing up. Forward-looking accountability acknowledges the mistake and the harm resulting from it, should lay out the opportunities (and responsibilities!) for making changes so that the probability of such harm happening again goes down.[46]

In 2021, the ICAO produced a significant Manual on Human Performance (HP) aimed at ensuring the integration of human performance considerations in the planning, design and implementation of new technologies, systems and processes as part of a safety management approach, and to facilitate the integration of human performance elements in competency-based training programmes throughout professionals' careers.[47] A prime purpose was 'to make it easy for people in the aviation system to do the right thing and avoid negative safety consequences'. The approach builds on systems thinking – viewing systems in a holistic, integrated manner, rather than as isolated components or parts – and integrates human performance principles, on the basis that '[w]ithin a complex system, it is the human contribution that often provides the important safety barriers and sources of recovery'.

OBCR Case Studies

We have seen in earlier chapters that the *purpose* and *function* of regulation is to provide *protection* from unacceptable risks and harms and involving a number of distinct regulatory *systems* in doing so. Each system is individual and distinct, and has particular features, even though the architecture and details of what might be called families are similar. However, their existence as distinct systems have limitations, including not achieving the desired outcomes or, in instances, generating competing outcomes.

Chapter 4 introduces the concept of functions of a regulatory system as being holistic and comprehensive about controlling activities and risks. It suggests a better way to think of regulation as a *system* that achieves desired protections, avoiding harm and achieving desired outcomes. Viewed as a system, a regulatory space inherently becomes a collaborative *enterprise* between the relevant actors. It is only possible to make a system work, and to achieve all the desired outcomes, if all of those who perform core functions within the system, however modest they may be, perform their roles adequately. Otherwise, the system will not work. Achieving effective collaboration means we have to think of regulation as a horizontal exercise, in which different actors engage with each other in order to achieve their shared goals and outcomes. Such collaboration requires mutual respect and trust between the actors if it is going to achieve much. In reality, it will become necessary to provide for the integration of multiple systems.

For example, food safety needs to be looked at in the overall context of food security; SDG Target 2.1 says, 'By 2030, end hunger and ensure access by all people, in particular the poor and people in vulnerable situations, including infants, to safe, nutritious and sufficient food all year round.'[48] If one were to regulate some of those outcomes, one would need to be regulating across systems.

Several initiatives are currently underway globally that are involved in testing and implementing OBCR as a viable regulatory approach, especially when tackling the challenge of regulating as a system. Many of these initiatives are targeted at addressing significant global challenges including climate change, sustainable development goals such as food insecurity, reduced poverty and inequality, wherein regulations have a major role to play. The following provides a brief synopsis of those initiatives to provide a flavour of the successes and challenges in applying OBCR.

Climate Change and Environment

Scotland's ambitious climate change legislation has set a target date for net zero emissions of all greenhouse gases by 2045. The Scottish Government must deliver this statutory target, and do so by seizing the economic opportunities this ambition presents, in a manner in keeping with its commitment to realise a just transition for all of Scotland.[49] This requires the design of a regulatory system that would aim to achieve multiple outcomes representing the net zero target and Just Transition goals. It would therefore involve multiple systems of stakeholders, regulations and regulators. The Scottish Environmental Protection Agency (SEPA), with financial support from the UK Government, has chosen the OBCR framework as the basis by which it aims to assist in achieving the regulatory outcomes of this transformational initiative. It has initiated a pilot study in the community of Grangemouth (considered to be the highest industrial emitter of greenhouse gases and with one of the highest levels of poverty and unemployment) and is making significant progress in that regard. Through a collaborative process involving multiple regulators, industry, community and government, SEPA has achieved several strategic milestones in its progress towards a successful implementation of OBCR. SEPA stated in its report on OBCR:[50]

the project has provided SEPA and its partners with a valuable opportunity to take a concept for an outcome based collaborative approach to regulation and turn it into a practical model and then experiment in using the model. It also provided an opportunity for partners to share experience in managing and sharing data, generating valuable recommendations for digital and other solutions. This leaves a considerable legacy in the form of shared learning, practical tools and recommendations for future work.

Food Safety and Security

Food systems[51] are generally assumed to consist of various actors, their interactions and enabling policy environments and the cultural norms that exist along the food value chain. Food systems are broad, spanning input supply and production of crops, livestock, fish and other agricultural commodities to transportation, processing, retailing, wholesaling and the preparation of foods, through to consumption and disposal. Ideally, the desired outcomes of a food system, typically set through policies at a national level, align with the broader goals of society, ie improved nutrition, health, safety, productivity, efficiency, environmental sustainability, climate-smart and inclusivity.

Food regulatory systems tend to be part of the overall food system, but generally operate at sub-national levels, are primarily focused on protecting and improving public health and safety, whilst enabling consumer choice and supporting the existence of a sustainable industry. It is expected that food regulatory systems operate in alignment with the broader objectives of the overall food system to ensure that they deliver the desired outcomes.

Queensland, Australia, currently has two broad regulatory systems in place to administer the Food Act and the Food Production (Safety) Act. The purpose of the two pieces of legislation is primarily to ensure that food and primary produce are safe and fit for consumption (humans and/or animals). The Food Production Act is administered by Safe Food Queensland (SFQ). In its desire to future vision its regulatory delivery model to not only meet new and emerging risks but to address the various inefficiencies in the current regulatory system, SFQ has established an OBCR-informed regulatory delivery framework (RDF). Safe Food's new RDF is designed to support the agency's future operating model and strategic priorities, both of which require an outcome-based collaborative approach to regulatory delivery. The RDF[52] provides both the structure and adaptability required for the agency to deliver, measure and report on its regulatory activities into the future as businesses and industry sectors innovate in response to changing industry demands and environmental conditions. On implementing the RDF, SFQ aims to maintain a collaborative regulatory environment that fosters industry and regulatory best practice (system performance). This objective takes SFQ and its accreditation holders 'beyond a traditional regulatory approach, to one that promotes best practice for industry as a means of achieving sustained compliance and to reflect the increasing interrelatedness of supply chains and regulatory systems, and the need to balance social, economic, and environmental outcomes'.⁵³

Reducing Regulatory Barriers to Trade in Developing Economies

Citizens of countries in developing economies, and especially in sub-Saharan Africa, rely on small-scale traders and cross-border trade for access to essential commodities such as food and medicine. These traders, and cross-border trade in general, are subject to several barriers including regulatory requirements that are cumbersome, conflicting and not serving desired outcomes. One such border exists at Kasumbalesa between the Democratic Republic of Congo and Zambia. Data in 2017 indicated that goods valued at over $30 million were traded at this border, many of which involved fresh food produce, medicines and essential consumer products.

Goods that cross the border post from Zambia to the DRC and vice versa come in consignments of varying sizes and pose different types of risk to consumers in the DRC, including risks from fraud, smuggling and/or accidental importation of diseases and other health and safety threats. Regulatory agencies on both sides of the border had the enormous responsibility and challenge not only to monitor the movement of these goods in a manner that protects consumers from health and safety threats, but also to do so in a manner that increases timely market access to the products and enhances economic protection and impetus to small businesses. Multiple regulatory agencies ranging from customs, public health, food and drug authorities, product safety and standards authorities operate at the border to try and provide the necessary protection and assurance but do so independently.

With support from the German Government, an initiative was introduced using an OBCR framework to create an outcome-focused collaborative model involving regulators, businesses, trade associations, civil society organisations, community organisations and governments to help protect the ecosystem and ensure prosperity in the region. Key learnings from that project, which led to several interventions and where regulatory changes were identified, included that a collaborative and co-creative approach to develop an integrated framework increased the level of trust between the various stakeholders (which was previously absent). It empowered the stakeholder to take ownership of the issues and solve them, and it enabled the creation of timely and localised interventions. It also enabled traders to become more resilient to adverse effects of climate change as they were able to rely and share information and practices amongst each other.

Key Points

- Maximising the achievement of outcomes requires trusted actors and relationships. This is as true of regulation as it is of business or social activities.
- We can increase trust between stakeholders in a system if every actor produces evidence that they are trustworthy. The lens of trustworthiness goes beyond the traditional requirement of compliance with rules and procedures. In those regulatory systems that can achieve this, enhanced collaboration is truly transformative in terms of outcomes and efficiency.

---

[1] M Bertness, *A Brief Natural History of Civilization. Why a Balance Between Cooperation & Competition Is Vital to Humanity* (Yale University Press, 2020).
[2] See S Dekker, *Just Culture. Balancing Safety and Accountability* (Ashgate Publishing, 2007) 103; RL Helmreich, 'Building safety on the three cultures of aviation' in *Proceedings of the IATA Human Factors Seminar* (Bangkok, 1999) 39–43; D McCune, C Lewis and D Arendt, 'Safety Culture in Your Safety Management System' in AJ Stolzer, CD Halford and JJ Goglia (eds), *Implementing Safety Management Systems in Aviation* (Ashgate, 2011).
[3] NA Christakis, *Blueprint. The Evolutionary Origins of a Good Society* (Little, Brown Spark, 2019).
[4] M Heffernan, *A Bigger Prize. Why competition isn't everything and how we do better* (Simon & Schuster, 2014); ME Stuke and A Ezrachi, *Competition Overdose* (Harper Business, 2020).

[5] JE Stiglitz, *The Price of Inequality: How Today's Divided Society Endangers Our Future* (WW Norton, 2012).

[6] ME Stuke and A Ezrachi, *Competition Overdose* (Harper Business, 2020) 233.

[7] G Hardin, 'The tragedy of the commons' (1968) 162 *Science* 1243; E Ostrom, *Governing the Commons: Evolution of Institutions for Collective Action* (Cambridge University Press, 1990).

[8] *OECD Regulatory Policy Outlook 2021* (OECD, 2021).

[9] O O'Neil, *A Question of Trust* (Cambridge University Press, 2002). Many other sources include N Luhmann, *Trust and Power* (John Wiley & Sons, 2018); BA Misztal, *Trust in Modern Societies* (Polity Press, 1996); AB Seligman, *The Problem of Trust* (Princeton University Press, 1997); P Sztompka, *Trust. A Sociological Theory* (Cambridge University Press, 1999).

[10] EO Wilson, *The Social Conquest of Earth* (Liveright Publishing, 2012); J Haidt and J Graham, 'When morality opposes justice: Conservatives have moral intuitions that liberals may not recognise' (2007) 20(1) *Social Justice Research* 98–116; J Haidt, *The Righteous Mind. Why Good People are Divided by Politics and Religion* (Penguin Books, 2012).

[11] FBM de Waal, 'How Selfish an Animal?' in PJ Zack, *Moral Markets. The Critical Role of Values in the Economy* (Princeton University Press, 2008) 66.

[12] LD Molm, N Takahashi and G Peterson, 'Risk and Trust in Social Exchange: An Experimental Test of a Classical Proposition' (2000) 105(5) *American Journal of Sociology* 1396–1427.

[13] EJ Lawler and J Yoon, 'Commitment in Exchange Relations: Test of a Theory of Relational Cohesion' (1996) 61 *American Sociological Review* 89–108.

[14] E Goffman, 'On Cooling the Mark Out: Some Aspects of Adaptation to Failure' (1952) 15(4) *Psychiatry* 451–63; D Gambetta, 'Mafia: The Price of Distrust' in D Gambetta (ed), *Trust. Making and Breaking Cooperative Relations* (Basil Blackwell, 1988); T Frankel, *The Ponzi Scheme Puzzle: A History and Analysis of Con Artists and Victims* (Oxford University Press, 2012); G Hosking, *Trust: A History* (Oxford University Press, 2014).

[15] JC Gibbs, *Moral Development and Reality*, 4th edn (Oxford University Press, 2019).

[16] NA Christakis, *Blueprint. The Evolutionary Origins of a Good Society* (Little, Brown Spark, 2019).

[17] ibid.

[18] M Jenkins, *The relationship between business integrity and commercial success* (Chr Michelsen Institute, 2017); PM Nichols, 'The Business Case for Complying with Bribery Laws' (2012) 49(2) *American Business Law Journal* 325–68; *The case for purpose-driven business* (ReGenerate, 2020) ch 3.

[19] *Sustainable investing: resilience amid uncertainty* (BlackRock, 2020).

[20] RD Putnam, *Making Democracy Work* (Princeton University Press, 1993); RD Putnam, 'Turning In, Turning Out: The Strange Disappearance of Social Capital in America' (1995) 28(4) *PS: Political Science and Politics* 644; F Fukuyama, *Trust: The Social Virtues and the Creation of Prosperity* (Penguin Books, 1995).

[21] A Fox, *Beyond Contract: Work, Power and Trust Relations* (Faber, 1974); LG Zucker, 'Production of trust. Institutional sources of economic structure 1840-1920' (1986) 8 *Research in Organizational Behavior* 53–111.

[22] M Stevens, JP MacDuffie and S Helper, 'Reorienting and Recalibrating Inter-organizational Relationships: Strategies for Achieving Optimal Trust' (2015) 36(9) *Organization Studies* 1237–64.

[23] EO Wilson, *Sociobiology. The new synthesis* (Harvard University Press, 1975); J Haidt, *The Righteous Mind. Why Good People are Divided by Politics and Religion* (Penguin Books, 2012).

[24] J Henrich, *The Secret of Our Success: How culture is driving human evolution, domesticating our species, and making us smarter* (Princeton University Press, 2016); J Henrich, *The Weirdest People in the World. How the West Became Psychologically Peculiar and Particularly Prosperous* (Allen Lane, 2020).

[25] C Hodges and R Steinholtz, *Ethical Business Practice and Regulation: A Behavioural and Values-Based Approach to Compliance and Enforcement* (Hart, 2017) ch 9.

[26] AC Edmondson, *The Fearless Organization* (John Wiley & Sons, Inc, 2019).

[27] *Government response to the digital identity and attributes consultation* (DCMS, 10 March 2022).

[28] DH McKnight and NL Chervany, 'Conceptualizing trust: A typology and e-commerce customer relationships model', Proceedings of the 34th Hawaii International Conference on System Sciences (IEEE, 2001); DH McKnight and NL Chervany, 'What Trust Means in ECommerce Customer Relationships: An Interdisciplinary Conceptual Typology' (2001) 6(2) *International Journal of Electronic Commerce* 35–59.

[29] DH McKnight and NL Chervany, 'Conceptualizing trust: A typology and e-commerce customer relationships model', Proceedings of the 34th Hawaii International Conference on System Sciences (IEEE, 2001); DH McKnight and NL Chervany, 'What Trust Means in ECommerce Customer Relationships: An Interdisciplinary Conceptual Typology' (2001) 6(2) *International Journal of Electronic Commerce* 35–59.

[30] D Sull, quoted in 'Bartleby. The dark matter of organisations', *The Economist* (21 June 2025) 66.

[31] C Hodges and R Steinholtz, *Ethical Business Practice and Regulation. A Behavioural and Values-Based Approach to Compliance and Enforcement* (Hart, 2017).

[32] G Burchell, C Gordon and P Miller (eds), *The Foucault Effect: Studies in Governmentality* (University of Chicago Press, 1991).

[33] M Bovens 'Public Accountability' in L Ferlie, C Lynne and C Pollitt (eds), *The Oxford Handbook of Public Management* (Oxford University Press, 2007) 182.

[34] *Statement on the Financial Conduct Authority's further investigative steps in relation to RBS GRG* (Financial Conduct Authority, 2018).

[35] ICAO Annex 19.

[36] D McCune, C Lewis and D Arendt, 'Safety Culture in Your Safety Management System' in AJ Stolzer, CD Halford and JJ Goglia (eds), *Implementing Safety Management Systems in Aviation* (Ashgate, 2011) 195.

[37] AJ Stolzer, CD Halford and JJ Goglia, 'Introduction' in AJ Stolzer, CD Halford and JJ Goglia (eds), *Implementing Safety Management Systems in Aviation* (Ashgate, 2011) xlviii.

[38] See definition in *Communication from the Commission to the Council and the European Parliament. Setting up an Aviation Safety Management System for Europe*, COM(2011) 670, 25.10.2011, p 3: 'a pro-active system that identifies the hazards to the activity, assesses the risks those hazards present, and takes action to reduce those risks to an acceptable level. It then checks to confirm the effectiveness of the actions. The system works continuously to ensure any new hazards or risks are rapidly identified and that mitigation actions are suitable and where found ineffective are revised.'

[39] Numerous salutary stories are quoted in S Dekker, *Just Culture. Restoring Trust and Accountability in Your Organization*, 3rd edn (Ashgate Publishing, 2017).

[40] S Dekker, *Just Culture* (Ashgate Publishing, 2007) 15.

[41] Commission Regulation (EU) No 691/2010 of 29 July 2010 laying down a performance scheme for air navigation services and network functions and amending Regulation (EC) No 2096/2005 laying down common requirements for the provision of air navigation services, Art 2(k).

[42] Regulation (EU) No 996/2010, recital 24.

[43] RL Helmreich, 'Building safety on the three cultures of aviation' in *Proceedings of the IATA Human Factors Seminar* (Bangkok, 1999) 39–43; D McCune, C Lewis and D Arendt, 'Safety Culture in Your Safety Management System' in AJ Stolzer, CD Halford and JJ Goglia (eds), *Implementing Safety Management Systems in Aviation* (Ashgate, 2011).

[44] The implications for organisational culture are illustrated by comments from senior airline executives: *Keeping the aviation industry safe: Safety Intelligence and Safety Wisdom. 16 aviation industry senior executives reflect on how they run a safe business in a commercial environment. A Future Sky Safety White Paper* (European Commission, 2016).

[45] C Hodges and R Steinholtz, *Ethical Business Practice and Regulation. A Behavioural and Values Based Approach to Compliance and Enforcement* (Hart, 2017).

[46] S Dekker, *Just Culture. Balancing Safety and Accountability* (Ashgate Publishing, 2007) 9.

[47] *Manual on Human Performance (HP) for Regulators* (International Civil Aviation Organization, 2021), Doc 10151.

[48] See www.undp.org/sustainable-development-goals.

[49] Scottish Government, 'Just Transition: Grangemouth', September 2023.

[50] grangemouth-obcr-project-final-report.pdf.

[51] International Food Policy Research Institute, "Food Systems".

[52] Safe-Food-Reg-Delivery-Framework-Report_Final_2024.pdf.

[53] ibid.

PART B
Operating a Regulatory System Approach

6

Transformation of Practice on Interventions and Enforcement

How should the findings of behavioural science in the previous chapter be applied in a regulatory context?

This chapter gives an overview of evolutions in the practice of 'enforcement' and the shift to 'supportive intervention' directed at well-intentioned actors.

It identifies different 'families' of law (criminal/public, administrative, private/civil) and the traditional approaches to enforcement.

It sets out a modern, evidence-based policy that integrates 'enforcement' and 'supportive intervention' modes.

This chapter builds on the summary in chapter 2 of multiple strands of evidence on how and why humans behave. Here, we summarise the evolution in thinking and regulatory practice in recent decades that runs alongside the growing realisation of the importance of behavioural science in revising previous theories – from enforcement and deterrence to more supportive interventions and practices. Broadly, the trajectory started with violent and authoritarian control over others, to actions aimed at supporting improvements in behaviour, competence and performance, whilst still maintaining effective protection against bad or incompetent actors. We are currently at a major turning point in the evolution of these issues. This leads us to propose an updated (re)statement of policy on the Principles, Purposes and Objectives of Regulatory Intervention and Enforcement.

The Traditional Legal Enforcement Architecture

Categorisations and Differences between Criminal/Administrative/Civil/Private Law

State enforcement tools are traditionally classified under different types of law, namely criminal, civil, administrative or regulatory. Each of these has different institutions, principles, procedures, burdens of proof, and sanctions/remedies.

Public/Criminal Enforcement

Public enforcement is action taken by or on behalf of the state in response to a breach of the criminal, regulatory or administrative law. The traditional mode is that a public prosecutor institutes a criminal case in the criminal courts, or sometimes a case in an administrative tribunal. If the case is established, sanctions can be imposed such as orders, fines, restrictions, licence conditions or loss of licence, or imprisonment. It can involve prosecution in a criminal (or magistrates') court. The legal trigger is non-compliance with legal requirements (breach, infringement), whether of general or specific law or licence conditions, or possibly of a code provision if this is legally enforceable. The occurrence of harm rarely triggers an enforcement provision as such; some other specific infringement is usually required. In recent years, many regulatory authorities have been given power to impose (some, usually less serious) sanctions themselves without going to court, although the defendant can appeal to a tribunal or launch proceedings for judicial review of the authority's decision in a court. The standard of proof in criminal proceedings is that the evidence of infringement of a rule must be 'beyond reasonable doubt'.

Actions that are classed as *criminal* trigger the application of criminal law, a high standard of proof ('beyond reasonable doubt'), criminal courts, processes and judges, the stigma of a criminal conviction, and a particular range of penalties. That set of responses is broadly referred to as *public enforcement*, by public authorities (police or authorised regulatory or enforcement authorities). (In rare cases, private citizens may be permitted to bring public prosecutions, subject to intervention by the Attorney General.)

Enforcement of criminal law involves a strong core of upholding compliance with the law through *punishment and deterrence*.[1] Punishment should only be imposed by a state[2] (as opposed to any other originator) in response to breach of that state's law.[3] In order to be principled, punishment should be 'justly deserved', proportionate to the crime, so as to cancel out the offender's debt to society[4] by paying the appropriate 'price' for the offence (desert theory).[5]

The use of sanctions on a person should be consequential on their having done something wrong. Criminal law typically requires someone to have a 'guilty mind' (*mens rea*). But some offences are only based on the fact of breaching a rule (strict liability). Other legal concepts sometimes applied are that actions were deliberate, reckless, negligent or careless. Those descriptions are implied states of mind. The 'deliberate' end of that spectrum would normally trigger more serious consequences, which diminish towards the 'careless' end.

The historical approach was that all regulatory prosecutions had to be referred by a regulator or the police to the state prosecuting authority, which would decide whether to institute a prosecution in a criminal court (or specialist tribunal). Over time, regulatory authorities have been given powers to make their own decisions on prosecutions, and to bring them themselves. This delegation has given rise to various inconsistencies and scandals,[6] and is likely to be revised.[7]

Administrative Enforcement

The area of *administrative law* covers actions brought by citizens against public authorities to 'judicially review' whether the latter are acting legally, such as in following correct procedures or acting in ways that are 'so unreasonable that no reasonable authority could make them'. A further category of decision-making occurs in tribunals, which are like courts but usually less formal and sometimes where decisions are reached by a panel comprising a legally qualified chair and other experts who have professional or technical expertise in the subject matter. An example is the Competition Appeal Tribunal, which hears appeals from decisions of the Competition and Markets Authority. Another example is where a regulator brings proceedings, such as the Solicitors Regulatory Authority bringing proceedings against regulated solicitors in the Solicitors Disciplinary Tribunal.

Private/Civil Enforcement

Private enforcement is action taken by private citizens in *civil* courts. The claimant has to prove breach of their rights or a duty under private law that will typically lead to a judgment that the defendant should pay damages to the claimant. An example is a claim for financial payment (known as damages) to compensate harm caused. There can also be an action for an injunction to stop or prevent the occurrence of harm, but that sort of response would normally be taken by an authority under public law provisions. Nowadays, redress can also be sought through an Ombuds or other dispute resolution system, which may be more efficient and speedier than through the courts.

Some regulators are now authorised to use *civil sanctions*, for which the standard of proof is 'on the balance of probabilities', such as:

(a) fixed monetary penalties (fines);
(b) discretional requirements, including:
   (i) variable monetary penalties;
   (ii) compliance notices;
   (iii) restoration notices;
(c) stop notices, requiring a person to cease an activity that is or is likely to cause serious harm or is likely to give risk to regulatory non-compliance;
(d) enforcement undertakings, where a person agrees with a regulator to take specific corrective actions.

The power of an authority to use civil sanctions can be subject to requirements, such as that the authority is in compliance with the 'Principles of Good Regulation' (colloquially known in the UK as being 'Hampton compliant') and that they were transparent, accountable, proportionate, consistent and targeted only cases where action was required.[8]

Overlaps

Another distinction is whether enforcement powers must be exercised *by a court or tribunal* after public proceedings, or whether they may be exercised *by an authority* itself. The landscape is quite confused. Some regulators must bring prosecution proceedings in criminal courts (which are typically delayed, lengthy and costly), or in a Chamber of the First-tier Tribunal, whereas other authorities may typically themselves impose administrative and civil sanctions against the safeguard that a company may appeal to a tribunal.

For some authorities, the administrative step of opening a formal investigation has significance, for example triggering use of other powers, including an ability to impose the costs of the investigation on a regulatee if the authority concludes that there has been an infringement (eg Office for Students).

Many regulators are now themselves empowered to impose fines or other sanctions, such as to remove licences (eg finance, aviation, nuclear, medicines). Some regulators are authorised to exercise civil sanction powers. Reasons for this are to achieve speed of response to threats, consistency of approach, and to save money. Wide recognition of regulatory action supports perception by the general public that the law is being upheld, that others are subject to the same rules, hence triggering psychological motivation for observing the same laws and legal system.

The long-existing matrix of criminal law procedures and sanctions were adopted when regulatory authorities were created, largely in the later 20th century, to which have been added further powers and remedies (under the broad categorisation of administrative law). Power to bring proceedings to disqualify and ban directors can be granted to authorities. Some administrative powers are to inspect, take samples, and require information. Administrative sanctions and remedies may include imposing fines, removing or imposing conditions on licences, and banning defined actions. The suite of 'civil sanctions' inspired by the Hampton/Macrory Review of 2005 includes powers to agree resolution of cases with businesses, accept an undertaking to do or not do something, or order redress to be made (a sensible holistic approach that accords with the functions of the Regulatory Functions Model (RFM) set out in chapter 3).

Sanctions

A general categorisation of sanctions that may be held by state authorities in their toolbox of sanctions includes:

- *Formal/criminal*: prosecution, leading to imprisonment, imposition of a fine or other disqualifications or conditions, removal of licence to operate.

- *Civil*: orders to cease doing something, not to do something, to pay people money, to approve arrangements.
- *Investigative powers*: to enter premises, to inspect, to take things away and test, to take samples.

The traditional classification of criminal/administrative/civil/private therefore has two aspects: different procedures and institutions, and different sanctions in remedy powers. This siloism has confused thinking and the delivery of holistic responses. As indicated above, there has been a considerable cross-fertilisation between the silos, with criminal prosecutors and courts being empowered to order private redress, and with regulators being empowered to use 'civil sanctions' that cover behaviour, culture and redress, as well as imposing fines or removing licences.

The main tools, related to particular objectives, are:

Table 6.1 Intervention Tools for Specific Objectives

Function/objective	Powers
Ban	Prohibition notice Cease and desist (stop) notice for an activity Remove approval or licence for company or individual, completely or from an approved list
Change/improve/support	Give encouragement and advice, and focus on achieving outcomes Require, or agree, changes, eg in training, competence, behaviour, processes, systems, supervision, monitoring, advertising, or culture Promote assistance in training, change Compliance notice, that the subject is to take steps to restore compliance with the law Impose operating conditions Monitor that relevant changes and improvements have occurred satisfactorily
Sanction	Reprimand Impose financial penalty Ban/disqualify a manager or director Imprison an individual Remove or qualify a licence
Repair	Order or agree redress or repair or rectification Remove illicit gains

John Braithwaite and Ian Ayres identified a hierarchy of sanctions in 1992.⁹ Their enforcement pyramid is not applied universally but is helpful in illustrating the hierarchy of enforcement tools, providing an escalating response. Figure 6.1 shows an example from the Civil Aviation Authority's 2012 Enforcement Policy.¹⁰

Figure 6.1 Enforcement Pyramid of the Civil Aviation Authority 2012

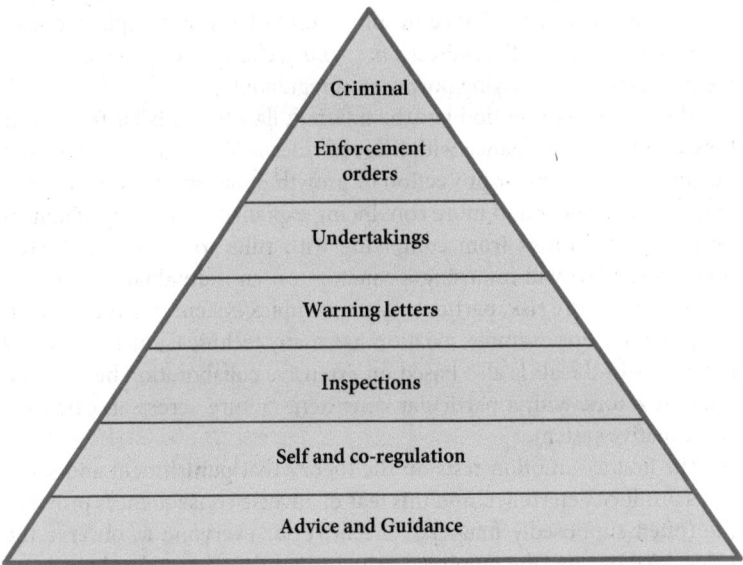

There is a need to provide adequate safeguards against abuse of power or collusive agreements. The extent to which that consideration may be important, and hence the degree of controls, will be affected by the general culture of the society, and the extent of consistent regulatory practice and level of corruption. Some countries may invest regulatory authorities with extensive discretion if there is a good level of confidence that it will be exercised legally and fairly. The general requirements are for strong governance, transparency, independence, accountability, professionalism and observance of sound principles and values, as set out in the Regulatory Delivery Model (RDM).

Purposes and Justifications of Enforcement of Rules

We now look at the traditional purposes of regulatory enforcement, or action, and the justifications for it. The background to the traditional approach is to enforce compliance with legal rules.

There are two assumptions here. First, that enforcement will generate full (or adequate) compliance by all. Second, that it is compliance with rules that will deliver the protection, stability, clarity and consistency that are the primary underlying purposes of regulation.

The second assumption has the inherent flaw that it is far from clear how requiring compliance with a set of rules achieves the fundamental outcomes, like safety or protection or growth of fair markets. Surely one would need a wider and more convincing explanation of the mechanism by which one jumps from complying with rules to achieving desired outcomes? How will imposing a sanction on an individual be effective in reducing future risk, particularly if a complex system is involved, with many actors? For example, aviation has many technical rules, but keeping planes in the air is also based on extensive collaboration between all relevant actors, with a particular consistent culture across an extensive coordinative system.

The first assumption rests on the theory that punishment and sanctions produce deterrence, and this fear of adverse consequences provides the (often supposedly financial) incentive for everyone to observe the rules. We consider the empirical evidence on that theory in chapter 2 – it is not at all strong or convincing. Justifying a forceful response to someone who has caused *intentional* harm is usually unproblematic, but what sanction or response may be appropriate, or bring about change in behaviour or reduction in future risk? These deep flaws in traditional theory and practice have prompted the new approaches to regulation and interventions that are set out in this book.

Traditional Principles Justifying Regulatory Action

The use of (monopolistic) force and authoritarian power by a state arises from its democratic mandate and social covenant of obligations as between citizens and the state. The core mandates are to maintain order and stability in the state. This is traditionally achieved by 'the rule of law', applied though due processes. Hence, the justification for the state, representing society, to intervene in the freedom of its members and use force on them is justified in accordance with the following principles:

(1) Force can only legitimately be used by a duly constituted legitimate authority to protect the ethical values, rules and order of society, and its effective functioning, especially of its regulatory systems.
(2) Any action must be in accordance with a duly constituted fair process in accordance with law and ethical principles.
(3) The purpose and effect of use of force must be to provide the objectives, especially protection. It is not to punish. It is illegitimate as a matter of constitutional and human rights principles for a modern ethical state to rule through fear or arbitrary use of power.
(4) Any measures taken must be proportionate to the need to protect society and to the maintenance of order.
(5) Any measures taken must be based on the best available scientific evidence of their effectiveness in reducing the incidence of future risk of unacceptable harm, and in achieving the legitimate outcomes of society.
(6) Measures should also be taken to make good any harm caused. This is usually achieved by those who have been harmed themselves bringing claims in the civil courts for damages.

Principles of Fair Enforcement

Decisions on when to impose a sanction, what sanction to select, and how severe a sanction should be, are subject to a set of principles and rules that rest on ideas of fairness, proportionality and due process, and ensuring justice and consistency, both in individual cases (responding to the circumstances of individual perpetrators and contexts) and across similar or all cases, so as to form a consistent matrix. Similarly, there should be consistency across actions taken by all regulators, and all courts. Thus, courts typically use standard sentencing guidelines, and regulators use published Enforcement Policies, covering the circumstances where they will take action and what considerations will govern their response. Mechanisms to review individual decisions are rights to appeal or to seek judicial review. Let us look at some of the factors that need to be taken into account in these decisions.

Proportionality: Mitigating and Aggravating Factors in Calibrating Sanctions

It is a basic principle of justice that people who break laws should be responded to more leniently or firmly as a consequence of the seriousness of their behaviour, competence, motivation and similar factors. Broadly, the principle is that a response should be calibrated to the level of culpability. Or, in other terminology, requirements and interventions imposed on offenders should be *proportionate* to non-compliance, harm caused, and risk. This principle is recognised not only in deciding the severity of sanctions but also, in regulatory contexts, in deciding which sanctions are appropriate. The principle of 'responsive regulation' involves proportionate and hence fair differentiation also based on factors relating to the size of an organisation, its degree of competence, capability and resource. But the achievement of protection may justify the prevention from operating of small and large businesses that carry high risk.

Practice across jurisdictions is far from consistent on such fundamental aspects of justice and fairness. A study published in 2021 found a range of practice on whether authorities take into account mitigating or aggravating factors in decisions on enforcement, sanctions or fines in the data protection sphere.[11] Some reported taking into account the existence of compliance frameworks of programmes,[12] whilst others did not take such compliance steps as mitigating factors[13] or as aggravating factors.[14]

The list of mitigating or aggravating factors can logically be extensive, and some lengthy examples have appeared. The EU's data protection legislation, the 'GDPR', specifies the following provisions regulating national administrative penalties:[15]

> When deciding whether to impose an administrative fine and deciding on the amount of the administrative fine in each individual case due regard shall be given to the following:
>
> (a) the nature, gravity and duration of the infringement taking into account the nature scope or purpose of the processing concerned as well as the number of data subjects affected and the level of damage suffered by them;

Principles of Fair Enforcement 159

(b) the intentional or negligent character of the infringement;
(c) any action taken by the controller or processor to mitigate the damage suffered by data subjects;
(d) the degree of responsibility of the controller or processor taking into account technical and organisational measures implemented by them pursuant to Articles 25 and 32;
(e) any relevant previous infringements by the controller or processor;
(f) the degree of cooperation with the supervisory authority, in order to remedy the infringement and mitigate the possible adverse effects of the infringement;
(g) the categories of personal data affected by the infringement;
(h) the manner in which the infringement became known to the supervisory authority, in particular whether, and if so to what extent, the controller or processor notified the infringement;
(i) where measures referred to in Article 58(2) have previously been ordered against the controller or processor concerned with regard to the same subject-matter, compliance with those measures;
(j) adherence to approved codes of conduct pursuant to Article 40 or approved certification mechanisms pursuant to Article 42; and
(k) any other aggravating or mitigating factor applicable to the circumstances of the case, such as financial benefits gained, or losses avoided, directly or indirectly, from the infringement.

The above list of required factors contains elements that fall into three broad categories:

(1) First, some elements relate to action by the infringer *before* or *at the time of* commission of the infringing act (eg items (e) previous infringement; (i) any previous orders; (j) adherence to approved code; (b) intention or negligence; (a) nature, gravity and duration of the infringement, purpose of processing, number of affected subjects, and level of damage suffered; (d) degree of responsibility; (g) categories of data).
(2) Second, some elements relate to the infringer's behaviour *after* the infringement (eg items (c) mitigating action; (h) manner in which the authority became aware; (f) degree of cooperation with the authority).
(3) Third, the final item is of general application, namely (k) whether there are any other aggravating or mitigating factors, such as financial benefits gained, or losses avoided, from the infringement. It is clear that the last item, (k), covers any aggravating or mitigating

factors, and not those of a type relating to financial benefits or losses, which are merely one possible example.

It is interesting to compare the GDPR's list of matters to be taken into account with a similar but different list of such factors that was enacted in 2019 to apply to the core EU consumer protection regimes.[16] Directive (EU) 2019/2161 specifies:

> Member States shall ensure that the following non-exhaustive and indicative criteria are taken into account for the imposition of penalties, where appropriate:
> (a) the nature, gravity, scale and duration of the infringement;
> (b) any action taken by the seller or supplier to mitigate or remedy the damage suffered by consumers;
> (c) any previous infringements by the seller or supplier;
> (d) the financial benefits gained or losses avoided by the seller or supplier due to the infringement, if the relevant data are available;
> (e) penalties imposed on the seller or supplier for the same infringement in other Member States in cross-border cases where information about such penalties is available through the mechanism established by Regulation (EU) 2017/2394 of the European Parliament and of the Council;
> (f) any other aggravating or mitigating factors applicable to the circumstances of the case.

This more recent consumer protection list is arguably clearer than the GDPR list, and the catch-all 'any other aggravating and mitigating factors' produces the result, in theory, that the factors that may be taken into account under either list are identical in nature and scope. There does not appear to be any significant difference in policy between the two lists. It can be commented that the overall objective is that fairness and justice should be done, by taking into account any relevant aggravating or mitigating factors.

The Relevance of Harm

In the traditional enforcement mode, the scale of an infringement may be relevant (see the GDPR example above), but is the extent of harm caused relevant in enforcement and to the severity of a sanction?

The occurrence, nature, scale and severity of harm often affect popular reaction to a disaster. People can say: 'They caused serious harm. That's dangerous. It shouldn't happen. Who's to blame? Whoever caused this should be severely punished.' But is the desire to inflict harm on those who are perceived to have caused harm essentially a retributive, punitive response and – critically – does it lead to changes or future behaviour that reduces future risk? We know that a blame-based approach is in fact counter-productive in preventing sharing information, learning and improving. Based on what we now know about how to achieve good outcomes, is a punitive, retributive response helpful? Using fear as a means of social control does not support building engagement through cooperation, trust, learning, and change. None of this undermines the need to take strong measures to protect against serious risk and harm, but how we do this matters in achieving good outcomes. We need to prevent and respond to enterprises engaging in serious risks without appropriate controls, but we need to analyse the effects of what we do in response. Motivation and competence remain the distinguishing factors between relevant regulatory categorisations and responses.

Competence

People and organisations must have the operational, technical and expert competence to undertake activities that can affect others. This is the rationale for regulation of many professionals. The criteria of competence, capacity and intention intersect powerfully in practice.

Compliance Programmes

Historically, the system based on imposing sanctions in response to breach of legal rules has led larger companies to create significant internal compliance systems and personnel. There has been scepticism whether these mechanisms are merely means of arguing for lesser sanctions. The empirical evidence on effectiveness and outcomes of compliance programmes has been equivocal. The mere existence of a compliance system is of little use in delivering compliance; the culture and behaviour of an organisation is of greater relevance.

Research by Andreas Stephan found evidence suggesting that competition law compliance programmes have been ineffective in preventing cartels or protecting firms from high fines.[17] The evidence reviewed suggested that cartels involved a small number of individuals who knew that what they were doing was illegal and took great pains to avoid being discovered through internal or external scrutiny. That suggested that the primary issue lay with the motivations of individuals (hence criminalisation was discussed) and the culture of an organisation (which was a point not then included in the debate). Indeed, Julian Etienne concluded in 2011 that no consistent or comprehensive compliance theory then existed, and there was only a collection of partial and incompatible theories.[18]

The OECD's *Best Practice Principles for Regulatory Policy* encourage compliance promotion, including through the use of appropriate materials such as regulatory guidance and compliance toolkits.[19] However, there is a distinction between encouragement and taking compliance efforts into account in enforcement. In enforcement of competition law in the EU, the European Commission said that it:[20]

> welcomes and supports all compliance efforts by companies .... But the mere existence of a compliance programme will not be considered as an attenuating circumstance. Nor will the setting-up of a compliance programme be considered as a valid argument justifying a reduction of the fine in the wake of investigation of an infringement.

The Australian Competition & Consumer Commission's 2020 policy is of positive encouragement of compliance, as stated in its compliance objectives:[21]

> To achieve our compliance objectives, we use four flexible and integrated strategies:
> - encouraging compliance with the law, particularly by educating and informing consumers and traders about their rights and responsibilities under the Act
> - enforcement of the law, including resolution of possible contraventions both administratively and by litigation and other formal enforcement outcomes
> - undertaking market studies, or reporting on emerging competition or consumer issues with a view to identifying any market failures and how to address them, and to support and inform our compliance and enforcement measures and identify possible areas for policy consideration

- working with other agencies to implement these strategies, including through coordinated approaches.

The ACCC is selective in the matters we investigate and the sectors in which we engage in education and market analysis. We use this policy to inform our decision making in this regard.

Similarly, different regimes and countries take different approaches towards acceptance of aggravating and mitigating circumstances in settling sanctions.

Regulating Discretion and Flexibility

The need to choose between regulatory responses, and especially the severity of any sanctions, raises the need for there to be a perception of consistency and principled fair behaviour by the public and those who are subject to regulation. Allegations of unfairness, inconsistency, arbitrariness, capture or corruption will undermine trust in the legitimacy of a system and its actors. Hence, a robust and ethical written policy is needed, that is demonstrably followed, that sets out the principles and procedures.

Major components of such a policy are consistency and predictability, proportionality, and observing procedural justice, treating like cases alike, in accordance with a tariff. These requirements arise both from philosophical inquiry and from behavioural research. As we note in chapter 2, Professor Tom Tyler has summarised his extensive work on the principal factors that lead to humans observing rules as follows:[22]

(a) The rules are made through a fair *process*; where people feel that they have had involvement, or a possibility for voice and input.
(b) The *substance* of the rule is perceived to be fair by the individual and most of the community, even if individuals do not agree with it.
(c) The rule accords with their sense of *values*; namely the values of the individual, the particular community or social group or organisation.
(d) The rule is *applied* fairly by/to all.
(e) Most people are *observing* the rule.

As with all activities of government, the decisions and processes operated by a public regulator are subject to review by the courts (judicial review) to ensure that they:

- observe the principles of natural *procedural justice* and constitutional requirements; and

- are in substance not ones that no rational authority would make (Wednesbury unreasonableness).

OECD's Best Practice Principles for Enforcement and Inspections

The OECD's 2014 *Best Practice Principles for Regulatory Policy: Regulatory Enforcement and Inspections*[23] set out a list of core principles on which effective and efficient regulatory enforcement and inspections should be based in pursuit of the best *compliance outcomes* and highest regulatory quality.[24] It asserts:

> A well-formulated enforcement strategy is one that provides correct incentives for regulated subjects as well as appropriate guidelines for enforcement staff, and minimizes both the monitoring effort and the costs for the regulated subjects and the public sector. To achieve this, any strategy needs to rely on a clear and sound vision of what the drivers of compliance are – both in terms of the effect of activities of the regulatory bodies, but also in terms of characteristics of the regulated businesses and of external factors (in particular market characteristics).

> The eleven principles addressing the design of the policies, institutions and tools for promoting effective compliance and the process of reforming inspection services to achieve results are shown in Box 12.1.

OECD International Best Practice Principles: Improving Regulatory Enforcement and Inspections

---

Evidence-based enforcement. Regulatory enforcement and inspections should be evidence-based and measurement-based: deciding what to inspect and how should be grounded on data and evidence, and results should be evaluated regularly.

Selectivity. Promoting compliance and enforcing rules should be left to market forces, private sector and civil society actions wherever possible: inspections and enforcement cannot be everywhere and address everything, and there are many other ways to achieve regulatory objectives.

Risk focus and proportionality. Enforcement needs to be risk-based and proportionate: the frequency of inspections and the resources employed should be proportional to the level of risk and enforcement actions should be aiming at reducing the actual risk posed by infractions.

Responsive regulation. Enforcement should be based on 'responsive regulation' principles: inspection enforcement actions should be modulated depending on the profile and behaviour of specific businesses.

Long-term vision. Governments should adopt policies and institutional mechanisms on regulatory enforcement and inspections with clear objectives and a long-term road-map.

Co-ordination and consolidation. Inspection functions should be co-ordinated and, where needed, consolidated: less duplication and overlaps will ensure better use of public resources, minimise burden on regulated subjects, and maximise effectiveness.

Transparent governance. Governance structures and human resources policies for regulatory enforcement should support transparency, professionalism, and results-oriented management. Execution of regulatory enforcement should be independent from political influence, and compliance promotion efforts should be rewarded.

Information integration. Information and communication technologies should be used to maximise risk-focus, co-ordination and information-sharing – as well as optimal use of resources.

Clear and fair process. Governments should ensure clarity of rules and process for enforcement and inspections: coherent legislation to organise inspections and enforcement needs to be adopted and published, and clearly articulate rights and obligations of officials and of businesses.

Compliance promotion. Transparency and compliance should be promoted through the use of appropriate instruments such as guidance, toolkits and checklists.

Professionalism. Inspectors should be trained and managed to ensure professionalism, integrity, consistency and transparency: this requires substantial training focusing not only on technical but also on generic inspection skills, and official guidelines for inspectors to help ensure consistency and fairness.

In order to be effective, the 'responsive regulation' approach also requires that the range of potential penalties available to regulatory enforcement agencies be sufficiently broad and differentiated to really treat different behaviours in a proportionate manner, but also to exert real deterrence when needed – with penalties that clearly will impose higher cost than the violation may have brought in undue profits to the business operator, and a process for imposing sanctions that uses administrative penalties (and not prosecutions in courts) for at least a significant share of violations so as to ensure more rapid and predictable enforcement. If sanctions provide insufficient deterrent, there is a high likelihood that 'rogue operators' will continue to commit major violations even after having been caught once (or repeatedly).

An Example of an Enforcement Policy

Authorities who enforce laws should be subject to legal requirements on how they do this, as well as to statements of operational policy (such as a Regulators' Code), and their own published policy statement that clarifies how they aim to act in the context of their specific domain.

An example of an Enforcement Policy is that of the Office for Product Safety and Standards (OPSS). It places strong emphasis on *prevention*, and steps taken by businesses to prevent and address non-compliance, and encourages cooperation by businesses through seeking advice and clarification (not mentioning deterrence). Its Enforcement Policy states:[25]

> 1.2 Our primary purpose, as explained in our Product Regulation Strategy, is to protect people and places from product-related harm, ensuring consumers and businesses can buy and sell products with confidence. Our strategy sets out our core objectives and the outcomes we seek to deliver for citizens, business and the environment.
>
> 1.3 We are committed to delivering regulation in a manner that is risk-based, proportionate and consistent and we aim to be transparent and accountable about our regulatory approach and activities, in accordance with the principles of good regulation …. We are guided by the Regulators' Code and recognise the importance of supporting businesses to comply and grow.
>
> 1.4 This policy sets out the approach we take to addressing non-compliance by those that we regulate and to product safety risks. It is intended to:
>
> - set the framework for our decision-making

- help those affected by our activities to understand how and why decisions are made

2) Our approach to addressing non-compliance and product safety risk

2.1 We aim to address non-compliance with the legislation that OPSS enforces, and any product safety risk, in a manner that is proportionate to:
- the nature of the legal obligation and the non-compliance or product safety risk
- the seriousness of the non-compliance or product safety risk, including in relation to harm caused or the potential for harm
- the associated circumstances, including the individual business context and the wider context

2.2 Our primary concerns when non-compliance or product safety risk has been identified are to ensure protection for people and the environment; and to ensure adequate steps are taken to address the issue and to minimise the likelihood of recurrence. We have a range of tools and powers available to us to hold businesses to their responsibilities, from discussing the non-compliance and providing guidance, or agreeing corrective actions, to serving enforcement notices, imposing sanctions or prosecuting offences. We will undertake sustained and escalating interventions where necessary, including to deter and disrupt careless and criminal behaviour.

2.3 Where a product presents a serious risk, we may ourselves act to address that risk by taking steps that a business could be or has been required to take, where the business is unable or unwilling to take appropriate action within the timescales required to protect public safety, for example by recalling products from consumers. In this circumstance, we may seek to recover any costs or expenses reasonably incurred in taking action, as appropriate, where the legislation makes provision for this.

2.4 We encourage businesses to approach us at an early stage to make us aware of any non-compliance or product safety risk that they have identified, including where there is an obligation for them to notify relevant authorities. We welcome approaches from businesses that seek advice and clarification on compliance related issues with a view to mitigating the impact of the non-compliance or product safety risk, or preventing recurrence, including from a business that is the subject of an investigation by us. When making any subsequent decision on appropriate enforcement action, we will take account of an early, positive and co-operative approach (see 4.3).

...

2.8 We are committed to treating those we regulate in a fair, unbiased and objective manner. ...

3) Conduct of investigations

3.1 When deciding whether to investigate non-compliance or product safety risk, we use our discretion, taking account of a range of factors, including:

- the impact or potential impact of the non-compliance or product safety risk on people and/or the environment
- the potential for OPSS interventions to significantly mitigate the risk of harm to the people and/or the environment and maintain public confidence
- the nature and seriousness of any potential non-compliance with legal obligations
- our current enforcement priorities
- whether others are better placed to intervene

3.2 When we decide to investigate, we do so with the aim of:

- gathering information and establishing the facts
- identifying non-compliance and understanding the causes
- determining appropriate interventions, including enforcement action

...

4) Decisions on enforcement action

4.1 In enforcing the legislation, we may use the full range of enforcement tools and powers available to us, which may vary according to the legislation that we are acting under. These enforcement tools and powers may be used in combination, including as an escalating response to continuing or recurrent non-compliance. They include:

- advice, guidance and written warnings (see section 5)
- accepting an undertaking (see section 6)
- serving an enforcement notice (see section 7)
- imposing a financial penalty (see section 8)
- offering a simple caution (see section 9)
- instituting criminal proceedings in England or Wales (see section 10)
- reporting a case to the Procurator Fiscal in Scotland or the Public Prosecution Service in Northern Ireland (see section 10), or
- referring the matter to another enforcement body

4.2 We exercise discretion and professional judgment to respond appropriately in each individual case, holding businesses to account including through the use of punitive actions. Our decisions on enforcement action are taken on the basis of the evidence available and are informed by a consideration of the following principles. We aim to:

- respond in a manner proportionate to the nature, seriousness and circumstances of the particular non-compliance or product safety risk

- tackle associated harm, where appropriate
- change the behaviour of the responsible business or businesses
- tackle any financial gain or benefit from non-compliance
- maintain confidence in the enforcement regime and deter wider non-compliance

4.3 The factors that we may take account of in determining the appropriate enforcement action(s) in an individual case include:

- the impact or potential impact of the non-compliance or product safety risk on people and/or the environment
- the ability and willingness of the business to address the non-compliance or product safety risk in an effective manner
- the steps taken by the responsible business to prevent the non-compliance and any clear reasons for the failure
- the willingness of the business to be open about the compliance failure or product safety risk, including its compliance with any notification requirements (see 2.4)
- the business's approach to co-operating with OPSS, both in its investigative activities and in ensuring that adequate steps are taken to address the issue and to minimise the likelihood of future non-compliance
- the willingness and ability of the business to meet relevant requirements, taking account of compliance history
- the maturity of the legal obligations and levels of awareness and understanding of technical requirements
- the likely impact of the proposed action in improving protections for people and/or the environment
- the likely impact of the proposed action on the responsible business
- the likely impact of the proposed action on the wider business community

4.4 We ensure our decisions as to the appropriate response to non-compliance or a product safety risk are taken in a manner that is objective, impartial and fair, without discrimination or bias.

Applying the Science

The Sociological Function of Enforcement

The sociological function of the concepts of rules, sanctions, punishment and deterrence is to maintain the cohesion of a group, by ensuring that all members adhere to the same values, and are seen to do so. The neurological and psychological mechanisms in most people work here to support self-motivation to observe the common rules of the group and a sense of their legitimacy, as well as satisfying a personal need to belong to the group and be accepted by its other members.

On one approach, legal moralism links the criminalisation of certain acts to their immorality.[26] On the other approach, criminalisation is based on the prevention of harm to others or to society.[27] However, enforcement is also an exercise of power by an authoritarian elite. This will be justified in a democracy if it is the proportionate and effective means of delivering protection. But it is not the means of enlisting the intrinsic motivation of citizens, which behavioural science identifies as the most effective mechanism for achieving valid shared objectives.

The use of power carries with it the historical ability of using force and the threat of force as a *coercive tool*. The use of certain types of force has declined, at least in democracies, but the spectrum, for individuals, includes death, imprisonment, banning and expulsion. The more modern equivalents here, especially in relation to organisations, are removal of a licence or freedom to operate, disqualification as a director or post-holder, imposing restrictions or qualifications on operation, requiring certain actions to be taken, imposing a financial penalty.

Philosophy of Punishment and Democracy

A lengthy deontological tradition considers punishment to be censure for a wrongful act, and stresses the need for the sanction to be proportionate to the seriousness of that act.[28] The imposition of punitive sanctions is essentially retrospective, constituting retribution imposed by a powerful society for breaking its laws, and so constituting an affront to the good order and rules of that society. Indeed, a principle is that punishment should only be imposed by a state[29] (as opposed to any other originator) in response to breach of that state's law.[30] In order to be principled, punishment should be 'justly deserved', proportionate to the crime, so as to cancel out the offender's debt to society[31] by paying the appropriate 'price' for the offence (desert theory).[32] The mere public condemnation of an offender for having committed an offence may constitute 'punishment', especially if it produces damage to reputation or other social consequences.[33]

But is punishment in contemporary society either effective or appropriate, especially in response to regulatory situations? We are no longer living in an authoritarian dictatorship but in a democratic state in which individual freedoms and human rights are core values. Controlling citizens by fear and arbitrariness (which is what deterrence and punishment involve) is no longer constitutionally acceptable. Neither, the empirical evidence shows, is it effective. But society is justified in taking proportionate, and evidence-based effective steps, to protect its citizens and values. The justification for regulation, and hence for regulatory enforcement and intervention, is that of *delivering protection* from unacceptable harm and risk. The means by which protection may be delivered vary, largely differentiated by the motivations, competence, resources, attention and cultures of those who are the proximate actors who cause harm, and of the systems in which they operate. All forward-looking activity is basically about *prevention*.[34]

Evolution in Understanding of Enforcement and Intervention

A number of regulators started undertaking significant divergence from formal enforcement approaches. Keith Hawkins' research highlighted that some British environmental inspectors reduced pollution by simply talking to operators rather than prosecuting them. A classic line was 'Buy a new pump, now, then I can leave you alone'.[35] Similarly, food safety in restaurants in London's Chinatown was transformed through a strategy of education of chefs and working with local culture.[36] This was useful, since many authorities found that they did not have the time or resources to prepare and institute prosecutions or other formal sanctions. Significant evidence has built up over some decades that the behaviour of a small business or farmer who is not complying with all the rules on tax or the safety of food, animals or work practices can be improved by a supportive intervention.[37]

Ian Ayers and John Braithwaite produced a hierarchy of enforcement tools in 1992, with the recommendation that most enforcement should start at the bottom with 'light' sanctions.[38] The implication was that a framework was needed to underpin which tools were used when, so that enforcement policy and practice remained principled and fair as between different actors. The lesson of Ayers' and Braithwaite's 'responsive regulation' is that enforcers should choose the appropriate sanction so as to *respond* appropriately to the offenders' situation and attitude to legal compliance.

A 2005 review of Better Regulation in the UK by businessman Philip Hampton created a policy shift based on the assumption that most businesses were trying to comply and do the right thing,[39] and that they only needed a light touch response when things went wrong, rather than punishment.[40] Evidence was produced that SMEs also often lack clarity about *how* to comply,[41] so can be helped to improve. The supportive approach was made a requirement for UK regulatory authorities under the Regulators' Code (originally 2007),[42] and an associated set of 'Penalty Principles' drafted in 2006 by Professor Richard Macrory.[43]

A rules-based approach started to be recognised as narrowing the vision and activities of enforcers. One study found that 'the mainstream practice of environmental health has become fixed on the delivery of a narrow agenda' and that participants expressed 'growing concern about the fragmentation of environmental health services, and lack of clarity on the nature of future environmental health roles and their contribution to health improvement and tackling health inequalities. [This] has resulted in environmental health officers having to take on predominantly technical and enforcement roles. This trend has been at the expense of effective practice of the wider principles of environmental health protection, and has had the effect of deskilling many in the profession, leading to both dissatisfaction among existing environmental health officers and a diminishing number of applicants for student training.'[44] There have been repeated examples of where an attempt to build a more collaborative dialogue or relationship between regulator and regulatees, focusing on outcomes, has been destroyed by the regulator's enforcement department maintaining an authoritarian deterrence-based approach to imposing sanctions for breaches.

A shift away from deterrence to more supportive and preventative policies has occurred in a piecemeal way across the globe and across sectors,[45] as dissatisfaction grew with the traditional approach. A leading enforcer at the US Commodity Futures Trading Commission described the traditional approach as a constant 'game of whack-a-mole – as soon as we bat down one violation, others just keep popping up.'[46] However, the official described the fresh approach in 2017 like this:

> CFTC are committed to working together with the companies and individuals we regulate to identify and prosecute wrongdoing that has occurred, and to stop future wrongdoing before it starts. In particular, we're committed to giving companies and individuals the right incentives to voluntarily comply with the law in the first place – and to look for misconduct and report it to us when they see it.

Moves Towards Classification of Behavioural Motivations

It can help to understand how ideas have changed here. From the 1980s, some regulatory authorities developed internal approaches that attempted broad categorisations of regulatees' supposed character or state of mind, in order to assist their enforcement choices. A widely quoted example of this is the spectrum of offenders' descriptors used around 2000 by the Scottish Environmental Protection Agency (SEPA). Each of the descriptors of character is linked with a broad response. The important points are, first, that only the 'criminal' person should be met by 'hit them hard'; second, that the direction of travel of all other categories should be based on 'encouraging improvement' up to 'promoting and rewarding best practice', through stages of education, enablement and engagement. Thus, a clear distinction was drawn between criminals (who should be dealt with firmly) and everyone else (who probably need to be supported).

Figure 6.2 Segmentation of Offenders: Spectrum of Compliance (Scottish Environmental Protection Agency)

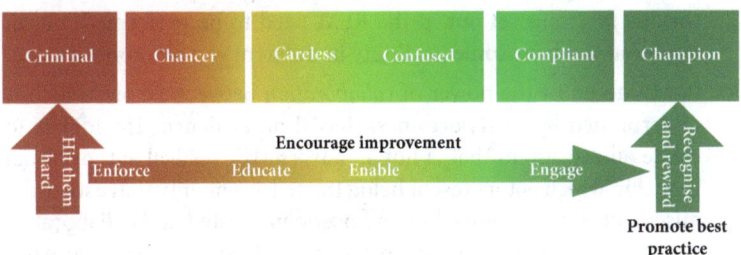

The model was a significant milestone in the evolution of thinking, but was somewhat simplistic. It has the disadvantages that it only focuses on broad categories of *motivation* and that these are *assumed generalised* descriptions of motivations. People are much more complex. Their behaviours are influenced by multiple influences. Individuals can behave in predictable and irrational ways at different times. General descriptors may not be accurate as summaries of a person's behaviour, especially in relation to organisations rather than individuals. A wider series of factors that are relevant to decisions on whether regulatory action should be taken would include factors such as competence, capabilities, resources, situations, and organisational influences.

Better Regulation and Regulatory Delivery

Chapter 3 set out the RDM, the RFM and the Outcome-Based Collaborative Regulation (OBCR) model. Key elements of these combine:

- first, to use a focus on achieving *outcomes*. Outcomes are visible and, if shared and ethical, will be both motivational and measurable. The whole focus of looking at rules, and even more restrictively on compliance with and breaches of rules, is shifted to the far wider and more positive vision of achieving desired outcomes – for individuals, organisations, communities and nations.
- second, to enlist the value of using two behavioural mechanisms: *intrinsic motivation* (values, beliefs, principles, objectives, outcomes) and the *social influence* of a cohesive group that shares the same values;
- third, to adopt a *systems-based* approach to regulation and outcomes. This can replace a vertical, authoritarian model of regulation and enforcement of rules, substituting an ecosystem in which every actor contributes to achievement of the common goals and outcomes. The various *functions* set out in the RFM need to be performed, but in ways that can have some flexibility in different sectoral contexts;
- fourth, to enlist the power of *collaboration* between actors, which is underpinned by trustworthiness, based on evidence. The idea is to create an ecosystem that is not an adversarial, vertical authoritarian model in which actors resent being treated as naughty untrustworthy miscreants by regulators, but an holistic integrated and collaborative system in which as many people as possible are motivated to work together to achieve the agreed common outcomes, improve performance, and control risk and respond to harm.

Adding Behavioural Science: Evolution from Enforcement to Supportive Interventions

As we saw in chapter 2, extensive behavioural scientific research has undermined the primacy of deterrence as both the practice and the theory underlying enforcement of breaches of legal rules, and instead identified the need for supportive leadership and interventions for most people. The scientific research about the effectiveness (or not) of specific *practices* prompts the need for fresh theories, policies and principles of the purposes and techniques of regulation.

The science identifies that there are particular ways of influencing someone else to modify their behaviour and do what you want. Broadly, the modes are: *supporting intrinsic motivation, providing information and support, intervening to stop or change things,* and *imposing sanctions*. These modes form a spectrum of what might generically be called interventions.

But which approaches or tools should be used when? The traditional Legal Model is that having identified a breach of a rule, *enforcement* action is taken, typically by imposing *sanctions*. This is on the theory (or assumption), first, that the objective is to ensure that actors comply with the rules and, second, that imposing a sanction will deter people from breaking the rules in future, and induce future compliance by those who are non-compliant and others. The theory is analysed in greater detail in chapter 1. This may be what many people believe – but there is extensive scientific evidence that it is incorrect.

The enforcement approach aimed at compliance with rules fails to address activities, performance and culture in general. Business schools have undertaken extensive research on what makes effective leaders and organisations, and the evidence is that one should start with motivating staff rather than making them afraid. Extensive research into human behaviour cements the importance of that approach. But it has only recently started to affect how we do regulation.

The behavioural science and related research set out in chapter 2 leads clearly to a set of conclusions in relation to what we used to call 'enforcement' and now need to think of more widely. Two key truths arise from the scientific evidence:

(1) First, the best way to affect people's behaviour is to engage their *intrinsic motivation* rather than to try to affect behaviour by rather crude external means. The *social influence* of others can also drive the behaviour of individual or aspiring members.
(2) Second, that someone in authority (and this can apply to teachers, managers, regulators and others) needs to *differentiate* between (at least) three different types of people. If you use the wrong tool on the wrong type of person, you will not succeed in getting them to 'comply' or be motivated to achieve the shared goals and outcomes

of society. You will run the risk of demotivating them, which may lead not only to failure to do the right thing, but a desire to do the wrong things.

Broadly, the three types of people who do not comply with rules are:

(a) Those who consciously aim to ignore the norms and rules in order to achieve their own selfish aims. These can be said simply to be criminals. They don't care about others; they just care about their own gains.

(b) Those who are incompetent, in other words unable to achieve adequate levels of protection and control over their activities, such that they represent a danger to others. They may be well-intentioned, but they might not have the technical ability, resources, training or systems to be reliable.

(c) Those who are well-intentioned and broadly competent. They might be distracted or less in control of some risks or situations over time. But they are essentially potentially trustworthy and think of themselves as law-abiding.

Thus, the science distinguishes between (at least) two contrasting modes of response:

(1) *A Supportive Intervention Response.* For those who are well-intentioned, those in category (c), the objective is to improve protection and reduce risk. Various kinds of supportive intervention should be used. However, use of the type of 'hard enforcement' tools that you need to use on criminals and incompetents may well produce exactly the converse of increased collaboration or compliance, since people who feel badly treated by authority when they believe they are trying their best tend to feel resentment and are demotivated to observe any rules. Feelings of fairness and justification are profoundly important to maintain.

(2) *A Protective Response.* For the criminal and the incompetent, the overriding objective of delivering protection means that robust enforcement action is needed, such as preventing them from operating. Only robust action will achieve protection. It is pointless to try to engage them in improvement or an OBC mode. So, this mode is essential enforcement as traditionally understood. This means using the formal 'enforcement' tools, selecting those that are appropriate but especially those that are effective, such as removing licences, disqualifying directors, and prohibiting activities.

At bottom, the two Responses outlined above differentiate between those who are ethical and trustworthy and those who are not. Criminals are clearly unethical. Neither they nor incompetents are trustworthy. Well-intentioned people are ethical, but can sometimes fail, or sometimes run into unexpected problems. They may experience challenges of resource, focus, lapses in control, be distracted by other things, or just be taken by surprise. There is quite a range of variables in this 'category' of people and organisations. In any event, the Supportive Intervention mode will help them put things right, reducing ongoing and future risk and delivering repair/redress, taking into account their capacities and competences.

But, in addition, adopting an OBC system can supercharge the system by adding continuing trustworthiness and focus on achieving desired outcomes. The OBC approach aims to raise standards to a higher level of competence, achievement, safety and fairness. In particular, it aims to increase motivation, especially by providing inspirational objective and measurable outcomes that people can pursue, and enlist them as members of a wider supportive community, which will result in operating in an 'open and just culture' so that problems are shared and addressed swiftly.

In addition, the RFM specifies that any harm that has been caused should be rectified as swiftly as possible. The objective of reducing risk is the flip side of achieving the legitimate desired outcomes of society – in this case the regulatory outcomes but also the full range of social, economic and environmental outcomes. Both outcome achievement and risk reduction aim at creating a society based on shared ethical values in which humans can flourish. It may be necessary to balance achievement of stated outcomes with reduction of particular risks. For example, overwhelmingly serious risks, such as responding to a pandemic, mean that some outcomes have to be put on hold until the risk is reduced to an acceptable level. This is, therefore, a situation in which risk-based prioritisation of response applies.

Restatement of Policy on Regulatory Intervention

The following is suggested as a general Policy applicable to regulatory supportive intervention and enforcement, based on the RFM and OBC principles.

Principles, Purposes and Objectives of Regulatory Intervention and Enforcement

(1) The Objectives are to deliver adequate *protection* and to achieve other legitimate goals of the society and regulatory system, such as fairness, predictability, stability, sustainability, growth, innovation and so on.

(2) Achievement of the Objectives is measured through achievement of specific agreed Outcomes.

(3) The selection and prioritisation of different Objectives and Outcomes is set through a deliberative consensus amongst relevant stakeholders (a Stakeholder Council).

(4) The Stakeholder Council will agree
   (a) The Outcomes.
   (b) Metrics, a strategy, and milestones by which the Outcomes are to be achieved, and performance in achieving them is to be demonstrated.
   (c) The design of the Regulatory Space, within which specific actors, institutions, mechanisms or means deliver the core Regulatory Functions.
   (d) The Policy on responding to risk or harm.

(5) The agreed Policy will deliver the following Functions:
   (a) To achieve the stated outcomes.
   (b) To identify harm and risk (and non-compliance) and their root causes.
   (c) To stop ongoing unacceptable harm (cessation).
   (d) To repair harm caused and restore balance (restoration). This means ensuring that redress is paid, and that all illicit gains are removed from those who have improperly benefitted.
   (e) To protect from future harm by preventing or reducing future risk (prevention). To make changes so that the same harm does not occur again, and/or the future risk is reduced. The nature of the relevant changes may be in behaviour, culture, the operation of the system or of controls, training, warnings, information or anything else relevant. The means by which they are undertaken are by responding effectively and proportionately, on the basis of the agreed ethical principles of protection, intervention, science, information and understanding, differentiating between actors who have had a role in the occurrence, based

on the evidence of their commitment to the ethical regulatory principles.

(f) To support confidence and trust in the system and its actors by demonstrating that the system is working to deliver relevant consequences (*just and effective culture*).

(6) The policy for responding to actors or events will be in accordance with these principles:

For actors:

(a) The goal of protection may sometimes need strong action (classic enforcement in style), such as removal or qualification of licences to sell or operate some or all products or services, or imposing bans on actors, activities or products.

(b) This is particularly so where the motivation of the infringer is to operate intentionally to make gains illegitimately, without due regard to causing harm to others.

(c) Well-intentioned actors should be encouraged to improve their performance, competence, behaviour or activities, and behave in accordance with the ethical rules of the society.

(d) Where relevant, intervention tools should be used that support ethical behaviour and achieving the stated common outcomes, making improvements in competence and performance, and reducing risk.

For society:

(e) All actions should comply with the constitutional principles of fair and legal process and be appropriate and proportionate in style and manner. Responses should be transparent and fair, so that the general population will perceive that others observe the rules, and that fair action is taken against those who (deliberately or recklessly, and maybe carelessly) break the rules so that society is protected, the rules are upheld, the cohesive fabric of the society is maintained and consistent, harm is repaired, and that lessons are learned and applied so that performance improves and risk is reduced (eg improvement in competence and performance, plus redress).

(f) All regulatory action should be in accordance with this Policy, and with detailed policies that are appropriate to the particular circumstances of individual regulatory regimes and situations.

(7) The preferred mode for resolution of formal issues between stakeholders in the Regulatory Space should be by *agreement* between *all* of them, and covering all relevant issues as a combined package, including cessation, actions to reduce risk and change culture, making redress or repair, and any changes or sanctions.[47]
Different approaches should be used on people depending on where they fall between the two extremes. For example, between regulators and traders, actions should aim to include cessation, reducing risk and changing culture, making redress or repair, and any penalties.

(8) The following considerations will be taken into account in deciding the response to individual actors where their activities or behaviour have led to risk or harm:

(a) Levels of competence or incompetence and resources relevant to activities and risk.

(b) Motivation and actions at the time of non-compliance. For example, did they:

    (i) Intend to do the right thing? Was the action a deliberate breach; deliberate blindness; recklessness; lack of focus on relevant risk; negligence; carelessness? To what extent can these supposed states of mind be accurately identified by others after the event? This is especially relevant in the case of organisations, or groups of humans.

    (ii) Focus on other worthy or unethical goals rather than on a causative factor or consideration that caused the harm/breach?

(c) Motivation and actions after the breach or occurrence of harm, up to now. For example, did they swiftly identify and stop the problem, involve relevant others such as experts or the regulator, act spontaneously to repair harm and to make changes so as to reduce risk? Or did they cover up the problem, obfuscate, frustrate or mislead the regulator or relevant others?

(d) Evidence of the trustworthiness, or lack of it, of the actor.

---

[1] See A Ashworth, *The Criminal Process: An Evaluative Study* (Oxford University Press, 1994) 24; J Gardner, 'Ashworth on Principles' in J Roberts and L Zedner (eds), *Principles and Values in Criminal Law and Criminal Justice: Essays in Honour of Andrew Ashworth* (Oxford University Press, 2012).

² See L Green, *The Authority of the State* (Oxford University Press, 1989); J Raz, *The Authority of Law: Essays on Law and Morality* (Clarendon Press, 1983); A Guinchard, 'Fixing the Boundaries of the Concept of Crime: The Challenges for Human Rights' (2004) 54 *International and Comparative Law Quarterly* 719; SJ Shapiro, *Legality* (Cambridge: Belknap/Harvard University Press, 2011).

³ J Feinberg, 'The Expressive Function of Punishment' in *Doing and Deserving: Essays in the Theory of Responsibility* (Princeton: Princeton University Press, 1970) 95–98 (arguing that imprisonment expresses public censure to a criminal); T Brooks, *Punishment* (London: Routledge, 2012).

⁴ GWF Hegel, *The Science of Logic*, trans AV Miller (Amherst: Humanity Press, 1999); a problem in reconciling the principles of equal treatment, consistency and proportionality is that the amount of pain that any punishment causes to an individual varies with their temperament and circumstances: TH Green, *Lectures on the Principles of Political Obligation* (London: Longmans, 1941), quoted in T Brooks, 'Punishment and British Idealism' in J Ryberg and JA Corlett, *Punishment and Ethics: New Perspectives* (Palgrave Macmillan, 2010) 16–32.

⁵ I Kant, *The Philosophy of Law: An Exposition of the Fundamental Principles of Jurisprudence as the Science of Right* (repr Clifton, New Jersey: Augustus M Kelly Publishers, 1974); GWF Hegel, *The Science of Logic*, trans AV Miller (Amherst: Humanity Press, 1999); A Ashworth, 'Is the Criminal Law a Lost Cause?' (2000) 116 *LQR* 225, 253–56; K Yeung, *Securing Compliance. A Principled Approach* (Hart Publishing, 2004).

⁶ Prosecutions by the Post Office against 900 or more sub-postmasters in wholly unjustified circumstances: *Post Office Horizon IT Inquiry: Report Volume 1*, HC 1119 (2025). Prosecutions by train operating companies adopting entirely inconsistent and unregulated criteria: see *Independent review of train operators' revenue protection practices* (Office of Road and Rail, 2025).

⁷ *Oversight and regulation of private prosecutors in the criminal justice system consultation* (Ministry of Justice, 2025).

⁸ The process is described in J Norris and J Philips, *The Law of Regulatory Enforcement and Sanctions. A Practical Guide* (Oxford University Press, 2011) ch 4.

⁹ I Ayres and J Braithwaite, *Responsive Regulation: Transcending the Deregulation Debate* (Oxford University Press, 1992).

¹⁰ *Civil Aviation Authority Regulatory Enforcement Policy* (Civil Aviation Authority, October 2012).

¹¹ *Organizational Accountability in Data Protection Enforcement. How Regulators Consider Accountability in their Enforcement Decisions* (Centre for Information Policy Leadership, 2021).

¹² They included Australia (ACCC and AFSA), Belgium (BIPT), Finland (TUKES), Malta (NRA), Netherlands (Education Inspectorate), Spain (CNMC), UK (OPSS, SRA and FSA).

¹³ Poland (UOKiK).

¹⁴ Brazil (CADE), Malta (NRA), Poland (UOKiK) and Spain (CNMC).

¹⁵ GDPR, Art 83(2).

¹⁶ Council Directive 93/13/EEC on unfair terms; Directives 98/6/EC on price marking, 2005/29/EC on unfair commercial practices and 2011/83/EU on consumer rights.

¹⁷ A Stephan, 'See no evil: cartels and the limits of antitrust compliance programmes' (2010) 31(8) *The Company Lawyer* 3.

¹⁸ J Etienne, 'Compliance Theory: A Goal Framing Approach (2011) 33(3) *Law & Policy* 305–33.

¹⁹ Principle 10, 'Regulatory Enforcement and Inspections', *OECD Best Practice Principles for Regulatory Policy* (OECD, 2014).

[20] European Commission, *Compliance matters – What companies can do better to respect EU competition rules* (November 2011), accessible at http://ec.europa.eu/competition/antitrust/compliance/, 19–20. In the UK, see *How your business can achieve compliance with competition law: Guidance* (Office of Fair Trading, 2011).
[21] *2020 Compliance and Enforcement Policy and Priorities* (ACCC, 2020).
[22] An excellent summary is: TR Tyler, *Advanced Introduction to Law and Psychology* (Edward Elgar, 2022).
[23] *OECD Best Practice Principles for Regulatory Policy: Regulatory Enforcement and Inspections* (OECD, 2014). See earlier *Consultation on Public Consultation Best Practice Principles for Improving on Enforcement and Inspections* (OECD, June 2013), para 2, available at www.oecd.org/regreform/regulatory-policy/enforcement-inspections.htm. This was published shortly after *Consultation on the Principles for the Governance of Regulators* (OECD, 2012), which specified such principles as role clarity, preventing undue influence and maintaining trust, decision-making and governing body structure for independent regulators, accountability and transparency, engagement, funding, and performance evaluation.
[24] The UK Better Regulation Delivery Office (BRDO) and the Dutch government had contributed a major input into the development of the final Recommendation.
[25] *Guidance: OPSS Enforcement Policy* (Department for Business and Trade, 2025) (updated 27 January 2025). See earlier *Enforcement Policy* (Department for Business, Energy and Industrial Strategy, Office for Product Safety and Standards, 2018) and *Enforcement Policy* (Department for Energy and Industrial Strategy, 2021).
[26] RA Duff, 'Towards a Theory of Criminal Law?', *Proceedings of the Aristotelian Society: Supplementary Volume LXXXIV* (2010) 1–28; RA Duff, *Trials and Punishments* (Cambridge: Cambridge University Press, 1896).
[27] Classically expressed by JS Mill, *On Liberty*, ed E Rapaport (Indianapolis: Hackett, [1895] 1978).
[28] A Bottoms and A von Hirsch, 'The Crime-Preventive Impact of Penal Sanctions' in P Cane and HM Kritzer, *The Oxford Handbook of Empirical Legal Research* (Oxford University Press, 2010); A Ashworth and L Zedner, 'Defending the Criminal Law: Reflections on the Changing Character of Crime, Procedure, and Sanctions' (2008) 2 *Criminal Law and Philosophy* 21–51, 22.
[29] See L Green, *The Authority of the State* (Oxford University Press, 1989); J Raz, *The Authority of Law: Essays on Law and Morality* (Clarendon Press, 1983); A Guinchard, 'Fixing the Boundaries of the Concept of Crime: The Challenges for Human Rights' (2004) 54 *International and Comparative Law Quarterly* 719; SJ Shapiro *Legality* (Cambridge: Belknap/Harvard University Press, 2011).
[30] J Feinberg, 'The Expressive Function of Punishment' in *Doing and Deserving: Essays in the Theory of Responsibility* (Princeton: Princeton University Press, 1970) 95–98 (arguing that imprisonment expresses public censure to a criminal); T Brooks, *Punishment* (London: Routledge, 2012).
[31] GWF Hegel, *The Science of Logic*, trans AV Miller (Amherst: Humanity Press, 1999); a problem in reconciling the principles of equal treatment, consistency and proportionality is that the amount of pain that any punishment causes to an individual varies with their temperament and circumstances: TH Green, *Lectures on the Principles of Political Obligation* (London: Longmans, 1941), quoted in T Brooks, 'Punishment and British Idealism' in J Ryberg and JA Corlett, *Punishment and Ethics: New Perspectives* (Palgrave Macmillan, 2010) 16–32.
[32] I Kant, *The Philosophy of Law: An Exposition of the Fundamental Principles of Jurisprudence as the Science of Right* (repr Clifton, New Jersey: Augustus M Kelly Publishers, 1974); GWF Hegel, *The Science of Logic*, trans AV Miller (Amherst: Humanity Press, 1999);

A Ashworth, 'Is the Criminal Law a Lost Cause?' (2000) 116 *LQR* 225, 253–56; K Yeung, *Securing Compliance. A Principled Approach* (Hart Publishing, 2004).

[33] An instrumental conception of law as a powerful normative order that can regulate social actors' behaviour and thus facilitate social change: P Legrand and R Munday (eds), *Comparative Legal Studies: Traditions and Transitions* (Cambridge University Press, 2003).

[34] *Regulation and Growth* (Better Regulation Delivery Office, 2016).

[35] K Hawkins, *Environment and Enforcement: Regulation and the Social Definition of Pollution* (Clarendon Press, 1984); K Hawkins, *Law as Last Resort* (Oxford University Press, 1992); BM Hutter, *The Reasonable Arm of the Law?* (Oxford University Press, 1988); R Baldwin, 'Why rules don't work' (1990) 54 *Modern Law Review* 321; J Braithwaite and P Grabosky, *Of Manners Gentle: Enforcement Strategies of Australian Business Regulatory Agencies* (Oxford University Press, 1987); H Genn, 'Business responses to the regulation of health and safety in England' (1993) 15 *Law and Policy* 219; BM Hutter, *Regulation and Risk: Occupational Health and Safety on the Railways* (Oxford University Press, 2001).

[36] Summarised in J Monk, *Reform of Regulatory Enforcement and Inspections in OECD Countries* (OECD, 2013), www.oecd.org/gov/regulatory-policy/Reform%20of%20inspections%20-%20Web%20-%20Julie%20Monk.pdf, para 53.

[37] See K Hawkins, *Environment and Enforcement: Regulation and the Social Definition of Pollution* (Clarendon Press, 1984); K Hawkins, *Law as Last Resort* (Oxford University Press, 2002).

[38] I Ayres and J Braithwaite, *Responsive Regulation: Transcending the Deregulation Debate* (Oxford University Press, 1992).

[39] *Drivers of Compliance and Non-compliance with Consumer Protection Law: A Report by Ipsos MORI Commissioned by the OFT* (Office of Fair Trading, 2010), OFT1225a, para 1.34.

[40] P Hampton, *Reducing Administrative Burdens: Effective Inspection and Enforcement* (HM Treasury, 2005).

[41] *Delivering Regulatory Reform: Report by the Comptroller and Auditor General* (National Audit Office, 2011).

[42] www.assets.publishing.service.gov.uk/government/uploads/system/uploads/attachment_data/file/300126/14-705-regulators-code.pdf.

[43] R Macrory, *Regulatory Justice: making sanctions effective* (HM Treasury, 2006); reprinted in R Macrory, *Regulation, Enforcement and Governance in Environmental Law* (Hart Publishing, 2010). Implementation was in the Regulatory Enforcement and Sanctions Act 2008. Subsequent codification occurred in the Consumer Rights Act 2015.

[44] S Burke, I Gray, K Paterson and J Meyrick, *Environmental Health 2012. A key partner in delivering the public health agenda* (Health Development Agency, 2002).

[45] C Hodges, *Law and Corporate Behaviour* (Hart, 2015). *Measuring the impact of regulation* (Stoke-on-Trent & Staffordshire Enterprise Partnership, November 2018).

[46] Speech of James McDonald, Director of the Division of Enforcement, Commodity Futures Trading Commission regarding 'Perspectives on Enforcement: Self-Reporting and Cooperation at the CFTC' (25 September 2017).

[47] This function is typically more swift, efficient and cheap than courts. Relegating private redress to private litigation, on the other hand, is ineffective and inefficient: see C Hodges and S Voet, *Delivering Collective Redress: New Technologies* (Hart, 2018); C Hodges, 'Collective Redress: The Need for New Technologies' (2019) 42 *Journal of Consumer Policy* 59–90. There is provision for the central role of a public body in the CPC Regulation: Regulation (EU) 2017/2394 of the European Parliament and of the Council of 12 December 2017 on cooperation between national authorities responsible for the enforcement of consumer protection laws and repealing Regulation (EC) No 2006/2004, Art 9(4)(c) giving a power 'to seek to obtain or to accept commitments from the trader responsible for the infringement covered by this Regulation to cease that infringement'.

7

Tools for a Regulatory System

Chapter 7 analyses how the functions identified in the *system model* in chapter 4 are delivered in practice. The basic point is that a regulatory toolkit should consist of all relevant means of delivering the desired preventions, controlling risks to acceptable levels, and achieving desired outcomes.

Controls need to be applied at different times: *before* the regulated activity takes place (such as before a product or service is marketed), *during* its marketing and use, or, subsequently, in order to *respond* to the occurrence of a problem/harm/non-compliance (before or after it has arisen). Other terminology that is used for the same idea is: *upstream, midstream, downstream*.

The aims of differentiating the different time points, interventions and tools are as follows:

(1) An *ex ante* system primarily aims at *prevention* of the occurrence of harm, and reduction of risk.

(2) An *ex post* system has three broad aims:

   (a) to maintain the expected *standards of performance* in terms of quality, safety and control;

   (b) to *identify* issues as they arise and be *able to respond* to them, and to respond to them properly, so as to prevent ongoing and future harm; and

   (c) to ensure that lessons are learned and relevant steps are taken to reduce the risk of future harm.

The Purpose of Tools in a Regulatory System: From Compliance to Outcomes

Many of the techniques and tools discussed here are familiar features that are required under existing regulatory regimes, and remain relevant. But the purpose and context have changed, as have the way in which the tools and techniques are used. A traditional approach might set rules, aimed at achieving compliance with the rules, and identifying and sanctioning non-compliance. The instructions might be:

- observe these rules;
- apply this procedure;
- operate this quality system, before, during and/or after a problem arises;
- behaviour: do not do this; treat customers fairly and with care and professionalism; observe this code of conduct.

However, under the Regulatory Delivery Model (RDM), Regulatory Functions Model (RFM) and Outcome-Based Collaborative Regulation (OBCR) approaches, rather than (just) focusing on compliance (especially for controlling those 'outside the circle'), we are now focusing (as between those 'inside the circle') on the following:

(a) Are the agreed outcomes being achieved or not?
(b) Is the system performing well?
(c) What problems are being identified that need to be addressed?
(d) Are all the required functions being operated effectively?
(e) Are all actors trustworthy and continuing their necessary actions to make the system work?
(f) Are proper responses being made to improving the performance of the system, and reducing future risk?

The viewpoint has changed here from 'regulation by regulatory enforcement' to 'an outcome-focused regulatory system'. The viewpoint is no longer just that from a regulatory authority. It is a viewpoint of the successful operation of a system, one that involves coordinated actors who collectively deliver the prescribed functions and outcomes. A major change is the reliance on the use of digitised data and the adoption of collaborative cultures, in which more information is shared and issues and actions are coordinated more closely, so as to monitor achievement of the agreed outcomes.

A. Before: Pre-Marketing

Objectives of Regulation before Marketing or Undertaking Activities

The objectives here apply *before* any regulated activity occurs. The rationale and objectives are essentially *preventative*. They aim to deliver adequate protection from unacceptable and avoidable harm, and allow for acceptable risk. Hence, the activity and the system will aim to:

(1) ensure that the regulatory objectives and outcomes are *likely* to be fulfilled; eg that products and services have a level of risk that is acceptable, and that activities, products and services:

   (a) have adequate design;
   (b) have been adequately tested;
   (c) will individually conform to the design specification;
   (d) so do not present unacceptable levels of risks;

(2) ensure that behaviour in markets will be fair and competitive;
(3) ensure that adequate monitoring, feedback and post-marketing systems are in place that will deliver the ability to respond appropriately and speedily if it becomes necessary to take action to control risk, prevent ongoing harm, or deliver redress.

The controls typically cover demonstration of the following aspects:

- an acceptable level of competence, capacity/capability and resource to undertake actions that are necessary or mandated so that harm will be controlled;
- a relevant control system, that covers the core activities and the manner in which they are to be undertaken, and/or requirements to take action if serious harm occurs;
- provision of adequate information, through specifications, instructions for use, storage and disposal, warnings and precautions, and advertising statements.
- increasingly, that one or more key individuals are considered to be ethically *responsible* and can be relied on to take decisions that accord with professional ethical codes and standards.

We will look below at these broad types of controls in greater detail.

We also need to note that formal state regulation and informal self-regulatory systems use different tools, albeit with some similarities. We will look at those two types in turn. Under formal regulation, we will distinguish between regulatory 'families', notably between safety regulation and economic regulation.

Many regimes may (or should) provide for requirements to be proportionately scaled to the nature and extent of risk, and the scale of the activity. Thus, requirements should accommodate and incentivise potential scale-up for small businesses:

- blocks of competence, resource, capacity, capability, motivation, intent, training;
- examples in food chains, energy and water in South Australia.

Licensing, Approval, Permits, Registration, Notification

Individuals or organisations carrying out specified activities may be required to do so only if they have been granted official *approval* to do so, such as by the grant of a licence or permission, on the basis of scrutiny of the safety and quality system data. The approval may be given by a state body, or involve elements of certification by an independent private certification body and assurance system, or (for low-risk products) by a manufacturer's own self-certification. Separate approvals may be required for different aspects or activities, such as a product/service type, or for the activities of manufacturing, distribution, marketing (including providing information) and advertising.

The techniques of licensing are aimed at controlling access to markets or the ability to undertake activities so that only approved services, products or activities that comply with pre-required standards of competence and resource are allowed. The approval may be issued by a public authority, or by a private (trade or professional) body. The difference is that a public permit is usually granted where acting without such a permit is illegal and may lead to public sanctions being imposed. So only authorised people or activities are allowed by law. Approval by a private body usually brings reputational advantages, and falling below the requirements may lead to censure or expulsion from the body, rather than prosecution or other public sanctions.

Registration or *notification* are less onerous techniques. They have the primary objective of confirming to the public authorities (and the public or markets) the identity and other details of who is carrying out an activity, in case they need to be contacted. For example, if a problem arises with an activity or product, the person who is responsible for it should be able to be identified to confirm matters such as its composition and risk, and to undertake remedial action, including warning people or ceasing further activity. Registration can have an anti-fraud and security function, such as requiring beneficial owners of a company or bank account to be identified.

Licences and permits for activities are usually issued subject to *conditions* that the licensee must observe. This is functionally equivalent to publishing such rules in general legislation, but it is easier to amend conditions, and to calibrate them to the circumstances of particular licensees. In many sectors (such as financial services, communications, and utilities), licence conditions can be extensive. Breach of the conditions will, of course, trigger the right of the licensor to take enforcement action.

The OECD suggests that licensing and permitting should be used only as a last resort, when notifications or reporting are ineffective and the risk is high.[1] I would say that the selection of any regulatory tool depends on the circumstances, including the relevance and effectiveness of the complete combination of *ex ante* and *ex post* activity tools that may be relevant. What is collectively effective and proportionate in managing and reducing risks? For example, codes and standards may be effective rather than legal rules, but a combination of the two may be appropriate.

Private Assurance Schemes

Some systems involve both public and private actors who exercise 'regulatory' functions and authority. Private assurance schemes originated in professional or commercial contexts, often as requirements of trade bodies, and have been assimilated into public regulatory schemes.

Accreditation and assurance schemes are extensive in food and product manufacturing sectors. Leading types are:

- *accreditation or assurance*, where use of private accreditation systems confers certain legal advantages or presumptions of compliance;
- *auditing or inspection*, where checking of systems or activities is required by a public or private body;
- *certification*, where a trusted professional employed or contracted by a licence holder (such as a Qualified Person in the medicines system) uses personal professional expertise to certify compliance with specific requirements.

Operators obtain prior or regular certificates that activities, processes and systems comply with requirements (such as compliance with standards, certification of compliance with standards or accreditation systems, audits, inspections).

There can be considerable efficiency in avoiding duplication of public and private systems and relying on a fused system with appropriate 'delegated' components, such as in the global regulation of food, when used by actors in supply chains. An integration of public and private bodies is facilitated where a regulatory space comprises trusted partners. A spectrum of assurance techniques is available to provide users with information and communication about systems using AI so as to enable justified trust.[2]

Requirements for credible private schemes are that they have independent governance, ensuring an absence of conflicts of interest by being owned or influenced by the private bodies that they are there to certify (no marking of own homework), and that they have transparency of processes and substance.

Professional Competence

For *professionals* (eg lawyer, architect, surveyor, doctor, nurse, pharmacist, accountant, actuary, engineer, teacher, and many others), the key issue is technical *competence*, also encompassing professional ethics, both at the point of qualification, certification, approval or licensing, and on an ongoing basis. Hence, there is often an *approval* stage (given by either a public or private body) based on passing a required standard in professional or technical examinations. There are usually requirements to maintain professional expertise through *ongoing* education: continuous professional development (CPD) or even re-certification. Provision of professional services may also involve extra requirements, such as inspection and certification (eg building work).

The International Standard on Accreditation Engagements ISAE 3000 (Revised),[3] includes:

- suitable criteria: the benchmarks used to measure or evaluate the underlying subject matter (exhibiting characteristics of relevance, completeness, reliability, neutrality, understandability) and enable professional judgment;
- sufficient and appropriate evidence: assessing evidence against materiality to inform the assurance engagement risk.

Issues of professionalism and professional standards raise issues of *professional ethics* as well as technical competence. Membership of professional or trade bodies has for centuries typically required observance of a code of ethics and conduct. All traders in Germany who are members of the Association of Chambers of Commerce (DIHK) are required 'to work to uphold the decency and morals of the honourable merchant'.[4] This principle underpinning fair and ethical trade has applied since mediaeval Guilds. Since 2012, as a consequence of the Global Financial Crisis, bankers in the Netherlands have been required to take a Bankers' Oath to act in accordance with an ethical code.[5]

Authorised Competent Persons

Authority to authorise or provide certification of activities can be delegated to individuals even within commercial organisations. An example of this is a 'qualified person' in medicines regulation, certifying designated activities such as manufacturing, expert approval of tests, batches or marketing materials.[6] The Qualified Person holds technical qualifications and is subject to the ethical requirements of their profession, such as pharmacy, medicine, veterinary medicine, chemistry, pharmaceutical chemistry and technology, or biology. Professional conduct and ethical rules apply alongside the regulatory rules. Other examples are various competent person schemes in the construction industry.[7]

The Qualified Person is typically an employee of or consultant to the commercial company. There is a clear potential conflict of interest for the individual, who is subject to influences from their employer and the general public interest. The theory is that the strength of professional ethics overrides the commercial or personal employment interests.

Economic Regulation

Restrictions on access to the market, and conditions on operation by monopolies or oligopolies, are mentioned below. Controls on competition through merger control are noted in chapter 1. Specific economic tools that are used in economic regulation include taxes, subsidies, auctions, quotas and permits, vouchers, and public procurement. The primary objectives are to maintain fair markets, with fully informed consumer choice (over matters such as quality, complexity, relevance, efficiency, safety, price, support and ongoing service), and protection from abusive behaviour of various types. In recent years, strict economic theories have had to take account of the fact that many consumers do not behave, as economic theory predicts, as rational actors. Behavioural science, such as 'nudges' and other incentives and irrational behaviours, has assumed increasing practical importance.

Safety Regulation in General

Safety regulation is concerned with the safety in use of products and services, so regulatory controls are directed at the micro level to products and services and particular safety aspects, and at the macro level, the controls form an integrated *system* of control and, indeed, a control of such a system. Different product and service types have systems that vary in complexity and scope.

The complex end of the range includes aviation, nuclear, major construction projects, medicines, some medical devices, all of which have very extensive sets of rules covering relevant activities in the chain of design, testing, manufacture, marketing and ongoing vigilance. Cars, food, biocides, cosmetics, machinery, toys and so on have somewhat simpler control systems. The model for motor vehicles involves certifying a specified design, and then having a system that each individual item conforms to the same specification (type testing). Tests on the basic type may be extensive, such as a destructive 'crash test' to monitor the extent to which a human in a vehicle would be injured in a crash of a specific impact force. For some low risk products (eg toys, simple medical devices), manufacturers may self-certify against the regulatory requirements.

At the lightest end are 'general' product safety requirements, of a generalised kind (such as a requirement to market and distribute safe products and to have the means to withdraw unsafe products). Health and safety in the workplace has a general requirement to operate a safe system of work, supplemented by detailed specific requirements for different activities. Within this broad matrix, there is a considerable range of tools, especially at the more complex end.

Wider criteria are used in practice than just safety, for example for medicines (safety, efficacy and quality) or medical devices (safety and performance). Specific requirements may be placed on producers, distributors, retailers and even users.

Products

For products, the approach is to ensure the safety in use of individual products or a class of products. Thus, we can use individual testing and approval mechanisms, but also a generic control system through reliance on a *quality management system*, which is itself certified, that can encompass:

- the design process, controlled as a system, such as recording design documents and standards that are applied;
- testing of products or services, eg for medicines, toxicology (animal tests) and clinical trials (testing in human volunteers and then patients);
- contents or ingredients that are approved or of proved demonstrable quality, such as conforming with standards, eg for chemicals, cosmetics, biocides, food (Codex Alimentarius), medicines (Pharmacopoeia);
- manufacturing controls, eg a production process, motor vehicle type-testing. This will involve checking, auditing and approving the process on an ongoing basis, perhaps with sampling of individual products;
- labelling, information and marketing requirements;

- reporting certain events to the authorities;
- operating a post-marketing safety vigilance system, involving collecting data on harm or problems occurring (eg medicines Yellow Card reports to the Authority);
- operating a system for receiving complaints and resolving disputes, providing redress and repair (traditionally enforcement of private law rights based on breach of duty and proof of damage);
- operating a system for collection of consumer complaints or questions searched on websites;
- having a system that can notify users of safety issues and recall dangerous products;
- authorising authorities to intervene to require actions or support improvement.

The objective is maintenance of performance, identification of problems or harms, and the ability to respond so as to limit damage and provide repair and the reduction of future risk. Depending on the nature and complexity of the product, approval of individual items produced might rest more on having a trustworthy quality manufacturing *system* than having to examine every item individually.

Testing

Typical techniques to identify and evaluate risk involve testing, monitoring and investigating. The 1960s Thalidomide tragedy led to the creation of a logical, linear system of testing for the safety, quality and efficacy of medicines. Principal steps require tests on compounds in laboratories, toxicology in animals, a series of trials in humans involving larger doses and numbers of human volunteers and then patients, before a public authority reviews all the evidence and makes a decision on the issue of a licence (or licences) for marketing, advertising and distribution.

This is a logical, sequential systematic approach. It studies the risk profile of the product through a series of controlled escalations in numbers of human subjects and in dosage, also studying interactions with other substances. (However, it is relevant to note that complaints are made that pharma companies try to restrict publication of trials where results are not adequately positive. Having transparent access to all relevant information is the objective.)

It is now possible to improve on the system, for example by telescoping stages to run concurrently, or by improving the post-marketing surveillance system to reduce reliance on pre-market testing.

Sandboxes

An updated approach to testing is now developing, based on phased expansion of scale under close collaborative scrutiny between innovators and regulators. A *regulatory sandbox* was developed in 2006 by the Financial Conduct Authority (FCA). Its objective is to test products in controlled situations before wide release, sometimes without any rules applying other than close cooperative study on effects and outcomes by the business and regulator involved. The sandbox technique has spread quickly around the world, in multiple sectors.[8]

There are various different forms of sandbox and, necessarily, no uniform approach so as to be able to cater to different situations. Further clarity needs to develop around a consistent understanding of different types, eg:

- suspension of all pre-existing rules;
- continuation of all rules, but close scrutiny;
- something in between, where some rules or procedures or data requirements are suspended.

Making full use of this significant regulatory technique requires power to be delegated from slow-moving legislative mechanisms (Parliament or Ministers) so that flexibility and discretion can accommodate reasonable responses to differing situations, in which some risk is accepted whilst there remains a guarantee that harms will be swiftly identified and responded to. Sandboxes also need trust to work, and this aspect is often overlooked.

Information and Disclosure

Regulation of information falls into two broad categories, as noted by Anthony Ogus: *mandatory disclosure*, which obliges suppliers to provide information relating to price, identity, composition, quantity or quality; and the *control of false or misleading information*.[9] Primary objectives for information regulation are to ensure that safety is maintained by or for users and bystanders, and that markets operate fairly. Thus, the Advertising Standards Authority aims to uphold the principles that advertising is 'legal, decent, honest and truthful'.[10] Statements should be prohibited that are, for example, untrue, unfair or unsubstantiated.

Some typical controls categorised by Ogus, depending on the particular type of product, service or activity, cover:

- *Mandatory Price Disclosure*, which is crucial for consumer choice and for efficient, competitive markets.
- *Quantity Disclosure.* Accuracy of weights and measures.
- *Identity and Quality Disclosure.* Composition and designation, or other quality indicators, eg energy consumption of domestic appliances, durability, reliability and safety, use of British Standard (BS) and Kitemark, a symbol that the product complies with the relevant standard and that the manufacturing process and sample items are periodically tested.
- *Securities and Financial Disclosure.*
- *Warnings and Instructions for Use.*
- *Controls on Misleading Information; Trade Descriptions.*

Both information provided *with* a product or service, and marketing and advertising information provided before, accompanying or after delivery of an activity or thing, are relevant and can be subject to general or regime-specific rules.

Financial Products and Services

Particular features of the recent evolution of financial services regulation have been to set ethical principles, and to try to supervise all staff, and especially senior officers, and the culture of regulated institutions.

Principles for Businesses

The FCA applies 12 Principles for Businesses to every authorised firm, either to part or all of its business, depending on the nature of the business it carries out.[11] Together, they outline the minimum requirements for conduct that an authorised firm must meet.

1 Integrity	A firm must conduct its business with integrity.
2 Skill, care and diligence	A firm must conduct its business with due skill, care and diligence.
3 Management and control	A firm must take reasonable care to organise and control its affairs responsibly and effectively, with adequate risk management systems.
4 Financial prudence	A firm must maintain adequate financial resources.
5 Market conduct	A firm must observe proper standards of market conduct.
6 Customers' interests	A firm must pay due regard to the interests of its customers and treat them fairly.
7 Communications with clients	A firm must pay due regard to the information needs of its clients, and communicate information to them in a way which is clear, fair and not misleading.
8 Conflicts of interest	A firm must manage conflicts of interest fairly, both between itself and its customers and between a customer and another client.
9 Customers: relationships of trust	A firm must take reasonable care to ensure the suitability of its advice and discretionary decisions for any customer who is entitled to rely upon its judgment.
10 Clients' assets	A firm must arrange adequate protection for clients' assets when it is responsible for them.
11 Relations with regulators	A firm must deal with its regulators in an open and cooperative way, and must disclose to the FCA appropriately anything relating to the firm of which that regulator would reasonably expect notice.
12 Consumer Duty	A firm must act to deliver good outcomes for retail customers.

Senior Managers and Certification Regime (SM&CR)

Following the Global Financial Crisis of 2008, a hierarchy of supervisory regimes was introduced for individuals working in financial institutions. This is described as follows:

> The SM&CR is an individual accountability regime. It aims to promote the safety and soundness of regulated financial services firms, reduce harm to consumers and strengthen conduct and market integrity by creating a system that enables firms and regulators to hold individuals within firms, and particularly senior decision-makers, to account.[12]

The Financial Conduct Authority later explained the regime like this:[13]

> *How the SM&CR works*
>
> The most senior people performing key roles in a firm need our approval before they can start that role. ...
>
> The basic principle of the SM&CR is about accountability and responsibility. A senior manager has to take responsibility for the activities under their control. Likewise, they should be accountable for that responsibility. ... Firms must also allocate specific prescribed responsibilities to individual senior managers. For example, being responsible for the policies and procedures for tackling the risk that the firm might be used for financial crime. Requiring a firm to allocate these prescribed responsibilities helps ensure that SMF holders are accountable for the key conduct and prudential risks that a firm faces.
>
> Every SMF holder must have a statement of responsibility, which clearly sets out their roles and responsibilities. Some firms must have a responsibilities map, which sets out the firm's management and governance arrangements. The responsibilities map must include details on who has overall responsibility for the firm's activities, business areas and management functions and how responsibilities have been allocated.
>
> The Certification Regime applies to staff whose roles mean they could potentially cause significant harm to the firm or consumers. People performing these roles do not need our approval before they start their job. However, firms need to check and confirm that these people are fit and proper to perform their role at least once a year, taking into account factors including their level of competence, qualifications and training. An example of a certification function is someone who gives advice to consumers, such as a financial adviser or investment manager.

The Conduct Rules are a new set of rules we can enforce that set out the minimum standards of good personal conduct against which we can hold people to account.

The UK hierarchy of rules is:

- *Conduct Rules:* these set minimum standards of conduct for all professional employees, together with additional rules applicable to Senior Managers.
- *Certification Regime:* this covers functions at the firm that are not Senior Management Functions (SMFs) and that have a material impact on risks to customers and the risk profile of the firm.
- *Senior Managers Regime (SMR):* Senior Managers hold one or more roles designated as SMFs. The individuals holding such roles are the firm's most senior individuals. These include executive roles, such as chief executives and finance directors, as well as some oversight roles, such as chairs of boards and their sub-committees and senior independent directors.

Under the SMR, individuals must be approved as fit and proper by their firm and the regulators, prior to appointment. In assessing fitness and propriety, firms and regulators consider three areas: honesty, integrity and reputation; competence and capability; and financial soundness.

In ensuring an effective system of individual accountability, firms and regulators need to be clear about the key responsibilities of each Senior Manager. To that end:

- Senior Managers must have a Statement of Responsibilities (SoR), a single document that sets out their responsibilities. This is prepared by the firm and shared with the regulators. The responsibilities include those inherent in a Senior Manager's role.
- Firms must also allocate a set of mandatory prescribed responsibilities (PRs) across their Senior Managers.
- Dual-regulated firms and enhanced solo-regulated firms must prepare and maintain a Management Responsibilities Map (MRM). This is a firm-wide document that contains summary information covering the names of each Senior Manager and their responsibilities, the allocation of the prescribed responsibilities among Senior Managers and details of the firm's governance arrangements.

The SM&CR approach was mandated under the Financial Markets and Services Act 2000 for all banks, building societies and credit unions. The approach was subsequently extended to cover designated investment firms in 2016 and insurance firms in December 2018. The regime was further extended to most other regulated financial firms from December 2019 and benchmark administrators from December 2020.

Official reviews of the SM&CR reported that they had supported higher professional standards and 'had brought about positive changes to behaviours'.[14] After a review of the regime agreed between banks and government in 2023,[15] it was announced in 2025 that the regime would undergo 'radical streamlining', including removing the Certification Regime from legislation, and reducing those subject to pre-approval under the Senior Managers Regime by around 40%.[16]

The UK approach has been copied in other leading jurisdictions. Australia introduced its Bank Executive Accountability Regime (BEAR) in 2018, Ireland established a Senior Executive Accountability Regime (SEAR), and proposed guidelines were issued by the Monetary Authority of Singapore (MAS) with a view to implementing a similar accountability regime.[17] Hong Kong's Securities and Futures Commission (SFC) introduced a Managers-in-Charge (MiC) regime in 2017, and the Hong Kong Monetary Authority (HKMA) has been developing a bank culture reform programme.

Culture

Evidence of motivation within organisations requires evidence of their culture. Culture is a general qualitative summary description of the prevalent behaviours of individuals in a group, predictive of future behaviour. Extensive research by business schools into effective companies has identified the importance of organisational culture – and especially whether an ethical culture exists or not – as relevant to whether or not a firm is successful, and also whether it has a high risk of generating breaches of legal rules.

As Edgar Schein said, the concept of culture implies 'structural stability, breadth, and patterning or integration' which results from the fact that culture is a learned phenomenon for a group.[18] After a lifetime studying different cultures, Geert Hofstede described culture as the collective programming of the mind that distinguishes the members of one group of people from another.[19] It is shown in patterns of thinking, feeling and acting, based on what a person considers to be right and wrong, and to be normal, rational and logical. Hofstede believed that such programming is a product of two factors: social environment and the experiences collected during life.[20] He noted that culture is a means of comparing societies, whereas values compare individuals.[21]

Benjamin van Rooij and Adam Fine analysed why the corporate cultures at BP, Volkswagen and Wells Fargo had become 'toxic', and concluded that the causes were less to do with deliberate law-breaking but lay in the fact that the accumulated strength of the social norms and culture overpowered the external legal rules.[22] In all three companies studied, the causative combination of factors was described as leading to cultures: (a) that condoned, neutralised or enabled rule breaking; (b) that disabled and obstructed compliance systems; and (c) where actual practices contrasted with expressed compliant values. They noted literature on unethical climates that highlighted: (a) the way organisations deal with errors and their type of management culture; (b) how differentiation between employees can be perceived as unfair and give rise to envy and disengagement; and (c) dysfunctional ethical climates.[23] They concluded that organisations should address the *structures, values and practices* that enable violations and obstruct compliance within an organisation, as well as move away from a singular focus on liability management (ie, assigning blame and punishment) to an approach that prioritises promoting transparency, honesty, and a responsibility to initiate and sustain actual cultural change.

Poor corporate culture was identified as a major cause of the 2008 Global Financial Crisis. From around 2010, the Dutch Central Bank led a series of interventions with banks, especially attending board meetings.[24] Many financial regulators around the globe subsequently made attempts to control, or influence, the cultures of the banks.[25] The problem is that the particular culture of any organisation is an artefact of its *internal* values, behaviours and leadership. It cannot be regulated externally. One of the most powerful tools was created in the Netherlands, where all bankers are required to swear a Dutch Bankers' Oath, which is taken very seriously.[26]

However, three highly significant streams of regulatory responses occurred. First, a duty of directors to promote 'the desired' culture of a firm, and ensure that it is aligned with its purpose, values and strategy, has been included in corporate governance codes, such as core requirements of the 2016 revision of the UK Corporate Governance Code.[27] This development is linked with the spread of corporate attention towards 'corporate social responsibility' (CSR) and environmental, social and governance issues and outcomes (ESG).

Second, major institutional investors (such as BlackRock and State Street) have increasingly insisted that companies must focus on corporate culture as a requirement for investment sustainability.

Third, financial regulators around the world instituted attempts at 'controlling' organisational culture. However, these attempts have had limited impact. Bankers in, for example, the UK,[28] the Netherlands and Australia[29] have introduced ethics-based codes, but there has been little to counteract the effect of the target and remuneration cultures. Some financial regulators have imposed regimes requiring assessment and accountability of staff, such as the UK's SM&CR noted above.

The Financial Conduct Authority said in 2016 in relation to the SM&CR that:[30]

> The aim of these regimes is to reduce consumer harm and strengthen market integrity by making individuals more accountable for their conduct and competence. The regimes are designed to:
> - encourage a culture in which staff at all levels take personal responsibility for their actions, and
> - ensure firms and staff clearly understand and can demonstrate where responsibility lies.

In 2018 it explained its 'focus on culture and governance' as follows:[31]

> We look at what drives behaviour within a firm. We address the key drivers of behaviour which are likely to cause harm. These include the firm's purpose (as it is understood by its employees), the attitude, behaviour, competence and compliance of the firm's leadership, the firm's approach to managing and rewarding people (eg staff competence and incentives), and the firm's governance arrangements, controls and key processes (eg for whistleblowing or complaint handling).

The Financial Stability Board issued in 2018 the following list of tools, in which there are multiple references to cultural 'drivers of misconduct' and one reference to 'desired cultural features':[32]

<u>Mitigating cultural drivers of misconduct</u>

Firms

Tool 1: *Senior leadership of the firm articulate desired cultural features that mitigate the risk of misconduct.*

Tool 2: *Identify significant cultural drivers of misconduct by reviewing a broad set of information and using multidisciplinary techniques.*

Tool 3: *Act to shift behavioural norms to mitigate cultural drivers of misconduct.*

National authorities

Tool 4: *Build a supervisory programme focused on culture to mitigate the risk of misconduct.*

Tool 5: *Use a risk-based approach to prioritise for review the firms or groups of firms that display significant cultural drivers of misconduct.*

Tool 6: *Use a broad range of information and techniques to assess the cultural drivers of misconduct at firms.*

Tool 7: *Engage firms' leadership with respect to observations on culture and misconduct.*

<u>Strengthening individual responsibility and accountability</u>

Firms and/or national authorities

Tool 8: *Identify key responsibilities, including mitigation of the risk of misconduct, and assign them.*

Tool 9: *Hold individuals accountable.*

Tool 10: *Assess the suitability of individuals assigned key responsibilities.*

National authorities

Tool 11: *Develop and monitor a responsibility and accountability framework.*

Tool 12: *Coordinate with other authorities.*

<u>Addressing the rolling bad apples phenomenon</u>

Firms

Tool 13: *Communicate conduct expectations early and consistently in recruitment and hiring processes.*

Tool 14: *Enhance interviewing techniques.*

Tool 15: *Leverage multiple sources of available information before hiring.*

Tool 16: *Reassess employee conduct regularly.*

Tool 17: *Conduct 'exit reviews'.*

National authorities

Tool 18: *Supervise firms' practices for screening prospective employees and monitoring current employees.*

Tool 19: *Promote compliance with legal or regulatory requirements regarding conduct-related information about applicable employees, where these exist.*

In 2021, the UK's FCA accepted that culture is difficult to measure and assess and that it is still developing its role in relation to approaching culture, for the moment viewing it through four lenses – purpose, people, leadership and governance – and using a range of supervisory and enforcement tools to address any issues it identifies, whilst seeking assurance from firms that they are guarding their organisations' culture against threats.[33]

The FCA said that its SM&CR 'supports firms' development of *a culture of responsibility* to identify the harm developing from their behaviour and take steps to address the *risk*' (emphasis added).[34] The FCA applies five conduct rules:[35]

- act with integrity
- act with due care, skill and diligence
- be open and cooperative with the FCA, the PRA and other regulators
- pay due regard to the interests of customers and treat them fairly
- observe proper standards of market conduct.

Limitations in Harnessing Culture as a Regulatory Tool

How effective have these approaches been? Despite considerable effort being expended on means of measuring and delivering ethical cultures, challenges remain high and results are as yet unclear.[36]

A significant finding by the FCA in 2019 was that: 'Firms have found it challenging to find appropriate ways of measuring culture and the effort to do so is continuing. Firms told us that the regime is having an impact on the mindset of senior managers. However, SM&CR is primarily enabling firms to improve their controls environment, which they expect to lead to improved behaviours. It is not clear to what extent the regime has been linked to culture.'[37] The FCA's 2020 review found that speaking up was still unsafe, and it reported pertinent findings on the timing and substance of responding to good and poor behaviour.[38]

The Group of Thirty (G30) concluded in 2019[39] that there had been some changes in the accountability regimes of senior management, in performance management, incentives and remuneration, in staff training, and much talk of 'tone from the top' and little on 'tone from above'[40] and on embedding culture awareness and stewardship at all levels of the organisation. But overall, the outcomes were 'slow progress and uneven results'. It even referred to there being 'culture fatigue'.

The Australian Bank Executive Accountability Regime (BEAR) is reported to have produced greater clarity, and an empowering effect, so decisions get made, problems get resolved and there is greater care and diligence.[41] However, these changes were related to personality types, and a 'fear effect' was also noted.

Major problems are that culture is very difficult to measure or control (certainly by external or regulatory means). The most important influences on an organisation's culture are internal, such as actions by leaders and between colleagues, and the core beliefs of all. Some influences, such as incentives for employees to focus on particular goals, will distract or 'crowd out' other (maybe more ethical) behaviours. Thus, a strong focus on achieving financial targets, especially if linked to triggering any, or high, remuneration, may distort behaviours and drive particular cultures.

Surely, the real point is to focus on trusted individuals and trusted institutions and systems. This needs not just competent but trusted individuals who have reputations for behaving well and professionally.

Open and Just Culture in Aviation Safety

As noted in chapter 4, a critical element of the maintenance of safety in aviation is the adoption of an 'open and just culture' across and within *all institutions* involved in the system. It is this culture that is essential in allowing everyone to take responsibility for the performance of their functions, for sharing all information however embarrassing, and hence for the maintenance of mutual trust between all actors. Identifying relevant learning needs multiple perspectives to understand systemic and situational root causation, so everyone's observations will be important to contribute. The culture of open sharing is possible because everyone feels psychological safety.[42] The major point here is that all the organisations and actors are motivated to adopt and maintain the required 'open and just culture'. They nurture it; it is not imposed on them.

Regulatory Culture

The UK's 2014 Regulators' Code specifies the following principles:[43]

1. Regulators should carry out their activities in a way that supports those they regulate to comply and grow

2. Regulators should provide simple and straightforward ways to engage with those they regulate and hear their views
3. Regulators should base their regulatory activities on risk
4. Regulators should share information about compliance and risk
5. Regulators should ensure clear information, guidance and advice is available to help those they regulate meet their responsibilities to comply
6. Regulators should ensure that their approach to their regulatory activities is transparent

The New Zealand Productivity Commission identified the following attributes of 'favourable regulator culture':[44]

- embrace the organisation's role as an educator and facilitator of compliance (rather than simply an enforcer of rules)
- place a high value on robust, evidence-based regulatory decisions
- value operational flexibility and adaption to changes in the regulatory environment
- value continuous learning at all levels of the organisation (ie, 'learning cultures')
- internal debate is the norm and where a 'speak-up' culture empowers staff to raise issues
- stress the importance of being open, transparent and accountable
- place great value on organisational independence and impartiality
- recognise the significance of the civic responsibility that comes with using the coercive powers of the state
- subcultures align with the overarching objectives of the organisation

By 2020 New Zealand had devoted significant effort in developing the idea of professionalism amongst regulators, working with a three-pillar model of people capability, organisational capability and the development of a professional community.[45]

Using Trust as a Regulatory Tool

In systems involving multiple actors and data sources, evidence of the trustworthiness of each actor and data source powerfully supports reliance and enables collaboration. Where adequate evidence of trustworthiness of actors is demonstrated, it may well lead to opportunities to slim down traditional requirements, thereby reducing barriers and burdens.

If trust is present, reliance on the need to check compliance with multiple rules can be deconstructed.

Traditional evidence of compliance with rules would include: appliance of certain standards; operation of management systems for financial probity, design and manufacturing quality systems; accreditation against assurance systems plus periodic inspections/audits; annual reports; compliant systems and so on.

Under a trust-based OBCR regime, evidence of trustworthiness should be provided by all actors, to demonstrate their competence, resource, intent and commitment to achieve the desired outcomes, behaviours and track record. The exact nature and extent of such evidence will vary from sector to sector, and with the nature and scale of the outcomes and of the relevant actors. Data produced by the ecosystem that demonstrates the collective achievement of the agreed outcomes, and the contributions of different actors to such delivery, will be powerful and transformative.

A number of private sector schemes aim to provide third party verification of 'trusted company' status, such as Good Corporations, BCorp and TrustMark. These can include evidence such as feedback and surveys from staff, experts, customers, investors and stakeholders. Powerful evidence can be found in how people react when things go wrong, such as unexpected harm occurring: was it misbelieved, ignored, buried, or was it properly assessed and appropriate changes instituted?

Key Points

- The purpose of *ex ante* controls is to identify risk and reduce harm in advance.
- This can traditionally give rise to requirements for extensive testing.
- There are currently various ways in which duration, scope and requirements for advance data can be produced more quickly. Sandboxes and other forms of close collaboration and scrutiny are being widely adopted. A system that identifies potential harm swiftly, including in the post-marketing phase, may reduce pre-marketing requirements.
- Other techniques focus on the trustworthiness of senior managers, and of regulatory and organisational cultures. These can be developed further.

B. During: Monitoring and Surveillance

The Objectives of Monitoring and Surveillance

The purposes here are to identify problems, issues, occurrence of harm, and an increase in risk, or occurrence of risks not previously identified. What's going on, and what's going wrong? What could be improved? This approach contrasts with the traditional approach, which aims to monitor that systems are being operated in accordance with the rules.

It has long been recognised that pre-market evaluation of test data only gives a certain level of confidence in the safety of a product or service in widespread use, and that constant ongoing evaluation is necessary. The pharmaceutical example is the Post-Marketing Vigilance (PMS) system, in which data on use in patients (but, curiously, not necessarily *from* patients themselves) is collected and reviewed. Many safety systems (aviation, nuclear, food, water, retail products) entail the analysis of data at different 'levels', involving companies, third parties and regulators.

The truth is that many harms and risks simply cannot be identified without the contribution and involvement of all types of stakeholders. This is especially true given the pace of events and technologies in the world we now live in and its Fourth Industrial Age. How are we going to know quickly enough of the harms that might be produced by innovative AI, quantum technologies, engineering biology and other things *unless* we get a complete and swift picture of what is happening? If children are harmed by online abuse, or scientists undertake unethical experiments, or our political views are affected by fake news, *how* is this going to be identified? Someone always knows. But do they pass on this information? How will they do this quickly and effectively so that the problem will be identified and action taken?

There are two main traditional tools here: *inspecting* and *reporting*. Inspections can be by public officials and/or by private accreditation or auding bodies. The outputs may identify a list of non-compliance with particular legal rules, procedures or standards, and perhaps a certification of compliance. Reporting involves manufacturers and distributors observing a rule to notify specified types of information or events, perhaps only yearly, to a public authority or in a public report. But these techniques are now, by themselves, out of date. It is difficult to see that either technique will deliver anything like an adequately responsive system in the face of 21st century risks. The OECD concluded: 'Comparative research has shown that a high number of inspections do not guarantee greater levels of compliance, and many sanctions do not necessarily safeguard the public.'[46] How will the traditional objective of achieving compliance with rules deliver adequate control?

The aim now should be to *monitor what's actually happening*, good and bad, and identify what needs attention – in systems, outcomes, risks and harms. We currently have a critical opportunity to shift from collecting data by manual means and inspections to a mode of constant collection of data by digital systems. We need to use digital tools on a systemic basis. We need to have a system that gathers data from all relevant sources – and this requires a collaborative ecosystem. Everyone should contribute. This is exactly what OBC aims to achieve. It recognises that collaboration in monitoring, sharing information and taking action is essential. Inspection, auditing, certification and reporting remain relevant, but as tools in a bigger picture.

So, in summary, the objectives in monitoring and surveillance are:

(1) To ensure that ongoing activities and systems deliver appropriate protection:
  (a) Control systems operate as they should.
  (b) Systems that may be needed to respond to unexpected risks or harms are fit for purpose.
(2) To ensure that problems, harms and risks are *identified swiftly*, and notified to those responsible for scrutinising them.
(3) In systems involving OBC relationships, to ensure that the agreed Outcomes are being achieved as intended.

Under a systemic approach, there are three main types of activities: *monitoring*, *investigating*, and *assessing*. In each system, it needs to be decided who takes responsibility for performing these functions. In a systemic model of a sophisticated regulatory space, they are not just functions of a public authority. They can be shared between public and private actors. The monitoring function, especially, can be a shared responsibility between the primary regulatees, accreditation and auditing bodies and public bodies. The following chart summarises the three functions and the powers associated with them that need to be available (usually powers of a public authority, but sometimes powers authorised by statute or membership of a trade/professional body). However, the powers should be regarded as invoked as a long stop, since proper collaboration between actors to achieve the three functions should take place automatically.

Table 7.1 Powers Needed to Deliver Specific Objectives

Function/objective	Powers
Monitor: to identify harm and risk; and to measure achieving the desired outcomes	A comprehensive data collection system Checking that systems and procedures are being operated satisfactorily Taking samples and testing Operate a post-market surveillance system: defining who performs what functions Review data on individual and market practices
Investigate: verify	Triggered by noting signals Undertake an investigation to verify facts and root causes Enter premises Require answers to questions
Assess risk and harm	Ability to involve multiple experts, usually in standing expert committees, sometimes international

Data Collection

The monitoring function operates on the basis of data. The core questions are: who has the relevant data that is needed to monitor the system and its outcomes, how is it shared, and who keeps it? In many regulatory systems, data needs to be held confidentially by a trusted independent organisation, which can guarantee that confidential and sensitive data remains only available to those who are authorised to see it, but that the totality of the data, where necessary anonymised, is available to authorised persons so as to provide an accurate and swift presentation of what is happening in the system.

Data should be generated automatically by a production/supply system or by feedback from use and the market. Data can be created constantly about the operation of any process or system, and can identify effective operative performance or the existence of problems. Auditing, inspection and certification may still be needed and results should be recorded. There needs to be agreement on what data is escalated to what level in the control system, and what is made public.

Public portals can be efficient places to provide information to users and be self-monitoring tools. For example, a public register of all properties that are rented will be useful verified information for tenants and contain uploaded certificates on insurance and fire control.

The UK Drinking Water Inspector aggregates testing data from every water company to produce a risk matrix across all suppliers.[47]

If such a system is to operate well, it needs to be designed to capture as much data as possible. Thus, it needs to be a simple, easily identifiable, single, central collection point of data on questions, complaints and disputes. It is essential that data should not continue to be collected by multiple unconnected points in a system, such as by different websites, or by a regulator as well as an Ombuds. The system should produce aggregated data that enables an overview to be taken of the extent to which outcomes are being achieved, and unacceptable harms are occurring. The data controller could continue to be the regulator, but it is more efficient and effective in many contexts if the data controller is independent. Independence gives confidence to both consumers and traders. It helps if multiple Ombuds acting in different sectors form an integrated network, as in Belgium.

Some Examples of New Approaches

Ombuds

In consumer markets, data from consumer complaints have been collated for some decades by consumer associations, but especially by sectoral Ombuds. Clearly, aggregation of data from individual complaints is powerful evidence of what consumers see about the behaviour, safety and quality of goods and services that they use. Ombuds have aggregated this data for some years, and used it highly effectively in holding up a mirror to traders about their activities. Ombuds typically relay their aggregate data regularly to companies to identify issues that companies should attend to, about a wide range of market behaviours.

Having a single consumer website (such as that of the Belgian Ombuds) provides a useful focus for attracting extensive consumer information, and it can also signpost a portal for making complaints. It attracts and collates extensive data on what consumers are concerned about, for example through use of AI analysis of the questions that consumers ask, which provides powerful evidence in revealing issues that consumers are concerned about.

Safe Food Production Queensland

The following recent experience of adopting an OBCR approach has kindly been contributed by Brian Witherspoon of SFQ:[48]

> The traditional regulatory toolkit includes: accreditation, verification studies/surveillance, food safety programs, audit (incl. third party), investigations and enforcement, and inspection. In our transformation, we have developed our regulatory toolkit more towards using a different set of tools, such as:
>
> - Preferred Supplier Arrangements (PSAs), such as with dairy. We no longer do routine audits: they do. They share data with us and we work together if concerns arise
> - Food safety notifications; business identifies an issue and tells us, then we work with them, on the basis of 'Let's problem solve this together'. This has worked well, and has built up a lot of trust.
> - Food safety assessment (Compliance Assessment System) rather than audits. This involves a commitment to manage those risks, effectively a culture management approach.
> - Online accreditation register for transparency and to help businesses and consumers verify what businesses are accredited.
> - Food safety management statements: short sharp documented system, as opposed to detailed, complex food safety programs.
> - Co-created baselines: with industry. The first was with poultry suppliers, for all activities in the supply chain. Questions were: Does this reflect your operation? How do you see yourself in this, making it work? This helped SFQ understand what *they* do. What control points apply? Stability of the system. Industry agreed all the targets (not in legislation). We worked out the baselines. The sequence of best practice is in stages with baselines; compliance just falls into place.
> - Data sharing (Central Information Management System). Data is already being collected – we want to use this, not just get people just to

collect data for us. We are continually improving the system, and this involves more and closer engagement. The businesses are sharing more information amongst themselves, recognising that this is in their best interests.

SFQ found that 'one size does *not* fit all' actors, and there needs to be an approach tailored to activities, resources, competences and risks. In order to shift to new approaches, SFQ has undertaken a Digital Transformation Programme (DTP) based on the strategic priorities of: expanding its positive influence and impact; leading the way in regulation innovation; transforming its corporate capabilities; and strengthening its scientific contribution. The components of the DTP have been: a new regulatory delivery framework; a new operating model; a workforce strategy, and a digital platform. The new regulatory delivery framework (and evolution of the pre-existing approach) was created to harness digital technology; recognise the importance of genuine collaboration and engagement with all food supply chain participants; proactively manage risk; and recognise that food safety is critical, but only one element in Queensland's broader food system. It enables a circular, joined-up system, and includes the United Nations' Sustainable Development Goals.

A co-creation approach with the horticulture industry resulted in a new code-based system with the goal of being:

> a collaborative regulatory environment in which:
> - all participants understand their roles and responsibilities in ensuring our food is safe, and
> - work together to problem solve and overcome the challenges we face now and into the future.[49]

UK Food Standards Authority

The UK Food Standards Authority launched a project with five supermarkets, agreeing a data management programme to replace multiple inspections of local branches across the country. Local environmental health inspectors (EHIs) typically spent 95% of their time inspecting supermarkets. But the supermarkets had high standards and significant in-house expert resources. The 'Alternative Business Compliance' (ABC) project[50] was independently assessed as entirely successful.[51] The arrangements included the features of a systematic data management system (which not all supermarkets outside the trial possessed, and involved some changes that were agreed for those taking part in the project), the type and nature of the data that the supermarkets would collect, and who would scrutinise this and raise issues with others. General reviews take place at six monthly relationship meetings. In practice, data scrutiny is constant and is undertaken by trusted partners.

This project demonstrates the power of transforming systems through use of digital data systems and trustworthy partnerships. There would be a realignment between public and private actors of functions in the regulatory space, no diminution in safety, but considerable increase in efficiency. The same approach could be envisaged in many other sectors. For those businesses that are scrutinised by multiple regulators, there are considerable opportunities for efficiency by using a single data set of material that demonstrates trust and performance.

Future Opportunities

It is possible to envisage extension of these projects both 'horizontally' across other major retailers, involving food and other products, and 'vertically', involving manufacturers, farmers and down supply chains. A single global governance structure can be envisaged, combining representatives of all groups of stakeholders. National or supranational governments would be represented, but need not all be actively involved in delivering or controlling every activity.

Markets and Economic Regulation

The three domains that we identified in chapter 1 – competition law, economic regulation and consumer protection – all have distinct modes of control and 'enforcement'.

Competition law is largely *reactive*. It is a classic rule-breach-enforce model. Thus, it has no pre-marketing requirements as such, other than that it is expected that large companies will need to undertake internal measures to deliver compliance, such as having monitoring systems, training and responsible officers. The basic assumptions of this area of law are that companies can dominate markets, which can lead to behaviour that is unfair and restricts competition, and to prices being artificially high, a chilling of innovation, and keeping new and disruptive players out of the market. Competition authorities exist in every advanced state to guard against such abuse and bad outcomes. They need to have state authority to be able to stand up to powerful businesses. They are typically empowered to undertake a market inquiry to determine if the law has been broken – this can be a complex technical inquiry. Proposed mergers must be *notified* to the authority, which may undertake an investigation to determine if the result will be an unacceptable concentration of market power, and thus ban or impose conditions on the merger.

Economic regulation rests strongly on imposition of conditions and requirements in marketing licences, breach of which may trigger penalties. It also controls prices that can be charged through the mechanism of periodic reviews of whether prices are fair and justified in terms of the need for effective operation, investment and making profits that can be paid to shareholders.

Controls aimed at *consumer protection*, outside the area of prices, have developed to cover the *behaviour* of providers of regulated utilities and unregulated traders towards consumers. For example, aspects might include: delivering a consistent level of service; responding swiftly, politely and effectively to interruptions in service and to requests or complaints; and treating people well and considering their viewpoints and needs.

Key Points

- The purpose of controls during the marketing of a product or service, or the operation of a market, is to identify risk and reduce harm through monitoring and surveillance techniques.
- The essence here is collection and analysis of data.
- Traditional techniques of requiring reporting of certain occurrences, or of inspections, are being transformed by more comprehensive systems of data collection from multiple stakeholders.
- Collaborative systems, involving comprehensive collection of data and its management by independent data controllers, offer potentially huge benefits.

C. After: Responding to Problems

The Objectives of Regulatory Interventions

Expanding on the RFM, the guiding objectives of responding to problems in a post-marketing context are as follows:

(1) Overriding objectives:
- To achieve the goals and outcomes of the particular protection regime, especially increasing safety and fairness.
- To deliver appropriate protection from risk and harm.

(2) Looking forward:
- To cease specific ongoing harm or risk that has been identified, so that the previous equilibrium of safety and fairness is re-established.
- To make relevant changes (whether in behaviour, systems, procedures, codes, rules and how things are done) so that ongoing and future risk is reduced. This involves:
  - investigating and collecting and collating relevant data;
  - analysing the root cause of the issue (which may involve looking at an issue from multiple viewpoints);
  - identifying effective and proportionate steps to reduce risk to an acceptable level;
  - ensuring that appropriate changes are implemented, so that the same harm does not occur again, and/or the future risk is reduced;
  - monitoring to see if any further changes are needed, and implementing them.
- To encourage the collaboration, motivation, commitment of, and effective actions by, the actor(s) to deliver protection and compliance in future, particularly by doing the right thing, and produce evidence of trustworthiness.

(3) Looking backward:
- Aim to ensure the commitment of, and effective actions by, the actor(s) to rectify and redress harm or loss caused by their non-compliance.

- To rectify and repair harm or imbalance in markets.
- Ensure that any financial gain or benefit from non-compliance is removed.
- Repairing harm caused. This means ensuring that redress is paid, and that all illicit gains are removed from the perpetrator.

A simple slogan might describe the basic outcomes that people want to see as: STOP, REPAIR, PREVENT, PROTECT, SIGNAL.

Comments on the Objectives

The list of objectives above contrasts with the traditional approach, which might simply impose sanctions in response to non-compliance with rules, on the assumption that that will increase compliance and deter non-compliance. As we've seen above, that simplistic approach is fundamentally misguided: the evidence is that it neither achieves protection nor other desired outcomes. The aim is *not* to deter or punish. It is to protect, and to demonstrate that the ethical values and rules are being observed and upheld. The response from bystanders to effective responsive regulatory action should be: that's right and fair.

The list of steps set out above should form the basis of the agreed common approach to problems, guiding regulators, regulatees and stakeholders as to how they should act and work together. It should also provide the matrix of accountability for any actor, such as a regulatee who has not entered into an OBCR commitment, and should provide the matrix against which such responses as occur are evaluated. Regulators should have powers to order or achieve all of these functions, as a fallback in case regulatees fail to respond in cooperating to deliver them.

These steps will be best achieved through full collaboration and sharing of information and expertise between relevant actors and the authority. Such collaboration, or its absence, will be a relevant factor to take into account in determining if any formal consequence, such as a reprimand or sanction, is used.

Markets and Economic Regulation

The practice of economic regulation has been dominated by economic theory. This has a number of consequences. It can lead to the following problems:

- Failure to conceptualise interventions and enforcement in any terms other than imposition of sanctions, especially financial sanctions. In economic theory, fines and damages have equivalent effect on companies. But this may simply be ineffective in terms of affecting behaviour towards consumers. It can be expensed as a 'cost of business'. Fines on public organisations penalise taxpayers or the users of public services (such as patients).

- Emphasis on the public law aspects and imposition of public sanctions can overlook the importance of achieving redress for consumers, and hence leave consumers, SMEs and others to claim damages in court or bring other civil procedures. This can lead to consecutive public and private litigation, leaving deserving individuals uncompensated for many years.

Cessation and redress should be the first priorities. There can be too much emphasis just on enforcement and sanctions. Some authorities have powers to order or approve redress to multiple consumers, but not all authorities use them.

Distinguishing between Actors: Two Modes

The conclusions from Part A of this book are that in responding to actors who may be involved in regulatory problems or harm, we need to distinguish between different types of people and organisations, and to select the right mode of engagement and tools. In chapter 6, we identified a distinction between two modes of engagement: a Supportive Intervention Mode and a Protection Mode. Let us summarise the approaches to each.

Supportive Intervention Mode

In this mode, we are responding to problems where something has gone wrong that involves honest, well-meaning, honourable people trying to do their normal productive job to contribute to society. There could be quite a few reasons why things have gone wrong, such as lack of focus, resource, time, expertise, competence, experience, or just inadvertent mistakes and bad luck.

The objectives here are the core ones identified above of putting things right: to repair and to learn what might cause something similar to occur again, so as to institute changes that reduce future risk (a prospective, preventative function). What is needed is support or intervention to bring about the right changes that will rectify things and reduce future risk. It should be possible to agree the required changes spontaneously or through collaborative engagement between stakeholders, if necessary led by a regulatory authority. The responses should if needed be discussed and agreed, and implemented, swiftly and without the need for any form of coercion. That occurrence is itself powerful evidence that the parties deserve trust.

All relevant issues should be resolved, as part of an integrated package of responses, including cessation, actions to reduce risk and change culture, making redress or repair, and any penalties.[52] Accordingly, the basis for an outcome-focused and collaborative regulatory regime should be to *incentivise* actors to *action* and *agree* the appropriate and proportionate responses to risk and harm. The concepts of enforcement of rules, punishment and deterrence should all be alien and unnecessary in this mode. A regulator's job should be an oversight one to ensure that all the right actions are taken.

Protection Mode

The situation here is that risk or harm is occurring at a level that is unacceptable, and an authority is justified in taking formal action to deliver protection of people, society, markets, the environment and others. Much of the traditional approach to 'enforcement', more accurately now characterised as 'intervention', as discussed in chapter 4, and the traditional toolbox of 'enforcement' tools, remains valid not just for the 'enforcement mode' but also as a background to the 'supportive mode'. The powers should always be available to be invoked in whatever situation arises, but it should be very rare that they would need to be invoked in Supportive Intervention Mode. It is worth stressing that the objective here is not revenge or punishment. The justification and purpose of preventing people from harming others is all that is needed, and it can be applied in a less emotional and possibly more consistent manner.

Private Regulatory Schemes

Private self-regulatory systems are typically highly unlikely to be able to deliver all of the functions in the circular model. Their primary function is often restricted to setting technical requirements and codes of behaviour. They may have some form of complaints system, and some form of sanctioning mechanism.

The major differences between the possible mechanisms lie in their governance, transparency, applicability, coverage, compliance and enforceability.[53] A major issue in practice is whether the risk of unacceptable harm(s) is such that formal requirements are required to be mandatory for all specified traders or activities.

By definition, trade, accreditation or code bodies do not possess the authority to impose the sanctions of a state, such as imprisonment, disqualification or (usually) fines. The typical sanctions would be:

- in an accreditation scheme, removal or qualification of certification;
- in a self-regulatory trade or professional scheme, imposition of certain conditions or requirements (eg for further training) or expulsion from membership.

Many private 'regulatory' schemes exist, and they operate well in their contexts. Criticisms of these private sanctioning mechanisms are that the sanctions are ineffective to affect behaviour (before or after they are imposed) and that the governing bodies are subject to incentives not to 'rock the boat', by being lenient or even blind in response to evidence of infringements. The absence of trust in the effectiveness of a system can be a major factor leading to the imposition of a system of public regulation. Equally, the circumstances can be such that private regulatory schemes can operate well enough if there is adequate trust and independent governance. Some schemes follow the good practice of having committees for making decisions on infringements and imposition of sanctions that contain some or complete membership from outside the trade or profession itself.

Ensuring that Change Occurs

Whether the mode is Supportive Intervention or Protection, it is usually necessary to ensure that appropriate actions are taken (prospectively and retrospectively) so that real change occurs to prevent repetition of harm or of a problem, and to reduce future risk. This is a major flaw in the traditional 'enforcement approach: it *assumes* that change occurs if a sanction is imposed, and it usually fails to provide a mechanism to check what change has occurred, but crucially it fails to engage with what actually needs to be done – and is done – *so that* relevant and effective change in fact occurs.

The necessary steps are:

- Decide what changes are necessary.
- Who is to do what.
- Ensure that all relevant changes are implemented.
- Monitor what happens.

As the RFM illustrated in chapter 3 showed, the functions of monitoring performance and outcomes, and responding prospectively and retrospectively, need to occur constantly. It requires a continuous loop of feedback and response. This requires expertise and oversight, usually supported by analysis of relevant data. All relevant sources of data need to be contributed, aggregated and evaluated. This needs not just traditional reporting of adverse events, but scrutiny of data that is more detailed and closer to actions and events. A huge digital transformation is under way, from inspection of compliances to constant monitoring of systems.

Then there is oversight of what relevant changes should occur, and that such changes are in fact implemented. This is essentially a regulatory oversight function, and regulatory authorities need powers to ensure that change occurs, or that enforcement action is taken if risk continues unaddressed. However, the governance and oversight mechanism in an OBC system should involve co-oversight by all relevant stakeholders, and be mandated by their inherent authority.

Shocking recent examples can be cited of where no monitoring took place on the reality of what was occurring, or curiosity as to the accuracy of reports of problems, even to the extent of denial of any problems in the face of evidence to the contrary – cultures of closed minds and an inability to listen to feedback. This led to failure to learn and change. Such behaviours and cultures have been the cause of many disasters. Recent examples in the UK are infected blood (deaths and permanent injuries), Grenfell Tower fire (deaths) and Post Office Horizon IT problems (wrongful convictions of 900 people plus bankruptcies and other consequences).

By contrast, the vast number of planes stay in the sky because multiple kinds of data are constantly reported, and considered at different levels of committees and expertise, depending on the seriousness of a risk. Typical tools aimed at reducing future risk might include providing teaching on ethics, technical training, information, support, changing procedures, systems or culture. These interventions might be provided by people other than managerial or regulatory authorities: new ecosystems of information and support can emerge. It may be important to achieve improvements in the culture of an organisation. This is not something that can be achieved by external requirement or force. Only those working within an organisation – at all levels – can behave in certain ways, and change their behaviours, so as to add up to a particular culture. This needs an understanding of the behavioural drivers of actions and the levers that affect culture.

An Inadequate Feedback System

In some sectors, there may be a lack of a proper feedback or supportive mechanism that effectively promotes improvement in performance. Inspection and grading of educational or clinical healthcare establishments afford examples. The UK system for education involves qualification of teachers (competence in subject matter and in the art of teaching) and inspection of an institution (school), leading to a grading of the institution. There has been much criticism of this system. The origin of grading was to provide parents (and school management) with an overview of the quality of the school. However, the use of single word gradings ('failing', 'requires improvement', etc) proved to be far too simplistic and led to awful consequences. A single word fails to reflect the range and complexity of activities and outcomes involved. After a headteacher committed suicide when her generally good school was given a low grading based on inadequate attention to one aspect, the system was changed to introduce gradings under various categories. However, this form of control can be perceived as negative and demotivating by teachers and management, and fails to engage with the function of providing tangible helpful support aimed at improvement in performance. A system of mentoring and periodic peer development in a culture open to fresh insights would be far more effective than the authoritative, simplistic but damaging grading system.

Redress

An effective and principled regulatory system should aim to ensure that harm that occurs is rectified: damage caused should be repaired and financial redress or compensation paid. People expect to see this in a just and fair society. Indeed, swiftly delivering repair and redress where it is due is evidence of trustworthiness, and can reduce calls for sanctions, or the need for significant formal enforcement. If people acknowledge problems and agree or spontaneously initiate relevant actions, there may be no point in, or justification for, punishment or enforcement.

Traditionally, regulators would take (public) enforcement action but leave individuals who have been harmed to institute their own (private) enforcement actions for damages. That differentiation is unprincipled in a fair, holistic system. Combining the prospective and retrospective responses to resolution of a problem is not only more effective and speedier in achieving resolution, but it is also right. Ensuring the comprehensive resolution of issues that have given rise to harm is part of the function of a regulatory system, and hence of a regulator. It is not satisfactory for a regulator to leave those who have been harmed to institute their own civil actions for damages to recover their losses. This takes time and inflicts greater cost and effort (including emotional distress) on them. It is certainly more efficient if all aspects of harm can be resolved holistically, and there may well be some leverage in intervention or enforcement discussions, incentivising a comprehensive resolution of all actions.

A powerful example here is that infringements of competition law typically lead to imposition of sanctions (a large fine) initiated by a public authority, but those harmed are left to try to recover their individual damages (which may be individually small) in civil litigation, such as by joining together in a class action. But a principled response would begin with rectifying an unbalanced market by removing all illicit profit from a perpetrator of anti-competitive behaviour (and transferring the money as compensation to those harmed) and only then considering what public enforcement response is needed to reduce future risk.⁵⁴ Some regulators in some countries and sectors now adopt this holistic responsiveness, and it needs to spread.

Even without this integrated approach to behaviour and redress, widespread issues of delays and cost with civil litigation procedures have led to innovative and alternative approaches towards delivery of redress. A number of highly effective avenues for redress have been created, which can be used effectively alongside discussions with regulators about achieving a comprehensive resolution of a problem.

The avenues and the institutions that might be involved in delivering redress outside courts might include the following:⁵⁵

(a) A regulatory authority having a power to order redress to be paid. This can sit alongside a power to approve arrangements agreed to by a trader for delivering repair, redress or compensation of customers. The process may be undertaken by the trader, or it may involve a separate scheme or Ombuds. As said above, the major advantage is that this can provide resolution of *all* aspects of a problem – both public enforcement and private redress – in an integral package. This can encourage a responsible company to make appropriate proposals spontaneously and swiftly. The offer of redress can be a factor that influences the authority to take a more lenient approach to imposing a regulatory sanction.

(b) An Ombuds scheme, also involving mediation or conciliation, and a final stage of a decision by an Ombuds if the parties fail to agree. Ombuds typically have a number of clear advantages over other redress schemes. Firstly, Ombuds are typically independent from traders in their governance and operation. Secondly, use of an Ombuds is typically free to consumers, as their costs are paid by a sector (either voluntarily arrangements or under statutory requirements). Thirdly, Ombuds have the ability to perform the function of amassing data on consumers' experience of traders and markets, which can have considerable regulatory value. Countries vary on whether they have Ombuds and in which sectors. The UK and Belgium are the leaders in coverage of consumer or market Ombuds in Europe.

(c) An 'alternative dispute resolution' (ADR) redress scheme. These are typically created by trade associations in order to support their members' reputations. The techniques that might be available might be mediation, decision or arbitration, all involving an independent lawyer or panel.

> **Key Points**
> - Certain requirements are essential to control adequate responses to the identification of the occurrence of harm.
> - In an OBC context, they are also aimed at monitoring whether the desired outcomes are being achieved, and whether the regulatory system is operating well or has any gaps.
> - The responses, as outlined in the RFM, are to respond to problems prospectively (to stop harm and reduce ongoing risk, including through feedback and learning) and retrospectively (by repairing harm caused).
> - Applying the scientific evidence from chapters 5 and 6 leads to two approaches:
>   - a Supportive Intervention Mode, ideally applied in an OBCR environment and culture; and
>   - a Protection Mode (closely related to traditional enforcement).

---

[1] *Managing Risks and Incentivising Growth: Draft Best Practice Principles for Licensing and Permitting* (OECD, 2024).

[2] *The roadmap to an effective AI assurance ecosystem – extended version* (HMG, December 2021).

[3] See International Federation of Accountants, www.iaasb.org/standards-pronouncements.

[4] Art1.1 of DIHK's founding law (www.gesetze-im-internet.de/bundesrecht/ihkg/gesamt.pdf).

[5] JE Soeharno, *The Value of Oath* (eleven publishing, 2020).

[6] eg Directive (EC) 2001/83, Art 20.

[7] Competent person scheme – current schemes and how schemes are authorised, www.gov.uk/guidance/competent-person-scheme-current-schemes-and-how-schemes-are-authorised.

[8] *Regulatory sandbox toolkit* (OECD, 2025); Report. FinTech: Regulatory sandboxes and innovation hubs (ESMA, EBA and EIOPA, 2019); Issues paper: Regulatory sandboxing (Australian Energy Regulator, 2021).

[9] AI Ogus, *Regulation: Legal Form and Economic Theory* (Clarendon Press, 2004) 121.

[10] *The UK Code of Non-broadcast Advertising and Direct & Promotional Marketing* (Committee of Advertising Practice), www.asa.org.uk/type/non_broadcast/code_folder/preface.html.

[11] www.handbook.fca.org.uk/handbook/PRIN/2/1.html.

[12] DP1/23 – *Review of the Senior Managers and Certification Regime (SM&CR)* (Bank of England, March 2023), para 1.3.
[13] *Report on the Financial Conduct Authority's further investigative steps in relation to RBS GRG* (Financial Conduct Authority, 2019).
[14] *Evaluation of the Senior Managers and Certification Regime* (Prudential Regulation Authority, 2020).
[15] DP1/23 – *Review of the Senior Managers and Certification Regime (SM&CR)* (Bank of England, March 2023).
[16] *The UK's Modern Industrial Strategy. Financial Services Growth and Competitiveness Strategy* (UK Government), www.gov.uk/government/calls-for-evidence/financial-services-growth-and-competitiveness-strategy.
[17] Guidelines on fit and proper criteria for all relevant persons carrying out any activity regulated by MAS, www.mas.gov.sg/regulation/guidelines/guidelines-on-fit-and-proper-criteria. Guidelines on Individual Accountability and Conduct, www.mas.gov.sg/regulation/guidelines/guidelines-on-individual-accountability-and-conduct.
[18] EH Schein, *Organisational Culture and Leadership*, 5th edn (John Wiley & Sons, 2017).
[19] G Hofstede, *Culture Consequences. Comparing Values, Behaviors, Institutions, and Organizations Across Nations*, 2nd edn (Sage, 2001) 9.
[20] G Hofstede et al, *Cultures and Organizations: Software of the Mind – Intercultural Cooperation and Its Importance for Survival*, 3rd edn (New York, McGraw Hill, 2010).
[21] ibid 15.
[22] B van Rooij and A Fine, 'Toxic Corporate Culture: Assessing Organizational Processes of Deviancy' (2019) 8(3) *Administrative Sciences* 23.
[23] See summary in W Scholten and N Ellemers. 'Bad apples or corrupting barrels? Preventing traders' misconduct' (2016) 24 *Journal of Financial Regulation and Compliance* 366–82.
[24] *Supervision of Behaviour and Culture: Foundations, practice & future developments* (DeNederlandscheBank, 2015).
[25] *A New Paradigm. Financial Institution Boards and Supervisors* (Group of Thirty, 2013).
[26] *How to bring the professional oath to life in daily practice* (DeNederlanscheBank, 2024).
[27] *The UK Corporate Governance Code* (Financial Reporting Council, 2018): 'The board should establish the company's purpose, values and strategy, and satisfy itself that these and its culture are aligned. All directors must act with integrity, lead by example and promote the desired culture.'
[28] The Banking Code was established in the UK in 1991, the voluntary Business Banking Code was introduced on 31 March 2002, and is revised regularly. See www.bcsb.co.uk/.
[29] *Banking Code of Practice* (Australian Banking Association, 2019).
[30] *Our Future Mission* (FCA, October 2016), www.fca.org.uk/news/press-releases/fca-mission-consultation.
[31] *FCA Mission: Our Approach to Supervision* (Financial Conduct Authority, 2018).
[32] *Strengthening Governance Frameworks to Mitigate Misconduct Risk: A Toolkit for Firms and Supervisors* (Financial Stability Board, 2018).
[33] S Mills, 'A regulatory perspective: measuring and assessing culture: now and in the future, the role of purpose and the importance of D&I', speech at the Investment Association, 22 September 2021.
[34] *Our Future Mission* (FCA, 2016). Official evaluation of the SM&CR has been broadly positive: *Senior Managers and Certification Regime Banking Stocktake Report* (Financial Conduct Authority, 2019); *Evaluation of the Senior Managers and Certification Regime* (Prudential Regulation Authority, 2020); and comment 'PRA evaluation of the senior managers and certification regime' (DLA Piper, 27 January 2021).
[35] COCON 1.1.2R sets out who COCON applies to.

[36] R Miles, *Culture Audit in Financial Services. Reporting on Behaviour to Conduct Regulators* (KoganPage, 2021).

[37] *Senior Managers and Certification Regime Banking Stocktake Report* (Financial Conduct Authority, 2019), www.fca.org.uk/publications/multi-firm-reviews/senior-managers-and-certification-regime-banking-stocktake-report.

[38] ibid.

[39] *Banking Conduct and Culture. A Permanent Mindset Change* (Group of Thirty, 2019).

[40] ibid: 'By "tone from above" we mean the signals being sent by an employee's manager or supervisor. Cultural norms are felt and transmitted most directly by a worker's immediate supervisors. The worker in a large firm is unlikely to have regular contact with senior managers or their CEO. This is why the task of embedding the desired conduct and cultural norms throughout an institution is so important.'

[41] E Sheedy and D Canestrari-Soh, *Regulating Accountability: An early look at the Banking Executive Accountability Regime (BEAR)* (Macquarie Business School, 2020).

[42] AC Edmondson, *The Fearless Organization* (John Wiley & Sons, Inc, 2019).

[43] *Regulators' Code* (Department for Business Innovation & Skills, 2013). Originally the *Regulators' Compliance Code: Statutory Code of Practice for Regulators* (Department for Business, Enterprise and Regulatory Reform, 2007). The Code is made under the Legislative and Regulatory Reform Act 2006, s 22(1).

[44] *Regulatory institutions and practices* (New Zealand Productivity Commission, 2014) 86–88.

[45] P Fentham, W Kale, K Manch, N McGirr, P Mumford and S Raj, *Professionalising regulatory practice. Lessons from the New Zealand G-REG Initiative* (Victoria University of Wellington and Government Regulatory Practice, 2020).

[46] *OECD Best Practice Principles for Regulatory Policy: Regulatory Enforcement and Inspections* (OECD, 2014).

[47] M Rink, 'Regulating Quality Outputs, an Approach Based on Provision of Data to Drive Behaviour' in G Russell and C Hodges (eds), *Regulatory Delivery* (Hart, 2019).

[48] See *The Outcome-Focused, Collaborative Approach to Food Regulation in Queensland* (Safe Food Queensland): from Report of the INDR Conference on Engagement by Regulators, Wolfson College, Oxford (20 November 2023) (on file with the author).

[49] This was based on *Future Visioning Safe Food's Regulatory Delivery Model* (PRISM Institute, 2022), www.safefood.qld.gov.au/wp-content/uploads/2022/08/Future-Visioning-Safe-Food-Production-Queenslands-Regulatory-Delivery-Model-PRISM-Institute-Report.pdf. Two supporting groups were created: an Industry Advisory Technical Group looked at 'how' through recognition of industry certification systems, and a Cross-Agency Reference Group looked at 'how' on the government side. Further information: Safe Food Production Queensland, www.safefood.qld.gov.au; Australia and New Zealand Food Regulation, www.foodregulation.gov.au; Food Standards Australia New Zealand (FSANZ), www.foodstandards.gov.au.

[50] www.food.gov.uk/about-us/achieving-business-compliance-abc-programme.

[51] *Evaluation of the Enterprise Level Regulation (ELR) Proof of Concept (PoC): Final report* (ICF, 21 June 2024), www.food.gov.uk/sites/default/files/media/document/Evaluation-of-the-Enterprise-Level-Regulation-Proof-of-Concept-Final-report.pdf.

[52] This function is typically more swift, efficient and cheap than courts. Relegating private redress to private litigation, on the other hand, is ineffective and inefficient: see C Hodges and S Voet, *Delivering Collective Redress: New Technologies* (Hart, 2018); C Hodges, 'Collective Redress: The Need for New Technologies' (2019) 42 *Journal of Consumer Policy* 59–90. There is provision for the central role of a public body in the CPC Regulation: Regulation (EU) 2017/2394 of the European Parliament and of the Council of 12 December 2017 on cooperation between national authorities responsible for the enforcement of consumer

protection laws and repealing Regulation (EC) No 2006/2004, Art 9(4)(c) giving a power 'to seek to obtain or to accept commitments from the trader responsible for the infringement covered by this Regulation to cease that infringement'.

[53] K McEntaggart, J Etienne and J Uddin, *Designing Self-and Co-Regulation Initiatives: Evidence on Best Practices: A literature review*, BEIS Research Paper Number 2019/025 (Department for Business, Energy & Industrial Strategy, 2019).

[54] C Hodges, 'A Market-Based Competition Enforcement Policy' (2011) 22(3) *European Business Law Review* 261; C Hodges, 'European Competition Enforcement Policy: Integrating Restitution and Behaviour Control' (2011) 34(3) *World Competition* 383.

[55] C Hodges and S Voet, *Delivering Collective Redress: New Technologies* (Hart, 2018).

PART C

Problems, Criticisms, Challenges and Future Solutions

8

Problems and Criticisms of Regulation

> Regulation attracts multiple criticisms and inherently gives rise to various challenges. This chapter summarises the main issues, and puts (some of) them into context, so we can see to what extent the problems are valid. Many comments about 'regulation' and not well-informed. We can only devise effective responses to genuine problems if we correctly analyse what they are, and what is causing them. At the heart of the conundrum is for a society to have a consensus about its attitude to risk.
>
> Leading historical attempts to reform regulation are noted, especially Better Regulation initiatives. Fresh ideas for 'improving regulation' are set out, starting with viewing regulation as a system.

Too Much Regulation?

The basic complaints about regulation are that it gets in the way, slows things down or even stops progress, and costs too much. But isn't this what protecting people has to involve? If I want to cross the road, or drive from A to B, doesn't it make sense that I and others should observe the traffic lights, speed restrictions and Highway Code, for my safety and that of others? The real question here is not about there being restrictions but whether they are *effective and proportionate*. How much regulation is necessary or too much? We usually don't manage to engage the answers to those points well enough, nor to provide effective solutions to them. Let's look in more detail at the list of complaints and criticisms. At end of the chapter, we can note some possible solutions.

Too Many Rules and Procedures

The complaint that there is 'too much red tape' can mean a number of things. If we are going to find a solution, we need to know exactly what the problem is. The criticism may be that:

(a) the content of a *rule* is unnecessary, or too burdensome, or even fails to adequately control a risk;
(b) the need to follow a *procedure* is unnecessary or too cumbersome or repetitive, especially if it requires assembling a lot of data or filling in forms or waiting for approvals;
(c) the *cumulative effect* of multiple rules and procedures is too great.

Each of these problems might be valid – or not – in a particular situation. But most rules and procedures are generic – they apply to everyone, and if we start to create exceptions, the regulatory landscape can mushroom into a very complex web that is confusing to navigate and may give rise to lots of arguments about which rules or procedures apply in which circumstances.

Many people may find that the individual and especially cumulative effect of complying with regulations is too burdensome. It takes too long. It costs too much. It's overwhelming. It's unnecessary (in my situation). One example may be a farmer who wants to get on with growing crops or herding cattle, but who has to obtain permits for chemicals and activities, fill in multiple repetitive forms, and follow health and safety and environmental requirements. Most workplace injuries occur on farms because farmers hurt themselves. But if a farmer is hurt, is adverse economic harm also caused to the farm? Other examples arise, often in relation to innovative technologies. New products, services, and ways of doing things, might not be permitted under existing rules, and might only be permitted after extensive evidence of safety has been produced – which might not be possible given the inability to undertake or fund the necessary research. So, the innovation is blocked.

In both situations, one hears complaints like: 'It's stupid, it stops me doing what I need to do, it's pointless, it slows me down unnecessarily, it completely prevents me from doing something beneficial, I can't afford it.' But the core argument here is usually not addressed:

- Is the restriction necessary, or effective, or proportionate?
- Is the restriction needed in some circumstances but not in others, which have not been adequately defined?

- How do we assess what is necessary, effective and proportionate in all of the relevant circumstances?
- How do we change things so that unnecessary barriers are removed, and necessary ones remain?

Cumulative Effects

A frequent problem is having to comply with extensive requirements from *multiple regimes and agencies*. This can give rise to duplication or inconsistency. The requirements might include detailed operational plans, financial assurances, and risk mitigation strategies: these 'may be pervasive and often excessive'.[1] It is easy to see how the cumulative effect of multiple rules and regimes can add up. A response to this problem would be to review and cull unnecessary rules, and to use online and AI procedures, plus integrated do-it-all-once techniques. For example, a business could have a single file that contains all its governance and financial details, which could be accessible to relevant authorities (and customers) and avoid repeating the same information for multiple authorities. Company registries have been making progress with this technique. The same approach can be applied for individuals (identity confirmation) and properties that are being let (a single portal, demonstrating ownership and compliance with fire, safety, insurance and other requirements).

After a business has satisfied one regulator, it can find that it also needs to satisfy another, operating another set of rules. An example was the conversation between producers of autonomous agricultural machinery who engaged with agricultural, environmental and workplace safety regulators, but were unaware until later that they would need to satisfy highway authorities in order to drive their machines to fields. This problem calls for coordination between regimes and one-stop-shops for advice and approvals.

A further problem may be that different regulatory regimes (or maybe their interpretation by different authorities) lead to inconsistency and duplication. 'One lot tell me to do this, the other says the opposite.' 'I've already given one agency most of this information, and now I've got to give it all again to another.' A solution here is to create a single repository of information, such as on a portal.

Different regimes may involve inspections, when they could be coordinated so that maybe even only one inspection might be undertaken. Frustrations here can generate a tendency to blame the regulatory authorities rather than conflicts between the regimes that they administer but cannot alter – the ability to change requires action by government.

In a digital world, much can now be achieved by providing data (once) through monitoring systems, possibly removing the need for physical inspections. Duplication also arises as between commercial selling and public procurement requirements, and in selling to different markets (eg CE marking in addition to UK marking).

Resource Problems for Regulators

An obvious cause of delay can be where an authority has insufficient resources to process applications or deal with issues quickly enough. Technical authorities complain that they do not have enough capacity, technical and digital infrastructure, expert staff (because industry pays more) and so on. There are only two sources of funds for public authorities – public allocations from the Treasury and fees paid by regulatees – both of which are subject to constraints and resistance. Similarly, after the UK exited the EU, there was a bottleneck because of increased demand for private accreditation service providers. Making the case for more funding is a constant activity of public authorities. Solutions 'outside of the box' may lie in, first, maximising use of digital technology and AI to monitor, control and process, and, second, more efficient reallocation of functions amongst the various public and private actors in a regulatory space.

Regulatory Creep

The cumulative effect of regulation gives rise to 'regulatory creep'. The argument is that regulations always proliferate and never reduce. We make many new rules, but we fail to remove ones that we no longer need. It is not difficult to see how regimes tend to be cumulative rather than refreshed. Possible reasons for regulatory creep, or its perception, are:

- New risks are identified and need to be covered.
- New controls (rules, processes) are identified and need to be added.

- A government and/or regulatory authority believe that they are exposed to reputational risk on a topic and wish to be seen to cover it.

A related phenomenon is 'government-sponsored voluntary regulation'.[2] This occurs where government leans on a sector to adopt voluntary controls as a means of avoiding legislation, which gives a Minister the opportunity to say that an issue has been dealt with, but still adds compliance costs to the sector.

Only recently have some governments begun to address the historical mountain of legislation. What is the process for undertaking a systematic review of existing legislation and the ability to amend or remove it? Some states have introduced a 'sunset clause' in new legislation at the time of creation. The problem with that is the amount of legislative time that might be needed to review, amend and repass existing laws: ironically it would be to create a colossal regulatory monster! The task of culling and modernisation is vast. Under a Parliamentary system, it might take a century even if it moves quickly. Does this not suggest that we should adopt a new way of making and reviewing regulatory laws?

Gaps and Silos – Inconsistency between Regulators

The opposite of duplication is the existence of a gap. Some risks are not addressed because individual actors, authorities or government departments do not consider that they are responsible for them, so the problem falls into the gap until it blows up in a crisis. The Cumberledge Report highlighted serious consequences of siloism in the healthcare system's care of new babies and mothers – and gaps between regulatory silos, leading to consistent failure to identify problems and harm.[3] Similarly dysfunctional and unintegrated systems were causes of the Grenfell Tower fire[4] and many other disasters.

What is needed here is a mechanism to identify inconsistencies, conflicts and gaps, and resolve them. The UK Regulatory Horizons Council has developed useful experience of doing this as an independent investigator and problem-solver, but its remit is limited to regulation affecting innovative technologies. *Having an independent investigative and problem-solving body could achieve a great deal if it had a wide, general remit.*

Specific Issues Arising with Economic Regulation

Economic regulators were created to ensure fair behaviours in markets, especially fair prices. When faced with any set of restrictive rules, company behaviour will include seeking to circumvent, appeal and renegotiate them. They can complain that the system of setting the prices they can charge their customers does not provide the stability they need to attract or deliver the long-term investments they require. Price control periods can be a few years, whereas investment decisions typically take a far longer trajectory. The system is inherently authoritarian, and can involve imposition of significant financial penalties. This induces a distrustful and confrontational culture. Appeals are common, such as in the UK to the Competition Appeal Tribunal and the General Regulatory Chamber of the First-tier Tribunal.[5]

Several economic regulators have been criticised for failing to prevent harms. The water story is summarised below. Another was high and fluctuating energy prices after the Russia-Ukraine war led to global disruption in energy supply. The system was designed on the assumption of economic and market stability, and encountered challenges when those assumptions fell.

'Failure of Regulators': The Water and Sewage Problems

Water and sewerage services were privatised in 1989. An economic regulator (Ofwat) was created to control price increases and regulate fair market behaviour so as to protect consumers. Like other economic regualtors, it controlled amounts allowable for investment. But it was also intended to permit shareholders attractive profits, so as to attract investment to the UK, and to support those shareholders who were pension funds. Some companies leveraged funds through borrowing to maintain levels of profit and remuneration. So, there were inherent conflicts, not least bewteen dividends, investment, and prices. The Environment Agency also regulated emissions that harmed the environment. In times of excess rain, the water system had inadequate capacity, and permits were issued for the level of foul water (including sewage) to be discharged into rivers and the sea.

The system had inadequate capacity, and extensive public concern arose at excessive pollution of rivers and beaches, and flooding. Water companies and regulators were demonised for excessive uncontrolled pollution whilst maintaining significant shareholder dividends. But were the root causes an inadequately integrated and defined system? Should reforms be directed at controlling directors, or regulators; or reviewing privatisation of a public good; or taking a longer term view; or inadequate control over all the relevant critical nodes of the system (borrowing, investment, profit distributions) as well as an inability to respond to evidence of a manifest problem (infrastructure).

In 2025, the Cunliffe Independent Review covering England and Wales recommended wholesale reform of every aspect of the system. It started with recognising that the water system is a *system* and needs to be managed, regulated, owned, operated and maintained in an effective integral manner. The problems lay with the system as a whole, and blame was not attributed to any particular actors.

Among the list of 88 recommendations were these. First, in order to regulate a system effectively, there should be a single regulator. Hence it was proposed that Ofwat, the Drinking Water Inspectorate (which was highly regarded), and the water environment functions of the Environment Agency and Natural England be combined into a new organisation in England. In Wales, it was proposed to embed new economic regulatory responsibilities within Natural Resources Wales.

Second, the ownership and management of public assets needed stronger oversight and accountability. Examination of whether privatised assets should be transferred to public ownership (which existed in Wales and Scotland but not England) was outside the terms of reference of the Cunliffe Commission, but it recommended new regulatory controls in areas like corporate governance, ownership and transparency, dividends and remuneration, senior management accountability (a regime similar to the Senior Managers Regime for financial institutions, but more restricted), and reviewing decisions and behaviours in the public interest.

There were various references to achieving outcomes and to collaboration, but no more detailed examination of those concepts. Strategic direction and planning remained as conceived in a top-down manner, with wider consultations, rather than on a genuinely stakeholder approach.

A system in which regulators of privatised companies administering public goods (water, rail, energy) are encouraged to pay dividends (often to prop up teachers' pension funds but sometimes to shady, dubious shareholders), whilst consumer prices are controlled, but without allowing for adequate investment in infrastructure, will fail. In these circumstances, the 'fault' does not lie with regulators, who are only doing what they were told, operating within their defined and narrow remits.

As Colin Mayer has said,[6] 'alignment of private profit with public interest, namely [through] regulation, has been found to be seriously deficient in avoiding abuses of monopoly and promoting efficiency in the delivery of public services. ... there is a limit to what regulation can achieve in a context in which there is such divergence of interest between the regulator in public benefit and corporations in the private pursuit of profit.' He also cites the similar dilution of promised intensive regulation after the financial crisis in the light on subsequent economic and political realities.

It is a mistake to fail to involve adequately all the relevant distinct issues and people involved. A lack of collaboration and consensus about purposes, such as just through consultation on some issues and limited representatives on committees, is too limited and unholistic an approach. Further, it fails to focus on outcomes, how they are achieved, and how progress towards them can be measured.

Impeding Growth and Investment

The view of businesses and governments that regulation is a barrier to economic health and growth arises regularly, especially in times of economic stress. It is very easy for people to blame regulators without correctly analysing the root of a problem, and understanding why regulation has been introduced in the first place.

A related complaint by governments is that imposing significant fines on companies can make a jurisdiction unattractive for foreign investment, and deter companies from setting up. The opposite view is that companies need to be deterred from dangerous and unfair activities that cause harm. How are these views (and some between the extremes) to be reconciled into consistent and fair policy decisions?

In reducing regulatory burdens, governments can overlook the purpose of regulation and may only increase the risks and costs. The Australian Productivity Commission said in 2025 that 'Government's role in producing a more dynamic and resilient economy can be achieved through taxation, spending, or regulation' and recommended 'immediate concrete reductions in regulatory burden'.[7] This approach views regulation just as an economic lever, and fails to take account of the fundamental purpose of regulation, namely protection, or of the inevitable consequence of reducing regulation, namely increase in risk and harms. What happens when people, businesses and markets are harmed? Who pays? Is the harm avoidable if more sophisticated policies are pursued?

Major questions here are: If the national economy is paramount, do you lower your standards of protection? Should we accept increased risk of being harmed? Who decides? Or should we aim for global consistency in standards, so that countries cannot compete by having lower rules (regulatory arbitrage)?

The Underlying Issues

Proportionality

Complaints are often made about having to incur the cost and time involved in regulatory compliance *at all*. The reaction may be an ideological resentment about *any* interference with individual freedom. A response is that if multiple individuals have to live together in a pluralist democratic society, each person cannot do exactly what they want. They have to moderate their actions, or the society will degenerate into chaos or self-destruction (the traffic rules referred to above). Achieving things together requires collaboration, and this has to involve everyone observing the same values of behaviour and rules. But beneath this, there may also be a point that some risk is illusory or negligible, and more importantly that the cost and time of carrying out regulatory checks are *disproportionate* to the *risks*.

It is easy to make a complaint about the existence of a barrier, or to make an allegation of disproportionality, but often difficult to substantiate or investigate or rectify it. An objective analysis would need to consider extensive evidence of *risk, benefits, costs and time* involved, and evaluate them carefully and objectively, in the relevant circumstances. This needs answering: risks, benefits and costs to whom, and in what different circumstances? There are usually *multiple* risks, benefits, costs and lost opportunities, involving different people or organisations. Investigating and proving whether disproportionality is a valid criticism or not may necessarily involve detailed evidence and consideration of particular cases.

It is rare that any regulatory system has a mechanism to respond effectively here: such mechanisms do not exist at the operational level of people who are affected – you're either subject to the rule or you're not. Is it possible to make decisions at a policy level about what should apply in every situation, and what exemptions or modifications there ought to be? Do decisions weighing risk, benefits and burdens need to be taken in the real practical context of different operations? But how can a system of rules be flexible enough to enable rational application of authoritative and objective delegation of risk decisions?

In particular, what is the system for evaluating the possible *benefits* that are being prevented from being realised? Do regulators (or does someone) have the authority to create exceptions, or the discretion to allow exemptions, to general rules? Surely, waiting years for Parliament to get round to making new rules is way too long for the realisation of the benefits of most new technologies. The source of the problem here is not with regulators or regulatory regimes, which are required by Parliament to observe the laws that apply to them, but with the cumbersome *Parliamentary system* of making laws.

Is evaluation of the proportionality of controls best reviewed by people who are close to the risk and activities, rather than at a remote high level? But it needs to be based on sound data.

Risk Perception

It can be that those subject to regulation simply fail to observe the rules. They may not be aware of them, they might not think the rules are important, or they do not care, or they argue that they are in fact complying with a rule (creative compliance), or they don't care and positively aim to evade observance and identification, and so on.

Humans have a well-recognised ability to underestimate risk and the ability to self-justify their actions: 'it will never happen to me', 'what I see is all there is', 'it's not dangerous', 'everyone else does this'.[8] A number of different root causes are worth examining:

(a) a lack of understanding and communication about risk: the absence of realisation why a rule or procedure exists and may be justified, given the risks;

(b) the regulator may have no flexibility in applying the rules: regulatory authorities typically have no power to remove or bend a rule or procedure – it is required by Parliament to apply it, because it is part of delivering the protection that Parliament requires the authority to deliver;
(c) absence of a mechanism to review or change the rules, speedily or at all.

There are in fact so many possible situations that it is not only difficult but also not helpful to generalise about why non-compliance occurs. Situations usually need to be considered in their particular contexts. But solutions lie in addressing communications about regulation, increasing flexibility, and introducing mechanisms for review and change.

Risk: Attitudes and Appetite

Realisation that controls should be proportionate to risk raises the questions: How much risk does/should society accept, and who decides this?

Risk, or the perception of risk, has a significant political element in relation to regulation. In considering risk and regulation, it can be helpful to consider *who* perceives *what risks*, and how they respond to them. Public perception of risk is particularly susceptible to stories of harm suffered by individuals (life stories) that trigger a magnified sense of actual risk. Fears of new and unknown risks inherently arise in relation to new technology.

It is no accident that complaints about excessive regulation are heard in three situations. Firstly, after disasters occur, involving major harm (especially death) to individuals (although this may conversely be a complaint about lack or regulation). Secondly, in time of economic or financial stress, where resources are tight and people want to do things, especially to make or save money. Thirdly, in societies that stress political and individual freedom, where constraints are resisted on the basis that the risks are exaggerated.

Some major, and conflicting, response mechanisms involving different groups are as follows:

(a) *Consumers* or *societies* can perceive that certain things give rise to major risks, from which they need to be protected. This is the origin of all legislation on regulation of any type and many self-regulatory

regimes. The concerns are most frequently around safety issues (the risk of harm and damage) but can be on ethical issues (whether certain activities should be allowed).
(b) In response to (a), *governments* not only pass legislation that is intended to provide protection from the perceived risks, but also adopt policies on risk. An example of such a policy is the EU's 'precautionary principle' that was adopted in response to the BSE/'mad cow' risk to food safety and public concerns about GMOs. Recent examples are legislation aimed at delivering protection from perceived risks of AI and online media.
(c) *Innovators* find that existing regulation or precautionary policies are a barrier to research and development.
(d) In response to (c), *governments* take steps to reduce such barriers, especially at times when economic conditions are constrained or as matters of political ideology (Brexit and now Trumpian assertions about constraints on freedom). This leads to claims that societies – and regulators – are 'too risk averse' or ruled by 'safetyism'.

In response to (d), are the regulatory regimes and authorities created by legislators merely doing what they were supposed to do to deliver adequate protection? Academics talk about the need for a society to decide its 'risk appetite', but this can be highly influenced by public perception and the media, and be subject to inconsistencies. There can be both a pendulum effect, and policy inconsistency based on different perceived risks occurring at the same time. In 2025, we are currently experiencing a broad swing away from situations (a) and (b) in many technologies, with situations (c) and (d) leading to calls for deregulation, whilst at the same time other concerns (about AI) prompt demands for regulation for protection. In any event, perceptions of regulation and risk are subject to public perceptions and become significant political issues. Risks (a) and (c) become *political* risks, forcing governments to react with (b) and (d).

Various attempts have been made to produce a balanced approach, under the banner of making 'Better Regulation' (see below), but without obvious success. One of the major missing elements in legislative tools for either governments or regulators is the ability to respond quickly enough to changing circumstances so as to increase or decrease regulatory controls. (Various barriers of this kind that can be experienced by innovators are noted at the start of chapter 9.[9])

Logically, a society ought to agree its risk appetite. This concept is never discussed or even acknowledged, and certainly not measured. But different societies across the globe do have different attitudes to risk. The calls for precautionary or proportionate approaches are simple manifestations of this. (We discuss the precautionary principle in chapter 9.)

Some political discussion in the 2020s has talked about a 'risk aversion ratchet'. This is said to comprise three components. Firstly, 'a political culture that is increasingly "safetyist", which privileges risk-mitigation and security over other imperatives, and which expects the government to eliminate risk from people's lives. Secondly, a bureaucracy on which it is remarkably easy and ostensibly "cheap" to generate new regulations. And finally, a complete lack of incentives to remove redundant regulations from the rulebook.'[10] The argument is heard that it is a duty of government to establish a basic level of security from harm, but that the regulatory apparatus 'has extended into realms that far exceed this remit'.

The rhetoric here seems to be that political imperatives of delivering economic growth lead to a public policy of prioritising safety over risk. The logical consequence of allowing more risk should be the occurrence of more harm – more people get hurt and more crises occur. But if a regulatory system is in place that identifies and responds to the occurrence of harm swiftly, then the society should be resilient, and able to accept risk and to promote innovation. This thinking points to adoption of the Regulatory Functions Model in chapter 3. It accepts the reality that we are unable to predict crises or the risks of much new technology, but we can control unknown risk if we are able to react quickly enough when harm occurs, so as to reduce their impact.

Many Decisions are Political

Regulators and regulation are often criticised when the underlying issue relates to matters outside their control, as the examples of sewage and energy prices above, and many others, show. Dissatisfaction with a particular rule, or set of rules, or a perceived regime, is easily attributable to a particular authority, or to regulation as a whole. But this is a situation of 'blame the messenger'. The underlying frustration is often a symptom of a problem with the system, how it is designed and how it is required to be operated. Hence, the solutions to this problem lie with ensuring that the system is better designed and reformed, and that the realities of responsibility for root causes are communicated and better understood.

The claim that regulators should take more risk, and hence be less of a barrier to innovation, omits recognition that it is politicians and governments who need to respond to the regulatory barriers around innovation, and to empower regulators to disapply existing protective rules where there are good reasons to do so. The regulators are only doing what they are legally obliged to do by applying the rules made by Parliament to protect us. They cannot just ignore the rules – they would be subject to public and legal criticism for failing to apply the rules in accordance with their duties.

The massive (governmental) elephant in this room is being missed. Governments should create a mechanism under which existing barriers can allow for exceptions, exemptions, sandboxes, or 'ways through' that can be operated *more quickly* than through a slow legislative process. Who should have the power and flexibility to decide this? Ministers, committees, regulators?

Complaints about regulation often align with political, social and academic thinking, preoccupations, and viewpoints. Viewpoints are strongly influenced by world views, such as either freedom from interference or protection from risk. And they reflect a lack of understanding about how complex systems work – or fail to work well. Regulators were criticised for failing to solve problems for which they had no remit or powers. They were expected to solve every problem, but within the limits of a legal straitjacket (enforcement through judicial review and subject to criticism by politicians, the media and the public with little ability to reply).

In many countries, there has been a trajectory from the later 20th century of outsourcing political decisions to regulators followed by criticism of regulators' performance that is misdirected. The main advantage of delegating power to regulatory authorities was perceived to be operational independence, which would enable decisions to be made more quickly than if multiple decisions had to be taken by Ministers. But with that delegation of power came the ability for politicians to off-load criticism onto regulators when things went wrong. By the early 21st century, there were many claims that regulators were responsible for too much red tape, were impeding sensible business, making nations unattractive to foreign investment, and presiding over disasters. In short, regulators were said to have failed. By the 2020s, this political criticism, fuelled by elements of business, had reached a point of demonising regulators and regulation.

This anti-regulation agenda was closely linked in the UK with the EU, which was painted as a slow, legalistic juggernaut, creating ever more rules that could not be challenged. The need for economic growth and investment, and barriers to scientific and technical innovation, working alongside populist political slogans of 'taking back control', fuelled widespread dissatisfaction in regulation. Regulatory budgets were constrained by many nations, and the most dramatic action was to cut whole regulatory regimes under President Trump. Where regulators remain, governments have made various attempts to control or direct them. The tools have ranged from imposing more legal duties on regulators to Ministers issuing 'policy steers'.

At different times, particular goals are prioritised, and also deprioritised. Important examples of changed goals arise from planet sustainability, environmental protection, Sustainable Development Goals, human rights, and diversity, equity and inclusion (DEI). These wider social goals tend to be deprioritised by governments and societies in time of economic distress, or conflict, but are never removed from regulators.

One solution to these issues is to identify more accurately those decisions that are political and those that are operational within a defined regulatory framework. Other responses are to enable the regulatory and political frameworks to work better together in a more integrated way, and to enable rules and regimes to be changed more swiftly. The specific issue of regulation and innovation is addressed in chapter 9.

The underlying problem here is that it is *the system* of making and amending rules that is too cumbersome and slow. We have no effective mechanism for changing requirements quickly enough. This has become a real barrier to innovation.

Attempts to Control Regulation

A number of responses have been made to the problems identified above. *Deregulation* is the concerted attempt to reduce the extent of regulation, usually focused on the number of existing regulations. We look below at some systematic attempts to do this, through bureaucratic constraints.

Reduction Techniques

Removal of Regulation or Regulators

Cutting resources so as to constrain regulatory activities is a familiar governmental technique. However, the Trump rhetoric of 'dismantling the Deep State' and ending 'Weaponized Government' whilst returning 'Self Governance to the People' reached 'wrecking ball' proportions in 2025 in its extreme aversion to regulation – wholescale removal of regulatory staff, agencies and regimes. President Trump's Director of the Office of Management and Budget, Russell Vought, was reported as saying in October 2024 before appointment:[11]

> We want the bureaucrats to be traumatically affected. When they wake up in the morning, we want them to not want to go to work because they are increasingly viewed as the villains. We want their funding to be shut down so that the EPA can't do all of the rules against our energy industry because they have no bandwidth financially, to do so. We want to put them in trauma.

It will be interesting to see whether some businesses and sectors respond by taking initiatives to control risks themselves, or just ignore risks of causing harm.

Removal of a public body was also undertaken at the same time by the UK Government, with the abolition of NHS England being justified on the basis of duplication, so the Government 'took back control' into the Department of Health. One may wonder if this shift was the right way round. Are politicians and officials good at managing? A long history of big government disasters might suggest that professional managers might be better.[12] Would a succession of Ministers, each lasting a relatively short period in office, with limited experience or expertise of management or policy, lead to professional, consistent and continuity in operations?

Risks with Deregulation

There are some obvious risks with deregulation. If one removes rules, the protection that they should offer is also removed. So, risk and harm may increase. How much risk are we comfortable with? Take a look again at the areas that are typically subject to regulation, listed in chapter 1. Which ones do you want to get rid of? In which could you live with a lesser degree of protection? How would you react if regimes were eased but you or others then suffered harm? The history of so many disasters in corporate and public fields includes a lack of vigilance by those subject to regulation and/or regulators. Examples include Thalidomide; Grenfell; Boeing 737 MAX (delegation without trust); explosion of the Challenger Space Shuttle; unsafe cladding at Grenfell Tower (death of 72 people) and *other* buildings; infected blood; the wrongful conviction of 900 sub-postmasters and mistresses.

As stock markets showed in 2025 after the Trump destabilisations, lack of predictability and especially a lack of stability are critical in markets across the globe.

Some may argue that protection is maintained because the cost of litigation (private enforcement) is a deterrent to companies. That mechanism is simply not credible as a means of prevention in general, or ensuring that adequate steps are taken in prevention. But it remains true that if you deregulate, you are likely to increase, some time later, the incidence of litigation, when harm occurs. That may be the only mechanism open to those who have been harmed, but they might well prefer not having been harmed in the first place. The spread of concern about risk and of stories of harm is not exactly good for supporting confidence in society, governments, regulators or businesses.

A significant insight here is that regulation does not *impose* costs; it merely *reallocates* costs. Without regulation, harm is caused, which incurs costs on victims, markets, society, and (subject to effective redress systems) reallocation costs on those who are responsible for causing the damage. On this view, regulation reallocates who pays and when.[13] Hence, the purpose is to make producers internalise the cost of risk reduction at an early stage rather than allow other externals later to suffer the larger costs. The point is that absent effective *ex ante* steps required by regulation, such steps will not be taken and harm will occur, which cannot then be undone.

Controls on Making Law and Rules

Reduce the Flow of New Rules by Controlling the Regulatory Process

The mechanism of imposing constraints on legislators is widespread. Many countries require a Regulatory Impact Assessment (RIA) to be produced before a legislative or subsidiary regulatory implementation is permitted. The RIA typically requires an analysis of the costs and benefits of the new rules, and that the balance of benefit over cost should be positive. A major problem here is that of predicting with any accuracy what the costs or benefits may be, where the implications can be highly complex. There is much that is speculative. Business frequently responds to calls for quantification of proposals that they cannot know in advance of clarity of what the final rules might be (after it has gone through a Parliamentary process) or in advance of them actually having to comply with them and how they are implemented. It makes more sense to carry out a subsequent review of costs and benefits, which has not been attempted until recently.

A very simplistic tool that has been used is to require those who propose new rules to also remove one or more other rules as a condition of being permitted to proceed ('one-in, x-out'). Germany instituted a federal Programme for Bureaucracy Reduction and Better Regulation in 2006.[14] After reform in 2011, a 'one-in, one-out' rule was introduced in 2015.

This approach does little to target the reduction of serious costs or delay, or address any specific serious problem, which merely remains unaddressed, while the easiest candidate for withdrawal is selected, irrespective of its useful or unhelpful effects. The simplicity of 'one-in, x-out' reveals more about achieving catchy political headlines than real engagement with a particular problem.

The most extreme example so far is President Trump's 'one-in, 10-out' order in February 2025.[15] This idea reveals the depth of lack of understanding about regulation at policy-making levels. Regulation is not about numbers of rules; it is about outcomes and protection. Rules may be needed in one situation, but not in another – that is a level of sophistication that is completely missing from this simplistic knee-jerk approach.

In Trump's first term, whilst applying a 'one-in, two-out' rule, the administration imposed annual regulatory costs averaging $10 billion, compared to $111 billion for the Obama administration and $43 billion under George W Bush. But the key point is that the regulatory burden continued to rise, not fall.

Another technique is to require new rules to be time-limited (sunsetting) and requiring positive legislative action to continue them. In Idaho and Texas, the use of sunsetting for both individual regulations and agencies themselves has been claimed to have had 'a remarkable disciplining effect on the regulatory state.'[16] But the sunset technique may need significant extra legislative time in reviewing and re-enacting the same, or reformed, legislation. It also fails to provide business or society with predictability or continuous protection. Texas reviews agencies' mandates every 12 years (by the Sunset Advisory Commission), but does it have objective data on burdens, and benefits and risks, or is the decision subject to political whims?

Reduce Existing Stock of Rules

Various governments have attempted to cull existing rules, usually through public invitations to contribute to a 'bonfire of regulations'. The logical approach would be to establish a baseline of what rules exist, such as a comprehensive database of regulation – as was done in Germany in the 2010s. This was said to increase transparency and accountability.

The UK Government undertook a 'Red Tape Challenge' to reduce the estimated 21,000 pieces of regulation as of 2011. It estimated that review by a 'star chamber' led to at least 3,000 regulations being scrapped or reduced. It has been estimated that the combined use of gateway conditions and the Red Tape Challenge 'drove a £14.59 billion reduction in the regulatory burden between 2011 and 2017 when adjusted for inflation'.[17] However, complaints about regulatory barriers and burden continued subsequently after the 2016 Brexit vote and with the 2024 Labour Government's growth mission. The same deregulatory policy kept being repeated with renewed urgency, which suggested that little deregulatory impact had been achieved.

A general cull may remove ancient, unused rules, but does not necessarily address whether the vast majority of the stock remains useful or proportionate. It fails to address the problem of rules that may be useful in some circumstances but are unhelpful or disproportionate in others. That sort of sophisticated analysis has not been widely attempted, possibly because the task is so huge and the nature of the inquiry can be extremely complicated. It needs to be undertaken close to the 'front line' rather than at a high policy level.

Examples of Combinations of Techniques

Governments usually use combinations of regulatory-reduction techniques. Here are some reported stories.

In British Columbia, the regulatory code was cut by 37% in three years through cuts in departmental regulatory budgets.[18] In 2001, the Government of British Columbia counted the number of 'rules' by undertaking a 'regulatory requirement' measure. The count could now be undertaken largely by AI. Between 2001 and 2004, it reduced the number from 382,139 to 268,699. The principal mechanism was a 'one-in, two-out' rule, although some regulators worked to 'one-in, five-out'. The slimming process was reported to have maintained high levels of environmental quality and safety, and to have significantly improved British Columbia's ranking for economic growth amongst peer provinces. Three essential lessons from the process were stated as: political leadership is required; simplicity matters ('too often, regulatory measures become so complex that they are too expensive for governments to use broadly or communicate simply'); regulators are an important part of the system.[19]

Significant programmes have been undertaken in the USA at state level. The Idaho Red Tape Reduction Act and Licensing Freedom Act of 2019 required every state agency to designate an employee to review all of its existing regulations, and stipulated that prior to any new regulatory measures, an agency would be required to carry out an impact assessment and identify two regulations to cut. The Licensing Freedom Act required the Idaho Division of Financial Management to identify annually five professions regulated by the state and review the appropriateness of the existing regulations on these occupations. It also imposed a presumption against the creation of new state professional regulations under a 'sunrise clause'. After political gridlock in 2019, a Bill authorising the continuation of all 8,200 pages of Idaho's legislative code failed to pass, and an urgent review was undertaken on what to keep, rather than what to scrap. This resulted in scrapping 139 chapters entirely, removing parts of 79 chapters, and rewriting 31 chapters. The Governor claimed that the regulatory burden had been reduced by 75%. Subsequent moves required state agencies to review their rules every eight years, carry out impact assessments and justify ongoing rules. After the pandemic, a Governor's Executive Order required agencies to justify restoring regulations that had been suspended. As a result of these and other measures, Governor Brad Little claimed to have reduced Idaho regulations by 95% since taking office in 2019. Idaho was ranked as the least regulated state in the USA.[20]

In Florida, an Office of Fiscal Accountability and Regulatory Reform (OFARR) was created in 2011 and extended in 2019 to oversee activities on deregulation.[21]

Virginia's State Government created an Office of Regulatory Management (ORM) in 2022 that offered credits for agencies that cut words or reduced burdens. The ORM estimated that by 2024 agencies had cut or streamlined 17.6% of the requirements in the Virginia Code and 34.9% of the words in guidance documents. The following are some examples.[22] The Virginia Board for Barbers and Cosmetologists reduced cosmetologist training hours from 1,500 to 1,000, and received a 33 per cent credit. The Virginia Department of Housing and Community Development eliminated requirements from its 2021 building code that were claimed to cut over $24,000 from the cost of constructing a new house. The Department of Environmental Quality simplified the stormwater permitting process and provided new compliance pathways, claiming to save Virginia businesses $124 million per year. The Marine Resources Commission introduced a streamlined type of permit for working in subaqueous bed, claiming to save businesses $47 million per year. The Department of Environmental Quality introduced an online dashboard on which any citizen could track one of its permits, showing each step in the process, how long it was supposed to take, and how long it was actually taking. This site was said to cut permitting process times by 70 per cent in three years.

In 2024, the Australian State of Victoria's policy of 'making it simpler to do business' included these initiatives:[23]

1. Halve the number of business regulators by 2030.
2. Speed up Environmental Effects Statement (EES) processes, targeting assessment review of no longer than 18 months.
3. Deliver new priority assessment teams within key regulators to fast-track the assessment of priority projects.
4. Use digitisation and AI to speed up government.
5. Streamline liquor and planning approvals for hospitality businesses.
6. Remove the need for a planning permit for outdoor dining on public land.
7. Slash the regulatory burden for businesses to the tune of $500 million by 2030.

This is a typical example of political rhetoric that fails to explain *how* things are going to be done systemically (other than using more AI). Is this optimism or ignorance? Clarity is required on 'regulatory delivery' but this is usually missing at political level.

The questions underlying these stories are: Did the cut in historical rules have much impact on either reduction in contemporary business costs, or reduction in protection? Were they long overdue culling of redundant historical legislation? What was the impact on effort and on harms? Importantly, what was the impact on outcomes – especially levels of protection and harms, and on economic growth? The evidence on these points seems missing.

Better Regulation Techniques

Make Better Regulations

There has been a long trail of attempts to find the Holy Grail of a better way of doing regulation – so far largely unsuccessful! Various important steps have been taken, but they have not been focused in a complete solution; neither have individual positive elements yet been developed to their logical conclusions.

Different labels have been used over time, such as 'smart regulation' or 'agile regulation', but they remain mostly aspirational, with little clarity on how they are to be achieved.

Regulatory Reform Principles

There are plenty of examples of lists of the *principles* that regulators and regulation should follow, such as the post-Brexit policy that regulation should be proportionate, forward-looking, outcome-focused, collaborative, experimental and responsive.[24]

The focal points in the UK Regulatory Horizons Council's 2022 Report, *Closing the gap: getting from principles to practices for innovation friendly regulation*, were as follows:

- Regulation should adopt a proportionate approach to risks and benefits
- Regulation and innovation should embrace ethics and public engagement
- Regulation should take account of commercial considerations and the need to attract investment
- Regulatory design and implementation should consider alternative forms of regulation
- Regulation needs to get the timing right
- Regulators should foster a culture of openness and a growth mindset

Interesting conclusions emerged from the 2022 *Independent Review of Research Bureaucracy* on academic research.[25] It proposed seven principles for cutting unnecessary bureaucracy:

Harmonisation	Reducing the volume of administration through the use of common processes between different funders to make essential work easier.
Simplification	Reducing the complexity of individual processes to address unnecessary bureaucracy.
Proportionality	Ensuring that the obligations placed on researchers and institutions are commensurate with the size of the risk or reward.
Flexibility	Supporting and embracing excellence wherever it is found and not excluding research that does not fit within narrowly defined parameters.
Transparency	Communicating the rationale for systems and processes which have a bureaucratic burden.
Fairness	Developing approaches to systems and processes that support fairness, rather than erode it.
Sustainability	Cutting bureaucracy in ways that avoid destabilising the system to deliver a more efficient system over the long term.

Questions here are: Do principles like those set out above have much practical impact? Do they clarify what should be done?

Regulation of Regulators

Having created independent regulators, governments then try to control them. Structural controls exist through the definition in the governing legislation of objectives and duties, and the definition of powers (which may not empower certain activities). In addition, there has been a growth in the provision of Ministerial 'strategic steers'. A range of other attempts to 'regulate regulators' has also emerged. This is ironic, given that such attempts usually arise in response to claims of excessive regulatory burden. Is creating more at a different point in the system the right response? Other techniques include affecting how regulators operate by imposing a Regulators' Code, and creating coordination and learning mechanisms.

Codes, Duties and Steers

Most legislation creating a regulatory authority imposes duties on the authority. An authority can be held to account by Parliament, and be subject to judicial review by businesses and citizens if it fails to act in accordance with those duties. Ministers can also impose 'strategic steers' on regulators, to prioritise particular government policy. However, duties often conflict. How is a regulator to prioritise a growth duty (which probably involves being lenient and less controlling) with the core duty to deliver protection? The GDPR imposes 49 duties and powers on data protection authorities. Isn't that far too many?

A major change in approach to regulatory enforcement in the UK occurred in 2014, when a 'growth duty' was added to the requirements on regulatory authorities in a revision of the Regulators' Code. The 2014 Code specified the following principles:[26]

1. Regulators should carry out their activities in a way that supports those they regulate to comply and grow.
2. Regulators should provide simple and straightforward ways to engage with those they regulate and hear their views.
3. Regulators should base their regulatory activities on risk.
4. Regulators should share information about compliance and risk.
5. Regulators should ensure clear information, guidance and advice is available to help those they regulate meet their responsibilities to comply.
6. Regulators should ensure that their approach to their regulatory activities is transparent.

The primary duty here was to *support compliance and growth*. This shift had profound consequences on how regulators should act, which have yet to be fully realised. Some obvious implications are that both regulatory requirements and enforcement interventions should be targeted to *provide support*, and to use less formal civil sanctions that can cover behavioural and redress elements and include agreed undertakings, especially in consumer protection.[27]

The need for economic growth was re-emphasised by the UK Government in a series of initiatives from late 2024. These included calling on regulators to review their activities to support growth, requiring government departments to review regulators,[28] and imposing fresh strategic steers to support growth.[29] However, some underlying aspects of the policy were unexplained. First, the requirement to take greater risk implied reducing protection, which would logically lead to increased harms. Was more harm publicly accepted, and how would it be responded to? What about the people and businesses that were harmed? How is a regulator supposed to comply with its primary purpose and duty to deliver protection, if it is to deal more leniently with some risky activities by some people on the basis that this might assist growth? Had the regulators' primary purpose and duty been changed to permit them to be more lenient in some cases, and in which cases? Second, one underlying concern was that heavy *enforcement* is bad for growth (large fines make the UK look an unattractive jurisdiction to big business). But again, how should regulators be more lenient with some (foreign?) businesses than others whilst still maintaining credible consistency in their work? Does all this reveal a disconnect between high-level economic policy and the role and methodology of regulation?

'Performance' of Regulators

Some governments think that they can 'regulate regulators' by setting requirements for their professionalism, supposed 'maturity level', or 'performance'. Australia has been working since 2015 on performance reporting and working towards maturity levels. These approaches are usually a distraction, ironically adding to regulatory burden on regulators without achieving improved outcomes. The proposed metrics are usually around outputs rather than outcomes.

The problem here is that regulators are operating within the system, confines, duties and powers prescribed for them by Parliament. They cannot just change what they are established to do, nor in many circumstances how they do it. They cannot just 'go outside the box' and start to make things up, or fail to uphold the law that they have been created to uphold. They are at risk of attack from judicial review, and being called out by Ministers, Select Committees and the media. They are usually subject to a series of duties and 'steers', but rarely have a set of outcomes that could be used to measure their effectiveness.

All are attempts to use top-down authoritarian methods to 'control' regulatory authorities, the same mindset as in trying to rely on an authoritarian model by which authorities try to control the behaviour of regulatees. It's all the wrong approach, however intuitively apparent it might seem.

Regulatory Relationships: Enforcement or Support?

In 2011, government noted that businesses had told it that what was needed was a more mature relationship between business and regulators, a more transparent system of local regulation, and a simpler and more understandable regulatory landscape designed more around those who are regulated and protected, rather than Whitehall priorities.[30] A series of subsequent reviews showed excellent practice by some regulators, but also examples of overlapping, conflicting and duplicated regulatory requirements, delays, incomprehensible guidance, and companies wanting to comply left frustrated and bewildered as to where to turn.[31]

This line of thinking highlighted a disconnect between a traditional regulatory mode of imposing sanctions for non-compliances with rules, and a supportive mode of identifying problems, learning and improving (see chapters 3 and 4). These two modes are both valid – but apply in different situations. The lessons are clear but have yet to be applied widely in regulatory practice. This disconnect is a major factor holding back the achievement of regulatory outcomes and economic growth.

Consistency, Networking

Responses to inconsistency between different regulatory agencies lie in improved systems for communication and collaboration. More is needed, but some examples are as follows:

(a) A mechanism for engagement between national level businesses and multiple local authorities is the Primary Authority scheme, which creates a prioritised communication channel between the business's national head office and Primary Authority, providing advice that can be relied on.[32] This has proved to be an effective mechanism, but should be embedded across the entire regulatory landscape in order to eradicate all inconsistencies and gaps.

(b) Mechanisms for coordination between different sectoral regulators include the following:

    (i) National fora of regulators. Examples are the Canadian Federal Regulators Forum, the Forum of Indian Regulators, and the Australian National Regulators Forum. These need to be run so as to provide training and enough challenge and exchanges of information and techniques, without being perceived as attempts by government to control or manipulate regulators. Hence, they are often more effective if run as professional associations but with enough independent (and academic) challenge and governance.

(ii) UK Regulators Network (economic regulators: Financial Conduct Authority, Financial Reporting Council, Ofcom, Civil Aviation Authority, Ofgem, Regulator of Social Housing, Ofwat, Pensions Regulator, Payment Systems Regulator, Single Source Regulations Office, Information Commissioner's Office, Office of Road and Rail, Utility Regulator).

(iii) The (UK) Digital Regulators Cooperation Forum (Competition and Markets Authority, Information Commissioner's Office, Ofcom, Financial Conduct Authority). This provides a one-stop shop for advice to innovators, and a forum for consistency in policy. It has been notably successful, but a major reason is the small number of agencies involved.

(iv) The (UK) Financial Services Regulatory Initiatives Forum (Bank of England, Financial Conduct Authority, Prudential Regulation Authority, Payment Systems Regulator, Competition and Markets Authority, Information Commissioner's Office, Pensions Regulator, Financial Reporting Council; HM Treasury is an observer member).

Regulatory Delivery: Do it Better

In essence, much of the challenge is not about 'regulatory policy' but about 'how you do regulation' – regulatory delivery. The Government highlighted the importance of regulatory delivery in achieving not only regulatory outcomes but also business growth.[33] But this remains a largely untapped seam. As explained in chapter 3, the essence of the Regulatory Delivery Model revolves around six elements: Prerequisites – Governance framework, Accountability, Culture; Practices – Outcomes, Risk-based prioritisation, Intervention choices. The differentiation between enforcement and support made above is implicit in use of the term 'intervention choices' here, rather than 'enforcement'.

Huge power in improving the purposes of regulation could be unleashed by simply focusing on *outcomes*. No legislation requires regulators to focus on outcomes – statutes merely refer to duties. A focus on outcomes generates not only practical solutions for the achievement of the multiple desired outcomes (using the Regulatory Functions Model in chapter 3), but also the data that will establish if the relevant outcomes are being achieved or not. It is also highly likely to support collaboration between the different stakeholders. The outcomes of protection, profit and growth could be achieved more swiftly by using this simple approach.

How Much does Regulation Cost?

Complying with rules and procedures causes cost and delay. The cumulative cost and delay may be significant. Is it worth it? Cost and the value of regulation are important issues. But do we know what the costs are of complying with regulation? Do we know what the added costs are of unnecessary regulation?

We have a very limited understanding of how much of a burden new regulations are imposing. Vitali and Marsh studied over 1,200 new regulations introduced between 2014 and 2024, related to seven regulatory bodies: Natural England, Ofcom, Financial Conduct Authority, Food Standards Agency, Competition and Markets Authority, Financial Reporting Council, and Care Quality Commission. Fewer than two in 10 new regulations came with a Regulatory Impact Assessment.[34]

In 2024, 'the [UK] Government suggested that the administrative costs of regulatory compliance may amount to around £70 billion per annum, or 3-4% of GDP. Some of that will be the cost of funding the regulatory state itself: there are some 130 "bodies that regulate" in the UK (including regulators but also professional bodies), and in 2022-3, the largest 17 regulators had an annual expenditure of £5 billion and a head count of 39,000 full time employees.'[35]

Solutions here would be to monitor the cost of regulation – the *actual* cost, rather than (just) the predicted cost/benefit before rules are introduced, or a reduction in the calculated cost of individual regulatory authorities. The cost that is important is the cost felt by business – but that is difficult to measure. Further, the cost needs to be balanced against the risks and the benefits – do we do that?

Challenges of Globalism

Many commercial activities and organisations are now global. But rules and enforcement remain either at the level of an individual state or maybe a group of states. This presents barriers to trade between states, including regulatory barriers, which can be addressed by bilateral trade agreements, or those covering multiple states (such as the EU or the World Trade Association), providing for mutual recognition or equivalence. The objective is to avoid multiple compliance requirements and approvals, thereby reducing costs for businesses.

In mature activities and regulatory systems, there is an evolution towards establishing harmonisation of either or both of international standards and procedural certification requirements, and also regulatory rules, especially technical rules. Examples of organisations that produce globally accepted standards or harmonised legal requirements are:

- Basel Committee on Banking Supervision (BCBS):[36] see Core principles for effective banking supervision[37]
- International Organization of Securities Commissions (IOSCO)[38]
- International Maritime Organization
- International Civil Aviation Organization (ICAO) and International Air Transport Association (IATA)
- International Conference on Harmonisation of Pharmaceuticals for Human Use (ICH)
- World Health Organization (WHO)
- World Intellectual Property Organization (WIPO)
- International Telecommunication Union (ITU)
- International Atomic Energy Agency (IAEA)
- Global Agreement on Tariffs and Trade (GATT)
- International Accounting Standards Committee (IASC)

- United Nations Commission on International Trade Law (UNCITRAL)
- International Medical Device Regulators Forum (IMDRF)
- Codex Alimentarius Commission (food).

Will regulation succeed? Or will it be constantly playing catch-up? Governments, markets, societies and populations face a series of big challenges. Will life on earth continue to be viable if we fail to control global warming (let alone war)? Can we grow economies and afford pensions, social and health care? How do we support innovation but control its risks? Global platforms, global finance, AI, engineering biology, quantum, space and other developments know no boundaries.

The world is becoming increasingly VUCA (volatile, uncertain, complex and ambiguous), and regulatory development is somewhat fragmented and the processes often too slow. Major threats include a crisis in climate regulation, shifts in the global regulatory landscape due to war in Ukraine and the Middle East (leading to sanctions and trade restrictions, energy trade adjustments, export controls on dual-use goods, food security measures, reconfiguration of supply chains, and so on) and deconstruction of regulation.

Individual states are no longer able to control things based on the limitations of their geographical boundaries of jurisdiction and enforcement. More geographically far-reaching mechanisms are needed, but these are slow to form and to act. New technologies arrive at speed, and the pace of controls based on legislation and a Legal Model will not keep up. The opportunities for international crime are extensive. There is a definite need to develop regulatory mechanisms as the global economic and technology environments change rapidly. Further, the increasing threat of regulatory arbitrage may bring increased instability.

There remain considerable opportunities to develop effective controls, and to reduce duplicative rules and procedures, at international level. Reduction in repetitive tests or evidence of compliance can be achieved by closer alignment between public regulation and private accreditation systems – provided they are trustworthy and have sufficient independent governance and transparency. Increased reliance could be placed on trust-based collaborative networks of relationships, that have genuine legitimacy[39] and independent governance. There are significant opportunities for international supply chains to be based on trusted, holistic digital systems. It can align requirements of competence, resource, capacity, capability, motivation, intent and training with the size of a businesses. This approach offers huge potential for developing countries to make progress in economic and sustainable development goals.

How to do Regulation Better

It's easy to criticise regulators. But this is often a case of 'don't blame the messenger'. The causes of frustration usually lie elsewhere – with the system and those who create it (politicians) and the fact that almost no regulatory systems are capable of swift evolution, change and flexibility. Generalised criticisms of regulation are unhelpful because they undermine the confidence that a society needs to have in its system of providing many protections.

Remember Why

Before we sound off against regulation, we need to remember why it's there – to protect us. Much regulation is created in response to public outcry arising from major disasters that people do not want to see repeated. Examples of major scandals are:

- UK: Thalidomide, Equitable Life, PPI, BSE and mad cows, Northern Rock, Global Financial Crisis, Windrush, infected blood, Grenfell Tower fire, Post Office Horizon IT, motor finance commissions.
- UK NHS: Bristol children's heart hospital, Dr Harold Shipman, Mid-Staffordshire hospital care failure, Morecambe Bay neonatal care failure, Cumberlege Medicines and Medical Devices Safety Review, Winterbourne View elderly abuse.
- Abuse within various church, care and educational contexts.
- International financial fraud: Enron, WorldCom, Satyam Compute Services, Wirecard, Libor manipulation, Forex manipulation.
- Financial misrepresentation and fraud: Madoff's Ponzi scheme, Lehman Brothers collapse, 1Malaysia Development Berhad (1MDB), Wells Fargo fake accounts.

- Other corporate: Volkswagen emissions (Dieselgate), Boeing 737 MAX Manoeuvring Characteristics Augmentation System failure, Facebook–Cambridge Analytica Data scandal.

Some of the scandals listed above are failures in regulation as well as failures by those who were regulated. The failure of the model or practice of regulation, with differences in each case, shows that things do need to be improved. And we need to remember that the root causes of these disasters lay with their *originators*, rather than with regulators.

In 2025, the UK Prime Minister criticised regulation with the example that a housing development next to a cricket field was prevented because a risk assessment of cricket balls was not undertaken by an approved person. But in many contexts, such as the Grenfell tower fire, requiring assessment by an approved person is critical. Let's not write off regulation. Let's instead learn and get better at it. It's there to protect us:

- We *want* someone to protect our children from being groomed, abused, robbed and terrorised online.
- We *want* someone to stop sewage being pumped into rivers, beaches and the sea.
- We *want* someone to protect our markets, businesses and jobs from instability and unpredictable harm.
- We *want* to prevent children being born with phocomelia or other conditions, and to be prevented from illnesses through vaccination; and to prevent people being killed or injured on roads, at work and in the home.
- We *want* someone to speak up, listen and respond when computer systems are relied on to wrongly prosecute people (the Post Office) or unsafe cladding is installed on buildings (Grenfell Tower) or avoidable mistakes are made in delivering babies (Mid-Staffordshire) or caring for the elderly (Winterbourne View).

How to Address the Real Problems

It is undoubtedly true that many rules and procedures cause cost and delay, sometimes significant, both individually and cumulatively. This is especially a problem for SMEs and innovators, who have limited resource to satisfy extensive bureaucratic requirements. A possible response here is to operate a staged system, where the requirements are proportionate to the competence, resource, risk and trustworthiness of different sizes of enterprise. A number of proposed responses to 'the regulatory problem' have proved to be pointless. But the following functions are worth concentrating on.

Flow

Evaluating new regulation is not just about trying to make theoretical economic predictions about costs and benefits (RIA) but about an ongoing engagement with the effectiveness of the regime as a whole. There has been almost no attempt to consider or review the effectiveness of new rules on the *behaviour* of those subject to them (a Behavioural Impact Review), either in relation to specific actions or wider holistic effects and effectiveness of new requirements, or of the regulatory regime. This ought to demonstrate that a focus on having just a system of legal rules plus their enforcement to achieve 'compliance' misses the point in many cases.

Stock

An important issue for almost every state is to address the stock or regulations. Are they still needed, or are they disproportionate? Does the system of rules work? Are there better ways of achieving their protective purposes? So far, most attempts to reduce regulatory burden by removing outdated rules have been largely simplistic, and have had little impact on current ongoing burdens.

Proportionality

How much risk is acceptable? Regulation is there for a purpose. It protects us from harm, and from causing harm to others. People inherently underestimate risk. An assessment of risks versus benefits has to be undertaken objectively. But regulation costs money and delays things. The basic point is to be able to balance protection against activity that might entail risk. How do you find the right balance, and what is it?

Logically, whether the challenge of disproportionality and excessive cost or delay is valid is an issue that can only rationally be evaluated against the relevant evidence in a particular context. But we rarely do that. Indeed, we usually do not have the data or mechanisms to do that. Instead, generalised claims about 'regulation' and 'regulators' are bandied around, which are impossible to evaluate.

It is increasingly being realised that there is a conflict between the core role of regulators in delivering protection from harm, and multiple conflicting and genuine socio-economic goals. Goals like 'saving the planet' recede and 'accepting greater risk' come to the fore in times of economic stress, when economic growth is paramount. What we do not have is a system to balance multiple high-level goals, whilst maintaining effective front-line level practical decisions. How can risk decisions be taken in a way that involves more people (who may have to accept increased risk) but still be effective in maintaining general protections? Might certain farmers (or others who undertake risky activities) be licensed to do some risky things if they demonstrate a heightened understanding of and care for avoiding harm? Should we have more graded generic approvals for small businesses against demonstration of increasing competence levels? Can we gain more accurate understandings of actual risk through wider use of data monitoring systems? Should those who are at risk be more involved in understanding the protections and balances that are struck? How is risk appetite to be better established?

Permanent Identification of Barriers, Overlaps, Gaps and Efficiencies

We should be able to identify the situations where unnecessary barriers exist in practice, and how we are able to respond to them. A large part of this is about coordination and consistency between multiple regimes that apply to individual actors or activities. Solutions would lie in having a system for permanent investigation of major barriers, and expert analysis of potential solutions – and then the ability to make changes. The Regulatory Horizons Council has been active here, but its remit has been limited to looking at barriers for early-stage scientific and technical innovations. The same investigative and imaginative problem-solving approach should be spread right across the regulatory and governmental landscape.

Agility

Above all, we need to address the issue of regulatory agility. We should have a mechanism for changing rules, procedures and practices that is far swifter than waiting years for new legislation. The whole system of making and amending legal rules is far too slow. One approach is to delegate power from Parliament to new structures or authorities. If this is not done, we are condemned to revolving too slowly and ineffectively on the same regulatory hamster wheel, while missing serious opportunities to innovate, improve and grow. Let's speed up! A second approach is to recognise that a system of legal rules is not the only answer, and to look for new ways of addressing risk, behaviour, culture and protection.

Achieving Outcomes

This is the big opportunity to do things differently. It would help if we accepted that there is always risk. Regulation is designed to deliver protection, but it can never deliver no risk, and no harm. We should recognise that reality, and accept that some people will get hurt. Sometimes, there may be a conscious policy of accepting greater risk, in which case this implies a possibly lower level of protection but certainly a higher likelihood of harm occurring. But whatever the risk appetite may be, the answer for a protective system is the same – as set out in the Regulatory Functions Model. We should operate an ecosystem that identifies harm swiftly, stops it continuing, delivers redress swiftly, and implements changes based on learnings that reduce future risk.

In particular:

- The ecosystem has to be collaborative and capable of identifying harm as swiftly as possible.
- There must be a pre-existing, efficient and convincing redress mechanism, which has to be swift and properly capitalised; a standing ombuds-like system, plus regulatory redress.

Profiting from effective ways of doing things, and delivering effective protection, do not lie in rules or bureaucracy, but in focusing on whether we are achieving the right outcomes.

Key Points

- Regulation exists for delivering adequate protection from harm. It necessarily imposes some controls on how people do things.
- But deciding how much control is enough, and how much constitutes too much cost and prevention of freedom to act and innovate, are difficult issues.
- Regulatory authorities are frequently blamed for doing what they are required to do by legislation and government.
- But the real issues are whether the system is properly designed, and how much risk a society is prepared to accept – which are issues that are not widely addressed.
- The cost of rectifying harm after it occurs is often omitted from complaints about regulation, or consideration of the benefits of action and doing new things.
- Traditional Better Regulation controls (on flow and removal of rules) have not been particularly effective. Neither will 'regulating regulators' be.
- Solutions lie in looking at regulation as systems, in increasing their agility and ability to achieve outcomes, and more open discussions about the acceptability of risk and provision of mechanisms for rectifying harms.

---

[1] *Managing Risks and Incentivising Growth: Draft Best Practice Principles for Licensing and Permitting* (OECD, 2024), paras 8, 14.

[2] C Decker and C Hodges, *Government-sponsored voluntary regulation in the British Retail Sector* (2014).

[3] J Cumberlege, *First Do No Harm – The report of the Independent Medicines and Medical Devices Safety Review* (2020).

[4] Grenfell Tower Inquiry Reports at www.grenfelltowerinquiry.org.uk/.

[5] Regulatory Enforcement and Sanctions Act 2008, s 54(1)(a). Administrative Tribunals were reorganised under the Tribunals, Courts and Enforcement Act 2007. See also the Tribunal Procedure (First-tier Tribunal) (General Regulatory Chamber) Rules 2009/1976.

[6] C Mayer, *Capitalism and Crises* (Oxford University Press, 2024).

[7] *Creating a more dynamic and resilient economy. Interim report* (Australian Government, Productivity Commission, 2025).

[8] See generally D Kahneman, *Thinking, Fast and Slow* (Allen Lane, 2011); D Ariely, *Predictably Irrational: The Hidden Forces That Shape Our Decisions* (HarperCollins, 2008). For more detail: D Kahneman and S Frederick, 'Representativeness Revisited: Attribute Substitution in Intuitive Judgment' in T Gilovich, D Griffin and D Kahneman (eds), *Heuristics and Biases: The Psychology of Intuitive Judgment* (Cambridge, 2002)

49; ND Weinstein, 'Unrealistic Optimism about Susceptibility to Health Problems: Conclusions from a Community-Wide Sample' (1987) 10 *J Behav Med* 481, 494; A Tversky and D Kahneman, 'Availability: A Heuristic for Judging Frequency and Probability' (1973) 5 *Cog Psych* 207, 221.

[9] *The Role of Regulation in Supporting Scaling-up* (Regulatory Horizons Council, 2024).

[10] J Vitali and Z Marsh, *The Rise of the Regulators. Reversing the Risk Aversion Ratchet* (Policy Exchange, 2024).

[11] https://documented.net/reporting/video-donald-trump-russ-vought-center-renewing-america-maga-new-trump-agenda.

[12] A King and I Crewe, *The Blunders of Governments* (Oneworld Publications, rev 2014); DC Grube, *Why Governments Get IT Wrong And How They Can Get It Right* (Macmillan, 2022); R Stewart, *Politics On the Edge* (Vintage, 2024); I Dunt, *How Westminster Works ... And Why It Doesn't* (Weidenfeld & Nicholson, 2023).

[13] Robert S Adler, 'Reflections of an Unapologetic Safety Regulator', *The Regulatory Review* (17 October 2022). This former Director of the US CPSC cited the agency's estimate that roughly 31,000 people die and 34 million people suffer product-related injuries in the USA every year; these events impose a cost on the US economy of roughly one trillion dollars annually.

[14] *A foundation for better law: five years of bureaucracy reduction and better regulation* (German Federal Government, April 2012).

[15] Executive Order 14192 of January 31, 2025 *Unleashing Prosperity Through Deregulation*; https://www.govinfo.gov/content/pkg/FR-2025-02-06/pdf/2025-02345.pdf.

[16] J Vitali and Z Marsh, *The Rise of the Regulators. Reversing the Risk Aversion Ratchet* (Policy Exchange, 2024).

[17] ibid.

[18] Laura Jones, *Lessons from the British Columbia Model of Regulatory Reform* (Mercatus Center, 27 September 2018), www.mercatus.org/research/federal-testimonies/lessons-british-columbia-model-regulatory-reform#:~:text=An%20overarching%20and%20important%20lesson,%2C%20safety%2C%20and%20environmental%20outcomes.

[19] J Vitali and Z Marsh, *The Rise of the Regulators. Reversing the Risk Aversion Ratchet* (Policy Exchange, 2024).

[20] See D Chambers and P McLaughlin, 'Idaho's Regulatory Landscape: Federal and State Rules and Some of Their Unintended Consequences' (Mercatus Centre, 2024).

[21] See www.floridahasarighttoknow.myflorida.com/regulation_rulemaking.

[22] RT Bull, 'The Virginia Model for Regulatory Modernization', *The Regulatory Review* (18 November 2024), www.theregreview.org/2024/11/18/bull-the-virginia-model-for-regulatory-modernization/.

[23] *Economic Growth Statement Victoria: Open for Business* (Government of Victoria, 2024), https://www.vic.gov.au/sites/default/files/2024-12/Economic-Growth-Statement.pdf.

[24] I Duncan-Smith, T Villiers and G Freeman, *Taskforce on Innovation, Growth and Regulatory Reform* (2012), www.gov.uk/government/publications/taskforce-on-innovation-growth-and-regulatory-reform-independent-report.

[25] http://assets.publishing.service.gov.uk/government/uploads/system/uploads/attachment_data/file/1094648/independent-review-research-bureaucracy-final-report.pdf.

[26] *Regulators' Code* (Department for Business Innovation and Skills, 2013). Originally the *Regulators' Compliance Code: Statutory Code of Practice for Regulators* (Department for Business, Enterprise and Regulatory Reform, 2007). The Code is made under the Legislative and Regulatory Reform Act 2006, s 22(1).

[27] Enterprise Act 2008, s 219A, inserted by the Consumer Rights Act 2015, s 79 and Sch 7, para 8.

[28] eg *Policy paper: A new approach to ensure regulators and regulation support growth* (17 March 2025, updated), www.gov.uk/government/publications/a-new-approach-to-ensure-regulators-and-regulation-support-growth. G Parker, O Aliaj and J Pickard, 'Rachel

Reeves to order audit of UK's 130 regulators in bid to cut red tape. Ministers will be told to look at whether some watchdogs can be scrapped', *Financial Times* (18 February 2025).

[29] eg *Strategic steer to the Competition and Markets Authority* (15 May 2025), www.gov.uk/government/publications/strategic-steer-to-the-competition-and-markets-authority/strategic-steer-to-the-competition-and-markets-authority.

[30] *Government Response to the Consultation on Transforming Regulatory Enforcement* (Department for Business, Innovation and Skills, 2011).

[31] Michael Fallon MP, *Speech: Deregulation and economic growth: priorities for government reform* (12 November 2013).

[32] See www.gov.uk/government/publications/primary-authority-overview.

[33] *Regulation and growth* (Better Regulation Delivery Office, 2016).

[34] J Vitali and Z Marsh, *The Rise of the Regulators. Reversing the Risk Aversion Ratchet* (Policy Exchange, 2024).

[35] Department for Business and Trade, 'Smarter Regulation: Delivering a Regulatory Environment for Innovation, Investment and Growth' (2024).

[36] www.bis.org/bcbs/.

[37] www.bis.org/bcbs/publ/d573.htm.

[38] www.iosco.org/.

[39] I Goldin, *Rescue. From Global Crisis to a Better World* (Sceptre, 2021) 96.

9

New Regulatory Systems to Support Innovation

> Innovators, their funders, and governments can find regulation to be an annoying barrier to doing and marketing new things. It is easy, here, to 'blame the messenger' in the form of one or more regulators, whose job it is to say 'sorry but you're not allowed to do that'. This chapter unpicks the underlying problems. How can innovators have clarity and support in developing a new technology and a market, whilst unacceptable harms are avoided. These questions have become highly topical, given the fundamental transformations that science and technology are unleashing in our Fourth Industrial Revolution. The pace of change is now way faster than traditional legal systems are capable of regulating. We no longer have the option of waiting to deploy a traditional rules-enforcement based regulatory system for most new technologies. The solutions lie in addressing problems with regulatory *systems* and how we operate them.

Challenges in Regulating Innovation

Regulation is typically thought of as a concrete formal system, backed by law, that applies to tangible products, services, activities and markets. In contrast, this chapter focuses on the stage *before* an innovative technology or science achieves maturity and is regulated by a specific, focused set of regulations. At that stage, the technology would typically not have become commercialised as products, services, activities or markets, and/or specific legal requirements have not yet been defined and enacted.

In this preliminary stage, a number of different situations and challenges may arise, notably:[1]

- There may be no rules or procedures, or a specific regulatory scheme or authority, that cover the products, services, activities or markets. It may just be a technology. Thus, it may be completely unclear what, if anything, people should do.
- Alternatively, there may be one or more existing regulatory regimes that apply, and these may give rise to barriers to developing or marketing the innovation. For example, the rules might ban certain things, or it may be difficult to apply the rules to the new use case, or there may be confusion over which requirements apply, and how. Issues of inconsistencies or conflict between regimes and requirements can occur and either constitute a significant barrier, perhaps because of lack of funding as much as time or evidence (the brick wall problem), or slow things down significantly.
- In between these two extremes (no regulation or some existing regulations), there can be quite a range of possibilities. For example, the existing rules may be unclear or inappropriate. Or there can be gaps in the requirements. Several existing regimes may apply, giving rise to overlapping or inconsistent requirements or constraints. The cumulative effect of different requirements can be significant.

Each of these issues (and they may arise cumulatively) may need different solutions, depending on the particular context. The situation may be made worse because of other factors, such as:[2]

- *Awareness.* Innovators may not be aware that they would need to satisfy regulatory requirements for their innovative product/service until late in the R&D stage. They then find themselves facing what seem like huge requirements to obtain data and may run out of money.
- *Irrelevance/alignment.* The regulatory requirements do not make sense for the new activity/product/service (because they were designed for different products/services); or they would not adequately control the risks.
- *Proportionality/cost.* The regulatory requirements are too onerous/expensive.

Principles

Precautionary and Other Principles

When we face unknown and new risks, should we proceed with caution until we can identify the risks and their causes, and control them in some way, or just press on and hope for the best? Is it more important to gain the benefits of innovation, or to have protection from harm? The obvious answer is: it depends! But our systems for making decisions are somewhat slow. In recent decades, arguments about innovation and protection in specific contexts have been generalised into broad principles, which have not tended to help matters.

The 'precautionary principle' started as 'the Vorsorgeprinzip' in German planning law around the 1960s, and was taken up by the EU in the context of chemicals regulation, particularly for organochlorine insecticides, where an extremely high standard of evidence was required before regulators would accept that organochlorines were disrupting the breeding success of birds. The point made was that we should have been more precautionary and accepted a lower standard of evidence in making the decision to ban organochlorines until we had gathered more evidence and could make a more considered judgement. The battle between the multinational chemical companies and the environmentalists was fought out on points of quality and quantity of evidence.

The EU responded to the 'mad cow' crisis by introducing a precautionary principle, which was that the public should not be exposed to risk unless there was adequate evidence-based scientific certainty.[3] Its origins were in environmental protection, but this was a political policy that prioritised safety and consumer protection over innovation, and much research was subsequently impeded. Subsequent discussions modified this by introducing an 'innovation principle' and adapting the approach under the long-standing EU 'proportionality principle'.

The exit of the UK from the EU included a political shift from the EU's precautionary principle to a proportionality approach. In other words, the notional juxtaposition was from a restrictive and protective mode to a more business- and innovation-friendly mode, whilst still aiming to deliver protection. Whether there is substance in this shift could be debated, and may depend on context, but it is at least politically important. Thus, the UK's suggested new proportionality principle in 2021 was that regulation should be proportionate to the level of a risk and ensure that regulation was based on outcomes.[4]

A problem remains that all of these high-level formulations would need to be worked out in practice in individual circumstances. This requires a person or body that has authority to make decisions on a balanced and principles-based approach, operating within a clear process. Achieving simplicity and certainty in practice are far from easy. Differences in viewpoints may remain contentious over the correct balance in both general and specific circumstances.

Principles and Responses in Regulating Innovation

The UK Regulatory Horizons Council (RHC) has looked at these challenges. Its 2022 Report, *Closing the gap: getting from principles to practices for innovation friendly regulation*, as noted in chapter 8, recommended the following focal points:

- Regulation should adopt a proportionate approach to risks and benefits
- Regulation and innovation should embrace ethics and public engagement
- Regulation should take account of commercial considerations and the need to attract investment
- Regulatory design and implementation should consider alternative forms of regulation
- Regulation needs to get the timing right
- Regulators should foster a culture of openness and a growth mindset

The RHC's analysis of principles published by numerous bodies highlighted these strong overarching themes:

- The need for collaboration.
- Retaining a degree of proportionality, and adaptability.
- Adopting an outcomes-focused approach.
- Being future facing; proactive in anticipating and monitoring future technological innovations.

The RHC's subsequent 2024 Report focused on activities to support the scaling-up of technological innovations and associated small businesses.[5] It made this important statement about the value of regulation:

We strongly believe that regulation – when designed and enacted well – can be an important *enabler* for start-ups. A well-designed regulatory environment can support start-ups and scaleups to scale their businesses to the next level, for example through:

- Shaping the development of safe and effective new products and services, and supporting start-ups and scaleups to gather the necessary evidence to demonstrate such credentials;
- Providing confidence in a sector to support access to finance and investment for scaling; and
- Facilitating the creation of new and trusted markets in the UK and internationally through promoting competition, fostering public acceptance and encouraging international harmonisation of requirements.

Regulation of financing models, infrastructure development and intellectual property also play a great role in influencing the other factors mentioned above that are important to start-ups and scaleups. However, for the sake of this review, we are focusing on the regulation of the *applications of the products and services* that are being developed, rather than the wider ecosystem.

The RHC made the following key points.

(a) One should not try to regulate a technology: one should regulate products, services, activities and markets. Hence, one should not try to regulate too soon. This may stifle innovation and development of applications and use cases, and it may entrench restrictive regimes or ones that favour established incumbents to the detriment of smaller innovators. But horizon scanning and planning remain critical.

(b) In the RHC's experience, innovation should not be regulated until it attains a certain level of maturity, such as Technology Level 6 (see below).[6] This point needs explaining.

The UK Government set out a 'pro-innovation approach' to AI regulation in 2023,[7] with a framework underpinned by five principles to guide and inform the responsible development and use of AI in all sectors of the economy:

- Safety, security and robustness
- Appropriate transparency and explainability
- Fairness
- Accountability and governance
- Contestability and redress

The Government proposed that its regulatory framework would be:

- **Pro-innovation**: enabling rather than stifling responsible innovation.
- **Proportionate**: avoiding unnecessary or disproportionate burdens for businesses and regulators.
- **Trustworthy**: addressing real risks and fostering public trust in AI in order to promote and encourage its uptake.
- **Adaptable**: enabling us to adapt quickly and effectively to keep pace with emergent opportunities and risks as AI technologies evolve.
- **Clear**: making it easy for actors in the AI life cycle, including businesses using AI, to know what the rules are, who they apply to, who enforces them, and how to comply with them.
- **Collaborative**: encouraging government, regulators, and industry to work together to facilitate AI innovation, build trust and ensure that the voice of the public is heard and considered.

Stages of Maturity

Useful analysis has been done on Technology Readiness Levels (TRLs), which suggests a point *before* which regulation is not helpful.[8] (Attempts have been made to extend the analysis to Market, Societal, Organisational, Legal and other Readiness Levels,[9] with varying degrees of success.) The TRLs can be described as in Table 9.1.[10]

Table 9.1 Technology Readiness Levels (TRLs)

Phase	Level	Stage	Description
Research	TRL1	Basic Principles	Specific technological idea is formulated
	TRL2	Invention and Research	The technology idea is explicitly described
	TRL3	Proof of Concept	Experimental proof of concept
Development	TRL4	Bench Scale Research	Technological elements tested and validated in lab or simulated environment

(continued)

Table 9.1 (Continued)

Phase	Level	Stage	Description
	TRL5	Pilot Scale	Integrated technology tested and validated in lab or simulated environment
	TRL6	Large Scale	Technology demonstrated in relevant environment
Deployment	TRL7	Inactive Commissioning	System prototype demonstrated in natural environment
	TRL8	Active Commissioning	Product tested and validated, and the functionality is being optimised
Operations	TRL9	Operations	Actual system proven functional in natural environment

Different types of standardisation might help at different stages of development of technology.[11] It is, therefore, important to consider in each particular context: what needs standardising; and how different types of standardisation can help at different stages and with different types of innovations.

Analytical work on the impacts of regulation on innovation also distinguishes between generic and specific types of regulation.[12] In economic regulation, it can be difficult to identify immediate specific impacts of regulation that foster innovation, whereas positive impacts are clearer in social regulation, which can stimulate innovation because they require compliance innovation.

The RHC proposed, in considering the platform technology area of engineering biology, that a systemic framework approach be adopted, which could subsequently lead to more specifics that would probably need to be customised for different types of subject matter.[13] It said that innovators, government, regulators and others should work together to devise appropriate governance as technologies developed, using networks like a Biotechnology Regulators' Network and the Biosecurity Leadership Council. Companies should be encouraged to make a formal commitment to responsible innovation.

It is, therefore, critical that government and regulators, together with academic institutions, funders and supporters of innovation, and others, undertake constant horizon scanning for new ideas as they emerge and are developed, and maintain communications about options for support, standardisation, commercial applications, regulation and so on. The following section sets out some techniques that have proved to be useful.

Lyall and Tait have suggested the idea of 'tentative governance' in the development phases of a new technology, as new rules of engagement are developed and revised, involving a shift in the governance mode to a second generation of governance approaches.[14] They also note that it may not be possible for consensus to be reached involving all stakeholders, meaning that full ongoing participation may not be possible as technology use cases mature.

Tools

Building Pathways: Standards and Private Accreditation Mechanisms

As an innovative technology develops, much can be done on a cumulative basis by those involved in developing an appropriate regulatory regime for it. The concept of *governance* may be more useful in this 'pre-regulation' phase rather than that of 'regulation'.[15] The typical discussions are inherently exploratory, rather than mandatory, but involve increasing clarity and solidification of what may end as legal rules.

Tools that are highly effective in building consensus, consistency and data around effective and appropriate elements of control are private systems of standards-making,[16] codes and private accreditation systems (see chapter 1). As the RHC said:[17]

> ... the building blocks of standards, tests, conformity assessment and so on can be crystalised over time. In this way, an evolving pathway around safe and effective use, risk and harm, and their evaluation and control, can identify the essential elements of what will become a regulatory system. Such a system can also emerge as stages of private and public elements, and regulators should consider opportunities to partner with academic institutions and innovative start-ups and scaleups when building this evidence.

It should be remembered that the main actors in a sector may have competing motivations in establishing a private regulatory system. They may wish to protect their reputations, or the reputation of their sector, by setting an expected standard of competence. They may wish to delay or avoid the imposition of a public system, which would remove a significant element of control and might involve significant cost. Any regulatory system may also erect cost and other barriers to entry, so tend to be protective of incumbents and restrict new entrants and also innovation.

Important questions might be:

- What common standards are required, for different aspects of product or service quality, consistency, efficacy and safety?
- What standards are needed to guide and demonstrate effective activities, behaviour, culture and control systems?
- What external verification or scrutiny is needed? Can this be done by private sector technical independent auditors or compliance systems, and what involvement of public authorities is required?
- What functions identify, control and respond to risk and occurrence of harm?
- What inconsistencies, overlaps, gaps and conflicts in the evidence need be filled?

Key issues are how to achieve a convincing *evidence-base* for the assessment of risks, how to achieve *consensus* on relevant issues, and how to build *international* consensus on such matters. What institutions and techniques are required? How can relevant dialogues, communications, debates and data be obtained and evaluated? How can such processes function with appropriate pace? Should data be held by independent trustworthy institutions?

The PAGIT Framework

A powerful tool is the PAGIT framework developed by Professor Joyce Tait and colleagues: Proportionate and Adaptive Governance of Innovative Technologies (PAGIT).[18] This consolidated responsible innovation framework (RIF) 'distinguishes between routine, company-specific aspects of responsibility, expected to be addressed within an organisation's standard operating procedures, and project-specific aspects requiring regular appraisal throughout the development of an innovation. It is designed to be simple and feasible for a company to implement within a commercial environment.'[19] Tables 9.2 to 9.4 set out the two component elements and the consolidated framework.

Table 9.2 Routine, Company-specific RI Elements related to Standard Business Practice

	Positive and negative drivers	Criteria
1.	Promoting sound practices in employment, business behaviour and ethics	Organisations should encourage principles of good business behaviour and ethics, including responsible sourcing, fairness, human rights, privacy, the avoidance of child or coerced labour, and accountable governance
2.	Absence of clear policies and procedures on bribery and corruption	Organisations should have appropriate policies in place, including guidance for employees
3.	Inappropriate use of human or animal products and substitutes	Partners should commit to adopting the appropriate codes and regulations
4.	Testing products on animals	Testing on animals should be kept to a minimum and should comply with Home Office guidelines
5.	Business in countries that violate the political and civil rights of their people	Where the market or components of the supply chain involve countries rated poorly in these respects, the organisations concerned should have effective policies on human rights
6.	Production or sale of weapons	Deriving revenues from this source outwith international treaties and/or for non-defence purposes is discouraged
7.	Addictive substances and behaviours	Projects leading to these outcomes are discouraged
8.	Familiarity and compliance with existing regulations relevant to the project	Organisations convicted of an offence within the last three years are not eligible for funding; organisations should demonstrate that they are familiar, and comply, with relevant regulations

Table 9.3 Project-specific Elements of RI Requiring Active Consideration and Monitoring as a Project Evolves

Source	Element
Positive drivers (factors in favour of supporting projects)*	1. Products and services that benefit society and/or human well-being 2. Making a positive contribution to the environment 3. Promoting sound practices in employment, business behaviour and ethics
Negative drivers (factors against supporting projects)*	4. End uses leading to social damage 5. End uses leading to environmental damage or pollution
Regulatory driver*	6. Regular reassessment of regulatory requirements and implementation of any necessary regulatory changes
Elements**	7. Anticipate – describing/analysing potential impacts relevant to the project 8. Reflect – on purposes of, motivations for and potential implications of the project and associated uncertainties 9. Engage – opening up visions, impacts and questioning to broader deliberation and dialogue 10. Act – using the above processes to influence the direction and trajectory of the research and innovation process.

* Proposed by the Technology Strategy Board (TSB, now Innovate UK) Responsible Innovation Framework.
** Proposed by the Engineering and Physical Sciences Research Council (EPSRC) as its anticipate, reflect, engage and act (AREA) approach.

Table 9.4 Consolidated RI Framework

Elements of RI	Issues arising during the project	Organisation responses Anticipate Reflect Engage Act
Societal element		
Environmental element		
Business practice element		
Regulatory element		

Responsible Innovation

In the initial phases of researching and developing innovation, *how and what* things are done is important. The observance of common values and consistency will support or undermine trust, and will allow early consideration of issues and implications. Professional or activity-based codes and requirements exist to guide and influence the performance of relevant behaviour.[20] Such requirements govern behaving in a *responsible* professional manner in accordance with the prevailing ethical norms and values of human society.[21] Companies and organisations should similarly ensure that their activities accord with *responsible* development of innovative products, processes and services.[22]

The PAS 440:2020 *Responsible innovation – Guide* sets out the approach. It follows a number of other precedents that specify the ethical and social responsibility principles that companies may commit to observing as part of their basic corporate governance. An individual example is BS ISO 26000:2020 *Guidance on social responsibility*, which specifies the following ethical principles:

(a) accountability for impacts on society, the environment and the economy;
(b) transparency in decisions that impact on society and the environment;
(c) ethical behaviour;
(d) respect for stakeholder interests;
(e) respect for the rule of law;
(f) respect for international norms of behaviour; and
(g) respect for human rights.

PAS 440:2020 provides a risk assessment matrix for recording evidence that demonstrates company-level social responsibility and a responsible innovation framework (RIF) for undertaking a baseline assessment of innovation-specific responsibility. The RIF can be reviewed over time. Responsible engagement guidelines are set out to ensure equitable treatment across all stakeholders, who all share a duty to behave responsibly, and to provide the basis of engagement between them, thereby achieving balance across diverse stakeholder perspectives. The guidelines accept that consensus may not be attainable, so expectations need to be managed accordingly, but say that the values and/or interests of one stakeholder group should not restrict the freedom of choice of others.

This approach recognises that the application of the guidelines in particular situations requires a process of achieving balance:

(a) across different sets of ethical principles, eg between innovation and precaution;
(b) between different power structures occupied by different stakeholders;
(c) between benefits and risks of innovations; and
(d) across the varied interests and values relevant to different stakeholder groups.

Issues around responsibility and ethics assume higher importance in an environment where trust and engaged relationships are needed between those involved.

Risk Appetites and Competing Values

Further issues are the *risk appetite* of a society and the application of *ethical values*. People may value some protections or risks differently, and may base their views on particular ethical principles. It is inherent in the nature of values that different values may be emphasised by individuals and communities at different times in particular circumstances (often without realising this, and its inconsistencies).[23] We have seen in recent years clear examples of this, with governments adopting a 'precautionary principle' and later imposing 'a growth duty' on regulators. What is missing here is a mechanism by which society, and its communities, reach a consensus on their risk appetite at a particular time. Such a mechanism needs to permit both democratic voice, debate and consensus, as well as the ability to state a conclusion that has binding effect on everyone *speedily*, and certainly more speedily than traditional Parliamentary legislative processes.

An Ecosystem for Identifying and Responding to Harm

In developing a regulatory system for something new, a key issue relates to the means of organisation and collaboration between various actors and institutions who will be involved in designing, supplying, using and monitoring it. The regulatory system itself is something that needs to be considered, and operated well. This requires a focus beyond the nature and properties of the innovation itself. Things like AI, quantum or biological engineering techniques may produce not only benefits but also harms that we cannot predict or design into our requirements in advance. So, our means of identifying problems, and responding to them, will be crucial.

The RHC posed these questions:[24]

> When developing new regulatory approaches for emerging technologies that take due account of all of these points, the basic questions that have to be answered are:
>
> - What is the system for identifying the risks and harms that occur with this product, service or market? Who will identify the relevant information, and how is it to be shared with others? Who needs to evaluate the data, and implement actions to manage it?
> - How will risks and harms be evaluated as acceptable (or not), and balanced with realistic potential benefits, and who needs to be involved? This typically involves technical expert evaluation, but it may also need the involvement of wider society if ethical considerations are involved.
> - How will risks be managed, so as to deliver successful and acceptable outcomes? What actions might need to be taken by whom?'

Too often the response to encountering a regulatory barrier to innovation is to blame the regulator. But the regulator is doing what it is legally required to do, in applying Parliament's laws. It may be that some regulators are slow to respond to the need to change and accommodate new things and new ways of doing them, and could identify new things and react to them more quickly, but ultimate responsibility lies with the *system* and its governance.

Having an ecosystem that responds quickly to new developments may be a powerful solution to the conundrum of deregulating so as to achieve some other goals (such as economic growth). What is essential is to have an effective and responsive Regulatory Functions Model (chapter 3).

Agility

So, we need an RFM that is agile and responsive. If our systems identify and respond to harm quickly, we should be able to face unknown risks and harms with greater confidence. We should be able to innovate more quickly. And we should be able to learn and make corrections in an iterative way, which typically characterises innovation.

A particular problem is making changes in existing legal rules so as to allow exemptions, suspend the rules in certain circumstances, change them, or repeal them. Regulators get blamed for this, but it is a responsibility of government and legislature. How should one allow flexibility and discretion in a regulatory system?

The RHC called this:[25]

> an important gap in the regulatory toolbox that should be available for all regulators, to facilitate pro-innovation culture and effective, speedy delivery. Such a mechanism would need to take account of and balance relevant considerations of protection, risk, benefits, innovation, growth and other aspects. But we recommend that changes can be made that observe considerations of constitutional governance, maintaining adequate protection, and delivering speedy support for innovation. Such a change would be a game changer, and no country has done it.

> The power to agree derogations or permit flexibility might operate differently in different contexts and sectors. It might, for example, be inherent within a regulatory structure, permitting operators flexibility in how they comply with essential outcome requirements through 'acceptable means of compliance' (a phrase used in aviation safety regulation), but many regulatory systems do not have such flexibility. In other contexts, there might be a power for a regulator to exercise discretion in permitting specific arrangements within a sandbox scheme, or to derogate or disapply existing rules in certain circumstances. Powers might be exercised subject to advice or approval by a suitable committee of experts and stakeholders. Alternatively, an independent committee might be empowered to make the decision, perhaps even a single centralised committee so as to avoid unnecessary

bureaucracy. Further, a Minister might have such [a] power, perhaps subject to notification and a 'negative resolution' procedure by Parliament.

Thus, a number of options might be relevant, some more swift and flexible than others. We recommend that all major sectors where innovation is relevant should review (involving business and other stakeholders, as well as regulators) what approach would be appropriate in their context so as to facilitate innovation. The review should invite views on the circumstances and conditions that should apply to the experiment, and what protections, how to decide what level of risk is acceptable, and what arrangements should exist for redress if harm occurs.

New Tools for Examining Risks

It will typically be the case that new technologies give rise to unexpected risks and unknown unknowns. The essential regulatory issues are to identify risks and, in some systems, to carry out a balancing evaluation as between risks and harms. This means that harms, risks and benefits need to be identified and evaluated. How? Chapter 7 sets out the main tools that are used in regulation, where the pre-marketing requirements for tests and trials are especially relevant.

The RHC noted various types of regulatory experimentation, especially sandboxes, testbeds, and digital simulation.[26]

Sandboxes are experimental approaches which offer supervised real-life or simulated test environments where innovators can [trial] new products, services or business models, often under relaxed regulatory requirements. They are designed and delivered independently by regulators and are not a tool for deregulation. These are particularly powerful when linked to data access.

Testbeds have a broader scope than regulatory sandboxes, often operating in environments with a significant industrial component, and do not always seek to create an appropriate regulatory environment, and may be developed primarily to test proof of concept. Regulators' involvement in a particular testbed can be useful to identify future regulatory implications, and is usually agreed between the regulator and the consortium driving the testbed forward, such as a local authority.

Digital simulation. Where products are in early-stage development and there are safety concerns surrounding testing their deployment even in controlled settings, digital approaches such as digital simulation or twins can be useful.

Digital models can be used to generate a virtual copy of a system in which interventions could be trialled. For example, virtual traffic models have been generated to test the interactions of autonomous vehicles, and the computational modelling has been used to better understand drug interactions.[27]

A *regulatory sandbox* seems first to have been used by the Financial Conduct Authority in 2006. Its testing of products in controlled situations, sometimes without any rules applying other than close cooperative study on effects and outcomes by the business and regulator involved, inherently rests on collaboration and trust. The sandbox technique has spread quickly around the world, in different sectors and countries.[28] There are various different forms of sandbox and no consistent understanding, such as whether *all* rules are suspended, all rules are continued under close scrutiny, or there is some ability to suspend some rules and procedures

Another tool is the 'delayed release' concept. This involves a minimum period of testing pre-release in an isolated facility and/or with controlled/licensed users during which one tries to break it (ie 'not what's the best it can do, but what's the worst it can do'). This information is then used to undertake an 'algorithmic impact assessment' to inform a decision as to whether the item is 'released' and what the conditions around it should be (an example is of *in silico* extrapolations).[29]

There may be real opportunities in developing further *private sector involvement* in providing regulatory functions, or some of them. This may be critical to overcome serious resource bottlenecks, or new areas where there is little expertise. It is not impossible to overcome issues of potential conflict with relevant governance and transparency arrangements. In some sectors, there is nothing unusual about extensive private accreditation, standards, auditing functions, either as part of a mixed economy of private and public mechanisms, or with private systems playing a major role. Indeed, in some systems (food) there is unnecessary duplication between private accreditation and public inspection regimes (an example of a pilot looking at this is the FSA's ABC project with supermarkets and local authorities). This technique may be more widely used in other sectors.

Opportunities from Collaboration

A key value of a sandbox is that it involves close collaboration between a regulator and innovators. This highlights the ideal that developing close and effective connection between all relevant actors *on an ongoing generic basis* is highly desirable. The RHC recommended a coordinated and collaborative approach to helping start-ups and to solving common problems across sectors.[30]

In traditional regulatory models, a number of innovative approaches may be possible, for example shifting the balance between pre- and post-marketing controls, which may significantly reduce the burden and time of producing extensive test data, transferring the means of scrutiny to real time monitoring. This may be facilitated where the ongoing monitoring ecosystem produces adequate data on how the regulatory system is operating and on identifying harms as they occur (in accordance with the RFM based on OBC). This shift in focus might be seen as a permanent collaborative sandbox.

An application of this approach would flow from the collection of all data on health outcomes in a given population. This might lead to relaxation of regulatory requirements on healthcare professionals, institutions, products and services, since easier identification of outcomes would flow from review of a complete healthcare system. Singapore has been considering this.

Providing Public Assurance and Trust

There is considerable scope for enhancing assurance that: (a) risks will be identified swiftly; (b) swift proportionate response will be implemented to reduce future risk; and (c) to provide care/repair/redress. The functions to deliver these goals are: (i) a suitably comprehensive vigilance system (involving users, business and regulators, all connected in an integrated data system, but also underpinned by a commitment to do the right thing under a behavioural code; and (ii) fresh insurance/pooling schemes and dispute resolution systems (replacing lawyers and courts with swifter and more responsive systems, integrating public investigative/enforcement regimes with private/compensation systems).

Providing Information to Innovators

Communication between innovators, regulators and government will assist on likely developments in science, technology and systems and possible regulatory implications. The UK Digital Regulation Cooperation

Forum (DRCF) has established a one-stop shop for coordinated assistance on identifying and achieving regulatory protections on digital issues, which has proved successful.

Key Points

- Regulation presents various barriers to innovation.
- Regulation can support innovation, if it is used properly.
- Don't regulate too soon. You can't regulate a technology, but you might need to regulate a product/service/activity or market. The rule/process distinction/dilemma.
- The solutions are:
  - To use a pathway and opportunity to construct standards and private certification controls through stages of maturity (PAGIT, PAS440 responsible development).
  - To ensure that the principles of responsible innovation (RI) are observed.
  - To operate a mechanism that captures the risk appetite of a society, and enables this to be debated and changed, but then drives regulatory decisions.
  - To have a regulatory system that is able to suspend and change rules, and make new ones: adaptability.
  - To have a regulatory system that identifies harm swiftly and responds to it (an RFM): agility.
  - Sandboxes and similar techniques are particularly useful, as can be reducing extensive pre-marketing testing, shifting some focus to ongoing surveillance.
  - As are one-stop shops that integrate access to, and responses by, multiple regulators.

---

[1] *The Role of Regulation in Supporting Scaling-up* (Regulatory Horizons Council, 2024).
[2] ibid.
[3] *Communication from the Commission on the Precautionary Principle* (Commission of the European Communities, 2 February 2000).
[4] *Taskforce on Innovation, Growth and Regulatory Reform* (2021) at https://assets.publishing.service.gov.uk/media/60c99a42d3bf7f4bd842e34a/FINAL_TIGRR_REPORT__1_.pdf.
[5] *The Role of Regulation in Supporting Scaling-up* (Regulatory Horizons Council, 2024).

⁶ *Closing the gap: getting from principles to practices for innovation friendly regulation* (Regulatory Horizons Council, 2022). I Bruno et al, 'Technology Readiness revisited: A proposal for extending the scope of impact assessment of European public services', ICEGOV2020. PH Kobos, LA Malczynski, LaT N Walker, DJ Borns and GT Klise, 'Timing is everything: A technology transition framework for regulatory and market readiness levels' (2018) 137 *Technology Forecasting & Social Change* 211–25.

⁷ *A pro-innovation approach to AI regulation* (DSIT, March 2023), CP815.

⁸ K Blind, 'Regulatory foresight: Methodologies and selected applications' (2008) 75 *Technological Forecasting & Social Change* 496–516. J-Y Ho and E O'Sullivan 'Dimensions of Standards for Technological Innovation – Literature Review to Develop a Framework for Anticipating Standardisation Needs' (Centre for Science, Technology and Innovation Policy, Institute for Manufacturing, University of Cambridge, 2015).

⁹ I Bruno et al, 'Technology Readiness revisited: A proposal for extending the scope of impact assessment of European public services', ICEGOV2020, https://ec.europa.eu/isa2/sites/default/files/technology_readiness_revisited_-_icegov2020.pdf. J Vik et al, 'Balanced readiness level assessment (BRLa): A tool for exploring new and emerging technologies' (2021) 169 *Technological Forecasting and Social Change* 120854. PH Kobos, LA Malczynski, LaT N Walker, DJ Borns and GT Klise, 'Timing is everything: A technology transition framework for regulatory and market readiness levels' (2018) 137 *Technology Forecasting & Social Change* 211–25.

¹⁰ The first three columns are taken from *Guide to Technology Readiness Levels for the NDA Estate and its Supply Chain* (Nuclear Decommissioning Authority, 2014). The right-hand column is from J Vik et al, 'Balanced readiness level assessment (BRLa): A tool for exploring new and emerging technologies' (2021) 169 *Technological Forecasting and Social Change* 120854. Alternative versions exist for different applications, such as in space flight.

¹¹ K Blind, 'The Impact of Standardization and Standards on Innovation', Nesta Working Paper No 13/15 (November 2013). PM Wiegmann, HJ de Vries and K Blind, 'Multi-mode standardisation: A critical review and a research agenda' (2017) 46 *Research Policy* 1370.

¹² K Blind, 'The Impact of Regulation on Innovation', Nesta Working Paper No 12/02 (2012), www.nesta.org.uk/report/the-impact-of-regulation-on-innovation/.

¹³ *The Governance of Engineering Biology* (Regulatory Horizons Council, 2025).

¹⁴ C Lyall and J Tait, 'Beyond the limits to governance: New rules of engagement for the tentative governance of the life sciences' (2019) 48 *Research Policy* 1128–37.

¹⁵ ibid.

¹⁶ J-Y Ho and E O'Sullivan, 'Dimensions of Standards for Technological Innovation – Literature Review to Develop a Framework for Anticipating Standardisation Needs' (Centre for Science, Technology and Innovation Policy, Institute for Manufacturing, University of Cambridge, 2015); K Blind, 'The Impact of Standardization and Standards on Innovation', Nesta Working Paper No 13/15 (November 2013).

¹⁷ *The Role of Regulation in Supporting Scaling-up* (Regulatory Horizons Council, 2024) 23.

¹⁸ J Tait, A Brown, I Cabrera Lalinde and D Barlow, 'Responsible innovation: Its role in an era of technological and regulatory transformation' (2021) 5(1) *Engineering Biology* 2–9.

¹⁹ J Tait, 'From responsible research to responsible innovation: challenges in implementation' (2017) *Engineering Biology* 1–5.

²⁰ PAS 440:2020 *Responsible innovation – Guide*.

²¹ J Tait, 'From responsible research to responsible innovation: challenges in implementation' (2017) *Engineering Biology* 1–5. J Tait, A Brown, I Cabrera Lalinde and D Barlow, 'Responsible innovation: Its role in an era of technological and regulatory transformation' (2021) 5(1) *Engineering Biology* 2–9.

²² J Tait, 'From responsible research to responsible innovation: challenges in implementation' (2017) *Engineering Biology* 1–5.

[23] SH Schwartz, J Cieciuch, M Vecchione, E Davidov, R Fischer, C Beierlein, A Ramos, M Verkasalo, J-E Lonnqvist, K Demirutku, O Dirilen-Gumus and M Konty, 'Refining the Theory of Basic Individual Values' (2012) 103(4) *Journal of Personality and Social Psychology* 663.

[24] *The Role of Regulation in Supporting Scaling-up* (Regulatory Horizons Council, 2024) 22.

[25] ibid 31.

[26] ibid.

[27] Catapult Transport Systems, 'Regulating and accelerating development of highly automated and autonomous vehicles through simulation and modelling' (2018), https://cp.catapult.org.uk/wpcontent/uploads/2021/07/00299_AV-Simulation-Testing-Report.pdf. A Frangi et al, 'Unlocking the power of computational modelling and simulation across the product lifecycle in life sciences: A UK Landscape Report', InSilicoUK Pro-Innovation Regulations Network (2023), doi: 10.5281/zenodo.8325274.

[28] *Report. FinTech: Regulatory sandboxes and innovation hubs* (ESMA, EBA and EIOPA, 2019); *Issues Paper. Regulatory sandboxing* (Australian Energy Regulator, 2021).

[29] See *Algorithmic impact assessment: a case study in healthcare* (Ada Lovelace Institute, 2022), www.adalovelaceinstitute.org/report/algorithmic-impact-assessment-case-study-healthcare/.

[30] *The Role of Regulation in Supporting Scaling-up* (Regulatory Horizons Council, 2024).

10

The Future of Regulation (and What We Need to do)

A Time of Transformations

We have identified in this book a series of transformations. Several have piled up at once, creating quite a challenge. Some of the evidence that change is needed may not be widely realised and may also be challenging to accept. 'We've always done it this way – what we've been doing must be right' is no longer a viable response. Our models and ways of doing things need to be rethought, applying the evidence of human science and what works. We need to engage with the realities of what the evidence tells us and the implications. If we do that, profoundly powerful ways of doing things better are within our grasp. But without this objectivity, application and change, we are heading for major problems and crises.

Background: Failures in the Traditional Models

A More Sophisticated Model: Adding Behavioural Science to Legal and Economic Assumptions

The Legal Model has to be replaced as the sole control mechanism. The traditional Economic Model of controlling through imposing costs on an actor, and hence a supposed lever of deterrence, is also fundamentally inadequate. These models of regulation are ineffective and out of date. Hence, the usual model of 'regulation is just a regulator enforcing rules' is out of date.

These models have multiple inadequacies. First, trying to get people just to comply with rules, on the assumption that 'compliance' is all that is needed for safety, is both inadequate as a risk control mechanism and very limiting, as it fails to engage motivation or to focus on increasing performance to do better than 'mere compliance' and hence to achieve innovation and growth.

Second, trying to control people's behaviour by a 'rule-breach-sanction' approach does not work for most people. Ideas of enforcement, and certainly deterrence, have limited effect as control mechanisms. 'Legal rules are designed for bad people whose burden is borne by good people.' Third, controlling people by fear in a democracy is philosophically unacceptable: the justification is unacceptable.

Compliance or non-compliance is a binary factual state (yes/no compliance with a specific rule). But it reflects a focus away from the more fundamental issues of the existence of risk or whether good outcomes are or are not being produced. This misses the reality of how safe an operation or organisation is (its general level of protection, or sustainable productivity), and whether its level of performance is improving or not. A compliance mindset produces the well-recognised problems of 'tick box' compliance in the focus of both operators and inspectors: it misses the point about risks, proportionality, improvements in performance through learning, and outcomes. It focuses on the micro level of compliance with individual rules, and is highly likely to miss the 'big picture', especially systemic risks and even multiple risks (a 'crowding out' effect).

Regulation (and regulators) need something more sophisticated, and wider. The answers are all there if we want to apply them – as some already do.

Behavioural science demonstrates how one needs to manage and interrelate with people so as to be effective – and the answer is *not* authoritarian enforcement. People will not share information without feeling psychologically safe. So, the whole traditional conception of law and regulation starts on the wrong foot. Behavioural science needs to underpin a *collaborative* approach: this leads to *Outcome-Based Collaboration* (OBC) as the ideal state, for those that can achieve it. There are outstanding examples of people doing this successfully. Aviation and nuclear safety have been doing it for decades.

Crucially, one needs to support and improve those who are well-meaning (who should be the majority) and enforce against those who have criminal intent or give rise to unacceptable risks through incompetence (prohibitions etc). Just using enforcement tools on everyone is positively destructive. The science on this is very clear – but the message is not widely understood, and people call for blame and accountability (where they mean punishment), in circumstances where it results in no one sharing information, or learning or improving.

Those who want to move on successfully will have to adopt new ways of thinking, behaving and speaking. Concepts like compliance, punishment, deterrence, even enforcement, need to be used very carefully and more precisely. Instead, language of outcomes, a regulatory system, trust, evidence, and data is both more accurate and more powerful in most circumstances.

Duties or Outcomes?

Imposing duties on regulators (which most politicians want to do) is also ineffective. The regulatory system and regulators need to be able to focus on *outcomes*. No legislation requires that, so this is quite a big and controversial political message, but using outcomes as the core focus is transformative. There are in fact a number of conflicting outcomes that need to be aligned, prioritised and achieved at once.

It's not a question of 'protection or growth' but of both – and more, such as business success, employment, Sustainable Development Goals, net zero and so on. The granular discussions on how to align all the outcomes need to happen at an operational level (not the high ideological policy level). Discussions about what controls, risks, activities and so on are necessarily detailed, and need to involve all relevant actors, within a series of (coordinated) communities of trusted stakeholders. This is another reason why a 'top down' model of regulation will fail: the involvement requires a 'horizontal' engagement between actors, based on respect and trust, rather than 'I'm government/regulator and I will tell you what to do'. This is a change that involves a fundamental shift in thinking, behaviour and structures. But it has solid grounding in science and evidence.

With many activities and risks, and certainly new technologies, the key issues are not 'Let's accept more risk, and therefore more harm, but it's all justified by growth'. Instead, we should think: 'We don't know what harms will occur, so what is our system to identify harms when they occur, and respond to them quickly?' The response will identify harm, be capable of stopping it, decide if it is reversable or acceptable (in terms of risk/benefit, including growth and experimentation), and be capable of repairing any damage quickly and of implementing changes to reduce further risk. This agility of response can accommodate high levels of risk. It is not fatalistic about the fact that some will get hurt, and there may be major disaster, but it plans in advance for identifying things and fixing them.

Solutions and the Way Forward

Solutions from Human Science

Regulation is ultimately about modifying human behaviour (so as to reduce unacceptable risk and harm). So, we should look for the core solutions in the science of how humans behave, and can be influenced, rather than in theoretical assumptions of legal philosophy and economics. When we do that, many solutions present themselves.

First, the problems noted above with an authoritarian approach and relying on enforcement are understandable – as are effective solutions. The most effective approach is as follows:

(a) Motivate people, with clear ethical objectives and outcomes, thus energising their inherent motivation (as opposed to external control tools). The mantra should be to satisfy human needs for *competence, autonomy and relatedness* (Self-Determination Theory). This applies in good management within any organisation just as much to relations between people in different organisations. There is huge power in group behaviour, and in-group cultures.

(b) Recognise that humans achieve more when the collaborate. Collaboration is based on shared goals and outcomes, and on relationships of trust. It is possible to define and achieve the (valid) outcomes of different people (eg prosperity, profit, protection and many more) by combining them into a shared plan and coordinated activities. Trust is based on humans' evaluation of the evidence of how others behave, so can be maximised where everyone in a group produces evidence that they can be trusted. The basis of trust is ethical values.

(c) Differentiate in responses and tools between those from whom society needs to protect itself and those who are well-intentioned.

This means being able to use firm interventions on the former, and a range of more supportive interventions on the latter. The right intervention tools must be selected for the right people, otherwise results will be counter-productive. The simplistic picture is of those outside and inside the system. Legal procedures are needed for the former; for the latter, outcomes, codes of behaviour and some mandatory rules are the core. Different mixes of 'good' and 'bad' actors exist in every regulatory space. So, a range of tools is needed that is relevant for the context. A 'top-down authoritarian' approach will not succeed for many people.

(d) Put greater effort into supporting behavioural codes that have independent governance (and associated decisions by independent Ombuds). This is an essential area that is distinct from law. The two areas need to complement each other. Thus, judges, ombuds and regulators should form a coordinated system.

The Power of Outcomes

Focus on outcomes and whether they are being achieved or not. This will tell you if a regulatory system is achieving its core purposes and delivering protection, growth, sustainability and so on. It will also guide you on how a regulatory system should interact with another. For example, a food product is only safe if it is produced, processed, packaged, transported, sold and consumed safely. However, all these individual outcomes may be part of multiple regulatory systems. Outcomes can be multi-level and multi-dimensional. We should identify, distinguish and ensure alignment between immediate regulatory outcomes (trends in compliance behaviours, tracking and managing near-misses etc) and longer-term impacts (reduced harm, improved products etc), especially when shifting from being reactive to proactive.

Monitoring outcomes is done through data. One needs to collect adequate relevant data over time. For example: how safe are activities/products now, and in a year's time? Is the outcome of multiple medical interactions (outputs) a healthier population? Is a system's performance improving?

A system that has comprehensive data may replace many individual requirements for detailed elements of a system. For example, comprehensive data on the health of a population could transform traditional silos of regulation of professionals (doctors, nurses, pharmacists, carers and others), hospitals and other institutions (laboratories), medicines, devices, diagnostics. It could identify holistically if interventions, treatments, products etc make people better or not, and clarify where changes should be made.

Relevant data will be held by different actors across a system. Is it shared, collected and examined? This suggests that the system will need to be a collaborative enterprise, if enough data is to be shared freely and swiftly. Certain types of data may need to be held securely and confidentially by a trusted independent data controller. The power of digitised data systems can transform traditional inspection and reporting models. It can also replace extensive pre-market testing with monitoring through early sandbox and ongoing collaborative systems. In short, data needs to be managed.

The Power of a Regulatory *System*

For highly functioning regulation, start by thinking in terms of *regulation as a system*. The system involves multiple coordinated actors, each playing their part (and who each needs to play their part). This will not be an authoritative model in which a single regulatory authority seeks to control the non-compliant activities of (the worst) actors.

Regulation is a *system*, which needs (a) various essential functions to be performed (more than in traditional assumptions); and (b) a collaborative approach involving all stakeholders. This is increasingly obvious when we contemplate the pace of new technologies, and hence serious risks and potentially big and fast-moving harms. Traditional approaches will just not work.

The Regulatory Functions Model (RFM) describes a continuous cycle of functions designed to deliver an effective regulatory space. The core aspects are that:

(a) the system is focused on achieving the agreed outcomes;
(b) the outcomes can only be achieved if the core functions are performed;
(c) each function can be performed by either public or private actors, or public or private regulatory tools and techniques, alone or in combination, depending on the context, risks, maturity of the actors etc;

(d) all actors need to take responsibility for playing their part in delivering the functions and outcomes;
(e) the system is most effective if it is a collaborative exercise – that needs objective transparent governance and accountability.

The core *functions* are as follows, forming a continuous holistic cycle, repeating Figure 3.2:

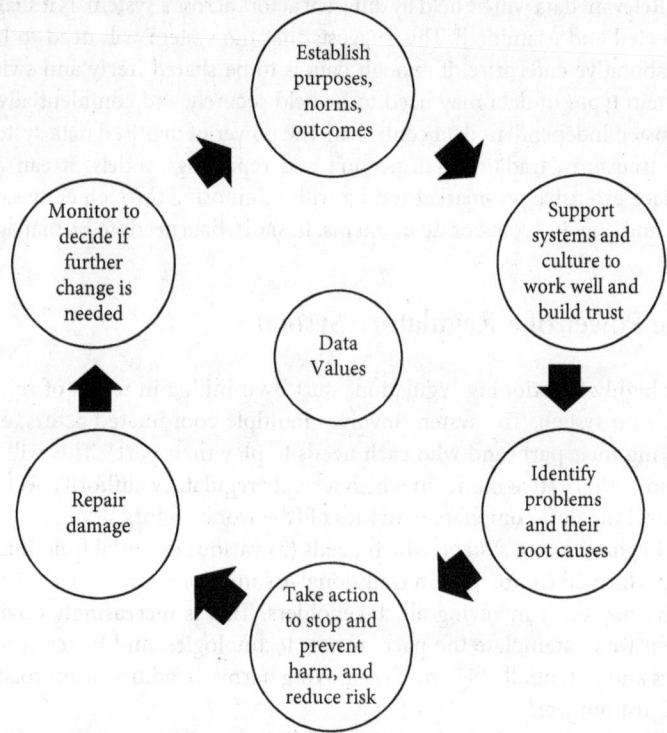

In designing regulation, one needs to think of a *'regulatory space'*, which can be flexible in terms of *public and private* components. Within this space, the basic question is: how do we make sure that the *core functions* are delivered? The answer will vary depending on the nature of each space, and may involve different configurations of public authorities, private accreditation and auditing systems, data management arrangements, complaints and resolution issues, and support/intervention and enforcement mechanisms.

If you have a system that gives you enough *data* about what is going on (outcomes, performance, harms) then this can simplify things no end. The issue is to be sure that you get all the relevant data. This is why Ombuds in consumer markets valuably perform dual functions of dispute resolution and data controller (in both cases as trusted independents).

The core questions in designing a system are:

(a) What are the purposes and objectives of the activities that are subject to regulation, and of the regulatory system?
(b) Who are the stakeholders, who need to be involved in system governance and accountability?
(c) What are the basic outcomes that the stakeholders wish to achieve?
(d) What are the functions that are needed to deliver the purposes, objectives and outcomes?
(e) How is each function to be performed? Who does what? What responsibilities does each have for performing their role? Do gaps need to be filled? What combination of public/private actors, institutions/systems is needed? Produced by whom?
(f) What data is required to demonstrate whether the agreed outcomes are being achieved, and the system is performing adequately? Who has that data and how is it to be shared and examined?
(g) What levels of risks and benefits, and of controls and costs, are agreed (risk appetite)?

A Quick Checklist

(1) What are the outcomes to be achieved?
(2) Oversight and governance of the *system*: who needs to be involved?
(3) What norms, values, codes of behaviour, rules (standards or legal), procedures, networks?
(4) What evidence of competence, performance and trustworthiness?
(5) What data will be needed to demonstrate competence, performance, achievement of outcomes, and of milestones?
(6) What evidence will demonstrate trustworthiness?
(7) Who produces what data?
(8) Who scrutinises?

Refreshment

On the basis set out above, all the traditional tools of regulation appear in a new light. Almost every traditional tool remains, but sometimes in a new context. Plus, there are some important new aspects to be added in.

In the pre-regulation phase, innovators can themselves develop both the emerging architecture of a regulatory space (especially through developing standards and accreditation) through stages of maturity (the PAGIT model) and PAS440:2020 *Responsible innovation – Guide*.

Many activities are now global. Indeed, some companies are so powerful that traditional nation-state control or enforcement is clearly ineffective. The solution lies with building communities of collaboration in the international context, based on shared norms and values, data, oversight/governance and systems. This is increasingly important and a major challenge.

A Systemic Solution to Risk

A regulatory system should *identify harms* as swiftly as possible, and then react to them effectively (stopping ongoing unacceptable harm, implementing changes based on sound learning that reduce future risk, and repairing damage). A community can manage considerable unknown risks if it has a system that does these things *swiftly* (an RFM that is *agile*). We can only do this adequately and swiftly if multiple actors work together to perform all the functions of identification, change and repair in the RFM. The logic points towards a coordinated system in which all relevant actors collaborate to achieve the goals and outcomes.

There is a big call to action here. Changes in legal rules that require Parliamentary authority will be too slow. New mechanisms for governance and change are needed that respond more quickly.

The Power of Collaboration

Humans achieve more when they collaborate. The outcomes approach, the RFM and the OBC model all facilitate this. They provide a framework in which multiple stakeholders can achieve multiple shared outcomes, through working together. This needs a bespoke framework that provides shared governance and commitment, accepting responsibility and accountability for performing their roles, and for contributing to the achievement of the agreed outcomes.

The relationships should be founded on mutual respect and trust. Each stakeholder should produce evidence that they are trustworthy. The basis of such evidence is how people actually behave, as well as what systems, governance, controls and values they demonstrate. The resultant culture should unavoidably be ethical. It will not be authoritarian, arm's length, adversarial or uncooperative.

Good regulation should operate as a checklist for good business; all private and public purposes, objectives and outcomes are balanced and aligned. Businesses and investors are not wasting their resources by pursuing activities that involve excessive risk.

INDEX

accidents, scientific research into 48-9
accountability *see also* blame; responsibility
  backward-looking 138
  collaboration 118
  deregulation 249
  enforcement 155
  financial products and services 197-8, 199, 203
  forward-looking 138
  future of regulation 299
  governance 94, 101
  government departments 102
  interventions 108
  joint stakeholders 89
  judicial review 102
  learning 292
  motivation 135
  Outcome-Based Collaborative (OBC) Model 123, 135-7
  Outcome-Based Collaborative Regulation (OBCR) Model 136, 216
  Parliament 17, 102, 254
  Regulatory Delivery Model (RDM) 101-2, 257
  Regulatory Functions Model (RFM) 88, 89
  regulatory system 297
  safety regulation 12
  sanctions 136
  scientific evidence 44, 61
  senior management 197-8, 199, 203
  transparency 101-2
  trust 126, 136
accreditation systems
  certification 3, 27-9, 31-2, 187, 189-90, 218, 259-60
  food safety and security 94, 285
  identity, proving 125
  innovation 276-7, 285
  inspections 285
  medical devices 94
  National Quality Infrastructure (NQI) 30
  private 3, 27, 28, 94, 187, 188-9, 219
    innovation 276-7, 285
    National Quality Infrastructure (NQI) 30
    public regulation, alignment with 260-1
    UKAS (UK Accreditation Service) 30
  reputations 276-7
  standards 31
  trust 83, 125
  UKAS (UK Accreditation Service) 30
actors, distinguishing between 217-18
administrative law 149, 151, 153
after regulated activities (downstream), regulation 108, 184, 188, 215-24
agility of responses 242, 245, 261
  crises, inability to respond to 116
  future of regulation 293
  innovation 282, 283-4
  Parliament, response of 119, 194, 235, 240-1, 265, 282, 298
AI *see* artificial intelligence (AI)
algorithmic impact assessments 285
Amabile, Teresa 41
anthropology 25-6, 122, 125
appointment, powers of 95
approval mechanisms 187-8 *see also* accreditation systems; assurance schemes; testing

arbitrage 239, 260
areas subject to regulation 3, 8–11
Ariely, Dan 41
artificial intelligence (AI)
  accreditation schemes 189
  data collection 35, 134, 211
  excessive regulation 233
  innovation 273–4, 282
  rules and laws, controls on
    making 250, 251
  standards 29
  surveillance 207
  trust 118, 274
assurance schemes 3, 27, 31, 138, 187,
    188–9
Australia
  Australian Competition & Consumer
    Commission 162–3
  Australian Productivity
    Commission 238–9
  Bank Executive Accountability Regime
    (BEAR) 199, 203–4
  codes of behaviour 201
  food safety and security
  Digital Transformation Programme
    (DTP) 212
  Food Act 141–2
  Food Production Act 141–2
  Safe Food Queensland (SFQ)
    141–2, 211–12
  Food Act 141–2
  Food Production Act 141–2
  Queensland, Australia 141–2
  performance of regulators 255
  rules and laws, controls on
    making 251
  Safe Food Queensland (SFQ) 141–2,
    211–12
  sectoral regulators, coordination
    between 256–7
authorised competent persons 190–1
authoritarian approach
  commons, maintaining the 58–9
  economic regulation 236
  enforcement 58–9, 149, 156–7,
    171–2, 174
  fear, control by 20, 24, 171
  future of regulation 299
  intervention choices 294
  learning 61
  power, use of 20, 115–17, 170
  psychological safety 53, 291
  regulators, regulation of 255
  regulatory system 295
  safety regulation 111
  scientific evidence 58–9, 291, 294
  traditional regulation 115–17
  use of force 29, 156–7
  vertical to the horizontal, shift
    from 74, 76
aviation safety
  accountability 138
  compliance-based approach 20
  culture 111–12, 137–9, 156
  data 221
  enforcement pyramid of CAA 155
  ICAO 93, 111–12, 137, 139
  information sharing 137
  Manual on Human Performance (HP)
    (ICAO) 111–12, 139
  open and just culture approach 39,
    111–12, 137–9, 204
  Outcome-Based Collaborative (OBC)
    Model 111, 291
  Performance-Based Regulation
    (PBR) 20, 137
  private safety audits 93
  safety management system (SMS)
    approach 137–9
  scientific evidence 39
  systemic cultural approach 20
Ayres, Ian 155, 171

barriers to entry
  agility of responses 245
  coordination and consistency between
    multiple regimes 264
  cross-border trade 142
  developing economies 142–3
  globalism 259
  identification 87, 264
  innovation 244–5, 270, 277, 282

Index 303

Baumeister, Roy   43
before activity commences (upstream), regulation   108-9, 184, 186-204, 222, 298
behavioural science   99, 149, 170, 173-7, 191, 290-2
Better Regulation techniques   172, 174, 252-3
bias   40, 109-10
Black, Julia   16
blame   161 *see also* accountability; responsibility
   counter-productive, as   45-6, 49, 59, 138, 161
   culture   49, 112, 122, 138, 200
   disasters   45-6, 49, 161
   individuals   20, 45-6, 59, 112, 122, 138, 161
   innovation   269, 282
   political decisions   243
   regulatory authorities   33, 234, 237-8, 269, 282-3
Boeing 737 MAX disaster   45, 115, 247, 262
Braithwaite, John   155, 171
brand reputation and endorsements   126
Brexit   249, 271-2
bribery   29
Brownsword, Roger   16
bureaucracy   243, 245, 253
Bush, George W   248

Canada   83, 256-7
capabilities   137, 173
capture   95, 110, 163
certification   3, 27-9, 31-2, 187, 189-90, 218, 259-60
change occurs, ensuring   219-22
Chatman, Jennifer   52
chemicals regulation   271
Chervany, Norman L   127
Christakis, Nicholas   41, 43, 122, 124-5
civil society organisations (CSOs)   10
clarity   15, 165, 172, 274

climate change and environment   140-1
commons, maintaining the   58
enforcement   171-3
Environmental Health Departments   18-19
environmental, social and governance (ESG) issues and outcomes   200
inspectors   171-2, 212-13
Just Transition goals   140
regulatory system, design of a   140-1
sustainability   4, 28, 99, 106-7, 140-1, 245, 253
codes of behaviour   15, 23, 25, 62, 135, 188
Codes of Standards in Public Life   110
Corporate Governance Code   200
culture   200-1
future of regulation   294
governments, imposed by   17-18, 28
innovation   276, 280, 286
Outcome-Based Collaborative Regulation (OBCR) Model   113
private regulation   27, 28
professional associations   18, 28
Regulators' Code   110, 204-5, 254-5
regulatory authorities   17-18, 253, 254
regulatory space, concept of a   79, 93
scientific evidence   294
self-regulation   219
trade associations   15, 18, 28, 93
values and principles   113
coercion   20, 118, 156-7, 170
collaboration *see also* cooperation; Outcome-Based Collaborative (OBC) Model; Outcome-Based Collaborative Regulation (OBCR) Model
AI   274
consistency   256-7
data   91, 295
enforcement   174-6
future of regulation   298-9
globalism   260

individual accountability   118
innovation   282, 285–6
interventions   110, 216
monitoring   208–9
networks   260
outcomes   86, 110, 265, 298–9
proportionality   239
Regulatory Functions Model
   (RFM)   86, 89–90, 258, 298–9
regulatory reform principles   252
regulatory space, concept of a   76
regulatory system   74, 77, 295–6
sandboxes   285–6
scientific evidence   293
trust   76, 89–90, 174, 205
commons, maintaining the   58–9, 122
communication
AI   189
consistency   256
cooperation, effective and
   continued   54
governance   101–2
innovation   275–6
outcomes   103–4
responsibility   244
risk perception   240–1
transparency   253
competence   103, 137, 161, 173, 176, 189–91, 206
competition law
abuse of a dominant position   14, 214
aggravating and mitigating
   factors   162–3
cartels   14, 162
class actions   222
collusive agreements   155
Competition Appeal Tribunal
   (CAT)   151, 236
compliance   161–3
cooperation   53–4
enforcement   213
European Union   162
fairness   13
fines   162, 222
large companies   213
mergers   14, 191, 213

monopolies   13, 191
oligopolies   191
Outcome-Based Collaborative (OBC)
   Model   122, 132–3
private regulation   31
reactive, as   213–14
redress   222–3
rule-breach-enforce model   213–14
trust   125
complaints   244 *see also* **Ombuds**
compliance
aviation safety   20
clarity, lack of   172
competition law   161–3
culture   129–30, 161
Economic Model   290–1
enforcement   161–3, 165, 171–2, 175–6
financial products and services   206
future of regulation   291–2
identification of non-compliance   3, 19–20
interventions   106
Legal Model   3, 290–1
mindset   99, 116–17
monitoring   208
objectives   162–3
outcomes   116–17, 185
programmes   161–3, 171–2, 175–6
sanctions   161–3
tick-box compliance   20, 291
toolkits   162
tools for a regulatory system   184, 208
trust   83, 129–30
conformity assessments   27–30
consensus, building   23, 25, 28, 33–4, 238, 276–7, 281
consistency
collaboration   256–7
communication   256–7
enforcement   157, 163
excessive regulation   233, 235
innovation   270, 276–7
local authorities, role of   18–19
objectives of regulates and
   regulation   114–15
regulators, regulation of   256–7

consumer protection 6–7, 15, 213, 214
cooperation 121–5 see also
    collaboration
  culture 43–4, 60–2, 111, 299
  enforcement 60–2, 159, 161, 166
  ethics 26, 42–4, 118, 125–6
  hierarchies 52
  individualism 53
  interventions 216
  outcomes 112–13, 133, 135
  reward systems 57–9
  scientific evidence 43, 53–8, 62, 118
  trust 125–6
  UK Digital Regulation Cooperation
    Forum (DRCF) 257, 286–7
co-regulation 27, 31
corporate social responsibility
    (CSR) 200
corruption 49, 109–10, 163
costs see costs of litigation; costs of
    regulation
costs of litigation 247
costs of regulation 33, 258–9, 262
  excessive regulation 232
  innovation 270
  monitoring 258–9
  proportionality 239, 263–4
  reallocation of costs 247
  redress 223
  regulatory authorities 258
  Regulatory Impact Assessments
    (RIAs) 247–8, 258
  rules and laws, controls on
    making 251–2
  small businesses 262–3
criminal law
  anti-bribery management systems 29
  corruption 49, 109–10, 163
  deterrence 151, 172
  enforcement 60, 149, 150–1, 152–3,
    173, 176
  ethics 177
  fines 153
  fraudulent trading 14
  incentives 41
  international crime 260

mens rea 151
  prosecutions 150–1, 152–3
  protection 176–7
  public regulation 31
  punishment 150–1, 153, 170–1
  sentencing guidelines 157
  siloism 154
  standard of proof 150
  strict liability 151
crises, inability to respond to 116
criticisms of regulation see problems
    and criticisms of regulation
cross-border regulation 118
crowding out 41, 57
culture
  aviation safety 111–12, 137–9, 156
  belongingness 43
  blame culture 49, 112, 122, 138, 200
  codes of behaviour 200–1
  confrontational culture 236
  controlling organisational
    culture 201, 204
  cooperation 43–4, 60–2, 111, 299
  delivery of functions 84
  enforcement 175
  ethics 41, 84, 199, 200–1, 299
  financial products and services 195,
    199–204
  functions, establishing a culture that
    will deliver 83
  future of regulation 299
  governance 103
  in-group cultures 293
  leadership 103, 129
  limitations in harnessing culture as a
    regulatory tool 203–4
  media 106
  open and just culture approach 109,
    111–12, 137–9, 204
  organisational culture 47, 52, 129–30
  politicians 106
  professionalism 205
  psychology 26, 44, 84, 204
  Regulatory Delivery Model
    (RDM) 103, 106, 257
  safety regulation 111–12

scientific evidence 43–4, 50–2
Self-Determination Theory (SDT) 51, 62
support 60–2
systemic cultural approach 20
tools for a regulatory system 204–5, 220
toxic culture 200
transformations 84
trust 52, 129–30, 204
values 42, 103
Cumberledge Report into healthcare of new babies and mothers 235
Cunliffe Independent Review 237
Curry, Oliver 42

damages 22, 152, 157, 217, 222
data collection
access, continuous improvements in 104
AI 35, 134, 211
anonymization 209
auditing 210
aviation safety 221
certification 210
collaboration 91
confidentiality 209, 295
data controllers 79, 210, 295
delivery of functions 84
digitised data systems 295
excessive regulation 234
future of regulation 294–5, 297
independence of data controllers 210
innovation 276–7, 286
monitoring 84, 208–10, 234, 295
Ombuds 79, 90, 210–11
outcomes 90, 134, 294–5
pre-marketing testing 295
public portals 210–11
registration 210
Regulatory Functions Model (RFM) 87, 89, 90–1
regulatory space, concept of a 93
regulatory system 297
risk-based prioritisation 105
single collection point 210
surveillance 207
tools for a regulatory system 209–13
trust 134, 212–13
data protection 158–60
de Waal, Frans 43
Deci, Edward 50–2
Dekker, Sidney 138–9
delay 22, 33, 223, 239, 258, 262–4, 285
see also **agility of responses**
delegation 33–4, 244–5, 265
delivery of functions 82–5 *see also*
Regulatory Delivery Model (RDM)
culture 83–4
data, use of 84
identification of problems and root causes 84, 108–9, 112
improve, taking action to 84
monitoring 84–5
motivation 135
operational management of the system 83
outcomes 84, 257
protection 74–5
regulators, regulation of 257–8
regulatory systems 82–5, 296–7
repairing damage 85
rules and laws, control on making 251
scientific evidence 174
stop and prevent harm, taking action to 84–5
system that will deliver functions, establishing a 83
trust 83
Democratic Republic of Congo (DRC) and Zambia, Kasumbalesa border between 142
demonization of regulators and regulation 237, 245
deregulation 245–52, 263
bureaucracy 245
costs of litigation 247
disasters 247
economic growth 239, 283
harm, increase in 246–7

innovation 283
litigation, increase in 247
making laws and rules, controls
  on 247–52
markets, effect on 247
predictability, lack of 247
proportionality 263
public authorities 83
reallocation of costs 247
regulatory creep 235
removal of regulation or
  regulators 246
risks 246–7
stability, lack of 247
techniques 246–52
design 74, 78, 93, 140–1, 192, 243–4,
  297
deterrence
behavioural economics 21
costs of litigation 247
criminal law 151, 171
Economic Model 3, 21–2, 23–4, 290
enforcement 21–4, 60–1, 149, 151,
  156, 169–70, 172
fear 24, 60, 156, 171
fines 22
future of regulation 290, 292
intentional harm 156
interventions 216
investment, impeding 238
Legal Model 19–20, 23–4
rational profit maximisation 21–2, 24
sanctions 156, 166, 171
scientific evidence 174–5
sociology 22, 169–70
developing economies 142–3, 261
digital technology see **artificial**
  intelligence (AI); technology
disasters and scandals
blame 45–6, 49, 161
causes 45–9
consistency 114–15
corporate disasters 45–6, 115
culture of organisations 46–9
deregulation 247
enforcement practices 58

excessive regulation 241
financial disasters 45, 47, 115
fire 45, 115
healthcare 45, 60
inquiries 45–9
prosecutions 151
psychological factors 46–7
purposes of regulation 261–2
risk factors 46–8
systemic factors 45–9
transport 45
wrong, what people want when things
  go 59–60
discretion 163–4, 283–4
dispute resolution schemes 27, 193,
  223–4, 286 see also **Ombuds**
disqualification of directors or
  office-holders 170
diversity, equity and inclusion
  (DEI) 245
Drinking Water Inspector 210
during regulated activities (midstream),
  regulation 184, 207–14

Economic Model 3, 21–2, 23–6, 98–9,
  110–11, 290–1
economic regulation 5–7, 10, 14–15 see
  also **Economic Model**
authoritarian approach 236
competition law 213–14
confrontational culture 236
economic growth 6, 7, 110, 238–9,
  254–5, 264, 283
enforcement 213, 217
excessive regulation 236–8
fairness 236
fines 217
innovation 275
interventions 14–15, 217
investment, impeding 238–9
licences 214
markets 213–14
network effects 15
private litigation 217
private profit with public interest,
  deficiencies in aligning 237–8

private regulation 27
protection 191, 239, 255
public utilities 14
purpose of regulation 238-9
sanctions 217
system, regulation as a 237
tools for a regulatory system 187, 191, 213-14, 217
trust 236
education establishments in UK, inspection and grading of 221-2
enforcement
  abuse of power 155
  accountability 155
  administrative law 149, 151, 153
  aggravating factors 158-60, 162-3
  authoritarian approach 149, 156-7, 170-2, 174
  Better Regulation 172, 174
  capabilities 173
  collaboration, power of 174-6
  competence 161, 173, 176
  competition 213
  compliance programmes 161-3, 171-2, 175-6
  consistency 157, 163
  consumer protection 213
  cooperation 60-2, 159, 161, 166
  corruption 163
  criminal law 60, 149, 150-1, 152-4, 157, 171, 173, 176-7
  culture 60-2, 175
  deregulation 22
  deterrence 21-4, 60-1, 149, 151, 156, 169-70, 172
  discretion 163-4
  Economic Model 23-5
  economic regulation 213, 217
  environment 171-3
  ethics 157, 177
  European Union 160
  evidence-based policy 149, 157
  fairness 13, 60, 157-66, 176-7
  families of law 149-53
  fines 153
  future of regulation 291-2, 298
  globalism 298

  harm, relevance of 160-1
  hierarchy of enforcement tools 171
  improvements, encouraging 173
  independence 155
  intervention tools for specific objectives 154, 171-2, 177-80
  investigations 152, 154
  judicial review 163-4
  justifications of enforcement 156-7, 176
  Legal Model 19, 23-5, 117
  mitigating factors 158-60, 162-3
  motivations 173, 174-7
  OECD *Best Practice for Enforcement and Inspections* 164-6, 176
  Outcome-Based Collaborative (OBC) Model 174, 176-80
  outcomes 156, 174, 176-7
  overlaps between categories 152-3
  policy 157, 166-9
  power, exercise of 170, 174
  principles of fair enforcement 157-66
  private/civil law 149, 152-4, 157
  proportionality 157, 158-60, 170
  protection 149, 156, 171, 176
  public law 149, 150-1, 154
  public regulation 31
  purposes of enforcement 22, 156, 178-80
  Regulatory Delivery Model (RDM) 155, 173
  Regulatory Functions Model (RFM) 153, 173, 177-80
  resources 173
  responsive regulation 171
  rule of law 157
  sanctions 3, 19, 60-1, 77, 157-66, 169-70
  science, application of 60-2, 118, 169-75, 293
  social influences 174-5
  sociological function 169-70
  supportive interventions 149, 174-7
  tools for a regulatory system 185, 218, 220
  traditional regulation 23-5, 79, 84, 116, 149, 150-7, 218
  trust 113-14

Index

types of people 175–6
use of force 156–7, 170
Engel, Christoph 44
engineering biology, platform technology area of 275
environment *see* **climate change and environment**
ethics *see* **morality and ethics**
Etienne, Julian 162
European Union (EU)
  anti-regulation agenda 244–5
  Brexit 249, 271–2
  competition law 162
  conformity assessments 30
  Enforcement and Modernisation Directive 160
  General Data Protection Regulation (GDPR) 94, 158–60, 254
  medical devices 94
  populism 245
  precautionary principle 34, 242, 271
  taking back control 245
evidence *see also* **scientific evidence**
  competition law 162
  culture 199
  enforcement 149, 164
  future of regulation 292
  innovation 277
  new models 99
  outcomes 117–18
  precautionary principle 271
  trust 98, 113–14, 121, 123–4, 125–30, 132, 299
    feedback systems 206
    Regulatory Functions Model (RFM) 89–90
    traditional regulation 205–6
excessive regulation 231–9
  consistency 235
  content of rules, not necessary to follow 232
  costs of compliance 232
  cumulative effect of multiple rules and procedures 232, 233–4
  economic regulation, specific issues with 236–8
  effectiveness of restrictions 232–3
  gaps 235

innovative technologies 232
  necessity of restrictions 232–3
  proportionality 232–3
  regulators, regulation of 253
  regulatory creep 234–5
  resources 234
  silos 235
experimental regulation 252, 284–5

fairness 7, 13–15, 75
  competition 13
  economic regulation 236
  enforcement 157–66
  markets 13–14
  principles 157–66
  processes 60, 157–66, 176–7
  regulatory reform principles 253
  repair 84
  rules 55–6
  sanctions 157–66
  unfair contract terms 15
fear 118, 156–7, 161, 241, 291
  authoritarian approach 20, 24, 171
  culture 204
  deterrence 24, 60, 156, 171
  motivations 134–5, 175
  psychological safety 53
  self-motivation, effect on 61
feedback systems 79, 206, 209–10, 220, 221–2
Fehr, Ernst 41
Feldmanm Yuval 24, 40, 41, 44
Financial Conduct Authority (FCA) 195–9, 201
  culture 201–3
  Principles for Businesses 195–6
  sandboxes 285
  Senior Managers and Certification Regime (SM&CR) 136–7, 197–9, 201–3
financial products and services 194, 195–204 *see also* **Financial Conduct Authority (FCA)**
  accountability of senior management 197–8, 199, 203
  Australia, Bank Executive Accountability Regime (BEAR) in 199, 203–4

310 Index

Basel Core Principles (BCPs) 93–4
compliance, evidence of 206
culture 195, 199–204
disasters 45, 47, 115
Dutch Bankers' Oath 190, 200
ethics 195, 199, 200–1
Financial Services Regulatory
    Initiatives Forum 257
fit and proper persons 198
global financial crisis 2008 197, 200
hierarchy of rules 197–8
Hong Kong 199
Ireland, Senior Executive
    Accountability Regime (SEAR)
    in 199
Principles for Businesses
    (FCA) 195–6
sandboxes 194
Senior Managers and Certification
    Regime (SM&CR) 197–9,
    201–3
Singapore, accountability regime for
    senior management in 199
standards 93–4
supervision 93–4
tools for a regulatory system 194,
    194–204
Fine, Adam 49, 200
fines and financial penalties 22, 31–2,
    152–3, 162, 170, 217, 222, 238
fire disasters 45, 115
**First-tier Tribunal, General Regulatory
    Chamber of** 236
food safety and security
accreditation 285
Alternative Business Compliance
    (ABC) project 212–13
enforcement 171
future opportunities 213
inspections 285
objectives 141
outcomes 140, 294
private accreditation 94
public regulation 94
Queensland, Australia 141–2
    Digital Transformation Programme
    (DTP) 212

Food Act 141–2
Food Production Act 141–2
Safe Food Queensland (SFQ)
    141–2, 211–12
Regulatory Delivery Framework
    (RDF) 141
silos 96
small food suppliers 15
standards 29
tools for a regulatory system 189,
    211–13
trustworthy partnerships 212–13
UK Food Standards Authority
    (FSA) 212–13, 285
vulnerable business groups 15
Foucault, Michel 133
fraudulent trading 14
Fuller, Lon 16
functions *see* **purposes/functions of
    regulation**
future of regulation 290–9

G30 203
game theory 58–9
gaps in regulation 87, 235
**General Data Protection Regulation
    (GDPR) (EU)** 94, 158–60,
    254
Germany 190, 248–9, 271
global financial crisis 2008 190, 197,
    200
globalism 259–61
barriers to trade 259
challenges 259–61
developing countries 261
enforcement 298
financial standards 93–4
future of regulation 298
harmonisation of standards,
    certification and rules 259
international crime 260
private accreditation and public
    regulation, alignment
    between 260–1
standards 93–4
supply chains based on holistic digital
    systems 260–1

VUCA (volatility, uncertainty, complexity and ambiguity) 260
governance of a regulatory system 94-6
  accountability 94, 101
  appointment, powers of 94-5
  capture, risk of 95
  culture 103, 202-3
  environmental, social and governance (ESG) issues and outcomes 200
  framework 100, 101, 103
  future of regulation 299
  innovation 276, 282, 285
  Ombuds 95
  PAGIT 277, 298
  power 133
  private regulation 95
  public regulation 94-5
  regulatory authorities, duties on 95
  Regulatory Delivery Model (RDM) 100, 101, 103
  regulatory system 74, 83, 95, 297
  tentative governance 276
  transparency 165
Grenfell Tower fire 45, 115, 220, 235, 247, 261-2
group identity 43-4

Haidt, Jonathan 41, 42-3, 125
Hampton Review 152-3, 172
Hardin, Garrett 58, 122
harm
  blame-based approach 161
  competence 161
  costs of regulation 247, 264
  deregulation 246-7
  disasters 161
  economic growth 255
  enforcement 160-1
  identification 265, 282-3, 284, 286, 298
  intention 156
  motivation 161
  outcomes 265
  regulatory system 76-7

rules and laws, controls on making 252
safety regulation 11
sanctions 160-1
stop and prevent harm, taking action to 84-5
unacceptable harms 75
Hawkins, Keith 171
health and safety standards 28, 192
healthcare systems
  Cumberledge Report into healthcare of new babies and mothers 235
  disasters 45, 60
  inspections and grading 221
  mad cow disease 242, 271
  medical devices 94, 192
  medicines 12, 190
  NHS England, abolition of 246
  Post-Marketing Vigilance (PMS) for pharmaceuticals 207
Henrich, Joseph 25-6, 44
hierarchy of regulations 17-18
Hofstede, Geert 199-200
Hong Kong
  bank culture reform programme (HKMA) 199
  SFC Managers-in-Charge (MiC) regime 199
human rights 25-6
human behaviour 39-62, 113, 293-4

identification of problems 84, 108-9, 112
improvements 61, 84, 136, 173, 231, 261-5
individual responsibility 20-1, 40, 46, 129, 138, 186, 188, 202-3
infected blood scandal 220, 247, 261
information, sharing 16, 84, 137, 165
  see also **transparency**
  blame culture 122
  confidentiality 209, 295
  disclosure 194-5
  false or misleading information, control of 194-5
  innovation 286
  portals 233

312 *Index*

private regulation 27
psychology safety 201
Regulatory Functions Model
 (RFM) 87
scientific evidence 175
single repositories of information
 233
injunctions 152
**innovation, new regulatory systems to
 support** 6, 7, 269–87
 accreditation schemes 276–7, 285
 agility 282, 283–4
 AI 273–4, 282
 algorithmic impact assessments 285
 barriers to entry 244–5, 270, 277,
  282
 challenges in regulating
  innovation 269–70
 codes of behaviour 276, 280, 286
 collaboration 282, 285–6
 consensus, building 276–7, 281
 consistency 270, 276–7
 costs of regulation 270
 data 276–7, 286
 delayed release concept 285
 deregulation 283
 digital simulation 284–5
 economic regulation 275
 enforcement 232
 ethics 280–1
 evidence of risks 277
 existing regimes, issues with 270
 experimentation 284–5
 future of regulation 298
 generic types of regulation 275
 governance, concept of 276, 282, 285
 guidelines, achieving balance in the
  application of 281
 harm, ecosystem for identifying and
  responding to 282–3, 284,
  286
 information, provision of 286–7
 insurance/pooling schemes 286
 maturity, stages of 273, 274–6
 monitoring 282, 286
 new regulatory systems to support
  innovation 269–87

 no existing rules or procedures, where
  there are 270
 overlapping or inconsistent requirements
  or constraints 270
 PAGIT 277, 298
 positive and negative drivers 278–80
 precautionary and other
  principles 271–2
 preliminary stages 269–70, 284–6,
  298
 pre-marketing requirements 284–6
 principles 271–4, 280
 private sector involvement 276–7, 285
 proportionality 270, 271–2, 286
 redress 286
 Regulatory Horizons Council
  (RHC) 272, 275, 282, 283–6
 regulatory system 269–87
 Responsible Innovation (RI) 274–5,
  277–81, 298
 risk appetites 281–2
 sandboxes 284, 285–6
 small businesses 272–3
 specific types of regulation 275
 standardisation 6, 275–7, 280–1
 Technology Readiness Levels
  (TRLs) 274–5
 testbeds 284
 tools 276–87
 transparency 285
 trust 286
 UK Digital Regulation Cooperation
  Forum (DRCF) 257, 286–7
 values 280–2
inspections 18, 27, 210, 234, 285
 accreditation schemes 189
 educational establishments 221–2
 environmental health inspectors
  (EHOs) 171–2, 212–13
 healthcare establishments 221
 OECD *Best Practice for Enforcement
  and Inspections* 164–6, 176
 surveillance 207–8
 trust 126–7
integrity 49, 125, 129–30
 accreditation 30
 commercial success 49, 125

Index   313

competence and capability, lack of 137
definition 136
ethics 129-30
Senior Managers 197-8, 201
trust 126-7
International Standards Organisation (ISO) 28-9
intervention choices
 accountability 108
 after regulated activities 108
 authoritarian approach 294
 backward, looking 215-16
 before activity commences 108-9
 bias 109-10
 capture 110
 categorisation 108
 change occurs, ensuring 219-21
 collaboration 110, 216
 deterrence 216
 economic regulation 14-15, 217
 enforcement 108, 257
 expertise 109
 forward, looking 215
 functions/objectives 154
 independence 109, 110
 licensing 105, 108
 objectives 215-21
 outcomes 108-11, 295
 present, past and future 108-9
 powers 153
 prevention 108-9
 Principles, Purposes and Objectives of Regulatory Intervention and Enforcement 149
 Regulatory Delivery Model (RDM) 100, 105-6, 108-11, 257
 Regulatory Functions Model (RFM) 215
 repair/restoration 108-9
 restatement of policy 177-80
 sanctions 106, 108
 scientific evidence 175, 293-4
 small businesses 171
 support 108, 110, 217-18, 257
 Supportive Intervention Mode 217-18, 219-20

tools for specific objectives 154, 171-2
investigations 152, 154, 168, 208
investment 198-9, 238-9
Ireland, Senior Executive Accountability Regime (SEAR) in 199

Johnson, David 53-4
Johnson, Roger 54
judicial review 102, 151, 158, 163-4, 254-5

Kahan, Dan M 44
Kahneman, Daniel 44
King, Martin Luther 122

leadership 103, 129-30, 175, 202-3
learning 60-1, 136, 218, 253, 265, 291-2
Leary, Mark 43-4
Legal Model 3, 19-21, 23-6
 authoritarian model, as 20, 24
 behavioural models 117
 compliance 3, 290-1
 deterrence 19-20, 23-4
 enforcement 19, 23-5, 117
 fear, ruling by 24
 future of regulation 290-2
 governance 94
 non-compliance, identification of 3, 19-20#
 outcomes 20, 106
 problems 23-6
 Regulatory Delivery Model (RDM) 110-11
 Regulatory Functions Model (RFM) 86
 rule of law 21
licensing and permits
 access to markets 187-8
 conditions 150, 153, 214, 288
 economic regulation 214
 intervention choices 105, 108
 removal 107, 150, 153-4, 170, 176, 179
 use of force 170
light touch regulation 93, 172
Lyall, Catherine 276

314 Index

Macrory Principles 153, 172
McKnight, D Harrison 127
Macleod, Sonia 60
mad cow disease 242, 271
making laws and rules, controls on 247–52
 combinations of techniques 249–52
 costs, reduction in 251–2
 delay, addressing 248
 existing stock of rules, reducing 248–50
 one-in, one-out rules 248
 one-in, two-out rules 250
 political rhetoric 251
 simplicity 250
 sunrise clauses 250
 sunset clauses 248–9
Mangalam, Srikanth 131
Manual on Human Performance (HP) (ICAO) 111–12, 139
markets 5–6, 10, 13–14, 247
Marsh, Zachary 258
Mayer, Colin 238
Meadows, Dona 77, 95–6
media 106
medical devices in EU 94, 192
Ministerial strategic steers 110, 245, 253, 254, 255
models *see* Economic Model; new models; Outcome-Based Collaborative (OBC) Model; Outcome-Based Collaborative Regulation (OBCR) Model; Regulatory Delivery Model (RDM); Regulatory Functions Model (RFM)
Molm, Linda 124
monitoring 83–5, 208–10, 220
 costs of regulation 258–9
 cultural transformations 85
 data 208–10, 234, 295
 delivery of functions 84–5
 financial supervision 93–4
 innovation 282, 286
 investigations 208
 outcomes 131–2, 294

 pre-marketing requirements 286
 public/private function, as 208–9
 self-monitoring tools 210
 traditional regulation 25
morality and ethics *see also* codes of behaviour
 compliance or integrity framework 129–30
 cooperation 26, 42–4, 118, 125–6
 criminal law 177
 crowding out 40
 culture 41, 84, 129–30, 201–2, 299
 deterrence 22
 enforcement 157, 177
 Ethical Business Practice (EBP) 129
 fairness 40, 157
 financial products and services 195, 199, 200–1
 frameworks and practices 84
 honesty 40
 innovation 280–1
 internal moral compass/knowing right from wrong 123, 125
 Outcome-Based Collaborative (OBC) Model 122, 136
 power 39, 43–4
 professional competence 189–90
 reasoning 42–3
 religion 25
 rule of law 21
 scientific evidence 40, 41–3, 49, 62, 118
 social norms as overriding ethical norms 44
 teaching 221
 trust 39, 40, 114, 121, 123–6, 128–30
 use of force 157
 values 41, 129–30
motivations
 accountability 135
 accreditation 276–7
 classification of behavioural motivations 173
 crowding put 41
 delivery 135
 disasters 47

enforcement 173, 174–7
external 39, 41, 134–5, 293
harm, relevance of 161
intrinsic 39, 41, 51, 57, 113, 134–5,
  174–5, 293
leadership 175
scientific evidence 24, 39, 41, 293
Self-Determination Theory 39, 51–2,
  293
self-motivation 61, 135
motor vehicles, safety of 191–2
Mullins, Daniel 42

Need-to-Belong Theory 43
Netherlands 83, 190, 200–1
networks 256–7, 260
new models 98–119
  behaviour, shift from law to 116–17
  compliance mindset 99, 116–17
  consistency between goals of regulatees
    and regulation, potential
    for 114–15
  inside and outside modes 116–17
  Outcome-Based Collaborative (OBC)
    Model 98, 111, 112–14,
    115–17, 298–9
  Regulatory Delivery Model
    (RDM) 98, 100–11, 115–17
  Regulatory Functions Model
    (RFM) 116–17
  rules to outcomes, from 99–100
  systemic behavioural
    approach 111–12
  theories to science, from 99–100
  trust and trustworthiness 98, 100
New Zealand 77–8, 205
NHS England, abolition of 246
Nowak, Martin 58–9
nuclear safety 45, 291

Obama, Barack 248
**OECD (Organisation for Economic
  Co-operation and
  Development)**
  *Best Practice for Enforcement and
    Inspections* 164–6, 176

licensing 188
Outcome-Based Collaborative (OBC)
  Model 122–3
principles 23
surveillance 208
Ofwat, failure of 236–7
Ogus, Anthony 194–5
Ombuds
  data 79, 210–11
  future of regulation 297
  governance 95
  outcomes 265
  private regulation 152
  redress 223
  single consumer websites 210–11
one-in, one-out rules 248
one-in, two-out rules 250
open and just culture approach 109,
  111–12, 137–9, 204
O'Reilly, Charles 52
Ostrom, Elinor 58, 122
**Outcome-Based Collaborative (OBC)
  Model** 98, 111, 115–17,
  121–43 *see also* **Outcome-Based
  Collaborative Regulation
  (OBCR) Model**
  accountability 123, 135–7
  achievement of outcomes 131, 134
  agreeing outcomes 133–4
  commitment 135
  competence and capability, lack
    of 137
  competition 122, 132–3
  creation of an OBC system 131–4
  data 134
  enforcement 174, 176–80, 185
  ethics 122, 136
  examples of OBC systems 137–43
  governance 133
  how people collaborate 123–30
  identification of outcomes 131
  improvement, processes of 136
  information sharing 122
  initiation 132–3
  measurement of performance 134
  monitoring 131–2, 208

motivation 134–5
new models 98, 111, 112–14, 115–17, 298–9
policy, restatement of 177–80
psychological safety 122
Regulatory Delivery Model (RDM) 115–17
Regulatory Functions Model (RFM) 135–6
Regulatory System Model (RSM) 95
responsibility 135–7
scientific evidence 291
tools for a regulatory system 185, 208, 220
transparency 133
trust 121, 123–30, 177
value of collaborating 121–3
values-based cooperation 112
Outcome-Based Collaborative Regulation (OBCR) Model 111, 112–15, 174
accountability 136, 216
case studies 139–43
climate change and environment 140–1
codes of behaviour 113
compliance 185
core regulatory functions, list of 112–13
developing economies, reducing regulatory barriers to trade in 142–3
ethics 113–14
evidence 113–14, 124
food safety and security 141–2, 211–12
function of regulation 139
intrinsic motivation, stimulating 113
interventions 216
prioritisation 113
purpose of regulation 139
regulatory space 139
regulatory systems 140
scientific evidence on human behaviour 113
support, provision of 113
trust 113–14, 124, 139–40, 206

outcomes, achieving 7, 19, 33, 35, 81–2, 265 *see also* **Outcome-Based Collaborative (OBC) Model; Outcome-Based Collaborative Regulation (OBCR) Model**
adequate analysis capacity 104
blame 161
collaboration 110, 265, 295, 298–9
compliance 116–17, 185
conflicts 107
data 104, 294–5
duties on regulators 292–3
enforcement 156, 174, 176–7
food safety and security 140, 294
future of regulation 292–3, 294–5
harm, identification of 265
improvements 84
interventions 108–11, 295
jurisdictional issues 107–8
learning 265
Legal Model 20, 106
measurement 100, 103–4, 117–18
monitoring 294
multiple shared outcomes 298–9
ombuds 265
proportionality 272
protection 265
redress mechanisms 265
Regulatory Delivery Model (RDM) 100, 103–4, 106–11, 173, 257–8
Regulatory Functions Model (RFM) 86, 258, 265
regulatory reform principles 252
regulatory system 76, 81–2, 297
retribution 161
rules 57, 99–100, 250, 291
scientific evidence 20
silos 295
tools for a regulatory system 185
top down model 292
transparency 110
trust 103, 206, 292

PAGIT (Proportionate and Adaptive Governance of Innovative Technologies) framework 277, 298

Index 317

Parliament
  accountability 17, 102, 254
  agility of responses, lack of 119, 194, 235, 240–1, 265, 282, 298
  civil servants 17
  committees 17–18, 34, 102, 110, 255
  delegation of powers 33–4, 265
  formal state regulation 26
  governance 95–6
  Legal Model 94
  ministers 17, 94, 110, 244–6, 253, 254, 255, 284
  National Audit Office (NAO) 102
  regulatory authorities 33–4, 95–6, 241, 244, 254–5
performance 20, 53, 84, 134, 137, 255–6
permits *see* **licensing and permits**
Picket, Kate 51–2
Pirie, Fernanda 20
policy
  accountability 17
  economic growth 7
  enforcement 157, 166–9
  Ministerial strategic steers 110, 245, 253, 254, 255
  private regulation 32
  proportionality 240
  public regulation 32
  publication 17
  restatement 177–80
  safety management system (SMS) approach 138
political decisions 243–5
  anti-regulation agenda 244–5
  barriers to innovation 244–5
  changes in goals 245
  delegation of political decisions to regulators 244–5
  reform of systems 243–4
populism 245
portals 78–9, 210–11, 233
post-marketing systems 23, 186–206, 286
Post Office Horizon IT scandal 45, 115, 220, 261–2
power 13–15
  abuse of power 155

  authoritarian approach 20, 115–17, 170
  collaboration, power of 174
  enforcement 170
  ethics 39, 43–4
  governance 133
  imbalance 13, 27
  interventions 154
  outcomes 294–5
  private regulation 27
  traditional regulation 115–17
  use of force 170
precautionary and other principles 33–4, 242, 271–2, 281
predictability 3, 5–7, 15, 46, 247, 249
pre-marketing requirements 186–206, 213, 284–6, 295
Primary Authority scheme 256
principles 6–7, 23, 25 *see also* **fairness; proportionality**
  AI 273–4
  enforcement 157
  FCA Principles for Businesses 195–6
  innovation 271–4, 280
  Macrory Principles 153, 172
  precautionary principle 33–4, 242, 271–2, 281
  Principles of Good Regulation 152
  regulatory reform principles 252–3
  traditional regulation 156–7
Prisoner's Dilemma 59
private regulation 3, 26–33
  accreditation schemes 3, 27, 28, 94, 187, 188–9, 219
  innovation 276–7, 285
  National Quality Infrastructure (NQI) 30
  public regulation, alignment with 260–1
  UKAS (UK Accreditation Service) 30
  advantages and drawbacks of 31–2
  assurance schemes 3, 27, 28, 30, 31, 187, 188–9
  aviation sector 93
  certification 3, 27, 28, 31–2

civil law 149, 152-4, 157
codes of behaviour 27, 28
competition 31
conformity assessments 27-30
co-regulation 27, 31
damages 152, 157
delivery of functions 83
economic instruments 27
financial penalties 27, 152
governance 95
information, guidance and
    education 27
injunctions 152
innovation 276-7, 285
level playing field, requirement for
    a 31
Ombuds 152
policy 32
power imbalance 27
public regulation 28, 31-2, 83, 111,
    188, 260-1
regulatory space, concept of a 78, 93
resources 285
sanctions 26, 31-2, 152-3
self-regulation 3, 26-7, 31, 79, 187,
    219
standard of proof 152
standards 27-31, 276
trade associations 188
problems and criticisms of
    regulation 231-66 *see also*
    excessive regulation
agility 242, 261, 265
barriers, identification of 264
Better Regulation techniques 252-3
control regulation, attempts
    to 245-52
costs of regulation 258-9, 262
delay 258, 262
deregulation 245-52, 263
Economic Model 23-6
flow 263
globalism, challenges of 259-61
how to do regulation better 261-5
identification of problems 84, 108-9,
    112
improvements 231, 261-5
Legal Model 23-6

political decisions 243-5
proportionality 239-40, 263-4
purposes of regulation 261-2
real problems, addressing 262-5
regulators, regulation of 253-8
risk 240-3, 264
underlying issues 239-45
professional services 9-10, 126-7
assurance schemes 188
certification 189
codes of behaviour 18, 28
competence 161, 189-90
continuing education 190
culture 205
ethics 189-90
fraudulent trading 14
integrity mechanisms 126-7
interventions 109
professional associations 14, 18,
    27-8
professionalism 109, 165, 205
training 27
profit maximisation 21-2, 24
proliferation of regulation *see* **excessive**
    regulation
proportionality 187, 239-40, 252-3
AI 274
collaboration 239
costs and time 239, 263-4
enforcement 157, 158-60, 165, 166,
    170, 232-3
innovation 270, 271-2, 286
outcomes 272
PAGIT 277, 298
Parliamentary system for making laws,
    problems with 240
policy 240
precautionary principle 271-2
risks, proportionality to 239-40
rule-breach-sanction approach 291
sanctions 151, 158-60, 170-1
protection, delivery of 3-5, 32-3, 35,
    74-6
costs of litigation 247
criminal law 176-7
economic regulation 191, 239
enforcement 149, 156, 171, 176
fairness 75

future of regulation   292
outcomes   265
Protection Mode   218, 219–20
Regulatory Functions Model
    (RFM)   265
scientific evidence   20, 62
traditional regulation   116
trust   114
psychology
authoritarian approach   53
cultural psychology   26
deterrence   22
disasters   46–7
fear, ruling by   53
Legal Model   20
safety   39, 53, 61, 84, 122, 125, 204,
    291
scientific evidence   39, 44, 50–2
Self-Determination Theory   50–2
values   118
public regulation   3, 10, 32 see also
    regulatory authorities
accreditation   260–1
actors, identification of   80
appointment, powers of   94–5
criminal law   31
disasters   45
enforcement   26, 31, 149, 150–1, 154
fines   31–2
governance   94–5
grading and inspections   27
mandatory rules   95
private regulation   28, 31–2, 83, 111,
    188, 260–1
regulatory space, concept of a   78–9,
    93
resources   234
sanctions   26, 31–2
subject to regulation, those who
    are   80
utilities   14
purposes/functions of regulation   3–5,
    35, 185 see also **fairness;
    protection, delivery of;
    Regulatory Functions Model
    (RFM)**
core functions   75, 79–81, 112–13
culture, establishing a   83, 202–3

disasters and scandals   261–2
economic regulation   238–9
enforcement   156, 178–80
fair markets goal   4–5, 6
interventions   154
Legal Model   19
outcomes   82, 139
regulatory space, concept of a   94
regulatory system   297
traditional regulation   19, 25, 74–5,
    156

Reason, James   48–9
Red Tape Challenge   249
redress/repair   222–4
ADR   223–4
competition law   222–3
consumer protection   15
costs of regulation   223
damages   22, 152, 157, 217, 222
delay   223
delivery of functions   85
economic regulation   217
enforcement   222–4
fairness and effective outcomes   85
future of regulation   292–3
injunctions   152
innovation   286
interventions   108–9, 218
Ombuds   223
regulators, regulation of   254
Regulatory Functions Model
    (RFM)   265
reform   231, 243–4, 252–3
regulation, definition of   3–36
areas subject to regulation   3, 8–11
hierarchy of regulations   17–18
outcomes   7, 19, 33, 35
principles   6–7, 23, 25
private regulation   3, 26–33
protection and freedom, achieving   3,
    4–5, 32–3, 35
public regulation   3, 26–7
purpose of and justification for
    regulation   3, 4–5
regulatory authorities, landscape of   3,
    18–19, 23
rules   22–3, 24–6

320 Index

safety regulation   7, 11–12, 23
state, activities of the   16
regulators, regulation of   253–8
authoritarianism   255
codes of behaviour   253, 254
conflicts of duties   254
consistency   256–7
coordination mechanisms   253
delivery   257–8
Ministerial strategic steers   110, 245, 253, 254, 255
networking   256–7
objectives and duties, definition of   253, 254–5
performance of regulators   255–6
Primary Authority scheme   256
regulatory authorities   3, 17–19, 23, 245–6
blame   33, 234, 237–8, 269, 282–3
codes of behaviour   17–18
consistency   18–19
costs of regulation   258
demonization   245
duties   18, 95, 292–3
enforcement   18, 19
governance   95
Legal Model   19
legislation, creation by   17, 18
local authorities, role of   18–19
Parliament   33–4, 95–6, 241, 244, 254–5
powers   17, 18
problems and criticisms   253–8
prosecutions   151
sanctions   18
scandals   151
sectoral regulators, coordination between   256–7
sponsorship by government departments   18
traditional regulation   47, 76–7
regulatory creep   234–5
Regulatory Delivery Model (RDM)   100–11, 115–17, 185
accountability   101–2, 257
culture   103, 106, 257
elements   100–1, 257
enforcement   155, 173
evolution   110–11
governance framework   100, 101, 103, 95
intervention choices   100, 105–6, 108–11, 257
joint responsibility   95
Legal Model   110–11
outcomes   106–11, 115–17, 173, 257–8
practices   100, 103–6, 257
prerequisites   100, 101–3, 257
risk-based prioritisation   100, 104–5, 257
transformation, significance of   106–11
Regulatory Functions Model (RFM)   74, 86–91, 116–17, 185, 215, 220
accountability   88, 89
actors   86–8
agility of response   283–4
collaborative system, as   86, 89–90, 258, 298–9
data   87, 89, 90–1
enforcement   153, 173, 177–80
innovation   283–4
interventions   215
key elements   86–91
outcomes   86, 135–6, 173, 258, 265, 295
policy, restatement of   177–80
regulatory space, concept of a   79–81
regulatory system   79–81, 295–6
responsibility   135–6
risk and responding   91
scope of the ecosystem   89
trustworthiness   89–90
Regulatory Horizons Council (RHC)   235, 272, 282, 283–6
engineering biology, platform technology area of   275
regulatory reform principles   252
scientific and technical innovations   264

Index 321

Regulatory Impact Assessments
  (RIAs) 247-8, 258, 285
regulatory space, concept of a 78-81
  bespoke regulatory spaces 93-4
  collaborative enterprise, as 76
  core functions 75, 79-81
  food safety and security 189
  innovation 298
  Outcome-Based Collaborative
    Regulation (OBCR)
    Model 139
regulatory system 76-8, 23, 140-1, 231
  see also **tools for a regulatory system**
  accountability 297
  actors, identification of 80
  amendment of systems 78
  authoritarian approach 76, 295
  bespoke design choices 74
  collaborative model 74, 77, 295-6
  continuous holistic cycles 296
  data 297
  delivery of functions 82-5, 296-7
  design 140-1
  economic regulation 237
  enforcement 77
  functions to enable system to work 80
  future of regulation 295-7
  governance 74, 83, 94-6, 297
  harm, avoiding 76-7
  innovation 282
  monitoring risks and harms 82
  outcomes 76, 81-2, 140
  post-marketing surveillance
    system 23
  regulation as a system 74, 76-8
  Regulatory Functions Model
    (RFM) 79-81, 295-6
  staged systems, operation of 263
  system, definition of 77
  system regulator, need for a 80
  systemic behavioural
    approach 111-12
  testing 23
  vertical modes of authority 76-7
religion 25

repairing damage see **redress/repair**
resources 100, 104-5, 109, 173, 234, 241, 285
responsibility see also **accountability; blame**
  collective responsibility 129
  communication of responsibility 244
  corporate social responsibility
    (CSR) 201
  culture 111, 129, 138, 200, 204-5
  delivery 82, 102
  financial products and services 197-8, 200-3
  gaps 235
  governance 101
  individual responsibility 20-1, 40, 46, 129, 138, 186, 188, 202-3
  innovation 274-5, 277-81, 298
  leadership 129
  monitoring 208
  multi and joint stakeholders 88-9, 95, 299
  Outcome-Based Collaborative Model
    (OBC) 135-8
  political decisions 244
  private regulation 95
  proportionality 159
  public regulation 77-8, 95
  Regulatory Functions Model
    (RFM) 135-6
  repair 85
  Responsible Innovation (RI) 278-81, 298
  Senior Managers 197-8, 201-3
  trust 126
responsive regulation 75, 165, 166, 171
  retribution 161
reward systems 41, 51-2, 57-9, 201
risk
  AI 92, 242
  assessments 105, 281
  attitudes and appetite 11, 34, 105, 241-3, 265, 281-2
  behavioural risk factors 46-8
  communication about risk 240-1

data, information and intelligence,
    need to use all 105
deregulation, effect of 246–7
disasters 46–8
economic growth 243
Economic Model 3, 23–4
excessive regulation, complaints
    about 241–2
factors 46–8
financial supervision 94
flexibility 241
future of regulation 298
governments, policies on risk by 242
harms, identification of 298
identification of risks 80, 91, 105, 193
innovation 242, 281–2
life stories 241
management 138
media 242
multiple risks 239–40
new tools 284–5
operational challenges 75, 91–2
pendulum effect 242
perception 240–2
political element 241–2
precautionary principle 33–4, 242–3
prioritisation 100, 104–5, 257
proportionality 33–4, 239–40, 243
Regulatory Delivery Model
    (RDM) 100, 104–5, 257
Regulatory Functions Model
    (RFM) 91, 243
relative risk 11
resources 100, 104–5
risk aversion ratchet 243
safety regulation 11–12
systemic risk 46–8, 298
transparency 105
unacceptable risks 4, 11–12, 33, 75,
    91–2, 108, 139, 171, 186, 218,
    293, 298
unknown risks 12, 75, 91, 104, 241,
    243, 271, 283–4, 298
rule of law 20–1, 157
rules 22–3, 24–6 *see also* **codes of
    behaviour; enforcement**
AI 250, 251
combinations of techniques 249–52

costs, reduction in 251–2
cumulative effect of multiple rules and
    procedures 232, 233–4
ethics 40
globalism 259–60
harm, impact on 252
harmonisation 259–60
hierarchy 197–8
Legal Model 3, 19
making laws and rules, controls
    on 247–52
mandatory rules 95
outcomes 57, 99–100, 250, 291
proportionality 291
reducing existing stock 248–50
rule-breach-sanction approach 291–2
scientific evidence 39, 55–7
sociological function of
    enforcement 169–70
sunrise clauses 250
sunset clauses 248–9
values 100
why and how we comply 39, 55–7
Russell, Graham 100
**Russia-Ukraine war and energy
    prices** 236
Ryan, Richard 50–2

safety regulation 7, 10, 11–12, 187 *see
    also* **aviation safety**
accountability 12
approvals 192
authoritarianism 111
complaints 193
complexity 191–2
culture 111–12
design process 192
digital harms 11
health and safety 28, 192
labelling, information and marketing
    requirements 192
manufacturing controls 192
medical devices 192
medicines 12, 192
motor vehicles 191–2
nuclear safety 45, 291
Office for Product Safety and Standards
    (OPSS) 166–9

proactive safety management 48
product safety 166-9, 192-3
psychological safety 39, 53, 61, 84, 122, 125, 204, 291
punitivenesss 111
quality management systems 192
risk 11-12
safety management system (SMS) approach 137-9
safetyism 242-3
systems 23
testing 192
trust 193
vigilance systems 193
vulnerable people 11
sanctions/punishment 118, 152-60, 185
accountability 136
aggravating factors 158-60, 162-3
categorisation 153-4
codes of behaviour 27
compliance programmes 161-3
criminal law 150-1, 153, 170-1
cross-border regulation 118
culpability 158
desert theory 151, 170
deterrence 156, 166, 171
Economic Model 23-4
economic regulation 217
enforcement 3, 19, 60-1, 77, 157-66, 169-70
fairness 157-66
fines and financial penalties 22, 31-2, 152-3, 162, 170, 217, 222, 238
future of regulation 292
General Data Protection Regulation (GDPR) 158-60
harm, relevance of 160-1
interventions 106, 108
Legal Model 3, 19, 23-4
mitigating factors 158-60, 162-3
new models 99
philosophy of punishment 170-1
private regulation 26, 31-2, 152-3
proportionality 151, 158-60, 170-1
public condemnation 170
public regulation 31-2
punitiveness 111, 170

regulatory space, concept of a 79
regulatory system 75, 76
rule-breach-sanction approach 291-2
scientific evidence 35, 175
self-regulation 219
sentencing guidelines 157
siloism 154
social punishment 44, 57-8
sociological function of enforcement 169-70
states, regulation by 118
technology, innovations in 118
traditional regulation 47, 76-7
trust 118
sandboxes 194, 244, 284, 285-6, 295
scandals *see* disasters and scandals
Schein, Edgar 199
Schwartz, Shalom 42
scientific evidence 39-62
accidents, scientific research into 48-9
accountability 44, 61
altering behaviour 16
application of science 169-75
authoritarian approach 58-9, 291
behavioural science 99, 149, 170, 173-7, 191, 290-2
bias 40
classification of behavioural motivations 173
cooperation 43-4, 52-8, 62, 118
culture, power of 43-4, 50-2
deterrence 21, 174-5
disasters, inquiries into 45-9, 60, 115
enforcement 60-2, 118, 149, 169-70
ethics 40, 41-3, 49, 62, 118
future of regulation 291-2
good management behaviour, business research into 52
human behaviour 39-62, 113, 293-4
motivations 24, 39, 41, 175
new models 98
nudges 191
outcomes 20, 291
protection 20, 62
psychological safety 39, 53, 291
punishment and democracy, philosophy of 170-1

responses, modes of 176–7
risk factors 46–8
rules 55–7
sanctions 35, 170–1, 175
Self-Determination Theory (SDT) 39, 50–2, 61–2
social influence, power of 43–4
social punishment 58
System I thinking 40
System II thinking 40
theories to science, from 99–100
trust 54–5, 61–2
understanding, evolution in 171–2
values 41–2
wrong, what people want when things go 59–60

Scotland
net zero target 140–1
Scottish Environmental Protection Agency (SEPA) 140–1, 173
Self-Determination Theory (SDT) 39, 50–3, 61–2, 293
self-regulation 3, 26–7, 31, 79, 187, 219
see also **codes of behaviour**
Selznick, Philip 16
Senior Managers 197–9
good management behaviour, business research into 52
Hong Kong SFC Managers-in-Charge (MiC) regime 199
Management Responsibilities Map (MRM) 198
mandatory prescribed responsibilities (PRs) 198
Senior Managers and Certification Regime (SM&CR) 197–9, 201–3
Certification Regime 198, 199
Conduct Rules 198
extension of regime 198–9
Senior Managers Regime (SMR) 198
Statement of Responsibilities (SoR) 198
silos 96, 154, 235, 295
simplification 57, 124, 248, 250–1, 253, 272, 297

Singapore, accountability regime for senior management in 199
small businesses 15, 171, 187, 272–3
social groups 5–6, 44, 55, 163
social regulation 26, 275
sociology 20, 22, 42, 118, 122, 169–70
Solomon, Robert C 41–2
space see **regulatory space, concept of a**
Space Shuttle Challenger disaster 45, 115, 247
stability 3, 5–6, 15, 42, 157, 247
stakeholder councils 83, 95, 133, 178
standard of proof 150, 152
standards 3, 16, 23, 31, 88
AI 29
aviation safety 93
certification schemes 3, 27, 29, 31
conformity assessments bodies 29–30
definition 28
designated standards 29
energy management standard 29
environmental management standards 28
financial supervision 93–4
food safety standards 29
globalism 259–60
harmonisation 30–1, 259–60
health and safety standards 28, 192
innovation 6, 275–7, 280–1
International Standards Organisation (ISO) 28–9
IT security standards 29
list of organisations 29, 259–60
medical devices 94
national standard bodies 28–9
Office for Product Safety and Standards (OPSS) 166–9
private regulation 27–31, 276
product standards 94
quality management standards 28
registers run by industries 31
regulated self-assurance 30–1
rules 23
self-regulation 26–7, 31
social responsibility, guidance on 280–1

trust 83
voluntary standards 28
Steinholtz, Ruth 129
Stephan, Andreas 162
strict liability 151
sunrise clauses 250
sunset clauses 235, 248–9
support
    culture 60–2
    criminal law 176
    enforcement 149, 174–7
    interventions 108, 110, 217–18, 257
    Outcome-Based Collaborative Regulation (OBCR) Model 113
    scientific evidence 39, 175
    Supportive Intervention Mode 217–18, 219–20
surveillance 23, 207–8
sustainability 82, 291–2, 294
    Better Regulation 253
    environment 4, 28, 99, 106–7, 140–1, 245, 253
    Sustainable Development Goals (SDGs) 5, 212, 245, 261, 292
system *see* regulatory system

Tait, Joyce 276, 277
technology *see also* artificial intelligence (AI)
    Digital Regulation Cooperation Forum (DRCF) 257, 286–7
    digital simulation 284–5
    PAGIT 277, 298
    single consumer websites 210–11
    standards 29
    states, regulation by 118
    supply chains based on holistic digital systems 260–1
    Technology Readiness Levels (TRLs) 274–5
    testbeds 284
Tenbrunsel, Ann 52
testbeds 284
testing 23, 30–1, 108, 191–4, 284–5, 295
Thalidomide disaster 193, 247, 261
tick box approach 20, 291

too much regulation *see* excessive regulation
tools for a regulatory system 184–224
    see also licensing and permits; monitoring; standards
    accreditation schemes 187, 188–9
    actors, distinguishing between 217–18
    after regulated activities (downstream) 184, 188, 215–24
    approval 187–8
    authorised competent persons 190–1
    before activity commences (upstream) 184, 186–206, 222
    change occurs, ensuring 219–22
    codes of behaviour 188
    competition 213–14
    compliance 185, 208
    consumer protection 213, 214
    culture 204–5, 220–1
    data collection 209–13
    during regulated activities (midstream) 184, 207–14
    economic regulation 187, 191, 213–14, 217
    enforcement 185, 218, 220
    ethics, teaching on 221
    feedback systems 220, 221–2
    financial products and services 194, 195–204
    food safety and security 189, 211–13
    information and disclosure 194–5
    interventions, objectives of regulatory 215–21
    objectives of regulatory interventions 215–21
    Ombuds 210–11
    outcomes 185, 208, 220
    pre-marketing 186–206
    product safety 192–3
    professional competence 189–90
    Protection Mode 218, 219–20
    purpose of tools 185
    redress 222–4
    Regulatory Delivery Model (RDM) 185

Regulatory Functions Model
  (RFM) 185, 215, 220
 safety regulation 187, 191–2
 supportive intervention mode 217–18
 surveillance 207–8
 testing 191–4
 trust as a regulatory tool, using 205–6
totalitarian/fascist regimes as distinguished from democratic societies 51–2
trade associations 15, 18, 28, 93, 135, 143, 188, 223
traditional regulation 23–5 *see also* Economic Model; Legal Model
 authoritarian approach 115–16
 crises, inability to respond to 116
 deterrence 23–4
 enforcement 23–5, 79, 84, 116, 149, 150–6, 218
 failures 290–3, 295, 298
 functions 19, 35, 74–5
 innovation 286
 interventions 216
 monitoring 25
 power, use of 115–17
 principles 156–7
 protection, delivery of 116
 refreshment 298
 regulatory authorities, creation of 18, 83
 sanctions 47, 76–7
 systemic approach, lack of 19
tragedy of the commons 58, 122
transparency
 accountability 101–2
 Better Regulation 253
 deregulation 249
 Economic Model 25
 enforcement 155, 165
 governance 165
 innovation 285
 Legal Model 25
 open and just culture approach 109, 111–12, 137–9, 204
 outcomes 110, 133

risk-based prioritisation 105
 testing 193
transport disasters 45
Treviño, Lee 52
tribunals 151, 236
Trump, Donald 242, 245, 246, 247, 248
trust and trustworthiness 4, 5, 123–30, 205–6
 accountability 126, 136
 accreditation systems 125
 AI 118, 274
 anthropology 125
 brand reputation and endorsements 126
 building trust 113–14, 121, 123–30
 collaboration, power of 76, 89–90, 174, 205
 competence 206
 competition, reducing 125
 compliance framework 129, 206
 criminal law 177
 culture 52, 129–30, 204
 data 134
 delivery of functions 83
 enforcement 113–14
 ethics 39, 40, 83, 114, 121, 123–6, 128–30
 evidence 98, 113–14, 121, 123–4, 125–30, 132, 299
  characteristics 126
  ethical organisational culture 129–30
  feedback systems 206
  internal moral compass 123
  Outcome-Based Collaborative (OBC) Model 121, 132
  Regulatory Functions Model (RFM) 89–90
  trusted company status 206
  traditional regulation 205–6
 evolution 124–5
 feedback systems 206
 finances 128–9
 food safety and security 212–13
 future of regulation 292, 299

innovation   286
integrity   125, 129–30
knowledge, lack of   123
leadership framework   129
list for trust in organisations   127–8
mechanism of trust   123–4
new models   98, 100
organisational culture   129–30
outcomes   113–14, 121, 123–30, 139–40, 177, 206, 292
professional integrity mechanisms   126–7
protection   114
psychological safety   125
purpose of organisations   127
quality management and inspections   126–7
reciprocal exchange   124
redress   222
Regulatory Functions Model (RFM)   89–90
relational exchange   124
responsibility   126
rules   83
safety regulation   193
scientific evidence   54–5, 61–2
self-regulation   219
social capital   124–5
spontaneous altruistic actions   124
standard-setting bodies, accreditation and compliance bodies   83
structures   125
supportive intervention mode   218
transactionally negotiated trust   124
trust and non-trusted systems   126
trusted company status, private sector third party verification of   206
values   90, 124–5, 129–30
Trust Government Framework, verifiability assurance functions under a   25
Tyler Tom   52, 55, 58–9, 163

Ukraine, Russia's invasion of   236
UNCTAD   85

United States
Commodity Futures Trading Commission (CFTC)   172
deregulation   248
rules and laws, controls on making   248–51
sunset clauses   248–9
use of force   20, 118, 156–7, 170
utilities   14, 213

values
actors   87
basic personal values, list of   42
codes of behaviour   113
competing   281–2
cooperation   44
culture   42
disasters   49
ethics   41, 129–30
evolution   42
innovation   280–2
internal values   200
mission and values statements produced by corporations   41–2
organisational values   41–2
Outcome-Based Collaborative (OBC) Model   112
proportionality   239
psychology   118
religion   25
rules   55–6, 100
scientific evidence   41–2
sociology   118
stability   42
trust   83, 90, 124–5, 129–30
van Rooij, Benjamin   49, 200
Vitali, James   258
Volkswagen emissions scandal   45, 49, 200, 262
Vought, Russell   246
VUCA (volatility, uncertainty, complexity and ambiguity)   260
vulnerable or disadvantaged groups   5–6, 11, 13, 15, 96, 140

Weber, Elke 44
Weick, Karl 48
Wells Fargo 45, 49, 200, 261
Whitehouse, Harvey 42
Wilkinson, Richard 51–2
Wilson, Edward 55, 125
Witherspoon, Brian 211–12

World Economic Forum (WEF) 24–5

Zambia and Democratic Republic of Congo (DRC), Kasumbalesa border between 142
Zuckerberg, Mark 92